Literacy through
Language Arts

Literacy through *Language Arts*

Teaching and Learning in Context

Edited by

Sharon Murphy
York University

Curt Dudley-Marling
Boston College

National Council of Teachers of English
1111 W. Kenyon Road, Urbana, Illinois 61801-1096

Staff Editor: Tom Tiller
Interior Design: Doug Burnett
Cover Design: Jenny Jensen Greenleaf

NCTE Stock Number 29668-3050

Library of Congress Cataloging-in-Publication Data

Literacy through *Language Arts* : teaching and learning in context /
edited by Sharon Murphy, Curt Dudley-Marling.
        p. cm.
Chiefly articles originally published in *Language Arts*.
Includes bibliographical references and index.
    ISBN 0-8141-2966-8 (pbk.)
    1. Language arts (Elementary) I. Murphy, Sharon, 1955– II.
Dudley-Marling, Curt. III. National Council of Teachers of English.
IV. *Language Arts*.
    LB1576.L565 2003
    372.6—dc21

                                            2002152812

Contents

V. Literacy Intersections: Multilinguality, Home, and Assessment

1 Introduction

Sharon Murphy

Curt Dudley-Marling

To say exactly what one means, even to one's own private satisfaction, is difficult. To say exactly what one means and to involve another person is harder still.

Jeanette Winterson, *Art Objects:*
Essays on Ecstasy and Effrontery

Meaning is at the heart of the language arts. That meaning can be the meaning one creates for oneself or the meaning one constructs in dialogue or interaction with texts. As Winterson (1995) suggests, there are arts involved in using language to mean. These arts are more than the components of reading, writing, speaking, and listening. The arts of language include such things as delicateness, deftness, and tact in the of use of language. They also include signifying to others emotional specificity, depth, and breadth, as well as appreciating how we need to modify what we want to say to take into account the background knowledge and sensibilities of our audience. In short, the study of the language arts, whether for children in elementary school or for adults learning how to teach those children, is the study of the fullness of language in use in particular contexts by particular people for particular purposes.

Our purpose in this book is to provide a resource for those who are thinking about how to assist children in learning the language arts. We do so by drawing from the articles published over the past twenty-five years or so in the journal *Language Arts*. We have deliberately chosen to draw from this journal because it has distinguished itself by its focus on language arts classroom practices that are demonstrations of teaching and learning the language arts in context and for varied purposes.

The Emergence of Today's Language Arts

We begin by presenting a brief historical overview of the teaching and learning of language arts in order to set the broader context for understanding the perspectives that are currently advocated by many scholars of literacy education. Our history is skeletal, intended to provide more an indication of the trajectory of the development of the field of literacy education than a fully fleshed out version of events.

According to Squire (1991), throughout much of the nineteenth and early twentieth centuries in the United States, literacy teaching and learning focused on reading. For instance, the McGuffey Readers, introduced in the 1830s, were one of the hallmarks of schooling. Spelling books were added, and, eventually, by the 1930s, writing books were introduced (with an emphasis on penmanship, manuscript form, and grammar and usage). Not until the 1950s, as a result of Dora Smith's work, did the idea of integrated language arts (reading, writing, speaking, and listening) become popular. In the 1960s there was some focus on composition, and this was developed even further as ideas about the writing process were introduced into elementary classrooms in the 1980s. Despite all of these developments, Squire (1991) asserts that the hold of reading over the language arts curriculum remained strong even in the 1990s, with about half of all language arts instructional time and 40 percent of all textbook expenditures devoted to it. Nevertheless, further reconceptualization of language arts occurred in the 1990s, when the National Council of Teachers of English and the International Reading Association copublished *Standards for the English Language Arts*, which included statements addressing visual literacy (National Council of Teachers of English and International Reading Association, 1996).

While there was steady evolution in what constitutes language arts across the past century, instructional methods followed varied patterns: Sometimes the same debates about methods arose cyclically so that once every few years the same topic received attention. At other times, new methods were misperceived as being the same as those of the past, even though the new methods were in fact substantively different. At still other times, little change occurred. We will use some examples from the teaching and learning of reading to illustrate.

An example of a cyclical topic can be found in the question of how much emphasis should be placed on sound-symbol relationships in learning to read. In the late 1800s, calls were made for an increased emphasis on phonics (see Feitelson, 1988). The 1960s also witnessed a call for an emphasis on phonics (see, e.g., Chall, 1967), and a similar call occurred in the 1990s. The research base driving each of these moves was quite different. In addition, recent calls have become entangled with other issues, as politicians and fundamentalist groups include reading instructional methods in their platforms. Despite the differences of time and context, however, the net effect—an emphasis on phonics in the elementary school curriculum—was similar.

The description of the whole language approach of the late twentieth century as the whole word approach, popular in the early twentieth century, is an example of superficial similarity misinterpreted as substantive similarity (perhaps caused by the use of the word "whole" for both approaches). "Whole word" refers to a method involving the memorization of words—the look-and-say approach (see Feitelson, 1988; Squire, 1991). "Whole language" refers to a complex set of practices, one part of which involves assisting children in using particular strategies to sample graphophonic, syntactic, semantic, and pragmatic cues as they read text (K. S. Goodman, 1986).

An example of the relative slowness of change in classrooms is the continued heavy reliance on basal reading anthologies—grade-level-specific collections of stories and poems for children that may have been adapted from children's literature or were written expressly for the purposes of teaching children to learn to read. Squire (1991) reports that in the 1970s, approximately 90 percent of all classrooms used basal readers. While shifts in the nature and use of basals arose subsequent to the 1970s, as a result of criticism of basals (e.g., K. S. Goodman, Shannon, Freeman, & Murphy, 1988), it was also the case that for many teachers change in their practice was much more difficult to effect (Murphy & Dudley-Marling, 1997).

Finally, even though considerable variety existed in instructional methods throughout the past century, it is also the case that certain movements persisted throughout the century. A given movement may have taken different forms at different periods, but the underlying premises were similar. Shannon (1990), for instance, reviews the history of progressive reading instruction in the United States, ranging from the influence of Dewey, to movements like child-centered learning or social reconstructionist literacy, to contemporary movements arising out of psycholinguistics like whole language. A more recently theorized progressive approach is the conceptualization of literacy as social practice (see Barton & Hamilton, 1998; Bloome, 1987), in which "literacy is not merely the capacity to understand the conceptual content of writings and utterances but the ability to participate fully in a set of social and intellectual practices. It is not passive but active, not imitative but creative, for it includes participation in the activities it makes possible" (White, as cited in Fleischer & Schaafsma, 1998, p. xiv). This description contains echoes of child-centered learning, social reconstructionist literacy, and Deweyan thinking. Indeed, such common ground underlying progressive methods makes them more alike than different. The persistence of such methods suggests that even when education seems to turn back on itself in regressive reform, there are core progressive ideas and ideals that are strong enough to persist and that make a contribution to literacy education. These progressive ideas and ideals, we believe, can contribute much to literacy education, and they are drawn upon by many of the authors in this book. In addition to these ideas about literacy education, we believe that recent conceptualizations of teaching and learning provide a rich base from which to begin language arts education.

Teaching and Learning Language Arts

Several developments in our understanding of teaching and learning have contributed to, or occurred in tandem with, developments in language arts education. The first development relates to our understanding of the relationship between teaching and learning.

No longer is a direct cause-and-effect relationship assumed between teaching and learning (see Chapter 2 by Lindfors). The fact that a learner can do the task the teacher is teaching about or regurgitate the knowledge that the teacher just presented may or may not be related to the teacher's teaching. For instance, a learner may have sufficiently strong background knowledge and experience to undertake the task or provide the knowledge from a lesson without the teacher's intervention of teaching. An obvious example can be found in the fact that teachers' knowledge of computing is sometimes surpassed by that of their students; numerous less obvious instances occur on a daily basis in classrooms.

Alternatively, a learner may learn something that the teacher doesn't realize he or she is teaching. A case in point might be when, as a consequence of observing interactions in a lesson, learners learn that the teacher speaks to those who interrupt more quickly than to those who hold up their hand to request a turn to speak.

A learner also may choose not to engage in the activity that is the focus of the teacher's efforts, and this choice may or may not be related to the difficulty of the activity. Sometimes learners choose to disengage completely while others engage in procedural display—superficially appearing to undertake the task required but actually being engaged in something else (Bloome,1987)—which is a form of strategic guilty refusal to comply with the lesson. And, finally, sometimes, because of attending to the teacher's lesson, the learner knows something that he or she did not know the day before.

The fact that the instances described above deserve mention, even though they appear quite ordinary, underscores the degree to which a particular image of teaching and learning in schools has taken hold. Within our culture, teaching and learning in schools is associated with relatively narrow visions of education, visions in which silent pupils sap up words of wisdom from the mouths of their teachers and the chalkboards at the front of the room. The image is so strong that it makes us forget the ordinary understandings we have of teaching and learning, and it is to these understandings that language arts educators must return in order to provide as many opportunities as possible for students to learn about knowledge and how to use it.

Indeed, part of what has contributed to our better understanding of teaching and learning in classrooms is the fact that increasingly, through their own classroom research, teachers are explicitly and publicly becoming students of their own teaching and of students' learning. The hallmarks of research—questioning, careful observation, thoughtful documentation, and systematic analysis—are a part of most teachers' daily activities; however, the movement to name these activities as research and offer an accounting to others outside the classroom is what distinguishes the teacher-as-researcher movement (see, for example, Allen, Cary, & Delgado, 1995; Hollingsworth, 1994; Murphy & Dudley-Marling, 1999; Patterson, Santa, Short, & Smith, 1993). This movement has not supplanted research on classrooms conducted by university academics and others, but it complements, challenges, and contradicts the work of these researchers whose principal occupation lies outside the classroom being studied. The complexity of teaching and learning portrayed in accounts authored or coauthored by teachers contains the thread of credibility that comes out of everyday experience. We have drawn upon such accounts as well as the accounts of university-based researchers to demonstrate what is involved in the teaching and learning of language arts.

Language Arts through *Language Arts*

As mentioned earlier, our vehicle for exploring the teaching of language arts is the journal *Language Arts*. Founded in 1924 under the editorship of C. C. Certain, the journal, then known as *Elementary English*, not only became a voice for elementary school teachers of the language arts but also proved to be a journal with a social conscience. C. C. Certain was not reluctant to comment on injustices of the day, and in doing so he demonstrated language use in its most powerful sense. Eventually the journal became officially associated with the National Council of Teachers of English, and the name was changed to *Language Arts* in 1946 to better reflect the scope of its interests.

We were coeditors of the journal from September 1997 to July/August 2001. During this period, the journal celebrated its seventy-fifth anniversary. We thought it a fitting tribute to select from the journal a set of articles that would reflect its impact and be of use to persons just beginning their work as language arts educators. But we were interested in more than creating a tribute to the journal. As teacher educators, we continuously found ourselves referring our teacher education students to the exemplary articles in *Language Arts,* and we knew of others who did so as well. We knew that our use of these articles hinged on their rich context, vivid examples, and directness in dealing with everyday classroom issues, and we felt that others might well appreciate our efforts in creating a text that would represent the vision of language arts that the journal offers.

We selected from the articles published since 1975, not because no worthy items were published before that time but simply because of the volume of material to be examined. Even within this time frame, it was difficult to choose items that would become a part of the text. We narrowed down our choice first to thirty-five articles and later to twenty-five. We also wanted to include some of the insights of other texts, and, as a result, we excerpted from over eighty other articles.

The book is divided into five sections. Much of the book follows relatively traditional curricular lines (e.g., talk, reading, writing); however, there is considerable overlap between sections of the text. So, for example, an article about literature circles might discuss written response as well as document the talk that occurred and, inevitably, focus on reading practices. We also included an introductory section dealing with varied contexts for the teaching of language arts and a later section on intersecting issues which reveal literacy in its complexity, whether through acts of assessment or acts of pedagogy.

Each chapter within the book is a whole article taken from *Language Arts.*[1] In addition, interspersed throughout the book are dialogue boxes of three different types which contain smaller excerpted portions of other articles from *Language Arts.* The three different types of dialogue boxes are:

- **Quotations**—These dialogue boxes contain short quotations of one to two sentences. The quotes bring home in a compelling manner some key principles to think of in relation to literacy learning.

■ **Reflections**—These dialogue boxes contain larger excerpts of text. They are given a title and are prefaced by *Editors' Text*. The function of the *Editors' Text* is to set the context for the excerpt and to challenge readers of the excerpt to consider it from specific perspectives.

■ **Strategies**—These dialogue boxes contain sets of strategies for teaching varied elements of the language arts. Like the Reflections dialogue boxes, these boxes are titled and are prefaced by an *Editors' Text* which sets the strategies in a context.

We believe that the dialogue boxes will provide quick reference material, and, should readers wish to consider the material in its larger context, we have included the reference to the full article.

A Final Comment

Jeanette Winterson (1995) says that "strong texts work along the borders of our minds and alter what already exists" (p. 26). We believe that we have collected a sampling of strong texts from *Language Arts*. These texts have much more than the potential to shape one's own thinking about language arts. Because these texts will be read by teachers and future teachers, they have the potential to change children's futures as well.

Note

1. This book is presented in the style of the American Psychological Association. However, because the publishing style of the journal changed across the period represented, some references are not fully compliant with APA style, since the original style did not include all of the information required by APA.

I Opening Contexts for Thinking about Teaching the Language Arts

2 How Children Learn or How Teachers Teach? A Profound Confusion

Judith Wells Lindfors

Editors' Text: Language arts instruction needs to be theorized within the broader context of teaching and learning. In this article, Judith Lindfors helps us think about the not-so-simple relationship between what teachers do (i.e., "teach") and what students do (i.e., "learn").

At the risk of being pedantic, I start with definitions of teaching and learning. By "teaching" I mean an individual's intentional efforts (e.g., planning, conducting activities, talking) to increase another's knowledge or skill. And by "learning" I mean an individual's own sense-making activity, what Frank Smith (1975) has called "building a theory of the world in the head"—constructing out of one's experience expectations of how the world works. There are many people who teach and learn as these are characterized here, and many places where teaching and learning occur. Right now, however, I want to focus on teachers as the ones who teach and students as the ones who learn, and to focus on the classroom as a place where teaching and learning occur.

In classrooms, instances of teaching and learning sometimes connect: teachers do sometimes provide experiences that particular children act on and shape in their own sense-making activity. Sometimes the connection is, in a general way, at least, the one the teacher intends. Often it is not. Consider the following example.

> T: *(Pointing to a triangle cut-out)* See, it has three sides so it's a triangle, isn't it?
>
> C: *(Nods.)*
>
> T: And here's another one so here's another trrr . . . , tri . . .
>
> C: Triangle.
>
> T: And if I put another one here now I have threeeee . . .

This essay appeared in *Language Arts* 61.6 (1984) on pages 600–606.

C: Triangles.

T: Right!

Here the teacher deliberately engages the child in a particular kind of talk, intending, thereby, to increase the child's semantic knowledge, extending it to include the concept of triangle and its label "triangle." It may be, however, that the kind of sense the child makes of this encounter has more to do with procedure than with content (concepts or labels): "When she looks at me that expectant way and pauses and her voice goes up and gets drawn out, I'm supposed to say 'triangle'(or whatever word she's big on at the moment)." This is a connection of sorts, but not the one the teacher has in mind. But often teaching-learning connections are not apparent at all, with teacher's efforts to increase children's knowledge and skills, and children's efforts to make sense of their world, going on quite independently of one another. The main point here is this: regardless of whether and in what ways they do or do not connect, teaching and learning as defined here, are two distinct ventures which often get confused with one another.

I don't know whether the confusion of learning with teaching is on the increase or whether I've just become more aware of this confusion recently. In any case, I want to describe here four encounters that I have had that I hope will demonstrate the confusion. The four encounters involve (1) a doctoral student in education, (2) a primary grade teacher, (3) a child, and (4) a sociolinguist. I choose these four out of many not because the parties involved are ignorant or insensitive. Quite the opposite. I choose these four precisely because the individuals concerned are knowledgeable, intelligent, observant, aware. If such individuals in education fall into this teaching/learning confusion, then it can, and probably does, happen to all of us at one time or another.

A Doctoral Student

Janet was a Ph.D. candidate in Early Childhood Education in whom the five of us on her doctoral committee had utmost confidence. A mature woman, fifty-ish perhaps, she brought to her formal study of education a rich and diverse background of experiences with children, including her own children now grown, and the children she had taught for years in Central America. She also brought to her graduate study personal characteristics that education professors hope for in their students: an active and inquiring mind, a keen sensitivity to children, an ability to use language effectively. On the day that Janet and her five committee members came together, it was to discuss the fine exam that she had written a week earlier as part of her doctoral qualifying exam. Now we were meeting for the rest of that exam, the oral.

As expected, the oral moved along smoothly. Then one of us asked the question:

> *Committee Member:* How do you think a young child goes about the business of learning to read—of making sense out of those little black squiggles we call "print"?
>
> *Janet:* Well, first the child learns to say the alphabet and then he or she learns which sound goes with each letter, what each letter *says*, and then—
>
> *Me:* Wait a minute. I think you're describing ways that parents and teachers have traditionally taught children. What I want to know is your thoughts about the kinds of processes *children* use in their learning, the kinds of experiences they have with print and the uses they make of those experiences in figuring out how print works to express meaning.
>
> *Janet:* Yes, well, it's like I said. First they learn the ABCs and then they learn, for example, that "t" says "tuh" and "b" says "buh" and then they learn to put the sounds together.

My face must have said something I didn't intend, for she said, somewhat shakily, "I don't think I understand your question."

Sensing her nervousness, I dropped the matter, inviting her to discuss it with me later in a less threatening situation. And discuss it later we did, focusing on the difference between *teaching*—what teachers do, the instructional activities and sequences they design with the intention of increasing children's ability to relate language meanings to printed symbols—and *learning*, what children do to make print make sense.

Teacher

I was eating dinner in a London dormitory for visiting scholars. Pam, an elementary school teacher from New Zealand, sat down beside me. We got to talking. It turned out that Pam had been teaching for seven years. I asked her what grade she taught . . .

> *Pam:* Well, I mostly teach second grade, but first grade is really my favorite because that's where you get to start children in reading and that's just so important. I think that's really the most important thing any teacher does.
>
> *Me:* I just finished reading a book you might be interested in—a wonderful book, for parents actually—called *Learning to Read* (Spencer, 1982). The author is a recognized authority in

children's literature (as well as reading) and is quite op-
posed to the "reading scheme" (what we call "basals" in the
States). She teaches children to read entirely through the use
of children's literature because she firmly believes—it's
really one of her major points—that *what* children read
determines their view of what reading *is*. I happened to be
talking with her the other day (She teaches over at the
University of London Institute of Education) and she was
telling me about the work she and some of her graduate
students have done with twelve- to fifteen-year-old non-
readers. They worked with these kids intensively for several
years, and she was saying that the main problem was
getting the kids to move from asking of print "What does it
say?" to asking "What does it *mean*?" Even though the "buh,
tuh, duh" sort of thing hadn't worked for them for six or
eight years, they kept hanging on to it, just wouldn't let go.

I watched Pam go increasingly stiff as I talked, and I knew I was in
trouble. She responded huffily and from a lofty height.

> Pam: *Phonics* wasn't the problem. The problem was how
> phonics was taught. I've taught for seven years and I've
> never had a single child leave my room unable to read.
> *Every* child learns to read in *my* room.

And she launched into a lecture, not about children's learning, but about
the reading curriculum (strikingly similar to the one I remembered being confronted with in my first public school teaching job twenty-four
years earlier).

> Pam: You see (*condescending tone in the voice and patronizing smile
> on the face*), in first grade they do individual letter sounds—
> consonants first and then vowels. Then in second grade
> they start with blends and then . . .

It went on and on and she reiterated the fact that "all my children learn
to read" this way, adding, as if it were proof positive:

> Pam: And it's not just that *I* think so. Not at all. All the children
> are *tested*—not with tests *I* make up, but with *standardized
> reading tests* and the reading test scores *show* that they have
> learned how to read.

I mumbled something noncommittal like "Hmm," and wondered what
she meant by "reading."

The main point here is not what the merits are of phonic approaches to reading instruction, though my understanding of children's
language development tells me that any approach that removes reading from purposeful language, the relating of meaning and expression

for reasons real to the learner, cannot help children become more effective readers, because reading is language. And though it requires almost superhuman restraint, I'll ignore for the moment the merits of standardized test scores as indicators of anything other than test-wiseness. I'll stick to the main point which is that what this teacher described is reading instruction, what *teachers* do, sequences of activities they move children through. She did not describe the learning process of *children*. She was not aware that she had confused the two. Indeed, she may have been unaware that there were two.

A Child

Some years ago I had a particular conversation with my son that haunts me still. It is a conversation that suggests that our profound confusion of teaching and learning may be transmitted to the child.

It was late afternoon and Erik, a second grader, and I were sitting on the couch, talking casually about this and that. Some comment was made about school which prompted me to say, "So tell me about yourself in school, Erik. What are you like in school?" He answered with no hesitation, "I'm not good in school. I'm not good in reading."

I was stunned! To hear these words from one I knew was not simply a child who "knew how to read" but who was a reader, one who *did* the thing—avidly and with many purposes, his own purposes—whether for fun or for information about dinosaurs or TV programs or how to assemble a toy. I thought of the many times he had read aloud to me, never by way of demonstrating that he *could*, but always by way of sharing with me some new discovery: "Lemme read you this one, Mom. It's *really* funny," or "Here's a good one. 'What do you get when you cross a . . .'"

But suddenly I remembered a bedtime scene that had occurred a few weeks earlier. I had found him crying when I had come into his room to kiss him good night, and when I asked him why, he had said, "I know I'll have to do long and short vowels in school tomorrow and I can't do it. I know what the words are—I can read 'em and everything—and I know what sounds the letters make, but I don't know which ones are 'long' and which ones are 'short.'"

I pulled myself back to the present moment.

> *Me:* What makes you think you're no good in reading? You
> read me stories lots of times.
>
> *Erik:* Yeah, but at school I don't finish the workbook pages and
> I'm no good at vowels.

The confusion again, this time from a child. He who had so effortlessly and confidently and naturally learned to read saw himself as an inadequate *learner* because he did not successfully move through the instructional sequence provided by the teacher. What he had done (learn to make sense of print) was effective; what the teacher was doing (sequencing and conducting activities towards a specific end) was, in this particular instance, counterproductive. But he believed, wrongly, that his learning *was* the business of carrying out the teacher's sequence. He believed that he was doing *his* thing badly (learning) because he was not doing *her* thing well (moving through her instructional activities).

Sociolinguist

Roger Shuy is well-known for his research on language in its social contexts, especially for his work on social dialects (including black English) and, more recently, on uses of language in classroom settings. He also is involved in the development of teachers' manuals for reading . . . which may be the problem.

In his article "What the Teacher Knows Is More Important Than Text or Test" Shuy (1981) stresses the importance of teachers' own knowledge bases—their knowledge of learning theory, of language, of children's individual learning styles, of the reading process. He argues that only such knowledge enables the teacher to use existing instructional materials appropriately and sensitively with individual children. He presents a set of "language accesses to reading" (p. 922): "letter-sound correspondences, word-parts, words, sentences, discourse" (p. 923) which "differ in cruciality to the process of learning to read at different stages in the acquisitional processes." (p. 922) These "accesses" are characterized both as "roughly represent[ing]" children's language, "their arsenal of strategies" they use in learning to read, *and* as representing "most approaches to the teaching of reading" (p. 926). (Possibly he means to suggest here, though this is not made explicit, that reading instruction is in tune with children's learning.)

However, the following two points suggest that, in fact, Shuy is describing teaching sequences which he inadvertently confuses with children's learning sequences (an "acquisitional process" of "learning to read"). First, he orders these "accesses" according to their "degree of cruciality," as one learns to read. We are to take this ordering only as suggestive, as ". . . an estimate of some sort of average learner's awareness" (p. 926). But the pattern is clear. Shuy argues for a developmental view of learning to read in which the developing reader engages in what

Shuy calls "a movement toward meaning" (p. 922). At the beginning of this movement the child relies more heavily on smaller access units (letter-sound correspondences, word parts) than on larger ones, and ultimately the child relies more heavily on larger access units (sentences, discourse) than on smaller ones. But this "movement toward meaning" view, while consistent with familiar teaching sequences, totally ignores an important and growing body of research on children's *learning* to read. This research, much of it focusing on children's learning in natural settings, does not suggest a "move toward meaning," with children using smaller bits more at first and larger bits more later, finally moving up to "meaning." Rather, that research suggests that in the child's construction of meaning in early encounters with print, it is attention to larger units, discourse and context, that is overriding and, in fact, provides a framework for the child's processing the smaller bits at all. Examples abound, including the child "reading" a story aloud long before decoding skills are in evidence, or the child "reading" "McDonald's" as "hamburgers," or Harste, Burke, and Woodward's (1982) three-year-old Nathan reading "Crest" on the toothpaste carton as "Brush teeth." Meaning in a real context is clearly present, while use of small print units is noticeably absent. "Moving toward meaning" by going from using smaller bits to larger ones is the teacher's way and reflects instructional sequences; it is not the child's way of making sense of print.

Secondly, the largest and most meaningful "access" of all is totally absent from Shuy's scheme, namely, the reader's purpose in engaging with the discourse at all. It is puzzling to me that a sociolinguist would overlook this "access" which alone gives meaning and purpose to the others. As Shuy takes care to point out, reading is a language process and children come to reading knowing language well. Surely one of the major knowings children have about language is that it is always purposeful. "The child knows what language is because he knows that language does" (Halliday, 1973). Communication purposes are present long before talk, and the presence of these purposes in all expressive forms of language (speech, writing, deaf sign) remains a constant. To overlook communicative intent as "access" is clearly to be focusing on teaching accesses, which typically offer only the teacher's purpose of "Today we are going to read X." X, the text, is Shuy's highest unit, "discourse." But though teaching accesses may stop at text (discourse) and ignore language purposes, learning accesses do not. It is the child's purpose in reading, as in all language encounters, that gives rise to, enables, and sustains all sense making involving print.

The four encounters described here all have to do with reading, an important area of sense making for young children in school. But the examples could have come from any curricular area: the child's "learning" in social studies which gets described as an instructional sequence, "We study the family first and then we do community helpers," or the child's "learning" in science which gets described as the instructional sequence "The earthworm unit comes at the beginning of the year and then we do bones and it's butterflies in the spring." And nowhere is there mention of children as active explorers and builders in a social and physical world.

If the goal of teaching is, as some believe, to support children's learning, to "respond to what the child is trying to do" as Frank Smith (1973) would have it, then we would do well to try to understand what children's learning is like, what the child is trying to do. At the very least, we must begin by distinguishing between the time-honored instructional activities of teachers, and the timeless sense-making processes of children.

REFLECTION: WHAT ARE THE LANGUAGE ARTS FOR?

Editors' Note: Perhaps the *fundamental question in thinking about teaching language arts is this: What are the language arts for? This question is taken up eloquently by eminent scholar Maxine Greene.*

———❧———

Language arts, like other related disciplines in education, are in large measure for enabling persons to make sense of their experience, to order it, to symbolize it, to attend to it with acts of mind. To work with storytelling, to tap the arts to set the imagination free, to break with the "normal" and taken-for-granted, maybe to give persons opportunities to open to one another and to see through other eyes. (p. 478)

In classrooms open to the space beyond, with teachers conscious of their being in the world, people may be provoked to take notice of a world of burnt-out buildings, homeless families, ceaseless wars, violence and violations of all kinds. (p. 479)

▷

The arts—novels, stories, poems, films, paintings, dances—also provide shapes of possibility for the young, images of what is not—what might or ought to be. (p. 479)

Source: Greene, M. (1988). What are the language arts *for*? *Language Arts, 65*(5), 474–480.

REFLECTION: SETTING GOALS FOR LANGUAGE ARTS IN A MULTICULTURAL SOCIETY

Editors' Note: Arguably, one of the principal goals of language arts instruction is to help students develop the skills needed to live in a culturally, racially, and linguistically diverse, democratic society. Rebecca Eller Powell offers some goals consistent with her democratic vision for language arts instruction.

The trivialization of the language arts in our schools results from our failure to acknowledge literacy as a fundamentally social process that is learned and constructed in various social contexts. Language . . . is basically a cultural expression that takes on different forms according to the social context within which it is being used (Collins, 1989; Ferdman, 1990). Hence it is erroneous to speak of literacy in singular terms as a single, fixed entity. Rather, each of us is literate to varying degrees, within different social contexts. All uses of language carry with them certain values and attitudes about what constitutes appropriate linguistic behavior; therefore, within any given context are particular norms and expectations for legitimate language use (Heath, 1983; Taylor & Dorsey-Gaines, 1988). Schools represent one such context, and as homogenizing institutions, they have established certain standards that guide the instruction and evaluation of language development. Hence those students whose discourse patterns conform to school norms generally succeed, while those with divergent linguistic behaviors generally fare poorly. . . . By emphasizing the mechanical aspects of literacy and denying the social and political implications of language use, schools effectively silence opposing voices. (pp. 342–343)

[Powell then offers the following goals for language arts instruction.]

Goal #1: All students are able to communicate effectively with all persons within a multicultural, diverse society. (p. 344)

Goal #2: All students learn to value linguistic diversity and celebrate the cultural expressions of those who are different from themselves. (p. 345)

Goal #3: All students see the value of language and literacy for their own lives and for social, political, and economic transformation. (p. 346)

Source: Powell, R. E. (1992). Goals for the language arts program: Toward a democratic vision. *Language Arts, 69*(5), 342–349.

REFLECTION: ORGANIZING LANGUAGE ARTS INSTRUCTION

Editors' Note: Frank Smith's classic article "Demonstrations, Engagement, and Sensitivity" has provided a generation of language arts teachers with guidance for constructing a general framework for language arts instruction. The text that follows is an excerpt from this article.

Demonstrations

The first essential component of learning is the opportunity to see how something is done. I shall call such opportunities *demonstrations*, which in effect show a potential learner "This is how something is done." The world continually provides demonstrations through people and through their products, by acts and by artifacts.

Every act is a cluster of demonstrations. A teacher who stands before a class demonstrates how a teacher stands before a class, how a teacher talks, how a teacher dresses, how a teacher feels about what is being taught and about the people being taught. A tired teacher demonstrates how a tired teacher behaves, a disinterested teacher demonstrates disinterest. Enthusiasm demonstrates enthusiasm. Not only do we all continually demonstrate how the things we do are

▶

done, but we also demonstrate how we feel about them. What kinds of things are demonstrated in classrooms? Remember the time bomb—children are learning all the time. What kind of writing do children see teachers doing? What do teachers demonstrate about their interest in reading?

Every artifact is a cluster of demonstrations. Every book demonstrates how pages are put together, how print and illustrations are organized on pages, how words are set out in sentences and how sentences are punctuated. A book demonstrates how every word in that book is spelled. What kinds of things do our artifacts in the classroom demonstrate? Is it possible that those continually learning brains are exposed to demonstrations that books can be incomprehensible, that they can be nonsense?

There are some interesting kinds of demonstrations that I do not have space to go into here. I would like to explore *inadvertent* demonstrations. In a sense, most demonstrations are inadvertent, but sometimes we can demonstrate one thing quite unintentionally when we actually think we are demonstrating another. Some simulations may fool ourselves—but those ever-learning brains? An important category of demonstrations is self-generated, like those we can perform in our imagination. We can try things out in the mind and explore possible consequences without anyone actually knowing what we are doing. But imagination has its limitations, it is ephemeral. Writing can offer the advantages of thought, and more. It can be private, without the disadvantage of transience. We can (in principle at least) keep writing as long as we like and manipulate it in any way we like to demonstrate and test all kinds of possibilities, without the involvement of other people.

The world is full of demonstrations, although people and the most appropriate demonstrations may not be brought together at the most appropriate times. And even when there is a relevant demonstration—for example a spelling that it might be useful for us to know—learning may not take place. There has to be some kind of interaction so that "This is how something is done" becomes "This is something I can do."

Engagement

I use the term "engagement" advisedly for the productive interaction of a brain with a demonstration, because the image I have is of

▶

the meshing of gears. Learning occurs when the learner *engages* with a demonstration, so that it, in effect, becomes the learner's demonstration. I shall give two examples of what I mean.

Many people are familiar with the experience of reading a book, magazine, or newspaper and stopping suddenly, not because of something they did not understand, but because their attention was taken (engaged?) by a spelling they did not know. They did not start to read to have a spelling lesson, nor could they have predicted the particular unfamiliar spelling that they would meet, but when they encountered it—perhaps a name they had only previously heard on radio or television—they stopped and in effect said, "Ah, so that's the way that word is spelled." At such a moment, I think, we can catch ourselves in the act of learning; we have not simply responded to a spelling, we have made it a part of what we know.

The second example is similar. Once again we find ourselves pausing while we read, this time not because of a spelling, and certainly not for lack of understanding, but simply because we have just read something that is *particularly well put*, an interesting idea appropriately expressed. This time we have engaged not with a spelling or even with a convention of punctuation or grammar, but with a style, a tone, a register. We are learning vicariously, reading as if we ourselves might be doing the writing, so that the author's act in effect becomes our own. This I think is the secret of learning to write by reading—*by reading like a writer*.

The two examples I gave were necessarily of situations in which we might actually be consciously aware of a learning moment. But such moments are I think rare. Perhaps we catch ourselves engaging with a new spelling because it is a relatively rare event, as most of the spelling we need to know we know by now. Children learning the sounds, meanings, and spellings of scores of new words every day of their lives are hardly likely to be stopped, like an adult, by the novelty of actually meeting something new. Instead, most of their learning must be like adult learning from the newspapers and the movies, an engagement so close and persistent that it does not intrude into consciousness.

We engage with particular kinds of demonstrations because "that is the kind of person we are," because we take it for granted with our ever-learning brain that these are the kinds of things we know. My explanation may sound simplistic, but I can think of no

▷

alternative. Obviously we can learn by doing things ourselves. With engagement we assimilate the demonstration of another (in an act or artifact) and make it vicariously an action of our own. What I still must account for is what makes us the kind of person we are; what determines whether or not engagement takes place.

Sensitivity

What makes the difference whether we learn or do not learn from any particular demonstration? I thought at first that the answer must be motivation, but have decided that motivation is a grossly over-rated factor, especially in schools where it is used to cover a multitude of other possibilities. For a start, learning of the kind I have been describing usually occurs in the absence of motivation, certainly in the sense of a deliberate, conscious intention. It makes no sense to say an infant is motivated to learn to talk, or that we are motivated to remember what is in the newspaper, unless the meaning of motivation is made so general that it cannot be separated from learning.

On the other hand, motivation does not ensure learning. No matter how much they are motivated to spell, or to write fluently, or to learn a foreign language, many people still fail to learn these things. Desire and effort do not necessarily produce learning. Indeed, the only relevance of motivation to learning that I can see is (1) that it puts us in situations where relevant demonstrations are particularly likely to occur, and (2) that learning will certainly not take place if there is motivation not to learn.

My next conjecture was that expectation is what accounts for learning. We learn when we expect to learn, when the learning is taken for granted. This I think is closer to the truth, but a *conscious* expectation is not precisely what is required. Infants may take learning to talk for granted, but not in the sense of consciously expecting it. Rather what seems to make the difference is absence of the expectation that learning will not take place.

This is how I propose to define *sensitivity*, the third aspect of every learning situation: the absence of any expectation that learning will not take place, or that it will be difficult. Where does sensitivity come from? Every child is born with it. Children do not need to be taught that they can learn; they have this implicit expectation which they demonstrate in their earliest learning about language and about the world. Experience teaches them that they have limitations, and unfortunately experience often teaches them this unnecessarily. Children believe their brains are all-potent until they learn otherwise.

Why is learning to talk generally so easy while learning to read is sometimes so much harder? It cannot be the intrinsic difficulty of reading. Infants learning to talk start with essentially *nothing*; they must make sense of it all for themselves. Despite the remarkable speed with which they are usually credited with learning about language, it still takes them two or three years to show anything approaching mastery. Reading should be learned very much quicker, as it has so much spoken language knowledge to support it. And when children do learn to read, whether they learn at three years of age, six, or ten, they learn—in the observation of many teachers—in a matter of a few weeks. The instruction may last for years, but the learning is accomplished in weeks. What is the difference? I can only think that, with reading, there is the frequent expectation of failure communicated to the child, so often self-fulfilling.

Why is learning to walk usually so much easier than learning to swim? Walking must surely be the more difficult accomplishment. Infants have scarcely any motor coordination and on two tottering feet they must struggle against gravity. Little wonder walking takes several months to master. Swimming, on the other hand, can be learned in a weekend—if it is learned at all. It is learned when the learner has much better motor coordination and in a supportive element—water. And it must be as "natural" as walking. So why the difference? Could it be that difficulty and failure are so often anticipated with swimming and not with walking?

The apparent "difficulty" cannot be explained away on the basis of age. Teenagers are expected to learn to drive cars—surely as complicated a matter as learning to swim, if not to spell—and lo, they learn to drive cars. In fact, for anything any of us is interested in, where the learning is taken for granted, we continue to learn throughout our lives. We do not even realize we are learning, as we keep up to date with our knowledge of stamp collecting, astronomy, automotive engineering, spelling, world affairs, the television world, or whatever—for the "kind of person" we happen to be.

Engagement takes place in the presence of appropriate demonstrations whenever we are sensitive to learning, and sensitivity is an absence of expectation that learning will not take place. Sensitiv-

▶

ity does not need to be accounted for; its absence does. Expectation that learning will not take place is itself learned. The ultimate irony is that the brain's constant propensity to learn may in fact defeat learning; the brain can learn that particular things are not worth learning or are unlikely to be learned. The brain is indiscriminate in its learning—the time bomb in the classroom—and like the incorrect spelling it can learn things which it would really do much better not learning at all. Learning that something is useless, unpleasant, difficult, or improbable may be devastatingly permanent in its effect.

If this is true, what is the consequence of all the tests we give at school, especially on the children who do not do so well on them? What is the effect of "early diagnosis" of so-called language problems, except to transform a possibility into a probability? Children's brains are not easily fooled. They learn what we demonstrate to them, not what we may hope and think we teach. (pp. 108–112)

Source: Smith, F. (1981). Demonstrations, engagement and sensitivity: A revised approach to learning language. *Language Arts, 58*(6), 103–112.

3 Scaffolding: Who's Building Whose Building?

Dennis Searle

Editors' Text: Student ownership has become a key concept underlying language arts instruction in many classrooms. This piece raises important questions about the role of teachers in the context of student ownership.

What has made the teaching of language arts exciting for me since I began in 1966 has been the continuing growth in our understanding of what language is and how it is learned. There has been a constant interaction between research into language and the teaching of language that has brought researchers into the classroom and turned teachers into researchers. This interaction is crucial but demands constant, critical evaluation. Recently, language teaching has picked up from research the concept of "scaffolding" and this concept has begun to be discussed in journals as a teaching strategy. I am concerned about how scaffolding is interpreted and what happens when teachers and consultants apply this notion to classroom teaching. At the base of my concern is the fundamental question of who is in control of the language.

Understanding Scaffolding

To understand how scaffolding can be misapplied it is first necessary to see what the concept was intended to describe. Bruner (1975) explains one form of interaction between a young child and its mother by saying, "In such instances mothers most often see their role as supporting the child in achieving an intended outcome, entering only to assist or reciprocate or 'scaffold' the action" (p. 12). Bruner and Ratner (1978) expand on the concept by identifying some features which contribute to effective scaffolding. These include a familiar semantic domain, predictable structures, role-reversibility, variability, and playfulness. Bruner's view that scaffolds give support to situations allowing children to interact and learn from their use of language seems to make

---

This essay appeared in *Language Arts* 61.5 (1984) on pages 480–483.

sense and was certainly picked up by other researchers including Scollon (1976) and Cazden (1979). Graves (1983) interpreted his approach to conferencing from a scaffolding point of view.

As a concept, then, scaffolding has an extremely respectable pedigree and it does help us understand some child-adult interactions. One of the keys to remember is Bruner's original statement that when scaffolding, the adult works to "support the child in achieving an intended outcome." Graves claims that "scaffolding follows the contours of child growth" (p. 271). The active, initiating child stays in control of the language and the experience while the adult operates effectively in response to the child.

Undoubtedly, this kind of responsive scaffolding can, and does, occur in school. Kreeft (1984) gives a good example in a written dialogue between teacher and student. The student is writing about a recent holiday in San Diego and the teacher uses the personal experience of a similar holiday to support the student's extended writing on the topic. By asking simple questions such as, "Do they still have the dancing waters?" the teacher triggers extended description and personal evaluation in the student's journal entries. Kreeft likens this dialogue to Wells' (1981) notion of the teacher as "leader from behind."

Ignoring Students' Intentions

Schools, however, are rarely effective in allowing children either to initiate topics or to shape the experience for themselves. As a result, scaffolding can more often become the imposition of a structure on the student. In Kreeft's article another example of scaffolding is shown. In response to a statement by the student about wishing to be a rock star, the teacher offers a set of career guidance information, such as "Do you play any musical instrument? Rock stars need to study music so they can interpret it and write their own." The student responds minimally to this scaffolding, because, I think, the original intentions have not been honored.

I have encountered other examples of this approach to scaffolding. In an address to the Canadian Council of Teachers of English Cazden (1981) suggested and demonstrated intervention in young children's show-and-tell sessions to help the children learn to speak in focused, extended narrative. In Cazden's examples, however, the children's understanding, valuing, and excitement of the personal experiences were negated as the children were led to report the experience in an appropriate form. Applebee and Langer (1983) advocate "instructional scaffolding" and provide examples in which teachers scaffold students' science experiment reports by providing a sheet of questions which outline the required steps. Undoubtedly, these outlines help the students report the experiment more completely, but do they really help them learn the purposes and nature of scientific writing? Why, for example, are the students performing and reporting the experiment? Whose intentions are being honored in the report?

In fact, it appears that the term scaffolding is being used to justify some long-standing and, in my view, questionable classroom interaction patterns. The following excerpt from a show-and-tell session observed in other research (Searle & Dillon, 1981) shows a teacher "supporting" a grade one student. Notice that the child's experience is taken from him and is molded according to the teacher's view of what is relevant and interesting.

> *T:* Oh, boy! What's that?
>
> *Ch: (Pause)*
>
> *T:* Maybe you'll explain to us about what this is. If you know, don't tell. Would you turn right around so we can all hear?
>
> *Ch:* A walkie-talkie.
>
> *T:* Do you just have one of them? How many do you have?
>
> *Ch:* One.
>
> *T:* How many do you need to listen?
>
> *Ch:* Two. My brother has one.
>
> *T:* I see. Can you show us how it works? You turn it on first. Is this where you turn it on?
>
> *Ch:* Um, that's where I talk to my brother.
>
> *T:* I see. That's called the *(inaudible)*. That's where you can talk to your brother. I don't imagine you can talk to him now. Did he bring his to school?
>
> *Ch: (Shakes head.)*
>
> *T:* And how do you talk? Let's pretend that Jason is talking. No? You are not going to show us? How many have used a walkie-talkie?
>
> *Ch$_1$:* I lost my walkie-talkie. *(Class starts to chatter.)*
>
> *T:* Just a moment, please. If you have anything to ask you can put your hand up. Yes?
>
> *Ch$_2$:* How long did you get it?
>
> *Ch:* Christmas.
>
> *T:* At Christmas.
>
> *Ch$_1$:* Yeah.

> *T:* We usually say, "How long *ago* did you get that?" Have you
>   had a lot of fun with it? Well, who would like to talk next?

This teacher described the teacher's role in such sessions as taking pressure off shy students and modeling questions and comments. In fact, the situation was changed into one in which the child was left to figure out the teacher's understanding and intentions. This feature of classroom life has been noted by other researchers, notably Barnes (1976) and Edwards and Furlong (1978). In understanding how scaffolding works outside the classroom setting, however, it is best to be reminded that "The routines of action and the rules behind them are accepted because of a co-operative motive, but they do not create the motive" (Trevarthen, 1980).

Scaffolding and Control

The adequacy of the metaphor implied by scaffolding hinges on the question of who is constructing the edifice. Too often, the teacher is the builder and the child is expected to accept and occupy a predetermined structure. Scaffolding, in this sense, provides a rationale for those who feel that children's language is deficient and therefore children need to be taught the "necessary" language. The notion of scaffolding, however, should not be used to justify making children restructure their experience to fit their teacher's structures. What we should be doing, instead, is working with children, encouraging them to adapt their own language resources to achieve new purposes which they see as important.

Wells has shown that schools differ from homes as environments for language learning in that there are fewer opportunities in school for children to initiate language activities and there is less response to these initiatives when they occur. This characteristic would indicate that schools are a poor environment for how Bruner originally conceived scaffolding to work by "supporting the child in achieving an intended outcome." Students have had little say in determining what counts as knowledge and how knowledge should be shaped in schools. Until teachers are ready to turn over more control to students, there appears to be no way in which scaffolding can be an effective classroom strategy for language development.

REFLECTION: CHILDREN ARE SMART

Editors' Note: One principle that ought to underlie all language arts instruction is this: "Children are very smart." Charles Read offers the following example of children's skill as language learners.

It has been estimated that a six-year-old knows about 8,000 root words in English, that is, forms like *house*, *run*, and *tall* excluding derived forms like *houses*, *running*, and *taller* (Carey, 1978). If we assume that the same child knew only about 50 words at eighteen months, then he or she has learned nearly 8,000 basic forms in about four and one-half years, or 1650 days. Simple division indicates that this child has acquired about five words per day, or about one word every third waking hour. . . . The size of this accomplishment increases our appreciation for a child's success as a language learner. (pp. 146–147)

Source: Read, C. (1980). What children know about language: Three examples. *Language Arts, 57*(2), 144–148.

STRATEGY: STRUCTURING STUDENT TIME

Editors' Note: Large blocks of time for reading and writing provide students with opportunities for extended reading and writing of texts and teachers with time to provide frequent, intense, explicit, and individualized support and direction appropriate to students' needs. Jacquelin H. Carroll and Charlene Noelani-Kahuanui Christenson offer some thoughts on how these "large blocks of time" might be organized.

[S]ome open blocks of time enabled students to think about and work on their goals. This flexible structure also gave Charlene time to observe her students, interact with them as individuals, and focus her instruction on their needs.

[Charlene's] students were given choices about what and how they would read and write. Students selected their own books for independent reading, chose from among books offered for literature

▶

study groups, managed many of their own small-group discussions, and wrote open-ended journal responses in addition to responding to some general questions given by the teacher. They also selected their own topics for writing, controlled the content and length of their pieces, and determined formats for publishing and sharing. These choices allowed students to consider their options and select materials and experiences to help them reach their goals.

Students were invited to take greater responsibility for their own learning and were held accountable for using their time to achieve their goals. At the end of readers' or writers' workshop, students were often asked to share what they had accomplished in working toward a current goal and how they felt about it. Other students' responses to one child's sharing were opportunities to develop a community of support for each other and each other's goals. Students also maintained their own portfolios, selecting work they thought reflected their progress toward their goals. (pp. 45–46)

Source: Carroll, J. H., & Noelani-Kahuanui Christenson, C. (1995). Teaching and learning about student goal setting in a fifth-grade classroom. *Language Arts, 72*(1), 42–49.

STRATEGY: FLEXIBLE GROUPING AND MINILESSONS

Editors' Note: In progressive language arts classrooms, skill instruction is often taken up in the context of small-group minilessons and individual conferences. Scott C. Greenwood suggests that learning contracts provide a means for organizing classrooms for this kind of support.

―――――― ✎ ――――――

Under the parameters of learning contracts, the teacher is afforded the time and opportunity to do lots of individual-skill teaching when conferencing. Additionally, there is clearly much opportunity to do brief, whole-group minilessons as the need arises. Finally, flexibly grouped minilessons are also called for. For example, if eight students in a class have negotiated to write original short stories, the teacher might group them for work on the mechanics or nuances of dialogue and dialect writing, using the specific needs of one of the student

▶

authors (with permission, of course). This group would then disband. In addition to flexible-needs groups, interest groups also form and re-form for specific instruction as needs dictate. (p. 92)

Source: Greenwood, S. C. (1995). Learning contracts and transaction: A natural marriage in the middle. *Language Arts*, 72(2), 88–96.

REFLECTION: PLEASURE AND THE LANGUAGE ARTS

Editors' text: In one of our editors' columns we explored why reading for pleasure is undertheorized in language arts.

———————⌖———————

> The teachers say they mean to consult our happiness in everything they do. But their "happiness" already seems to me like Father's: a dark affair of Conquering Sin and Doing One's Duty. Oh, Abial, I yearn to buffet the Sea of Pleasure, where there are poems on every wave and kisses in the curl of the foam.
>
> Farr, *I Never Came to You in White*

As we prepared the Editors' Pages for this issue, we began our exploration of the theme "Pleasure and the Language Arts" with Judith Farr's fictionalized account of the life of Emily Dickinson. Like the young Emily depicted in Farr's novel, we assumed the posture of critique in relation to the place of pleasure in education. Fueled by a climate in which learning in a technologically driven world is portrayed as "in-netscapable" and schools are viewed as either prep schools for industry or the training ground for tomorrow's consumers (Robertson, 1998), we seemed headed for yet another commentary on education in conservative times. And, for a while, the outlook for our Editors' Pages was bleak, until we decided to study the term "pleasure" and the life it has in contexts that are not announced as "educational."

　　Much of the writing in the language arts that deals directly with the concept of pleasure sanitizes it and turns it into something to be manipulated. The theorization of pleasure is drowned by an emphasis on skill development in well-meaning texts such as *Reading for pleasure: Guidelines* (Spiegel, 1981) or any one of hundreds of comparable essays. So, too, with writing—only more so.　▶

Yet, pleasure has been theorized upon since the time of the ancient Greeks and holds a prominent place in contemporary cultural studies writings. Pleasure and work (Kerr, 1962), pleasure and pain (Gosling & Taylor, 1982), pleasure and desire (Mercer, 1983), pleasure and diversion (Jameson, 1983), pleasure and frustration (Wallace, 1984) are among the binaries that characterize discussions about pleasure. Added to this list is the question of how writers work with the term itself. For instance, how does pleasure relate to value (Connor, 1992), satisfaction (Perry, 1967), gratification (Perry, 1967), or bliss (Barthes, 1975)?

In fact, it may be the presence of pleasure's many conceptual partners that results in educators shying away from pleasure's use in favor of using more muted or oblique referents. The company pleasure keeps is troublesome in an educational world demanding certainty and assurance. But, perhaps even more troublesome is the undercurrent of sexuality within the discourse of pleasure and the difficult knowledge that must be faced if a discourse of pleasure is to enter into educational writing. So, for educators, a discourse of pleasure can be multiply disconcerting, since it asks us to deal with an ambiguous concept that flirts with sociocultural taboos.

The Risks of Pleasure

> Danger is the sweet Heart
> Of Pleasure, and the thrilling Sister
> To Joy.
>
> (Farr, 1996, p. 121)

What might a discourse of pleasure look like? Imagine a discourse about reading where the conversation was not about character or plot or about word identification or vocabulary knowledge. Imagine, instead, a discourse about the risks of reading, the lure of the text, the feeling of losing oneself in a text, the loss of engagement and even melancholia that sets in once the reading is complete. Think about a discourse that considers the conjunction of a text's intensity, predictability, and availability (McBride, 1996) as descriptive of the potential pleasure that text might have for a reader. Such discourses demand a new pedagogy from educators and have attendant risks, such as shifting the responsibility for the interpretation of textual engagement to the reader. Similar discourses of pleasure might be considered for writing, discourses hinted at by comments like those of the poet and short story writer Rita Dove (1994):

> I run through all the different attributes of a word when I am trying to find the right one. A word not only has a meaning— it also has a sound, a feeling in the mouth, a texture, a history. Very often if a word has the right meaning, but not the sense, the deeper sense I need, I try to think of words that rhyme, or I look up its etymology. Writing for me means that intense plea- sure of dealing with language, working with the language like a potter works with clay. I think most writers have an almost shameless love of language, of words and the way they work. (p. 87)

What would writing instruction look like if the pleasure of the writer was the focus? How might the remembering of the pleasure of writing make the constructive work of writing desirable? These kinds of questions ask us to consider a more basic question: What might an explicit discussion of pleasure in the language arts unleash?

Discourses of Hedonism and Heartache

More than anything else, inventing a discourse of pleasure in the lan- guage arts would bring with it a recognition of the subjectivity of experience, the knowability of life at the personal, individual level. As Wendy Steiner (1995) puts it in her discussion of art criticism in *The Scandal of Pleasure: Art in an Age of Fundamentalism*:

> It has taken me a long time to admit that the thrust of criticism is the "I like," and whatever expertise I have accumulated con- spires in this admission. The authority of one's institution of higher learning, one's academic credentials, one's ever-increas- ing experience may establish "objectively" one's claim to be- ing an expert, but at the heart of any critical act is a subjective preference. (p. 7)

Once we open up the subjectivity inherent in the performance of the language arts, we must seriously consider that, from the per- spective of children's subjectivities, their experiences of pleasure may be outside our own. Research by Grace and Tobin (1997) and by Randi Dickson (1998) illustrates the risks, and perhaps the heartache, that adults must face when confronted with the perverse pleasures of children.

▶

When elementary school children were handed video cameras in the Grace and Tobin (1997) study, they were given choice—choice that went beyond the typical "choice" which really operated within the children's perceptions of the adult's view of what was school-appropriate. The result was not only a challenge to the video genre itself, but the production of videos that "often featured the parodic, the fantastic and horrific, the grotesque, and the forbidden. These scenarios enabled the children to locate a space where collective pleasures were produced" (Grace & Tobin, 1997, p. 169).

Grace and Tobin (1997) argue that the creation of the videos provided children a space to work through their worries, troubles, wants, and desires and to derive pleasure in the acts of creating and presenting their creations to others. The authors caution that the carnivalesque content of the videotape productions is not the desired goal of creating spaces for pleasure in authorship, but, in an echo of Farr's (1996) Emily Dickinson, it can be a place to remember that "the humor and everyday interests of children . . . have a place in the classroom, in the delicate, fragile, and shifting balance between excess and constraint" (Grace & Tobin, 1997, p. 185). This means that the discourses of pleasure need not be totally hedonistic where pleasure and value are identical, nor highly moralistic (Connor, 1992). Instead, possibilities such as those created by Grace and Tobin (1997) suggest that educators themselves should struggle with the pleasure and pain of opening up classrooms to a new discourse as they work with and think about the discourse of pleasure. (pp. 112–113)

Source: Dudley-Marling, C., & Murphy, S. (1998). Editors' pages. *Language Arts, 76*(2), 112–114.

II Talking about Talk

4 Discourse for Learning in the Classroom

Ken Watson

Bob Young

*Editors' Text: Drawing on the work of British educationist Douglas Barnes,
Watson and Young present portraits of typical whole-class discourse and
present examples of alternatives. Underlying this piece are questions of who
is in control of the discourse in the classroom, what teacher authority can look
like in varied models of discourse, and the assumption that students can and
do make unique, valuable, and knowledge-building contributions if provided
with the opportunity to do so.*

Teaching is essentially a process of transactional interaction during which, mainly through exploratory talk and writing, students clarify their ideas and forge links between new knowledge and their previous understanding. Some of the interaction occurs in small groups without the teacher, but the teacher's role is often still crucial in organizing resources, in insuring that individuals neither dominate groups nor sit back and let others do the work, in arranging for the sharing of insights between groups. The evidence is clear, however, that in the vast majority of classrooms throughout the English-speaking world the largest proportion of this interaction is to be found in the I.R.F. (Initiative-Response-Feedback) cycle or teacher question–pupil answer–teacher reaction cycle. In many studies more than half the official talk occurs in these cycles. They are the main way in which teachers engage their students in the process of exploration and rehearsal of new material. Where this form of interaction does not occur, it is not usually because some other oral communication, such as small-group work, has replaced it, but because the question/answer reaction pattern has been transferred into written form via the questions at the end of the relevant section of the textbook.

The evidence also suggests that this dominant pattern of classroom dialogue is ill-adapted to real learning, and teachers must take a critical look at current teaching practices.

This essay appeared in *Language Arts* 63.2 (1986) on pages 126–133.

Typical Classroom Discourse

If one reviews the evidence on teacher questioning, from Romiett Stevens (1912) to the most recent studies, one finds that teachers commonly ask as many as fifty thousand questions a year and their students as few as ten questions each. Further, about 80 percent of teacher questions are likely to call for memory processes only. Barnes et al. (1969), analyzing a series of lessons given to eleven and twelve year olds, found that factual questions predominated even in those lessons where the teacher's aim was to encourage the children to think; one of us found the same patterns of questioning at the highest levels of the secondary school. For example, of nineteen questions asked in one history lesson, only one required more than simple recall of facts. Even where the question itself was apparently an open one, both the form of the question and the teacher's intonation often signaled the required answer, as in this example from an English lesson:

> *Teacher:* Some people might say that the theme of the play is exploitation. Have we much evidence for that?
>
> *Students: (In chorus)* No.

With younger children, a great deal of the teacher's questioning, if the transcripts available to us are at all typical, is directed towards correct labeling of phenomena. It is not uncommon to find several pages of transcript devoted to the eliciting of a single word that the teacher has in mind and as an appropriate label for what is being discussed. The severely edited example which follows, arising from a child's reading of some lines from a poem, occupies forty-four lines in the original transcript:

> *Teacher:* Good girl! What did she put into that? Those few words. What did she add? What's the name of it? . . .
>
> *Pupil:* Strength? . . .
>
> *Teacher:* . . . The word I am thinking about starts with an *e* . . .
>
> *Pupil:* Exasperation?
>
> *Teacher:* I don't think so. Exasperation is when you're annoyed. . . . The question was, "What do you call it when someone is reading something the way X was." She didn't just read the words. She made them much more meaningful, because she added this dimension and it starts with *e*, the word I'm thinking about. There are other words for it. . . .
>
> *Pupil:* Exclamation?
>
> *Teacher:* Right. These are all on the right track, but not the one I'm thinking about.

Pupil: (Inaudible)

Teacher: Expression is the word. Expression!

At times, indeed, one is left with the distinct impression that the label is valued more than the idea behind it.

The pupil response phase of the I.R.F. cycle seems no more satisfactory. Transcript after transcript provides evidence that teachers are content with one- and two-word answers. Rarely do they invite pupils to elaborate on their answers. In a sample of thirty "discussion" lessons, eleven contained no examples of pupils being invited to develop their answers, and only seven had sufficient examples to suggest that the teachers were pursuing a deliberate policy of encouraging pupils to develop their replies (Watson, 1980).

A study we undertook of the feedback or teacher reaction phase of the cycle suggests that here, too, teacher behavior may be actively inhibiting learning (Watson & Young, 1980). After a pupil has replied to a question, the teacher normally makes an explicit metastatement such as "Good" or "No, that's wrong," and follows this with a statement in which the pupil's reply is repeated or reformulated in some way. We have identified a range of functions in these reactions: repeating a pupil's response so that everyone may hear; repeating it with positive approval because it is what the teacher wants; partial repetition of those parts the teacher wants to make use of; adding to, generalizing from, replacing terminology in, and otherwise transforming the pupil utterance. Our evidence suggests that in this stage of the cycle many teachers quite unconsciously alter pupil responses to fit their own frames of reference. Consider, for example, the following excerpt from a lesson with a class of thirteen year olds:

1. *Teacher:* Why do people have discussion?

2. *Pupil:* It's just natural, kind of—it's natural.

3. *Teacher:* That's right, it's natural to talk to people about things. But why? Why do people discuss?

4. *Pupil:* 'Cos it's easier than writing it all down on paper. *(Laughter)*

5. *Teacher:* Yes, it's natural to talk, but I think there's some other reasons too.

6. *Pupil:* To get each other's opinion.

7. *Teacher:* Good, to get each other's opinions.

8. *Pupil: (Inaudible)*

9. *Teacher:* All right, and to find out what each other thinks about things and perhaps to come to a . . . *(pause)*

10. *Pupil:* Agreement.

11. *Teacher: (Pause)* . . . decision about something. All right, you might have a problem, you discuss it with someone. They might help you to solve it. . . . What about if you're the speaker in the discussion? You're the one everyone's listening to. What sort of rules must you follow?

12. *Pupil:* Sometimes you've got to be careful what you say about people.

13. *Teacher:* All right, you've got to think about what you're going to say.

At two points in this sequence (11 and 13) the teacher has transformed the pupil's response into something different. By rejecting "agreement" and substituting "decision" the teacher is, surely, signaling that the response is deficient in some way. More seriously, perhaps, her response at 13 suggests that she is so enclosed within her own frame of reference that she fails to see that another, equally valid point is being made. Here is another, slightly different, example:

1. *Teacher:* OK. What do you think makes the foil spin round and what does that tell us?

2. *Pupil:* The air's getting hot.

3. *Teacher:* The air's getting hot. Yes, that's a very good answer. So what happens to the air? Tony?

4. *Tony:* It goes up and makes the foil spin.

5. *Teacher:* That's right. So for our conclusion what would we write about air? What did we find out about air? . . . hot air? We held the roll above the flame. The foil started to spin when held above the flame. So what does that tell us about hot air? Where does the hot air go? I think Lynette told us.

6. *Lynette:* Um . . . where the foil is.

7. *Teacher:* And where is the foil?

8. *Lynette:* On the stick. *(The aluminum foil was attached to a stick.)*

9. *Teacher:* But what happens to the air?

10. *Lynette:* It gets warm.

11. *Teacher:* Yes, it gets warm and what happens to it then?

12. *Anna:* It rises.

13. *Teacher:* So what happens?

14. *All:* Hot air rises!

15. *Teacher:* Right. So our conclusion is that hot air rises.

In this example, the teacher did not build on the correct but *particular* conclusion advanced by Tony at line 4 but engaged in a long and inefficient exchange aimed at eliciting the general notion (all hot air rises) or at least wording compatible with it, since we may be permitted to doubt whether the point of the exercise was really understood by the pupils. If, instead of focusing on the pre-decided correct conclusion, the teacher had focused on the pupils' answers, the answers would have been evaluated in their own right, rather than simply for the degree to which they did or did not match the answer the teacher had in mind. A possible move, following up Tony's answer and explicitly seeking the level of generality the teacher wanted, would have been:

Teacher: And do you think the air will *always* go up like that?

Pupil: If it is hot.

Teacher: Fine, would you go and write that on the board.

Even where there is no suggestion that the teacher is ignoring or distorting a pupil's answer to fit it into his or her frame of reference, it often seems that the cognitive work of the lesson is being done by the teacher instead of by the pupils. As has already been noted, relatively few teachers encourage pupils to develop or elaborate on their answers; instead, it is the teacher who does the work of analyzing, generalizing, synthesizing.

Teacher: And how does the boy in the poem feel about these rough boys?

Pupil: He wants to be one of them.

Teacher: Yes, he longs to join them: This is because, isn't it, he not only longs for companionship but because he feels that they are really living, that his parents, by keeping him away from them, are sheltering him from life's experiences, keeping him away from what life is really like. They are depriving him of the experiences that all boys should have.

It seems that the majority of teachers lack faith in their pupils' capacity to be active, constructive participants in their own learning. They feel that they must *tell* the pupils what they must know, *interpret* new knowledge for them, *make explicit* any generalization that can be drawn from the accounts of experience being presented rather than structure classroom experience so that pupils feel a need to develop their own accounts more fully. Even the computer and the video can also tell, make explicit and interpret—often more vividly than the teacher. They can be (to use Douglas Barnes's term) good teachers of the "transmission" kind (Barnes, 1973). But we now know enough about children's learning to make us reject the transmission model of teaching as inadequate.

An Alternative Discourse

The interactive nature of teaching must be informed by a model of classroom communication which recognizes the *active* nature of children's learning, which values exploratory talk and writing as the chief means by which children come to terms with new knowledge, which acknowledges that the links between old knowledge and new must be forged by the learners themselves. The Transmission teacher must be replaced by the Interpretation teacher, who

> will see discussion and writing as ways of helping pupils to think more effectively, and will credit them with the ability to make sense of experience for themselves by talking and writing about it. For him, knowledge is something that each person will have to make for himself. (Barnes, 1973, p. 14)

The move from Transmission teacher to Interpretation teacher is not an easy one. We suggest that the first step might be a constant encouragement to pupils to develop their answers, so that they are given frequent opportunities to "talk themselves into understanding" (Douglas Barnes's phrase).

> *Teacher:* You're saying that the school environment is a pretty violent one?
>
> *Pupil:* No, not necessarily, but they see it on television.
>
> *Teacher:* But that TV tape you saw said that violence on television didn't have much effect on people.
>
> *Pupil:* But that was just a theory.
>
> *Teacher:* You really think it does have some effect? OK.
>
> *Pupil:* I don't think that violence on TV and that, it'd influence us much because, er, we're really old enough to understand that it's going on for much larger issues than just a little difference.
>
> *Teacher:* And a desire for revenge?
>
> *Pupil 2:* Yes.
>
> *Teacher:* Such as Kirk suggested. Is it so much, let me come back to something Kirk suggested before we go on to this wider front, do you think it (violence between students) is for prestige reasons?
>
> *Pupil 3:* Well, sir, they might not have the verbal . . . er . . . power to express what they want to so they just hit out.
>
> *Teacher:* Lacking, all right, you're suggesting perhaps where you haven't got the, the verbal skills, is that what you are suggesting?

Pupil 3: Yes.

Teacher: Mark, would you agree with that? From what you said earlier . . . ?

Mark: I would think it was a matter of self-control.

Teacher: You think they lack self-control, so they hit out, rather than lacking the means of an alternative?

Here is a teacher of a year nine class developing a structure of opinion about a poem which deals with children fighting. Note that this teacher is doing three things which, in either the research literature or the body of the transcripts available to the authors, are quite rare: he is keeping track of who "owns" which opinion ("Such as Kirk suggested"), he is checking to see whether his understanding of each opinion is correct ("Is that what you are suggesting?"), and he is building a logical structure into which students can place their views and systematically interrelate them ("So they x rather than y"). We later find the same teacher making these moves:

Teacher: (After a student has argued that if we didn't fight with our friends, we might do something that would create even more damage) So vandals who destroy railway carriages are people who haven't got friends to fight with?

Pupil: (Changing his answer) Aw . . . no, I suppose . . .

Teacher: (Interrupting) I, no, no . . . I'm just trying to get you to test out your generalization . . . er . . . think it out and if you still think it . . .

What is particularly notable about the teacher's final move is that it is a rare example of a teacher making the logical or methodological assumptions of the talk quite explicit. The same may be done for value assumptions, value contrasts, or aesthetic relationships:

Pupil: When people get angry, it's very ugly.

Teacher: You think sometimes it's not nice to see people when they're like that. . . . Is it, do you think, sometimes people can be beautiful when they're angry?

Pupil: Yes . . . but I don't know, they're still ugly sometimes, too.

Teacher: What's the difference between the ugly and the beautiful angry people? How could we figure this out? Something being angry and beautiful at the same time?

Going even further, the teacher can actively work to relax the degree of conversational control that he or she exerts in the classroom so that it no longer becomes necessary for every response to be channeled through the teacher. It is possible to create a classroom climate in which pupils feel free to respond directly to one another without having to wait for the teacher's evaluative comment. In one of the transcripts available to us, a discussion of a poem, the teacher's conversational control is so relaxed that her question is often followed by comments from four or five pupils before she feels it necessary to intervene again:

Teacher: What are these children (in the poem) doing?

Pupil 1: Writing.

Pupil 2: And they're really getting into what they're writing about.

Pupil 3: And it's something the teacher didn't have to push onto them.

Pupil 4: Yeah, they're just doing it . . . by themselves.

Thirdly, a critical analysis needs to be made of the textbooks and packaged kits in use in the classroom. Too many of these, especially in the language arts area, simply reinforce the negative aspects of the I.R.F. pattern. (Here it is important to note that the stated rationale of the textbook may prove at odds with the contents. Many of the most widely used textbooks in the language arts area have introductions proclaiming the most enlightened educational philosophy, and yet the activities and exercises define knowledge in a way which suggests that it is completely objective and factual and discount the value of the pupils' own experience.)

Finally, there needs to be a much wider recognition of the fact that pupils need frequent opportunities to discuss new ideas in small groups. The work of Barnes and Todd (1977) has clearly demonstrated that small-group work can be very productive indeed, training pupils in collaborative learning, helping them to develop hypothetical modes of thinking, teaching them to rely on their own initiative and judgment. Barnes and Todd found that:

> When we played back the recordings to the teachers, their reactions were commonly of surprise and delight. They were surprised because the quality of the children's discussions far exceeded the calibre of their contributions in class; and were pleased to hear the children manifesting unexpected skills and competencies. (p. 9)

Barnes and Todd's findings have been partially replicated in a study by Michell and Peel (1977). In that study pupils working in groups were compared with conventional teacher-led discussion and pupil discussion where the teacher acted as "neutral chairperson." The main measures employed were measures of the frequency of "describing" and "explaining," which, although very crude, permit some conclusions about the cognitive level or complexity of talk. The amount of explaining in the pupil groups without a teacher present was much higher than in the conventional teacher-led discussion (of the kind found in many of the examples above), but there was an even higher level of explaining in the groups where teachers acted as "neutral chairpersons," taking responsibility for structure and relevance of the discussion but not for the content. The presence of the teacher may have a value after all! But a note of caution should be sounded. In comparing pupil groups working alone with the teacher-chaired group we may be doing something rather similar to comparing the writing or speaking of a foreign language (generative action) with the reading of it (recognition). The ultimate measure must have to do with what the pupils are capable of by themselves. Just the same, it suggests that an alternation between pupils working alone or in small groups and more actively teacher-structured pupil activities, such as chaired discussions, may be an appropriate strategy. No doubt there is room, too, for a variety of inputs of a more conventional kind, such as films or lectures. The crucial distinctions are not between one kind of activity and another but between situations in which the teacher sensitively provokes further development of the pupil's own active processes of making sense through talk and writing and the kind of situations, which are all too common, where teachers impose their own framework on a stratum of pupil talk artificially elicited for the occasion.

Conclusion

It is not particularly original to suggest that teachers should create more opportunities for students to possess and develop their own ideas in an atmosphere of encouragement. Nor is it unusual to hear it argued that to do this it is essential to provide opportunities for exploratory talk. Perhaps a little less often, we hear it argued that students will learn more quickly and efficiently if they can identify with the ideas they are learning, either fit them into their own frames of reference or recognize a need to change their views. The main trouble with the latter assertion, it is said, is that the presence of structure and organization in the learning materials is also closely related to learning efficiency. To gain the benefits which come from the active involvement of students in building their own world view, along with those that come from well-structured materials, is the aim of every educator.

Teachers may meet current challenges to their effectiveness, at least in part, by encouraging *pupils* to deliver more of the materials, while teachers take more responsibility for provoking pupils to improve the quality of their ideas and a similar responsibility for helping them to structure and compare and criticize accounts in the light of their own experience.

STRATEGY: THE BOOK TALK

Editors' Note: The book talk is a monologic form of talk. It may be demonstrated by teachers across several occasions, and, eventually, children may wish to present their own book talks utilizing the same principles. The book talk is unlike whole-class or small-group discussion in that it involves formal preparation and the development of an organizational framework for talking to a group.

—————— ✎ ——————

Purpose

The book talk can be an effective means for calling children's attention to authors, titles, and types of books in which they might be interested. The intent is not to give synopses of the books presented, but to tell just enough to intrigue would-be readers. (p. 416)

Organization

A book talk typically would include four to eight titles, and be presented to a group. More titles could cause confusion, making each less memorable. . . . Choose a unifying theme of some sort. . . . Within the chosen theme, select titles which, among them, will appeal to all members of the audience. (p. 416)

Once the titles are chosen, the means for presenting each must be determined . . . [e.g.,] simply telling something about the book . . . [or] reading a brief selection. . . . [A]ppropriate visuals may be shown. (p. 417)

The content of the presentation of a fiction book could be an introduction to its characters . . . , an exposition of the situation . . . , a typical and inviting episode from the book . . . , or an introduction to the setting. . . . For a non-fiction book, the way an author approaches a

▶

subject generally provides the content of the presentation; demonstration of a technique or actual audience participation can be used, as in how-to books. (p. 417)

At the end of the book talk, provide for an immediate follow-through, in which children are invited to help themselves to titles in which they are interested. (p. 417)

Source: Witucke, V. (1979). The book talk: A technique for bringing together children and books. *Language Arts, 56*(4), 413–421.

5 Authentic Questions: What Do They Look Like? Where Do They Lead?

Beverly A. Busching

Betty Ann Slesinger

Editors' Text: Questioning is often the focus of many beginning teachers' anxieties, and Bloom's Taxonomy is often presented as a tool to use in resolving this anxiety. However, Busching and Slesinger challenge Bloom's hierarchical scheme and suggest an alternative. Although the authors focus on their analysis of student questions in response journals, the applicability of their alternative to all classroom discourse is readily apparent.

must love the questions," Alice Walker (1983, p. 40) writes, and sometimes we do love questions, drawn by the "locked rooms full of treasure" they promise. But often we don't love questions—we don't love them at all. Perhaps that is why Walker titles her poem "Reassurance." Questions are not always welcome, especially if they are big, hard, and real. The promised rooms of treasure are often not a lure at all but a peril to be avoided. When we ask questions, we must deal with the answers— or our failure to find them—whether we are prepared or not.

Real questions are still rare in classrooms. The mighty force of the curriculum, once set in motion, does not easily pause for uncertainties and undetermined destinations. Teachers and students alike leave their important questions at home and reduce their wondering to the confines of preplanned "thinking" activities. We may thus create a more orderly school day, but our potential as inquirers is diminished. The space that we can grow into has been made very small indeed.

Are there ways to rethink curriculum so that we can invite an active pursuit of significant human questions into the classroom? The two of us, a middle school teacher and an education professor, began

This essay appeared in *Language Arts* 72.5 (1995) on pages 341–351.

to look at Betty's seventh-grade language arts class to see how she could create a learning environment that would stimulate students to raise and pursue their real questions. She was committed to an authoring cycle approach (Atwell, 1987; Harste, Short, & Burke, 1988) and decided that she wanted to extend this model to humanities inquiry. Her current approach of integrating personal and transactional writing with literature had provided a useful frame for active involvement of students across genres, but it did not provide sufficient scope for students to grow beyond their current interests and thoughts. Supported by a grant from the Rural Education Alliance for Collaborative Humanities (a division of Collaboratives for Humanities and Arts Teaching), we began to make plans for a multidisciplinary unit on the European theatre of World War II, involving students in fiction and nonfiction as sources for their learning.

Preparing for the Unit

We wanted students to see history full of the lives of people. It wasn't enough to know that 13 million people were killed in the Holocaust, we thought; they needed to seek the stories behind the numbers. We wanted students to address lifelong questions and challenge their television-derived stereotypes. We started by looking for our own real questions and found these: How can we study war in a way that leads to a commitment to peace? How can a Holocaust study avoid stimulating hatred for Germans or contempt for Jews? How can students find a personal connection to historical events? Will the unit lead to caring about injustice in their own world?

Although Betty had hoped for a block schedule that would give her extended time with the students, it was not possible this year. We needed to create the conditions for an authentic engagement with distant historical issues for five 50-minute language arts classes each day. We knew that an ordered sequence of teacher-planned questioning activities would not allow students to pursue their own questions in a thoughtful way (Atwell, 1991). So we turned to a model of immersion: extended student engagement in a variety of reading, writing, listening, viewing, and talking activities that immerses them in the topic from a variety of perspectives (Gamberg, Kwak, Hutchings, & Altheim, 1988; Short & Burke, 1991; Watson, Burke, & Harste, 1989).

Language arts objectives would be integrated into their work. We wanted the students to be engaged with both informational and fictional sources in an integrated, overlapping approach because we thought that the emotional immediacy of literature interacting with a factual background would promote stronger personal involvement than if each type of learning occurred in a separate phase. We planned a variety of ways for students to make connections between information and personal response as they read, viewed, talked, and wrote. They would share responses with each other and, even more importantly, be resources for each other. Face-to-face interactions, always limited by the five-period schedule, were supplemented with online dialogue in the computer room and by filling the walls with the results of each student's research. Refinement of their thinking in finished products would come through publishing their work for an audience.

Based on this preplanned framework, Betty filled the room with a wide variety of resources (see chapter appendix) and worked with the librarian and the social studies teacher in her unit to make additional sources available. Her weekly planning then became an interplay between preplanning and responses to student needs, interests, and suggestions. A summary of the resulting activities is shown in Figure 1.

The unit, described in more detail in Slesinger and Busching (1995), evolved into the following five phases over a period of six weeks:

1. The launch: A read-aloud of *Rose Blanche* (Innocenti, 1985).

2. Initial engagement and fact finding: The story of Anne Frank as a diary (Frank, 1958); a play (Goodrich & Hackett, 1989); and a biography (Lindwer, 1992). Teacher-directed geographical and historical study.

3. Student-directed engagement with fiction, family history research, and factual inquiry. Connections with current events.

4. Refining and sharing learning through student-selected projects.

5. Inquiry projects on racism and hate in their own community.

Studying Students' Questions

So that we could begin to understand how the unit stimulated student thinking, we tracked the students' questions through the various contexts in which they naturally arose. Betty asked students to record their questions in each of the written response formats they used, such as learning logs and online dialogue journals. In Figure 2 are two contrasting responses to the required sections of the journal (facts, personal feelings, questions, and author's strategies). Erica had already read *The Diary of Anne Frank* (Frank, 1958) and therefore reached out beyond the immediate circumstances of the Frank family. Her "facts" section made

Teacher-Planned Whole-Class Reading and Viewing

Teacher read-aloud: *Rose Blanche*
Partner reading: *Diary of Anne Frank* excerpts; companion informational article
Reader's Theatre: *Diary of Anne Frank* play
Analysis of painting: Picasso's *Guernica*
Videos giving informational background

Individual and Small-Group Work Shared with the Class

Facts and terms search
Family connections with World War II
Articles, poems, and artifacts (as discovered by students)
Investigations of racism and hatred in our community

Other Individual Work Shared in Small Group or with Partners

World War II novels (choice of 15 titles)
Background investigation for novels and final projects

Shared Information Formats (Classroom Displays)

Time line
European and world maps
Facts pockets (who, what, where) and facts charts
Questions

Peer Response Formats

Double-entry literature response journals
Summary paragraphs and character descriptions
Online dialogue responses to novels
Inquiry and authoring conferences

Final Project Choices

Book reviews
Scriptwriting
Interviews
Short stories, fictional diaries
Graphs, charts, and maps
I-Search papers and "big questions" essays
Reviews of World War II in current media

Figure 1. Summary of World War II inquiry unit activities.

Erica

Facts

Germany started war.
Germany invaded Holland.
Put Jews under restriction.
Had to turn in bikes, couldn't go to movies, school, and couldn't ride in cars.
Jews not allowed in German stores.
All Jews wore the Star of David to show they were Jews.
Many went into hiding for many years.
Jews were put into concentration camps.

Personal Feelings

I think some Germans didn't like what Germany was doing to the Jews. I think the characters were strong and brave for going into hiding. And the people were brave for helping them.

Questions

What were Anne's feelings towards Adolph Hitler?
What made Hitler do this?

Eric

Facts

They flew in a B-17, and its top speed was 170 mph.
It was so cold that ice formed on his mask.
A piece of flak can tear a man to pieces.

Personal Feelings

The experienced fighters teased the rookies.
They like to curse in the Air Force.
The first mission is usually the hardest.

Questions

Is it safe for someone so young to be flying that much?
How long will his luck last?

Author's Strategies (section added to the response journals during the unit)

The author described things, like the plane.
He took that and made you actually see the plane.
He made you feel like you were really there.

Figure 2. Two literature response journal entries.

strong intertextual connections with the data gathering efforts that had begun to fill the walls of the classroom. Her questions are empathetic, and they raise moral issues. On the other hand, Eric demonstrated his strong interest in the physical facts he learned about airborne warfare from his selected novel, *The Last Mission* (Mazer, 1979). Even though this entry comes after almost a month of study, his opinions and questions arise from the immediacy of his reading experience.

Betty invited questions in class discussions and shared her own real questions as a participant in these discussions. To further stimulate authentic questioning, she gave a mini-lesson on "digging deeper," showing an example of a lively student journal entry. A chart of student questions posted on the wall grew over time, and, before the final projects began, an important session was held in which students sought consensus about what were the most important questions they had raised. This resulted in the following list of questions:

1. Why did Germany go to war again so soon after World War I?
2. Why did Hitler hate the Jews so much and go after them?
3. How could Nazis threaten people so horribly?
4. Why didn't the Jews fight back?
5. Who helped the Jews, and what happened to them?
6. What were the strategies, plans, and hopes for D-Day?
7. Why is there a neo-Nazi movement, and what does it want?

Because we wanted to learn about how students used questioning, we tried to notice what was going on as they asked questions. We were especially interested in the talking, writing, and reading they were doing. We thought that this would help us understand not only the kinds of questions they asked but also what their questions meant and what role questions played in their learning (Christenbury & Kelly, 1983; Langer, 1992; Morgan & Saxton, 1991). We did not use a predetermined category system as a screen because we wanted to see what we would discover.

Some of what we report here was discovered while the unit was going on. As the students moved from one phase to another in their study, we saw new roles for questioning and new directions for their inquiry; these insights relieved some of Betty's concerns about allowing students to find their own way. Later, in the summer, we perused the piles of xeroxed journal entries and final projects and, of course, saw much more. The contrast between traditionally accepted categories of questioning and what we found significant about the students' thinking clarified several issues for us.

Rethinking What We "Know" about Questioning

Now it is clear to us that we must reject the constraints of a hierarchy of question types if we are to understand the significance of questions in teaching and learning. For too long we have used Bloom's Taxonomy to assign artificial values to certain kinds of questions. A hierarchical scheme that values "higher-order" questions over "factual" ones ignores the obvious truth that facts cannot be relegated to a lower order of significance. It is only when facts are the object of isolated, artificially constructed work that they have less to offer the learner. In real inquiry facts offer power and control. The search for an additional fact may be integral to constructing a theory or testing a belief. Facts are both the basis for beliefs and theories and the means for testing them. In the larger society the vital significance of facts is not discounted; think of the medical importance of diagnostic tests and the legal importance of evidence. It is time to bring this understanding into classrooms. Whether a question is about facts or concepts is less important than whether a question is a part of something significant. The outward form of the question may have little to do with the level, the depth, or the importance of thinking that has occurred.

We want to suggest new ways to think about school questions, focusing on the real questions of students. Our categories attempt to express the meaning of questions as they occurred, but it should be remembered that our analysis is only an outsider's view. The students' thinking was undoubtedly more richly varied than our present understanding can capture.

Questions of Unfocused Information Seeking

The unit was launched with the picturebook *Rose Blanche* (Innocenti, 1985), which tells the poignant story of an Italian child whose village is invaded by German soldiers. The text is a simple, direct narrative; but the detailed illustrations provide a stark chronicle of invasion, starvation, betrayal, and, finally, a prison camp full of thin, ragged children. The ambiguous ending to this story brought protests from the students. Rose had obviously disappeared, but what had happened? The flower caught on the barbed wire fence was not really an answer, and that detail was not even noticed by most of the students.

- Betty, instead of responding to the flurry of raised hands, asked students to write their questions in the reading response section of their notebooks. The written reader responses invited all students, not just the most bold, to verbalize their uncertainties and the anomalies in the text. They discovered the questions could be preserved for continued study and reflection. At least 33 different questions were raised, reflecting the incredible amount of detail that students had noticed in both the text and the pictures. We were struck by how much they needed to know in order to understand this one simple story. The following two sets of questions show the range of their puzzlement:

Carol's Response
Why do the soldiers wink at the children?
Where in Germany are they?
Where are the trucks going?
What were the children doing there?
Why didn't the car have lights on?
Who shot the gun?
Who were the people that spoke differently?
What happened to Rose?

Jennifer's Response
Why were there broken toys in the river?
What is this town called?
Why were soldiers there?
Is this a true stretched story that happened to someone the
     author knew?
Why did the mayor bring that boy back to the truck?
What were the children doing inside that barbed wire fence?
Why was everyone getting thinner?
What did the star symbolize?
Why did Rose keep returning to that clearing?
What happened to Rose Blanche?
Why was the mayor wearing a symbol but the soldiers weren't?
Where were the other soldiers coming from?
What happened to the old soldiers?
Why wasn't Rose caught and arrested for feeding the children in
     the prison?

These responses taught us the first of many lessons that we would learn as we followed the students' questions throughout the unit. It was startling that they knew so little about what adults consider general cultural knowledge of World War II. Many did not even know who the Nazis were and did not realize that the soldiers would obviously be a threat to the town. None of them understood what the betrayal of the mayor meant or that the children were in concentration camps. They asked primarily literal, information-seeking questions, but the results were far from superficial or sterile. The obviously perilous adventures of Rose had stimulated intense emotional involvement, and students needed a factual foundation in order to speculate and wonder. Without this initial foundation of specifics, very few would have been able to move on to more compelling questions. And without this early investment of their emotions, very few would have been interested in asking more compelling questions.

These questions posed a challenge to one of our assumptions about the students' literary reading. When students rejected the ambiguous ending to *Rose Blanche*, we assumed that they were unwilling to invest themselves as active readers, perhaps because television had dulled their ability to sustain simultaneous possibilities. When we studied their questions, however, we realized that the truth was that they *had* invested themselves, but they didn't have enough information to formulate alternative possibilities. Now we wonder how many other times we had assumed that students possessed background information when it was lacking.

The students' need for information continued past the first, fact-seeking phase of the study. Whenever their investigations opened up a new window on World War II, a stream of factual questions poured forth. For instance, those students who didn't already know the Anne Frank story needed time to understand what was going on. In contrast to the broadly speculative questions that Erica raised in her journal (shown in Figure 2), their journals were full of factual questions like these:

> Is Anne still alive?
>
> What was life like in the attic?
>
> Who found Anne's diary?
>
> Where were the Franks sent?
>
> What happened in the camps?
>
> What if the people who helped the Jews got caught?

Questions to Fulfill Requirements

Especially at the beginning of the unit, many students responded to Betty's requirement to raise questions with responses that seemed lifeless, such as these questions raised in computer dialogues about Anne Frank:

> Do you like studying about Anne?
>
> Do you think it was mean for the Nazi soldiers to kill the Jews?

As might be expected with the fragmenting, five-class daily schedule, some of the 125 students never seemed to find authentic questions. Some students missed significant blocks of time for disciplinary reasons; a few were emotionally withdrawn; some struggled just to read their novels; and others seemed to lack the confidence to take ownership of their work. Examination of journals and final projects showed that these students were in the minority and that even they, although marginally involved, learned a great deal about the World War II period from the public sharing of information and questions from enthusiastic students.

We gained additional insights into the process of finding real questions in interviews with three groups of students as the novel-reading phase was just getting underway. The students agreed that at the beginning of a novel it is harder to ask searching questions because "you [aren't] into it yet." Sometimes, they admitted, they just put something down. They showed us some of their early questions: "Will Jack meet Dotty?" "How long will Jack be able to keep his cool figure?" Later in the book they had questions they truly wanted to raise. Our examination of the response journals supported the students' comments. Looking through them, we found many more "What's-going-to-happen?" questions like, "How long will his luck last?" (See Eric's journal entry in Figure 2.) Although these questions were similar in form to the inauthentic questions the students had shown us, they seemed real to us. They did not address the larger issues of the unit, but they seemed to be part of the process of immediate engagement with the book.

Questions of Focused Information Seeking

As students amassed information and made personal connections, their informational questions seemed to change in purpose. As inquirers, they were more in charge of their focus and less involved with struggling for basic comprehension. Their new questions of fact seeking were based on integrated geographical and historical understandings and seemed to search for a missing piece of a larger conceptual framework that was emerging. When we noticed how dramatically the questions differed in content from student to student, we realized how poorly served these students would have been by teacher questions assigned to the whole class. For example, notice the diversity of focus in these questions from journals and discussions:

> When did the U.S. invade and free the camps?
>
> I wonder how many Germans were really Nazis.
>
> Why were the prisoners moved around?
>
> How were the Spitfires different?

Questions of Connected Understanding

The increasing sophistication of their connected knowledge led students to ask questions that sought to clarify anomalies arising from different sources encountered during the study. Nonfiction reading and family history interviews provided the informational background students needed to unfold the many layers of meaning in literature. Information allowed them to go beyond literal readings. With their new understandings, ambiguous endings and flashbacks were fascinating rather than confusing. For example, after students had a factual and visual background for the war, the crushing sequence of Nazi domination began to be clear to them. *The Devil's Arithmetic* (Yolen, 1988) group, especially, could appreciate Yolen's ability to foreshadow the coming desolation and to create a poignantly innocent ignorance of this future. Their novels led them to cycle back into atlases and historical source books, and this process of trying to put together a big picture raised more anomalies. These anomalies, in turn, began to raise informed "why" questions. They asked questions like these in their discussions:

> How can you invade if you don't have any bases to supply you?
>
> Why were the Nazis mainly after the Jews? Why not Christians or Blacks or the Indians or anyone else?
>
> Why didn't the Jews fight back?
>
> What is it like to live in constant fear of getting caught?
>
> Why did Germany go to war again so soon after World War I?

Sometimes students returned to their earlier understandings and used questions in order to reconstruct a reading that was now challenged by current information. For example, Sheronda asked after several weeks of study, "Why did Rose Blanche not get arrested for helping the Jews with bits of food?"

Questions of Psychological and Moral Reconstruction

Students, shocked by much of what they were learning, inquired intensely into the psychological and moral processes that could create such terrible events. Their attempts to find ways to live with the horror, a process Kimmel (1977) calls "facing the oven," haunted their journals in the third phase of the unit. They had bumped up against facets of humanity that were beyond their current beliefs, especially in relation to their experience of civic life. The interaction of fiction, nonfiction, and real-life stories of their own families played its part: This was not just imaginary. Grandpa had been there, and it was in the 1943 newspaper! They had to construct a "story" of what had happened during this particular time in the past that could make sense. And at the same time, they had to try to construct a theory of humanity that could encompass Hitler, Anne Frank, and themselves. They needed to reconfirm their belief in the goodness of adults. These were big tasks, and their searching questions reflected the authenticity of their struggles:

> Why did Hitler hate the Jews so much?
>
> Did Hitler feel guilty?
>
> Why did Hitler do this?
>
> How did Hitler feel that he had the power to kill Jews?
>
> I don't know why the Germans followed a man like Hitler.
>
> Hitler was blessed with not only artistic talents, but academic talents as well; how could such an intelligent person hurt the world so badly?
>
> How could anyone follow a man who would burn books?
>
> I wondered how cruel can people be, and could this ever happen to us?
>
> Are people so sick they can treat people like toys—something they turn off and on? Are we *really* that inhuman?
>
> The worst part of the book was when Otto beat the nice old man. It's awful that the Nazis had no respect for their elders, don't you think?

Not all of their psychological questioning addressed such big issues. Some of the novels raised questions about other facets of human life, such as physical endurance and transitions into adult responsibilities. For example, in the journal entry shown in Figure 2, Eric asked, "Is it safe for someone so young to be flying that much?"

Questions of Historical Speculation

As students lived vicariously in history, a few of them began rewriting history in their imagination, and they speculated about how things could have been different with questions such as:

> What if Dunkirk had failed?
>
> What if the Jews had revolted?
>
> What if the D-Day invasion didn't work?
>
> What if the people who helped the Jews got caught?

We were excited when students demonstrated, at least tacitly, that they understood the tentative and hypothetical nature of resolutions in inquiry. Steven, for example, realized that a book on war he was reading "attempts to answer questions that no one really knows the answer to, like, 'What if the Confederates won Gettysburg?'" Because they were personally engaged, history seemed to matter to them. Imagining historical alternatives did not seem to be an idle exercise; instead, it became a recognition of the critical importance of certain events for human outcomes. This historical speculation led some students to imagine alternatives to their own present circumstances (Giroux, 1992), strengthening their commitment to righting wrongs. Amy captured the concerns of other students about "letting this happen again" in a discussion. When she wondered if she was "like Anne because I hear and see racism all day just like she did," she stimulated a follow-up class project on hate and racism in their lives today.

Questions of Literary Imagination

Throughout the unit, some questions demonstrated a close identification with books, as if students had "lived through" the story with the characters (Rosenblatt, 1978). Katie felt close to Rose Blanche in her perilous adventures and wrote her first journal entry as a personal letter: "Dear Rose, I loved your book." Sally imagined Anne Frank developing as a writer like herself, and she wrote to Anne: "When did you begin to write your journal? Did anyone inspire you to write?"

We were also fascinated to see that some students wrote questions into characters in their final stories, plays, and reports. It was as if they understood the universal need to cry out in question form as a protest against dehumanizing circumstances. Kim, for example, wrote a play that evoked the courage and fear of concentration camp inmates as they faced the reality of their deaths. The questions in this whispered dialogue are haunting:

Clara: Reba.

Reba: Yes?

Clara: Will we have to stay here forever?

Reba: Shhh, don't get us in trouble!

*   *   *

Clara: Will we ever get out of here?

Reba: I'm not sure, but I hope so. Maybe. Someday.

Questions as Rhetorical Devices

Several students who chose essays as their final projects demonstrated that the emphasis on questions throughout the unit provided them with another rhetorical device that, as authors, they could reach for when needed. Brian, for example, skilfully used a powerful question to focus reader attention in the lead of his written report:

> My grandfather, George Wold Sr., enlisted in the navy in March of 1943 because he was going to be drafted. Why would he enlist if he was going to be drafted? When the U.S. Army drafts somebody, they choose what service he/she serves in, and they decide how long they serve. When someone enlists, they get to choose.

Jennifer and Laura opened a dialogue with their readers in the dramatic ending to their jointly written essay on why the Jews didn't fight back:

> We have explained our opinions. Take facts that you may gather. And add them to these. Research people like Hitler. Other good people to research are Anne Frank, Franklin D. Roosevelt, and Winston Churchill. Explain your opinions and conclusions. Tell us, why didn't the Jews fight back?

Questions to Focus Research

When Amy raised the question about racism that was quoted earlier, she helped Betty see that the students needed a way to work on their unfocused discomfort about intolerance as it exists today. They decided to look more closely at hatred and racism in their own time. Several groups of students chose to do surveys of students or teachers at the school. Their long immersion in the topic made the process of choosing appropriate questions a relatively easy task. Their surveys focused on questions like these: "Do you believe there is a lot of hate in the world today?" "Why do people hate?" "How do people show their hate?" "What can you and others do to stop hatred?" These questions reflected awareness of the pragmatic purpose—to elicit responses—but were not merely influenced by practical concerns. Their content was also shaped by authentic personal concerns that had evolved during the unit, and the class sessions on survey group reports were tense with feeling. Carol expressed the feelings of her group as she reacted to the reasons for hating others that their school survey had uncovered: "Some people don't even know why they hate. Personally, my group thinks all these reasons are pathetic."

Unstated Questions

Because of occasional cries for help that students voiced in the journals or in impromptu private conversations, Betty thought that this unit on persecution and injustice raised another kind of question, unasked but nevertheless very present for some students. These were the questions that could not be asked because they were too personally threatening to voice publicly. Preadolescent students can be haunted by secret worries about their own inadequacies and their treatment by others: Why do people tease me? How can I be a valuable person when even my family treats me so badly? The inclusion of issues of inhumanity in middle school inquiry units may provide a safe way for young people to work on these personal concerns.

Questions to Quest

Many of the final projects, poems, essays, and many different genres of fiction seemed to address deeply felt, large questions about what it means to be a citizen, what it means to be moral, and what it means to be human in the presence of inhuman acts. The seven "big questions" selected by the students provided a focus for their final projects, in particular for the essays that were one of the project alternatives. We wonder if the consensus-building session that created this list of questions might also have been influential in creating the depth of thought we saw in other projects. Perhaps the thinking that took place in selecting and assessing these big questions supported students in striving to comprehend moral complexities far beyond their initial understandings. When Brandi wrote a long poem entitled "We Are," she went beyond just expressing indignation about hatred. She put herself inside perpetrators of hate to express subtle ideas about their desperate need to avoid facing the consequences of their acts. The collective inner voice of these agents of violence is horrifyingly real: "We are the people who hurt others./ We wonder what it's like for them,/ then focus on our jobs./ We hear their cries to stop and help,/ but who cares?" Robert created a GI from North Carolina who writes home to his family from a ruined farmhouse in France where his platoon is bivouacked, and it seems as if Robert's own voice cries out:

> It hits me like a ton of bricks. I realize that we are too busy killing
> to realize we are killing families, women, children. When we bomb
> a country we bomb more civilians than farmers. We have ruined
> everything.

Stacks of this writing surround us, the outpouring of concern from five classes of seventh graders. The last section of Chris's poem catches our eye because of the strong connection he made between this study and his current concerns:

> The Ku Klux Klan, having their meetings,
> Talkin' about hurting Blacks,
> Starting fights and gettin' them in packs
> And beatin' and killin' them.
> I'm sorry to say that those are the facts.
> The KKK acting just like Germans,
> Walking around and preaching their sermons.
> The holocaust ended fifty years ago.
> But the KKK is here today,
> Killing in the USA.

Many of our hopes for the unit were fulfilled. The issues involved in World War II did turn out to be compelling and multifaceted, and students were engaged without focusing only on the hatred and violence. As the students repeatedly cycled back into the topic through many different perspectives, the mix of fiction, family histories, video, and informational sources provided access to powerful new learning and also stimulated a desire to reach for it. Perhaps the most important single force operating in this unit was student intent: The students were engaged in seeking information that they wanted to know. This intentionality created a mental process that was totally different from what happens when students are seeking information they have been told to find.

We have come to understand that short-term, higher-order-thinking assignments, with their preset boundaries and demands for instant response, have inhibited students' potential for thinking. Instead of focusing on the kind of thinking we want to elicit, we need to focus on whether students' thinking is part of something significant—a commitment, an investment, an investigation. In this unit, students' intentional thinking connected many kinds of mental activity into a purposeful flow that, over time and at different rates, extended beyond expected limits. Allowed some leeway to find their own direction, most of the students were self-impelled inquirers on a quest for understanding. The questioning that at the beginning was guided by teacher assignments became guided by their own curiosity and emotional involvement (Wilen, 1987). There was a synergistic energy in the room, with one student's enthusiasm fueling another's.

Our students' questions took them somewhere, and, for many of them, that meant moving through history to restructure personal beliefs—reaching out with their hearts and minds and returning to their own lives a little different. As Carol said in her survey summary, "We have to think beyond hate and look for at least some good in people. We can't have closed minds. If everyone hated certain kinds of people, the world would most likely fall apart." Some of them reported that now they felt different when they saw World War II movies on television. We knew that one student became an activist against racism in the student council, and we overheard several indignant conversations about the racist behavior of other students. These glimpses of connections to their out-of-school lives encouraged us to believe that the unit was not a brief moment of engagement but part of a continuing cycle of new understandings and personal commitments. Perhaps we are not stretching the truth too far when we say that in the midst of the frenetic middle school day, during the Valentine carnation sale and Spirit Week, our 12- and 13-year-olds were being philosophers.

Appendix: Student Resources

Fiction

Arnothy, C. (1987). *1 am fifteen—and I don't want to die*. New York: Scholastic.

Bishop, C. H. (1952). *Twenty and ten*. New York: Puffin Books.

Burch, R. (1974). *Homefront heroes*. New York: Puffin Books.

Butterworth, E. M. (1982). *As the waltz was ending*. New York: Scholastic.

Fry, V. (1968). *Assignment: rescue: An autobiography*. New York: Scholastic.

Greene, B. (1973). *Summer of my German soldier*. New York: Bantam Books.

Hautzig, E. (1968). *The endless steppe*. New York: HarperTrophy.

Laird, C. (1990). *Shadow of the wall*. New York: Greenwillow.

Levitin, S. (1987). *Journey to America*. New York: Macmillan.

Lowry, L. (1989). *Number the stars*. New York: Dell Yearling.

Matas, C. (1987). *Lisa's war*. New York: Scholastic.

Matas, C. (1989). *Kris's war*. New York: Scholastic.

Matas, C. (1993). *Daniel's story*. New York: Scholastic.

Moskin, M. (1972). *I am Rosemarie*. New York: Scholastic Book Services.

Orlev, U. (1984). *The island on Bird Street* (H. Halkin, Trans.). Boston, MA: Houghton Mifflin.

Ransom, C. (1993). *So young to die*. New York: Scholastic.

Reiss, J. (1972). *The upstairs room*. New York: HarperTrophy.

Reiss, J. (1976). *The journey back*. New York: Scholastic.

Richter, H. (1972). *I was there* (E. Kroll, Trans.). New York: Puffin Books.

Sender, R. (1986). *The cage*. New York: Bantam Books.

Serraillier, I. (1990). *Escape from Warsaw*. New York: Scholastic.

Ten Boom, C. (1971). *The hiding place*. New York: Bantam Books.

Wiesel, E. (1960). *Night*. New York: Bantam Books.

Nonfiction

Atkinson, L. (1985). *In kindling flame—the story of Hannah Senesh, 1921–1944*. New York: William Morrow.

Cowan, L. (1969). *Children of the resistance*. New York: Hawthorne Books.

Dupuy, T. N. (1965). *Combat leaders of World War II*. New York: Franklin Watts.

Hoare, R. (1973). *World War II*. London: MacDonald Educational Ltd.

Hurwitz, J. (1988). *Anne Frank—life in hiding*. Philadelphia: The Jewish Publication Society.

Lindwer, W. (1991). *The last seven months of Anne Frank*. New York: Doubleday Dell Publishing.

Meltzer, M. (1976). *Never to forget: The Jews of the Holocaust*. London: Harper & Row.

Rogasky, B. (1988). *Smoke and ashes*. New York: Holiday House.

Sullivan, G. (Ed.). (1988). *Great escapes of World War II*. New York: Scholastic.

Sullivan, G. (Ed.). (1991). *The day Pearl Harbor was bombed*. New York: Scholastic.

Young, P. (Ed.). (1981). *The world almanac of World War II*. New York: Scripps Howard.

Young, P. (Ed.). (1986). *The world almanac of World War II*. New York: World Almanac.

Zyskind, S. (1989). *Struggle*. Minneapolis: Lerner Publications.

QUOTATIONS

Personal narratives belong to the silent language that embodies thinking. Children need a place where seminal experiences, which often occur outside of school, move from silent contemplation into speech. (p. 173)

Source: Gallas, K. (1992). When the children take the chair: A study of sharing time in a primary classroom. *Language Arts, 69* (3), 172–182.

———✑———

[D]iscourse acquisition is the lynchpin of schooling; it is the point at which real educational equity occurs. . . . [R]eading or math skills are only the skin of the literacy process. (p. 253)

Source: Gallas, K. (1997). Story time as a magical act open only to the initiated: What some children don't know about power and may not find out. *Language Arts,* 74(4), 248–254.

REFLECTION: ON COLLAPSING AND CO-CONSTRUCTING SHARING TIME

Editors' Note: One student, Jiana, who had "the chair" for sharing time, told a story so fantastic that the teacher's response was to believe it wasn't true. The next day, Jiana was absent. The following account is a reflection on what happened.

———✑———

Sarah got up and shared a story about a swimming incident in which her sister fell out of a boat and swam with the dolphins. The story was obviously a complete fabrication, and a few children said, "That can't be true!" and turned again to ask me [the teacher], "Is that true?" But this time I didn't respond. During the questions and comments, the children cross-examined Sarah on the issue of truth and realism, refuting her story line. Sarah tried to maintain the story but got caught in inconsistent details. I asked myself what was going on. Was the power of the chair so great that it made you do anything to stay in it? Did some children secretly admire Jiana's story and emulate

▶

it? More importantly, I wondered why I had defined the sharing narrative to mean true stories. Clearly, I was lagging behind some of these 6- and 7-year-olds in my conceptualization of what sharing time was. That was how our exploration of "fake" stories began. The next day, I apologized to Jiana and the rest of the children for my behavior and told them that it seemed as if we needed to expand our format. (pp. 176–177)

Source: Gallas, K. (1992). When the children take the chair: A study of sharing time in a primary classroom. *Language Arts, 69*(3), 172–182.

6 What Is Sharing Time For?

Courtney B. Cazden

Editors' Text: This discussion of the routine of sharing time, a feature of many primary grade classrooms, asks us to consider how culture contributes to the different ways in which stories are told and how it can affect the ways in which they are understood. Companion pieces can be found that illustrate what happens when children are permitted to take charge of their own sharing time and how children use power in this setting (Gallas, 1992, 1997).

Jerry: Ummm, two days ago, ummm, my father and my father's friend were doing something over the other side, and my sister wanted uhhh, my father's friend to make her a little boat out of paper, and the paper was too little. He used his dollar and, ummm, my sister undoed it and we, ahhh, bought my father and my mother Christmas presents.

T: A man made a boat out of a dollar bill for you?! Wow! That's a pretty expensive paper to use!

Sharing Time, a routine event in many primary grade classrooms, is of special interest for several reasons. First, it may be the only opportunity during official classroom airtime for children to create their own oral texts: to say more than a short answer to teacher questions and to speak on a self-chosen topic that does not have to meet criteria of relevance to previous discourse. Second, because one purpose of Sharing Time is to allow a sharing of personal experiences, it is often the only official classroom airtime when out-of-school experiences are acceptable topics in school. Otherwise, talking to the teacher about out-of-school life may be restricted to transition moments such as before school or while waiting in line; in fact, a teacher shift from listening to not listening to such stories is a clear marker that school has officially begun: "I can't listen now, Sarah, we have to get started" (i.e., we have to enter a

This essay appeared in *Language Arts* 62.2 (1985) on pages 182–188. Further discussion, including teacher research on sharing time, appears in Cazden's *Classroom Discourse: The Language of Teaching and Learning* (Heinemann, 2001, 2nd edition).

different discourse world in which what you're talking about, no matter how important to you, is out of bounds). Third, in addition to Sharing Time's unique features in expected length and topic of children's speech, it is of interest as a context for the production of narratives—perhaps the most universal kind of text.

Given these features of what might seem a routine and unimportant part of the school day, important questions can be raised. What kind of narratives do children tell? Are there differences in the stories that seem related to different home backgrounds? What is the role of the audience—teacher and other children? In a series of studies begun by Sarah Michaels in California and continued with me in the Boston area, we have tried to answer these questions. I will report here only what we have learned about the kinds of responses that teachers make.[1]

Most teachers make some response—either a comment or question—to each Sharing Time narrative. The responses we observed can be placed along a dimension of the extent to which teacher and child share a sense of appropriate topic and appropriate way to tell about it. At one end is the enthusiastic appreciation of Jerry's teacher:

> A man made a boat out of a dollar bill for you?! Wow! That's a pretty expensive paper to use!

At the opposite end is another teacher's negative reaction to Deena's day:

> *Deena:* Um, I went to the beach Sunday, and to McDonald's, and to the park. And I got this for my birthday. My mother bought it for me. And, um, I had, um, two dollars for my birthday, and I put it in here. And I went to where my friend named Gigi—I went over to my grandmother's house with her. And, um, she was on my back, and I—and we was walking around by my house, and, um, she was heavy. She was in sixth or seventh grade—
>
> *T: (interrupting)* OK, I'm going to stop you. I want you to talk about things that are really, really very important. That's important to you, but tell us things that are sort of different. Can you do that?

Between these extremes are a variety of responses. I have ordered them into four categories, but readers are encouraged to consider alternate orderings and their reasons for them.

First, and closest to the appreciation end, are cases where the teacher has clearly understood the story and simply comments or asks a question for further information, as Carl's teacher did:

Carl: Well, last night my father was at work. He—every Thursday night they have this thing, that everybody has this dollar, and it makes up to a hundred dollars. And my—and you've gotta pick this name out . . . and my father's name got picked. So he won a thousand dollars—a hundred dollars.

T: Tell us what he's gonna do with it.

Carl: He's gonna pay bills.

A second kind of response leads to an extended collaboration between questioning teacher and reporting child that results in a more complete story about an object or event than the child would have produced alone. Here is an example about making candles:

Mindy: When I was in day camp, we made these candles.

T: You made them?

Mindy: And, uh, I, I tried it with different colors, with both of them, but one just came out. This one just came out blue, and I don't know what this color is.

T: That's neato. Tell the kids how you do it from the very start. Pretend we don't know a thing about candles. OK, what did you do first? What did you use? Flour?

Mindy: Um, there's some hot wax, some real hot wax, that you just take a string and tie a knot in it and dip the string in the um wax.

T: What makes it have a shape?

Mindy: Um, you just shape it.

T: Oh, you shaped it with your hand, mmm.

Mindy: But you have—first you have to stick it into the wax, and then water, and then keep doing that until it gets to the size you want it.

T: OK, who knows what the string is for?

When Mindy's teacher says, "Tell the kids how you do it from the very start. Pretend we don't know a thing about candles," she seems to be speaking from an implicit model of literate discourse—the way one should write to an unseen and unknown audience. In response to questions, Mindy was encouraged to be clear and precise, and to put more and more information into words, rather than relying on shared background knowledge about candles, or contextual cues from the candles she was holding, to communicate part of the intended message.

A third response is a question that expresses the teacher's perplexity, her inability to keep track of the thread of the story as the child tells it. In a third classroom, Leona told a long story about her puppy—about incidents at breakfast one morning, and how he always tries to follow her to school, and then a more acute problem:

> Leona: *(continuing)* And we took him to the emergency and see what was wrong with him. And he got a shot. And then he was crying. And la-last yesterday—and now they put him asleep. And he's still in the hospital. And the-the doctor said that he hasta—he got a shot because he was nervous—about the home that I had. And he could still stay, but he thought he wasn't gonna be a—he thought he wasn't gonna be able to let him go. He—
>
> T: *(interrupting)* Who's in the hospital, Leona?

Sometime later, we asked Leona's teacher about her problem in understanding Sharing Time stories. She answered from her experience as mother as well as teacher:

> It's confusing when you listen, because their time frame is not the same as ours. When my son was six, he would suddenly talk about something from months earlier, and I could understand because I'd been there; I could make the connection. It's different in class. It's hard to make the connection with so many different individuals.

When we consider the problems teachers face in "making connections" in time for an on-the-spot response, story topics can make a big difference. Some stories, such as Jerry's paper boat and Carl's hundred dollars, are about widely shared experiences with publicly familiar scripts. Carl's explanation about lotteries even has extensive problems of vague words: *this thing, this dollar, it makes up to, this name.* But adult listeners would get enough cues to some kind of lottery to clarify the vagueness on their own. The same might be true of Leona's puppy in the hospital, but she faced the difficult discourse problem of keeping straight the referents to two same-sex characters—the doctor and the puppy, and we know from other research (Bartlett & Scribner, 1981) that this causes problems for young writers throughout the elementary school years. Other stories, such as Deena's special day, are about the more idiosyncratic events of family living. It is impossible for the teacher, listening to such stories, to clarify relationships on the child's words alone.

Fourth and last, and closest to the negative end, is a response by the teacher that shifts the topic to one the teacher either understands better or values more highly. After the teacher's request for information about who's in the hospital, Leona explains that her puppy is there because he's "vicious." This leads to a discussion of the meaning of *vicious* and then a retelling by Leona of the hospital episode, ending with "I'll tell you Monday what happened." The teacher, presumably still not understanding that Leona's concern for her puppy is a matter of his life or death, ends with a comment on dogs' need for house-training.

Similarly, Deena's teacher follows her interruption of Deena's account of her day with a question about the scene of Deena's first sentence, the beach:

> T: *(Continuing)* and tell us what beach you went to over the weekend.
>
> *Deena:* I went to um-um-
>
> T: Alameda Beach?
>
> *Deena:* Yeah.
>
> T: That's nice there, huh?
>
> *Deena:* I went there two times.
>
> T: That's very nice. I like it there. Thank you, Deena.

The teacher's topical shift to the beach could have two motivations that, in this case, converge. The beach is the scene mentioned in Deena's first sentence and thus might be considered by the teacher as the topic that should have been sustained throughout; alternatively, going to the beach may represent the kind of familiar scenario that the teacher either finds more appropriate, or just more comprehensible, than activities among family or friends. Being able to pick up an older and larger child ("And she was on my back . . . and um she was heavy"), no matter how important to the child, may seem to the teacher ordinary or even trivial.

Here is another example where the teacher's attempt to change the focus of the child's narration is due not to any lack of comprehension, but rather to a conflict between child and teacher about the highlights of a family outing:

> *Nancy:* I went to Old Ironsides at the ocean. *(Led by a series of teacher questions, Nancy explains that Old Ironsides is a boat and that it's old. The teacher herself offers the real name,* The Constitution. *Then Nancy tries to shift the focus of her story.)* We also spent our dollars and we went to another big shop.
>
> T: Mm. And what did you learn about Old Ironsides?
>
> *Nancy: (Led by teacher questions back to Old Ironsides, Nancy supplies more information about the furnishings inside and the costumes of the guides, and then tries to shift focus again.)* I also went to a fancy restaurant.
>
> T: Haha! Very good!

Nancy: And I had a hamburger, french fries, lettuce and a—

T: (Interrupting) OK, All right, What's—Arthur's been waiting
   and then Paula, OK?

Narratives are a universal meaning-making strategy, but there is
no one way of transforming experience into a story. In the words of British educator Harold Rosen (1982), narratives are

> first and foremost a product of the disposition of the human mind
> to narratize experience and to transform it into findings which as
> social beings we may share and compare with those of others.
> (p. 9)

But, while "the story is always out there,"

> the important step has still to be taken. The unremitting flow of
> events must first be selectively attended to, interpreted as hold-
> ing relationships, causes, motives, feelings, consequences—in a
> word, meanings. To give order to this otherwise unmanageable
> flux we must take another step and invent, yes, invent, begin-
> nings and ends for out there are no such things. . . . This is the
> axiomatic element of narrative: it is the outcome of a mental pro-
> cess which enables us to excise from our experience a meaningful
> sequence, to place it within boundaries, to set around it the fron-
> tiers of the story, to make it resonate in the contrived silences with
> which we may precede and end it. . . . The narrative edits ruth-
> lessly the raw tape. (pp. 10–11)

Our potentiality and disposition to construct narratives is similar to our
potentiality and disposition to acquire language. In Rosen's words:

> If we are programmed to learn a language, we must still be ex-
> posed to a language in order to learn it and its socially consti-
> tuted use. In the same way, however universal our human bent
> for narratizing experience we encounter our own society's modes
> for doing this. There is no one way of telling stories; we learn the
> story grammars of our society, our culture. (p. 11)

Differences of cultural background, and differences in age between teacher and child, will affect how the raw tape of experience is
edited and transformed; and sometimes a teacher's comments reveal
these differences. Deena's teacher asked Deena to talk only about "things
that are really, really very important . . . things that are sort of different." Nancy's teacher expresses the same idea in other words to one of
Nancy's peers: "If you have something that was *special* for you, that you
would like to share with us, but we don't want to hear about TV shows
and regular things that happened." But who is to say what is "important," "different," and "special" or just "regular" to someone else? And

don't our finest writers (e.g., Welty, 1984) often make stories out of the most ordinary events of daily life?

How then should a teacher think about her role at Sharing Time? The first question to ask is what are the primary purposes for Sharing Time anyway? To build a community of children through the sharing of out-of-school experiences? To give children practice in speaking before a group? To serve as oral practice in the kind of compositions that children will later be expected to write? The best course of action for each teacher will depend on her or his answer to this question.

If you value a growing sense of community among children, then it may be better to divide the class into small groups for Sharing Time, as Moffett and Wagner (1976, pp. 73–74) suggest. That way, there can be more informal questioning by other children, and more sharers can get a chance. If, on the other hand, the primary purpose is seen as oral preparation for writing, then the important question is whether it would be more effective to work with a child in a conference over an actual written text (as described by Graves, 1983) rather than try to change patterns of oral narrative style. In such a conference, the child is no longer a performer to a mixed audience of teacher and peers. A long story that takes up a disproportionate amount of class time in oral rendition would be valued as a written composition; and the teacher can give a more considered response.

Teachers, like physicians and social workers, are in the business of helping others. But as a prerequisite to giving help, we have to take in and understand. Piagetian psychologist Eleanor Duckworth (1982) speaks of the importance of teachers "understanding learners' understandings." British sociologist Basil Bernstein (1972) puts the same idea in different words:

> If the culture of the teacher is to become part of the consciousness of the child, then the culture of the child must first be in the consciousness of the teacher. (p. 149)

Important elements of that consciousness are our expectations about text structures, and our presupposed knowledge about what texts are about. We usually think of the importance of these "contexts in the mind" (Cazden, 1982) when we are teaching children to read; but they are just as important when the texts are oral instead of written, and when the interpreter is not a reading child but a listening teacher.

Note

1. Michaels (1981) reports her study of a California classroom that included Deena and Mindy. Michaels and Cazden (in press) and Cazden, Michaels, and Tabors (in press) report our research in Boston-area classrooms that included Carl and Leona. Separate from our research, Dorr-Bremme (1982) had analyzed the social organization of Sharing Time as well as Worktime in another Boston-area classroom that included Jerry and Nancy.

REFLECTION: DELIBERATING ON DIALECT

Editors' Note: Many different dialects of English exist within English-speaking nations. A long tradition of research and study suggests how educators might view dialects.

Linguists have made it clear that language systems that are different are not necessarily deficient. This is to say that nonstandard should not be considered substandard. (p. 647)

A dichotomy exists between home and school tongues. An "alternative" strategy using Black dialect [or any dialect] to ease students into the mainstream has been suggested. The child's first language must be accepted; it does not work to try to obliterate it. (p. 648)

Source: Pillar, A. M. (1975). The teacher and Black dialect. *Language Arts, 52*(5), 646–649.

REFLECTION: SHOULD CHILDREN LEARN TO TALK LIKE TEACHERS?

Editor's Note: Behaviorism's influence on educational instruction can be seen in the lip service given to the importance and potential impact of modeling. Yet Shuy suggests that teachers may spend a lot of time "modeling" talk forms that students will not use and invites us to wonder how classrooms might be different.

▶

What are these language functions which the teacher carries out but which are blocked to students? The following is a partial list: *Opening the discourse. . . . Closing the discourse. . . . Keeping attention. . . . Seeking clarification. . . .* Many others might be cited including the function of denying permission, declining a proposition, requesting something, seeking praise, getting invited, and establishing solidarity. There is little reason to believe that teachers permit children to learn these functions by practicing them. . . . Learning to talk like teachers then, is an activity which has offered very little to children. In the first place, children do not appear to *want* to talk like teachers. Secondly, one can only wonder at the efficiency of the "models" approach, especially in relationship to the peer group learning which takes such precedence during the early school years. . . . Curiously enough, those aspects of teacher language use which would seem most useful to model, the ability to use language to get things done (language functions), are least accessible to the children because of the structure of our schooling process. . . .

If children do not learn from their teachers how to use language effectively to get things done, it may well be from a number of causes. Perhaps such learning cannot be learned from models. Or, perhaps, the traditional classroom learning situation does not permit the teacher to model effectively or at all. Or, finally, perhaps the teachers are not effective language users anyway and cannot use language to get things done themselves. But for those language functions which teachers must carry out daily such as opening, closing, keeping attention, and seeking clarification, the schools should develop a conscious effort to go beyond mere passive reception. (pp. 171–173)

Source: Shuy, R. (1981). Learning to talk like teachers. *Language Arts, 58*(2), 168–174.

7 "I know English so many, Mrs. Abbott": Reciprocal Discoveries in a Linguistically Diverse Classroom

Suzette Abbott

Claudia Grose

Editors' Text: Globalization means that all teachers must consider ways of supporting children with diverse linguistic backgrounds in their classroom. Abbott and Grose's examples from a first-grade classroom provide some starting points.

A fter we sang Happy Birthday to Andreas, Jeannette suggested we sing it in Chinese! Ming and Yen helped her lead the class. Mrs. Lopez had just come in to pick up her daughter Maria, and she promptly taught us to sing "Cumpleaños Feliz" in Spanish. For four months, I had featured the linguistic diversity brought to our class by three ESL children, striving to turn that diversity into enrichment for us all. With the spontaneous enjoyment at Andreas's birthday party, I saw the effort was paying off.

From early in the school year, Suzette realized the primary challenge of her Inclusion first-grade class: how to integrate into her program three children who spoke little or no English. As a daycare and public school teacher in New York City for 20 years, Suzette had already enjoyed the richness of a multiethnic student body. And years ago, she said, "I was a new immigrant myself—when I arrived from South Africa, I was surprised at how foreign I felt, even though I spoke English. I have always tried as a teacher to draw into the class those children who are potentially 'outsiders,' to assure that they are not seen as less knowledgeable or capable because they are different or speak another language."

    This time the challenge went further, beyond the three ESL learners, to encompass *all* the children. How could Suzette build on the op-

---

This essay appeared in *Language Arts* 75.3 (1998) on pages 175–184.

portunity of fortuitous language diversity to enrich the language experiences of the whole class?

The literature is full of evidence that a rich curriculum and a positive group environment support and enhance the learning of individuals, both first- and second-language learners (Altwerger & Ivener, 1994; Fox, 1983; Peregoy & Boyle, 1993). Further, as Lim and Watson (1993) write, "effective language learning, either native or second language, depends not on direct teaching of identified skills, but rather on a sound philosophy of learning and teaching, underlying a meaning-filled curriculum" (p. 393). Part of Suzette's philosophy, thus, included giving "children windows through which to see *many* worlds" (Kiefer & DeStefano, 1985, p. 171).

This is the story of Suzette's classroom. The elements described bring to life a theoretical basis for understanding how a rich language arts curriculum serves as fertile ground for the development of both first- and second-language learners as they are actively involved in constructing their deepening knowledge of English (Hudelson, 1994; Peregoy & Boyle, 1993). It also highlights the unanticipated benefits for all learners that emerge from the reciprocal learning in the classroom (Edelsky, 1989; Kiefer & DeStefano, 1985; Moll & Greenberg, 1990). We illustrate the range of scaffolding techniques (the temporary instructional supports—personal, curricular, and social) that help emergent language learners move beyond what they could do on their own (Cazden, 1992a; Boyle & Peregoy, 1990; Peregoy & Boyle, 1993), and we show the importance of teacher autonomy, which allows flexibility to respond to children's funds of knowledge (Moll, 1988; Moll & Greenberg, 1990).

Suzette's Story

I teach at a small public school in an urban community. The student body is predominantly White and middle class. It includes the children of academics and professionals associated with the many colleges and universities in the area. We also have a number of families recently arrived from China, Africa, Central and South America, and the Caribbean.

When school started, my first grade, one of two in the building, had fifteen children, four of them new to the school. Among the newcomers was Maria, dark bangs framing animated, brown eyes, who came from Venezuela during the summer. Then in early October, two new children appeared: Yen, quiet and serious, two years in America but speaking Mandarin Chinese at home, and Ming, slight in build, mischievous in his smile, who had just arrived from China. Yen could speak some English; Ming and Maria spoke no English at all.

Resources and Routines

Getting started, I knew I was not alone; I could muster the resources at hand—if I could figure out how to use them. First, naturally, there were the parents and caregivers of the children. I was also fortunate to be in touch with a volunteer literacy support program directed by a friend and former colleague. When Claudia heard of my Chinese students, she introduced me to a new volunteer, Mrs. Lu, born in China, educated at Wellesley, now aged 80 and interested in doing something new and worthwhile. As soon as this sprightly little woman came into my classroom, in blue jeans and cropped white hair, she plopped down on a tiny chair to engage Ming and Yen—but she quickly became a point of interest to the whole class.

Finally, there were the children themselves. I decided to address the challenge of the three second-language learners directly with the whole class. Just because these children spoke little or no English, I said, did not mean that they did not know anything. I asked the class to help Yen, Ming, and Maria learn the routines, just as they would help any of their classmates.

From the start, I sought to establish a relationship with the parents of my three second-language learners (Cummins, 1994), to show them my interest in their children's special qualities, to allay their concerns, and to gather information. I found that telephone calls or face-to-face encounters, before or after school, were more useful than sending notes home. Fortunately for me, all the parents spoke some English. In addition, Mrs. Lu was effective in helping me communicate with Ming and Yen and their parents. In my initial contacts, I sought feedback about how their children were talking about their school experiences. Ming's parents related that he liked "English school" because he could play. During this talk, I also learned that Ming was attending Chinese school where he was learning to read and write in Chinese, a useful bit of information for the future. Maria's mother, Mrs. Lopez, arranged her work schedule to spend time each week in the class, helping her daughter but also making books and materials for all of us.

Language arts in my classroom are integrated throughout the day and across the curriculum to give children experience with a variety of reading and writing activities in various pleasurable and comfortable ways. In the first weeks of school, I felt it important to establish the class routines. Knowing that there is a plan for the day and assuming responsibility for different jobs in the room helps all children build independence; it also supports the idea of a community that works together. These established routines and procedures serve as particularly valuable scaffolds for second language learners who are struggling to make sense of their new environment and language (Peregoy & Boyle, 1993; Sutton, 1989).

We begin with a morning meeting to lay out the day's plan and engage in interactive chart reading and various opportunities for children to share ideas and personal information. A written schedule shows the times each day for focused reading and writing activities, in large and small groups and independently. An important activity is reading the illustrated job chart which directs individual children's responsibilities. Mrs. Lu translated the words so that Ming and Yen could understand how they could participate alongside their classmates in this fundamental aspect of the community.

Fortunately, within the broad mandates of our district frameworks, I had the autonomy to develop my own curriculum, an essential component for making reciprocal learning work. Thus I could seize targets of learning opportunity, to build upon each child's knowledge and abilities. I sought ways to include and highlight the languages of the three ESL children. One morning, I invited Maria and her mother to teach all the class to count in Spanish. As they began, another child, Estella, whose father is Puerto Rican, I learned, joined in. We made a class chart with the English and the Spanish words, and from then on we often counted in Spanish as part of our math time. A few days later, Yen's mother came in to help him and Ming teach the children the numbers in Chinese. Jeannette, whose mother is Chinese American, was so intrigued with the Chinese numerals that she copied them all from the chart into her own writing folder.

Other children asked if their parents or relatives could visit too, and one thing led to another over coming weeks as children shared stories about hearing different languages in their extended families and contributed more samples to our growing collection of multilingual charts. Andreas often had a hard time settling into school, but his first moment of pride and success came as he, his mother, and his little brother stood in front of the whole class and counted in Greek. Following another counting lesson, inspired by Liza whose mother is Korean, an interesting discussion developed as the children studied and compared the Chinese and Korean number words written on two charts hanging next to each other. Some children commented on the intricacy of the individual Korean characters, wondering if it was more difficult to learn than Chinese.

In those early weeks, I relied on Mrs. Lu and Mrs. Lopez to translate during meetings and to make sure the children understood the schedule and special activities. Mrs. Lu also wrote the Chinese words alongside the English and Spanish words for the months of the year. Then we added the days of the week in Spanish and Chinese to the English word cards in our class pocket chart, making the daily calendar activity more accessible to everyone. Ming, Yen, and Maria could remind us how to read the Chinese or Spanish, and the rest of the class felt proud at reading another language besides English. Many times in those early weeks, I noticed Maria copying English words from around the room, or Ming referring to the daily schedule. Other children liked to copy the Chinese or Spanish or Haitian Creole number words as well.

Risks and Rewards: A Rich Language Arts Curriculum

Routines established, we set about creating a supportive classroom environment in which all the children, those who knew English and those who did not, would feel comfortable taking risks and working together to build their language and literacy proficiency. Reading aloud to the class was central to my language arts program. The children looked forward to this time each day when they could stretch out on the rug or curl up against the cushions, and enter the world of literature. I combed libraries and discount book sales for a variety of literature that would entrance the children while reflecting and extending their diverse experiences and linguistic knowledge (Natarella, 1980; Nurss & Hough, 1992).

Moon Rope (Ehlert & Prince, 1992), a beautifully illustrated Peruvian legend, is published in a bilingual format with Spanish and English texts side by side. I invited Mrs. Lopez to join me, asking her to read the Spanish text in turn, as I read the English. On another occasion, the two of us read alternate parts of Lynn Reiser's *Margaret and Margarita* (1993), about two girls speaking their own languages and finding a connecting point.

Some children became restless during the reading of the unfamiliar language parts. I initiated a discussion eliciting children's reactions. Maria expressed her delight at the chance to hear the familiar Spanish language. Estella beamed with pride and pleasure at her ability to understand both the Spanish and the English. Other children talked about the difficulty of paying attention, when it sounded so different. As the year progressed, we came back to this topic several times, as children thought more and more about what it was like not to understand what was being said, and what little devices or strategies would help.

Next, I found two books, *At the Beach* and *Snow*, by Huy Voun Lee (1994a and 1994b), in which a mother teaches her child to write in Chinese calligraphy. Ming and Yen read the Chinese characters to the class. Later, during independent reading time, I noticed two of the English speaking girls carefully copying Chinese characters from the two books. They asked Ming and Yen for help when they ran into difficulty

Jeannette brought in *Jingwei Filling the Sea* by Feng Jiannan (1991), which had Chinese and English texts side by side. "You can read the English and Mrs. Lu can read the Chinese, just like Maria's mother and you did," she proposed. At the conclusion of that reading, the children commented on how different the Chinese language sounded from English, and I overheard some of them experimenting with the tones—a nice variation on the usual first-grade language play (Cazden, 1992a).

In the late fall, one of the children asked me to read *My Father's Dragon* (Gannet, 1948). Conscious of the wide variation in linguistic sophistication in the class, I wondered how to make this engaging series of chapter books accessible to all. First, I gathered together all the animals and related objects I could find. We made the eighteen crocodiles with lollipops, for instance, from photocopies but with real lollipops taped to their tails. This use of artifacts and dramatization not only helped Yen, Ming, and Maria, it delighted all the children, as each reading was full of unexpected surprises. The children loved taking turns manipulating the characters as the stories unfolded. The experience was such a success that it led to a sustained interest in dragons that became central to our curriculum, culminating many months later in a grand celebration of the Chinese New Year.

Several times a week, I read poetry aloud, usually writing the poems on large charts, and encouraging the children to join in. Sometimes for the ESL children, I found it useful to ask their parents or Mrs. Lu to translate the poems I read in class. Once they understood the gist, they could enjoy the other elements of rhyme, and rhythmic patterns and imagery.

Pursuing the dragon theme, I found Lillian Moore's poem "Dragon Smoke" (Prelutsky 1986), a lovely example of metaphor on the idea of seeing your breath in the cold winter air. The children joked about breathing "dragon smoke" and quite literally showed Ming and Maria what was meant in the poem. A few days later, as we walked outside, Ming pointed to the exhaust from the cars driving by and, with a twinkle in his eye, said "Dragon smoke!" and then blew his own. He had truly understood the figurative and literal language, and along with the others, could enjoy the fun of it.

Poetry also inspired other connections. One morning, Jeannette came in to school grinning broadly as she displayed a large gap in her upper gum. Tim, who often had trouble staying involved during shared reading, recalled two poems about teeth that we had read before. Someone pointed out that the title of one of the poems had the Spanish word for tooth written next to it. I then asked for the Chinese word. Yen and Ming each responded, but with different words. After we tried to say both, Makeda offered to find Mrs. Lu to ask her which word was correct. We now had the word for tooth in three languages: Chinese, English, and Spanish, and we saw that there can be several words for the same meaning.

After finishing the books in the Dragons of Blueland series, we wrote and practiced reading a group message to send home asking for any dragon books, toys or pictures. This request led to the engagement of even more parents in the curriculum and opened new experiences and connections.

In February, Tim, a monolingual English-speaking child, brought in *Vejigante Masquerader* (Delacre, 1993), a bilingual story about a Puerto Rican boy who dresses up in a special mask and costume as part of the Fiesta during Carnival in Ponce. Estella was bobbing up and down with excitement. She said that she had a Vejigante mask at home, given to her by her father. When she brought in her mask, the children kept trying it on, and we made plans to make our own.

Talking about the mask, I started to say the word in my normal South African accent, but caught myself and changed my mouth into the American pronunciation. Sabrina, a child who rarely contributed to language arts discussions, looked up in fascination. "I know what you did. You started to say 'mah . . . ,' and then you changed and said 'mask.'" Eric quickly explained, "She talks like that because she comes from South Africa." Sabrina had picked up the nuanced accents, and Eric could explain why. I wondered if this kind of metalinguistic thinking would have happened without our ongoing focus on the rich language differences in the classroom (Moll, 1988).

In my class, writing and reading go hand in hand, each helping to reinforce the other. Whenever possible, I enlisted Mrs. Lu and Mrs. Lopez in helping the three emergent English learners with their writing. I explained that there were many ways to write and spell, and all were acceptable. Maria initially wrote in Spanish, sometimes dictating first to her mother and then translating with help. Ming and Yen drew many pictures, and labeled them using both English and Chinese. Some children wrote stories based on published books, or on personal experiences. Tim, a most resistant writer, was inspired one day by Yen's presentation to each child of a folded paper boat. Clutching the creation, he recalled a trip he had taken to Venice with his parents, and he struggled to produce a series of picture stories about gondolas—a first for him and the start of a collection of boat stories in the class.

Most children started using invented spelling and we had several class discussions, collecting suggestions for ways to figure out spelling. At first, Ming, Yen, and Maria hesitated to experiment in their writing. I realized that they were concentrating on gaining command of vocabulary to convey their ideas. It was premature for them to focus on the details of the sounds (Nurss & Hough, 1992). Instead, I helped them use picture dictionaries and other books, as well as the environmental print in the room. Our ever growing Word Wall of common sight words was especially valued by the two boys, and at one point Ming actually added some Chinese translations. I was confident that as they wrote more and gained confidence in their English language, they would eventually experiment with spelling, too.

Ming was a child who immersed himself in what interested him—mice, whales, outer space. Sometime in late October, I noticed that he was drawing pictures of mice in his writing folder day after day. One day during Writing Share, he showed everyone his drawings. The children were fascinated both by the humorous way he drew the mice and his delight in sharing. For Show and Tell on another day, he produced a photograph of himself in his mother's laboratory, wearing a surgical gown. Here was an outside resource that I could not have foreseen, for as he showed the photograph, he spoke one English word, "mice." Sure enough, there behind him were stacks of cages full of mice for the laboratory experiments.

For our next shared poem I chose one about mice and encouraged the class to write or draw a response to the last line, "I think mice are nice." The children studied Ming's stylized and whimsical mice, and learned from his technique as they made their own illustrations. He was now the expert! The children were so pleased by the results that two girls volunteered to arrange a display of the large poetry chart and all the children's writing and drawings to hang outside our room for all the school to see.

In preparation for a trip to the science museum to see a movie about whales, we poured over the pictures in whale books. Ming became fascinated, and his enthusiasm was contagious; soon his classmates recognized him as the killer whale expert. Thereafter, anyone coming across a picture or book relating to whales rushed over to show it to Ming for his assessment.

After I read William Steig's (1971) *Amos and Boris* to the class, Ming sat with the book, studying the illustrations and diligently copying the opening sentences describing the little mouse who loves the ocean. He highlighted the word "ocean" on his paper, as he drew his beloved mouse. A few days later, he drew a picture of himself watching the mouse happily riding on the whale's back. All three of his characters had speech bubbles: the Ming and Amos characters announced, "I like whales," and the whale replied, "I like Ming." I was not surprised at his picture, but very impressed that he had incorporated the dialogue format which we had only recently introduced in class.

One day during Writing Share time, the usually taciturn Yen spoke up shyly, "I want to show you something." He produced his writing assignment from Chinese School, marked with a large grade A. As his classmates scrutinized the unfamiliar Chinese characters, Yen's confidence grew and he told everyone that he has to "write them pretty." To my astonishment, he further explained that when he sometimes forgets a line or mark, "the phonics help me to remember how to write the Chinese." Later Mrs. Lu explained to me that many Chinese schools now use an alphabetic phonetic approach to teach reading and writing (Ho & Bryant, 1997). Here was a whole new discovery for me to pursue!

We studied Yen's writing sheet, noticing special accent marks, and discussed how these marks told Yen which way his voice should go. The children tried to follow, using their own voices. Seeing this homework sample, I suddenly understood how strange our writing process must have seemed, compared to his experience in Chinese School (Anderson & Gunderson, 1997). I was gaining insights at the same time as my children.

For Valentine's Day, the children had spent days planning a sale of art and baked goods. Maria noticed when she came in that day that the morning message had not yet been written. "I know what to write," she announced. With my help sounding out some words, and by looking around the room for others, she happily wrote on the chart: "Get ready for the Sale."

Risks and Rewards: The Social Environment

In the normal course of their interactions and play, the children were experimenting and making discoveries about language. As the second-language learners were taking risks and experimenting with English for the purpose of communication and social interaction, the other children were making discoveries about the nature of language, their own and others (Peregoy & Boyle, 1993).

Yen became entranced with the earth-moving machines, trucks and other vehicles in our gravel box which I had set up because of the children's interest in the road building going on outside the school. One day as he and several other children were playing, I overheard him asking, "What is 'worse'?" After a moment, I realized that Andreas had told Yen that he was "making it worse," an abstract concept, difficult for Yen to grasp. It also became clear that Andreas did not want Yen and the other children to play in the box. I stepped closer to hear what the problem was, and to see if the children could come up with a solution. They did: a bigger gravel box, so Yen and Andreas could work in parallel—a fine example of the children's problem solving, but also a social breakthrough for Yen.

Maria's language development was very much involved with her social relationships. In September and October, I would see her by herself in the playground, watching the other girls. She stayed on the fringe of small groups, using her drawing skills to communicate, at one point writing a wordless book about the weather. Soon she found Estella, whose Puerto Rican heritage and fluent Spanish made her a special ally. They often wrote and did other projects together. Maria was a keen observer of the social patterns in the class, often getting ideas from other children, and mimicking English phrases which she heard; a favorite was "cool . . . it's cool." One morning in mid year, Mrs. Lopez reported Maria's comment that "there are so many troubles" in the class, referring to the ebb and flow of relationships among the girls. Her parents reassured Maria that it was nothing new; it was just that Maria now understood enough English to follow the squabbles. On another day, Maria and Estella were playing near three other girls. The three were commenting that Ming and Yen were "so lucky, because they can tell secrets," since they spoke Chinese together. At that point, Estella spoke up, pointing out that she and Maria could tell secrets too, in Spanish.

Large group meetings were particularly difficult times for Maria and Ming in the early part of the year. They would wriggle and fidget, and I could see their frustration as they tried to make sense of all the English language around them. Ming would often lie down and tune out. Sometimes he seemed exhausted (Freeman & Freeman, 1993). Yen took it upon himself to confide in Mrs. Lu his concern that Ming turned his head away in the big group activities. During one whole-group math class, Yen saw that Ming was not understanding the task at hand. To the surprise of his classmates, he spoke up. "Let me explain to Ming," and proceeded to do so in Chinese. Without prompting, Yen had learned how he could help others, and set a fine example for the class (Forman & Cazden, 1994).

One day during Meeting Time, as we were looking at the ubiquitous dragon toys, it became clear that Ming had something to say about a particular little green winged dragon. He raised his hand and tried to speak, haltingly pronouncing the word "dragon," but trying to say something else as well. It happened to be a day when Mrs. Lu was there, sitting behind him. The children were used to hearing Ming and Yen speak together in Chinese. Now they heard Ming explaining his thoughts to Mrs. Lu. From their facial expressions, and their quiet attentiveness, it was clear that they were very eager to hear what "secrets" Ming had to convey. Mrs. Lu duly reported Ming's observation about the similarity between one little dragon and another animal, a dinosaur. The other children accepted his point with interest, and many agreed with him. They realized for themselves that Ming's difficulty in expressing himself in English did not mean he did not have knowledge to share.

Not too long afterwards, Ming's confidence allowed him to risk taking the next step. In a math discussion about different coins, he started to say something while pushing his hand back and forth in front of him. Listening very carefully, I made out the words, "quarter, my mother." He was enacting placing quarters in the washing machine coin slot! Once the other children understood his idea, and his participation was validated, he sat back with a smile of satisfaction.

From halting single words like "mice," to overgeneralizations— "I love that book . . . I love that whale . . . I love poems," he began to formulate spontaneous sentences and ask about words he did not understand. Following my reading of a story about a doctor giving a child a shot with a needle, Ming asked, "What's a needle?" Dora immediately responded, "It's when you get a shot. A shot with a needle, not shooting." As she spoke, she acted out receiving a shot with a needle. A chorus of children began explaining to Ming, and Yen added a further explanation in Chinese. Ming was able to ask for clarification and, at the same time, the other children recognized the potential semantic confusion that was posed.

A climactic moment came one day when I reentered the room; Ming looked up at me and asked in a matter-of-fact tone, "Where have you been?" After telling him, I commented on how much more he was speaking in class now. He beamed and replied, "I know English so many, Mrs. Abbott!" I could only smile back in full agreement.

Building on the Children's Experiences

In December, Yen went to China for a month. That gave us an excuse to study the globe—from Boston, Yen had traveled across the whole United States and the Pacific Ocean to China. Everyone was excited to receive a letter from Yen from China. The stamps were of special interest, but the important news was that he had lost a tooth, information that was quickly added to the classroom tooth chart. On his return, Yen and his parents showed photos and traced on the globe the places they had visited and the route of the airplane. This discussion helped Yen reenter the class, and all the children began to see themselves in relation to the greater world in a way that made sense to them.

Just before the December vacation, the two first grades planned a joint Peace Breakfast, inviting all the families to bring samples of their holiday foods to share with everyone. Using the children's dictated language, we typed a simple reminder which they could read themselves and which they illustrated individually, showing the foods reflecting their different celebrations. For the occasion, we learned "The Sharing Song" in English and "De Colores" in Spanish. The songs were written on large charts which the children illustrated to help them remember the words. We also practiced along with an audio tape to make sure we pronounced the Spanish correctly. Later Mrs. Lopez confided to me Maria's comment: "Mrs. Abbott is doing well with Spanish. But her accent—I need to work with her on her mouth." It must have been reassuring for her to see her teacher also struggling with another language.

In early January, at Estella's suggestion, we read *Three Kings' Day* (Zapater, 1992), in acknowledgement of her celebration of that holiday. The children in the book eat *arroz con leche* (sweet rice with milk) as part of their celebration. Estella told us how delicious this is, so I asked her family for the recipe (cooking was a regular part of our curriculum and we often cooked recipes inspired by stories we read together). Not only did Estella's family send in the recipe, but also all the ingredients! I wrote the recipe up on a big chart, with clear illustrations and few words so that all the children could read it as we cooked. As always, some children loved it, and others did not even want a taste—but everyone enjoyed the cooking.

In early February, our dragon theme reached fever pitch as we began to prepare for the Chinese New Year. I read aloud *Lion Dancer*

(Waters & Slovenz-Low, 1990) about a Chinese American child who learns to dance as part of the dragon. Jeannette's mother brought in a videotape of street dances in Beijing and some audio tapes of Chinese songs. Mrs. Lu picked a short, simple song to write out on a big chart, with small copies for the children's poetry folders. She wrote the Chinese characters on the top line over a phonemic transcription in English to help with the pronunciation. The third line of print was an English translation of the text. As we looked at the song on the big chart, I used the phrase "Chinese characters"; this led to a wonderful discussion about "characters" in books we'd read and how Chinese writing is made up of "characters."

Under Mrs. Lu's instruction, we practiced singing, and Yen and Ming helped us as well. Now they were the ones who were more language proficient than the rest of the class! As we worked to learn the Chinese words, a discussion arose comparing the sounds with those of the Spanish song we had learned earlier. Many children concluded that Spanish was easier for them because it sounded more like English. This led to further comments about how hard it must have been for Ming and Yen to learn English. By the looks on their faces I could see that this experience of trying to learn another language, especially one that is very different from one's own, had given many of the children their first clues about the complexity of language.

As the New Year approached, our preparations became more concentrated. Jeannette's mother came in twice to teach us the simple street dance. The other first grade made a large dragon of papier-mâché to hold over their bodies during the parade. We arranged with all the other grade-level teachers to let us parade through their classrooms on the Festival Day. As we continued reading our book about Ernie Wan's celebration of Chinese New Year, we discussed costumes and colors, and all the preparations that had special meaning: for instance, that red signifies good fortune.

On the long-awaited day, the children came to school dressed in red, as requested in the note we'd sent home. All the families were invited. The other first grade assembled under their elegant dragon, and led the parade. We followed close behind, waving our fans and scarves, dancing in and out of the classes, down the stairs, through the kindergartens, and to the cafeteria.

After catching our breath, we sang "Xiao Hu Die" (Little Butterfly) to the wonder of the assembled company. Then we dined on dumplings and oranges, traditional New Year's food donated by a parent, and Mrs. Lu shared her memories of New Years in China seventy years ago.

The diverse contributions of the second-language learners had become the property of us all. As all the children gathered themselves together, and opened their New Year's envelopes (a traditional feature contributed by a parent), they beamed and chatted all at the same time, tired, proud, and happy.

Discussion

Teachers are pushed and pulled in all directions, urged to try one approach here, another technique there. Nowhere is this more apparent than in the current debate about teaching English as a second language or, more generally, the challenges faced by the teachers in a classroom with diverse language learners (Nieto, 1996; Hudelson, 1990, 1994). Good teaching emerges from the teachers' solid convictions, identification of a goal, and adherence to that goal through the flow of classroom life.

Believing that language learning "is an active, constructive holistic process, [that is] inherently social in nature" (Strickland & Strickland, 1997, p. 203), Suzette's goal was creation of a classroom environment that would nurture the integration of first- and second-language learners for the reciprocal and profound benefit of both groups (Hudelson, 1990; Nurss & Hough, 1992). In her regular visits to the classroom as supervisor of literacy volunteers, Claudia brought a fresh perspective that helped them both reflect on all that was really going on in that lively setting.

The developing linguistic facility of the three second-language learners over the year was obvious, from Ming's risk taking in uttering the single word "mice," to, just three months later, his casual enquiry, "Where have you been?" (Urzúa, 1980). Equally apparent, though not as expected, were the spontaneous initiatives of the other first-graders that demonstrated growing awareness of their own language and, at the same time, their interest and confidence in exploring the other languages around them. Sabrina, an English monolingual speaker, found nothing strange about choosing to take home *Margaret and Margarita*, fully confident of her ability to read both the Spanish and English texts.

Suzette's class worked as a case study of the benefits of reciprocity in multilingual elementary education. Far from distracting from the teaching of monolingual learners, the presence of the ESL children in a curriculum and environment that acknowledged and engaged their contributions enhanced the learning for all. The "emphasis on substance and content facilitated the frequent occurrence of . . . metalinguistic and metacognitive events: the conscious examination of other's and one's own use of language and thinking" (Moll, 1988). The children's ability to talk about the elements of language grew; they became aware of the role of sounds, visual characteristics, intonation, and semantic flexibility. They learned to explain words like "worse" and "shot" in context (Cazden, 1992a).

At another level, the children came to understand more deeply the purpose of language, both oral and written, and the way people across cultures use language to organize information, communicate meaning, make sense of the world. As he tried to understand his new land, Yen was alert to comparisons and differences. By spring, as he became more comfortable in English in a classroom that encouraged examination and celebration of diversity, he could comment on the different physical features of Chinese and American people (Nieto, 1996). Ming, forever quantifying objects, proudly announced his love of Chinese history because it is "10,000 years old."

Creation of such an environment in which all children—second-language learners and primary English speakers—are challenged and encouraged to work together for reciprocal benefit depends on three broad circumstances:

1. The teacher's belief, demonstrated in matters large and small, that all children have funds of knowledge to share (Moll & Greenberg, 1990), are capable of communicating their information and can be understood, by one means or another, whatever their spoken language (Nieto, 1996; Urzúa, 1989);

2. The deployment of multiple forms of language and literacy scaffolding that encourage risk taking and that support experimentation, discovery, and communication (Boyle & Peregoy, 1990; Hudelson, 1990; Peregoy & Boyle, 1993);

3. An educational philosophy across the whole school that supports teacher autonomy in making curricular and pedagogical choices in response to the dynamic personality of the class (Moll, 1988).

Scaffolding in Suzette's class took many forms, from direct translation provided by parents, volunteers, and other classmates, to the establishment of set routines, to the use of pictures and multilingual print on the wall, to the dramatization of whole texts to make them vivid and memorable (Boyle & Peregoy, 1990; Peregoy & Boyle, 1993; Sutton, 1989). Important, too, was the way in which children sought out and found their own resources, turning to each other or asking others for clarification (Chomsky, 1980; Forman & Cazden, 1994).

Ming's successful struggle to convey his understanding of the use of quarters marked a big step toward community participation. It was Suzette's scaffolding, her close attention, her belief that she could understand, and her restatement for the class of Ming's message, that propelled him forward into other attempts at communication in English (Hudelson, 1990; Urzúa, 1980).

At the same time, her modeling of careful listening, patient attending, and clarifying comments was noticed and unconsciously appreciated by many others in the class. The shared experiences, discussions, and investigations encouraged all the children to explore differences, draw comparisons, and appreciate the variety and richness of their world. In a climate of mutual support and respect, they took steps toward understanding diversity and developing empathy (Nieto, 1996).

Routine displays of environmental print in several languages and sharing of bilingual texts were further forms of scaffolding. They served the vital purpose of validating the first languages of the ESL children, providing them with a place to show their own expertise, and broadening the linguistic awareness of the whole class (Ernst & Richard, 1994/ 1995; Freeman & Freeman, 1993).

From parent participation came a more subtle process: their sharing of their family language and culture emphasized for the children (their own included) the positive view of "knowing" something, rather than the negative point of "not knowing" English (Moll & Greenberg, 1990). Invitations to share language and culture conferred "official" status upon them (Nieto, 1996; Quintero & Huerta-Macias, 1990). For some of the children, this paralleled their own emerging feelings of having something positive to contribute, not just of being deficient in something that everyone else seemed to know. Maria thus expressed confidence that she could play the teacher role in helping Suzette improve her Spanish pronunciation.

Teachers have long known that parental participation is a key factor in children's success in school. Too often, though, parents feel uncomfortable or unwelcome in a vibrant classroom society; work or family commitments, or different cultural understandings about school and learning, may also deter direct participation in school activities (Nieto, 1996).

Suzette's success in this endeavor came from her ability to show flexibility and creativity to accommodate potentially interested and interesting relatives, or other representatives of the community, finding materials and activities appropriate for different families (Mrs. Lu was a special resource, of course, but hardly unique). Bilingual shared reading was a natural way to engage parents who might have felt uncomfortable otherwise: the spontaneous dragon curriculum opened other avenues; cooking and arts projects, preparations for the various celebrations, and simple requests for information or artifacts that reflected home cultures offered other ways for parents to participate. These opportunities strengthened the home-school connection, and gave parents a closer view and better understanding of classroom life (Anderson & Gunderson, 1997; Quintero & Huerta-Macias, 1990).

Recognizing that "writing, speaking, listening and reading all nourish one another" (Rigg & Allen, 1989, p. xiii), Suzette provided opportunities for children to engage individually and together in a wide variety of meaningful activities, providing the "warm bath of language" (Rigg & Allen 1989, p. xii) for the new English learners and allowing all children to construct their own understandings of how oral and written language works.

For this, teacher autonomy is the key. Ever mindful of the district-mandated curriculum frameworks, Suzette still was free to make choices that responded to who her students were, as individuals and as a group, choices that allowed them to "act as thinkers . . . not as passive givers and receivers of prepackaged curriculum" (Moll, 1988, p. 468). By following up on the children's interests and taking advantage of their experience outside the classroom, she helped the class make connections that enhanced their global awareness in ways that were appropriate to their developmental stages.

Late into the spring, the number charts and birthday songs labeled by the children were displayed outside the classroom, attracting interest from students of all ages, as well as their parents. By all measures, the total of this first grade's language experience amounted to far more than the sum of its parts.

REFLECTION: THE ROLE OF TALK ACROSS THE CURRICULUM

Editors' Note: When students have the opportunity to talk about content area subjects, they reveal their understanding through a variety of language forms. In the following example, the students' use of metaphor emerges as they use a pile of one-inch tiles, a specific number of which they have been

▶

asked to arrange into rectangles (e.g., use of twelve tiles yields rectangles that are four tiles wide and three tiles high, or three tiles wide and four tiles high, or six tiles wide and two tiles high, and so on). Students make a list of primes—those numbers that can be arranged in only two ways (e.g., a pile of three tiles can be arranged only into a three-by-one or a one-by-three array) and another list of composites—those numbers that can be arranged in more than two ways.

Rhiannon, as [the] [f]igure. . . [below] shows, contrasted the notion of primes as being like thin sidewalks and ladders to composite numbers as being *variety numbers* (that is, there are a variety of ways to construct rectangles using those numbers of tiles). . . . Rett, however, called primes *kin numbers* because "they can only go two ways and they look like they're related," underscoring the commutative property of multiplication. (p. 110)

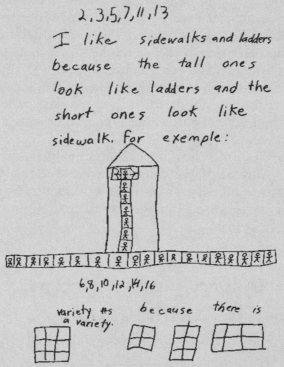

Source: Whitin, P. E., & Whitin, D. J. (1997). Ice numbers and beyond: Language lessons for the mathematics classroom. *Language Arts, 74*(2), 108–115.

REFLECTION: CAN OUR UNDERSTANDING OF TURN TAKING IN SMALL GROUPS HELP US RETHINK TURN TAKING IN LARGER GROUP SETTINGS?

Editors' Note: Talk in groups is predicated on the ability of participants to get a turn to say something. Steinberg reminds us that in classrooms such as the kindergarten she studied, the teacher controls much of the turn taking despite the fact that it appears that in smaller group settings these children have a variety of strategies for getting a turn.

Although the teacher requested the children to raise their hands to get a turn, the second most often occurring method of allocating a turn was to permit a child who has called out, to speak if what the child said was on the subject being discussed. . . . The third most used method . . . was for the teacher to name, point to, or nod at a child who raised his or her hand. . . . Other methods employed by the teacher to control turn taking included: (1) direct instruction on how to get a turn . . . (2) imposition of a turn on a nonparticipating child . . . [and] (3) ignoring a called-out turn not on the subject. . . . There was also tacit control by number of places, such as . . . six chairs placed at each table. . . .

The alternating of speakers or participants, with the next speaker being designated by the previous speaker, that characterizes other participant structures does not occur in these teacher-controlled turn-taking exchanges. . . . The child, in these exchanges, has no control over his own or others' turns. The teacher, as authority, makes all interactional decisions. . . .In contrast . . . , child-controlled turn-taking behavior allocated turns on a generally cooperative basis. The most often noted behavior illustrated the kindergarten child's ability to alternate turns in conversation. . . . Another method . . . was negotiation . . . for self or for another child. . . . Another method . . . was requesting a turn [or making] . . . an offer to help or cooperate. (pp. 160–162)

Source: Steinberg, N. R. (1985). Turn-taking behavior in a Kindergarten classroom. *Language Arts, 62*(2), 159–165.

III Reading about Reading

8 A Reading Program to Live With: Focus on Comprehension

Yetta Goodman

Dorothy J. Watson

Editors' Text: In this classic article, Goodman and Watson highlight some of the essentials for any literacy program. Using a socio-psycholinguistic view of reading as a point of departure, these authors outline, among other things, the importance of reading to children, as well as providing time for writing and individualized reading, and they discuss the use of strategy instruction to assist readers as they encounter texts.

In growing numbers, teachers are questioning the bases on which their reading programs are developed. These educators fear that they are asking students to spend time and energy on activities that, at best, have little to do with becoming good readers, and, at worst, are interfering with the reading process. Many of these teachers have faithfully attended to skill building, only to discover that while their students may improve on drill and skill exercises, they continue to struggle with written language, including social studies, math, and science materials; and rarely, if ever, become eager readers who enjoy a wide variety of literature.

As teachers become disenchanted with highly specific skill-oriented programs, they begin to rethink their own ideas about reading and learning. This has led them to discard some of their previous practices and to search for activities and procedures suitable to a reading program that is student-centered in nature, keeps language and thought intact, and has comprehension as its focus.

Before venturing into a new reading program, teachers should be able to articulate the program's theoretical base as well as to describe the activities found in it. To do this, teachers should answer four questions:

This essay appeared in *Language Arts* 54.8 (1977) on pages 868–879.

What is reading? How do children learn? What instruction is compatible with my views of reading and learning? and finally, What resources are available? We offer the following to those teachers who are in the disquieting process of answering these difficult questions.

What Is Reading?

Reading is a complex process in which readers bring their experiential background to the selection being read, just as the author did when the selection was written. Readers also bring expectations of their success or failure in handling the new material; these expectations are based on the reader's past experiences with print. Additionally, readers are influenced by environmental context; they expect a certain kind of language to be used in a science book, another on a baseball card, another in the TV guide, another on a graffiti-covered fence. In other words, reading begins before the book is open.

Teachers, as well as students, must realize that reading has limitations; even the most proficient reader cannot read everything. What the student is reading must be related to some degree to what the student already knows. The depth of the reader's knowledge and the extent to which the reader relates prior information to the author's message, as well as versatility with reading strategies, determine the depth and extent of the reader's comprehension. For example, a chemist reading directions on a can of flammable paint is likely to interpret those directions quite differently from the way a professional painter or a once-a-year consumer might interpret them. Differences in the background of consumers cause commercial writers headaches when it comes to producing directions.

Reading is an *active* process in which readers use the strategies of sampling, predicting, confirming or rejecting, and integrating information in order to derive meaning from the graphic, syntactic, and semantic cues provided by the author (K. S. Goodman, 1970). Reading takes place only when there is an interactive relationship between the reader and the author. If readers do not believe this, they are likely to be passive, unmotivated recoders (word callers) who think that rapid graphophonemic matching constitutes the act of reading. These are the readers who after finishing an impressive work by a fine author respond to the question, "Why do you think the author wrote this story?" with, "To teach me some new words."

Two characteristics of proficient readers are that they are active and that they are risk-takers; that is, they get wrapped up in interpreting their reading and consequently they are able to make good predictions about what the author has written. If their predictions miss the mark and can't be confirmed by past, current, or subsequent information, these readers do one of three things. Either they continue their reading remaining alert to cues that will fill in the gaps, they reread for missed cues, or they make an alternative prediction.

Finally, proficient readers build on integrated information (that which they bring to the passage and that which the author provides) in order to go beyond the ideas held prior to the reading encounter. In other words, reading/thinking continues after the book is closed.

How Do Children Learn?

Learning is an attempt to transform uncertainty into familiarity (Smith, 1975). Learners size up, make guesses, and construct meaningful patterns relating what they need to understand to what they already understand. Just as scientists do not know, prior to experimentation, whether hypotheses will be confirmed or not, learners do not always know if their predictions will prove to be appropriate. Consequently, learners, like scientists, must be encouraged to take risks, to learn from mistakes and to continue their pursuit for meaning. As the pursuit continues and as the learners interact with their surroundings they enlarge on their own concepts and experiences and gain important insights.

Teachers must understand that the way students perceive their surroundings is influenced by their background as well as by the total situation. Teachers must also realize that students learn more easily when they work in a meaningful, concrete setting. For example, if a reader comes on an unfamiliar morpheme such as *derrick* in a passage, meaning will not become apparent by focusing attention on the word's abstract letters or syllables, or even on its dictionary definitions. Rather, the reader needs to interrelate the significant context cues provided in the text with the developing meaning and syntax in order to understand the concept. The concept must be related to some previous experiences or to classroom experiences involving the use of *derrick* in relation to moving vans, ship loading, or oil rigs. Models, pictures, films, and the best learning experience of all, direct involvement, help the student construct the necessary important concepts. In such situations it is possible that the least proficient reader can help the most proficient readers by describing or explaining first-hand experiences with derricks which clarify the concept as presented in a passage or story being read. By using all available resources, the students discover a variety of ways derricks are used, what they look like, and perhaps how they have changed over the years. With such experiences the students will feel comfortable with the word when next they meet it in print. On subsequent encounters with the concept, students can judge whether their previous knowledge is appropriate, and raise questions about the authenticity of the new information (Smith, Goodman, & Meredith, 1976).

What Instructional Program Fits These Views of Language and Learning?—A Comprehension-Centered Reading Program

The one major concept which guides a meaning-centered program is that reading must be functional for the reader (Goodman & Goodman, 1976). People read in order to make their world more understandable, sensible, and ordered. A reading program based on this concept provides opportunities for students to read for purposes which are important to them and to make order and sense of their world. Children should not be expected to learn to read nonsense, and if they meet it they should learn to reject it.

The overall instructional program must place reading in its proper context. The instructional procedures and materials must help students focus on meaning for themselves as readers/thinkers; this is best accomplished by immersion in a total language arts program. Reading, like listening, speaking, and writing, is used to learn about the world. It is therefore important to keep reading as much a part of the total curriculum as possible and not an isolated, twenty- to sixty-minute daily lesson. When teachers keep in mind that they are teaching reading when they are focusing on social studies, science, math, art, or literature, it helps their students understand that reading is a functional part of everything one does in a literate society.

Reading to Children

Reading to children daily must be a part of every reading program. Not only is this an enjoyable, intimate activity, it has additional benefits. Children who hear prose and poetry written in a variety of moods and styles are being prepared to encounter and enjoy the writings of many different authors. When teachers encourage listeners to predict what will happen next in a story or to guess how a character might solve a problem, they are showing children a variety of ways to become actively involved in gathering information from the writer. Children can tell what might have preceded or caused a certain event; they can create their own endings; and they can go beyond the story by adding another event or episode. Each day they might quickly summarize or recall important events from yesterday's reading session. They can begin to understand the notion of plot by stating what they want to find out from the remainder of the story. Through such encounters children learn that reading is important (it must be—we do it every day), functional (it answers my questions), varied in content, style, and language (Shel Silverstein and Sharon Bell Mathis write different things in different ways), entertaining (some people prefer it to TV!), and worth the effort (I'll do it again).

Student as Author

From sunrise to sunset, children are bombarded with experiences that range from exciting to boring and from pleasant to miserable; many of these experiences are worth talking and writing about. Furthermore, children *can* talk and write about their lives if the teacher encourages and accepts the children's offerings told in their own language. Since the author and reader of a language experience story are the same person, the psycholinguistic gap between encoder and decoder is bridged, and the finished product is happily suitable and appropriate. Organized activities that are used as stimuli for language experience stories should be of high quality and well developed. A hurried walk around the playground, unrelated to anything else happening, usually won't inspire authorship; on the other hand, when an animal is brought to class and the children touch it, name it, and care for it, the students have something to write about. They can express themselves by writing letters, short stories, and poems about their new pet; charts will indicate the feeding schedule and other responsibilities involved in caring for the animal; a log of the pet's eating habits, weight gains or losses, and routine activities will be kept for future studies.

When children write, it is important that the teacher accept the experiences of the students as well as the language in which experiences are expressed. The language experience approach to reading provides insights into children's language; for example, children are expert dialect switchers. They can dictate a story in their own informal comfortable dialect, then after seeing their words in print, they may change certain forms to more formal English. This may happen on the first reading, perhaps a week or month later, and perhaps never. Teachers often find it difficult to refrain from tampering with students' writing, but when children show their own awareness of language, teachers are glad that they kept out of the way, valuing content above craft and allowing learners to make their own language discoveries. Evaluators of children's writing should react primarily to the quality of the writer's ideas and concerns, not to form of expression. Self-editing processes can be stressed after children are secure as writers.

Individualized Reading

A distinguishing characteristic of an individualized program is that children learn to read by reading—lots of reading, silently, and in a variety of materials. Obviously, a well-stocked library operated on a flexible, student-centered schedule and administered by an informed and helpful librarian is, to put it mildly, invaluable. In addition, a classroom collection provides the students with easy-to-get-materials and may be augmented by:

- requesting and frequently changing small collections from the public library.
- trading books with teachers in other rooms and in other schools.
- encouraging participation in paperback book clubs.
- pulling out good stories from unused basal readers and making "skinny books" of them.
- suggesting that parents give books to the class in honor of their child's birthday (nameplates can be pasted in the book indicating the honoree's name and birth date).

In an individualized program, time is scheduled for students to read silently every day. To promote independent reading, students are encouraged to draw on their own experiences and to use their own knowledge of language to help themselves become more efficient and proficient readers. When readers habitually depend on others for "the next word," they stop developing their own reading strategies, and lose faith in their own ability to contribute to the reading process.

Another characteristic of an individualized reading program is that the reading material is self-selected. Students should be allowed to choose their own fare, but teachers have the responsibility of encouraging readers to try different materials and to introduce them to a variety of literary forms. In fact, it is useful for readers to have three books in progress at once. Using a selection system called *Mine, Yours, Ours* will provide variety. This procedure allows both the student and the teacher a voice in selecting reading material. The student's choice, made without adult interference, is the *Mine* part of the procedure. *Mine* is usually material that meets a personal need—to be entertained, to find out something, or to gain status. The *Yours* selection is made by the teacher and is material that s/he believes will help the reader expand interests and develop reading strategies. The third selection, *Ours*, takes some doing, but is usually the most worthwhile as it is the one that is carefully examined, mulled over, and finally mutually agreed on by the reader and the teacher. Lists such as the ones developed by the Children's Book Council and the International Reading Association (see "Classroom Choices". . . in *The Reading Teacher*), and recommendations by librarians, can help the teacher and the student find appropriate reading material. It goes without saying that the teacher must be familiar with the rich and growing body of literature for children and young people if such a program is to be maximally effective.

Another characteristic of the individualized reading program is that a record keeping system is used. The simpler the better. Index cards on which students can record necessary information are easy to keep and don't frustrate the reader. It is easy for the teacher, in consultation with the readers, to develop record keeping forms which both find satisfactory. A card for very young readers might have on one side:

Your Name

_____

Book Title

_____

And on the other side:

Did you finish the book?

Yes ☐   No ☐

Did you like the book?

Yes ☐   Some ☐   No ☐

A card for older readers might have on one side:

```
Name —————————————————————————————————————

Type of material (book, magazine, newspaper, brochure, my own
story, class book, etc.): ——————————————————————

————————————————————————————————————————————

Title ————————————————————————————————————
```

And on the other side:

```
Did you finish the material?

If not, why not?

Would you recommend this book to anyone else?

Who? (Name names.)

What would you like to read (about) next?——————————

————————————————————————————————————————————
```

Reading Strategy Instruction

Proficient readers know intuitively that prediction and confirming are necessary reading strategies. While reading, they constantly answer questions: "What will happen next?" (*predicting*) and "Did it make sense?" (*confirming*).

Some children, however, feel that they are not really reading or that they are cheating if they cannot define every word, pronounce each phoneme, and master every syntactic structure. These up-tight readers will become more at ease and more willing to continue reading if they are encouraged to insert a bookmark at any trouble spot and to continue reading. At the close of the reading session the student selects one or two marked trouble spots and writes on the bookmark or in a log the sentence or sentences in which the problems occurred. The problem area should be underlined. At the end of the time set aside for this activity, the teacher collects and categorizes these self-selected miscues and from these, reading strategy lessons are developed. Such lessons are usually applicable to the problems faced by several students in a class and can be conducted in common-need instructional groups.

In addition to collecting self-selected miscues, the *Reading Miscue Inventory (RMI)* may be administered to students whose reading problems are not immediately apparent. The *RMI* provides a view of a student's reading performance that is very different from the ones provided by the traditional standardized reading tests or by informal reading inventories. During the *RMI* procedure, students read an entire story and their miscues (oral responses which differ from the expected response) are marked. Students receive no external help during the reading; they must rely on their own strategies. The miscues are then evaluated to see if the students are making appropriate use of syntactic and semantic information, as well as to determine what relationship they are making between letters and sounds. Additionally, miscues are evaluated to determine if they enhance the author's message and facilitate the reading process or if they are anomalous to meaning and disrupt the process. The *RMI* provides evidence of the reader's strengths as well as information about ineffective and inefficient uses of strategies. By using the *RMI* to study reading performance, teachers become aware that students often have more sophisticated knowledge of syntax and a greater awareness of the relationship between sounds and letters than other tests indicate. More importantly, the *RMI* provides the teacher with information about causes and quality of miscues. With such data the teacher need not make judgments about readers and their programs based on "error count" only (Y. Goodman & Burke, 1972).

The self-selected miscues and the analysis of reading through the *RMI* provide the basis for developing reading strategy lessons. For example, if a teacher learns that students attempt to sound out names like Dombrowski, Schochenitzch, or Izchuetichual; become discouraged in the process; and ultimately put aside the book because they think it is too difficult for them, s/he may choose to help these students with naming strategy lessons. In such lessons, a story with an unfamiliar person or place name is used. Students are asked to read the passage silently and not to be concerned with pronouncing the unknown name. Through discussion, the children realize that it is more important to determine what cues are available in the written material that can help them understand the character or nature of the person or place being described than it is to focus on how the name is pronounced. Except for the unusual person or place name, the language and concepts should be within the reader's grasp. Stories for strategy lessons may be selected from any materials that provide the language support needed to develop a particular strategy.

Teachers should try their hand at writing some stories for their strategy lessons. It not only makes them aware of the author's responsibility for making stories linguistically and conceptually supportive for the reader, but it also causes the teacher to carefully consider the problems children have when dealing with written language. Because different readers frequently tend to have similar problems, strategy lessons may be used again and again. For example, if a reader has consistent problems with pronoun references and antecedents, a selected-slotting strategy lesson might be developed. The first paragraph or two should be fully intact in order to provide appropriate buildup of context for setting, events, and character development. Then any references to the characters (proper name or pronoun) should be deleted. The reader should be asked to fill in the blanks and also to explain what cues were available in the story which made the particular choice possible. Selected-slotting strategies encourage readers to predict and to rely on their own language strength in reading. It helps readers understand that meaning is in the interaction between themselves and the language of the author, not in a particular word which they are unable to break down into smaller parts.

The following strategy story was written (by Kenneth S. Goodman) to help a student understand that it is not necessary to know every concept presented in a story prior to reading, nor is it necessary to know the correct pronunciation of a particular word such as *pali* while reading the story. The important strategy is to keep reading and build the knowledge of the concept through the story.

THE PALI

Several years ago, I saw a pali for the first time. Pali is an Hawaiian word, that everyone in the islands uses. The first pali I saw was very high. It was a pali near Honolulu that has great historical significance. They call it simply "The Pali." On this pali, King Kamehameha won a great victory. He trapped an enemy army at the top and drove it off the pali. The wind blows so hard up the face of the pali that you can hardly approach the edge. A local joke is that one day a despondent lover jumped off the pali and the wind held him up against the side of the pali until the fire department could come and rescue him.

It is important that the cues provided in the written material tell you what a *pali* is, so that readers can understand the material by having an image or picture in their heads. Some up-tight readers need to be convinced that it is more important to read the ideas than to read (recode) the words. Reading strategy lessons help readers focus on meaningful cues in their reading rather than on over-attention to word-attack skills.

Individualized Reading-Thinking Activities

These activities are designed to encourage the resourcefulness of students through "self-regulated inquiry reading." The first step in this activity is to identify a problem and to accompany this problem with a variety of questions concerning it. As well as serving as a motivating force, this self-proposed questioning technique allows students to look at what they already know about the topic under consideration. Following the question-forming period the students move naturally into hypothesizing solutions and outcomes. Another condition is that the readers have opportunities to share their findings with each other. In this activity the teacher functions as a resource person who helps gather materials and directs students to a wide variety of resources in and out of the school setting (Stauffer & Harrell, 1975). Strategies such as predicting, retelling, and summarizing force the reader to become actively involved in the reading process. Some children may find it necessary to retell what they have just read or to summarize briefly before they can proceed with their predictions. Readers who find it easy to make predictions usually do not need the retelling step and need to return to the text only to verify a point or to refresh their memories. Listening to a reader's predictions helps a teacher determine the degree to which that reader has understood the material.

Assisted Reading

This reading-in-unison procedure (Hoskisson, 1975) may be used with children who are having marked difficulty with their reading or during initial reading instruction. In this approach, sentences or phrases are first read by the adult (teacher, parent, aide, older tutor) and then by the child. An alternative (perhaps advanced step) is to have the adult read, stopping where a highly predictable word or phrase follows so that the reader can supply the appropriate language. The adult and child may read in unison with the adult fading out as the child gains confidence, and getting louder when the child becomes unsure of himself. The material, as in all other reading settings, must be of high interest to the reader and within his/her conceptual understanding; otherwise, the activity could become meaningless word calling.

Teachers in New Zealand and in parts of Australia often use a similar approach to beginning reading which they call "Shared Book Experience." This is characterized as learning to read in mother's lap. High interest books are read to children and the beginning readers are encouraged to read along with the adult. This is done in small groups and with stories the children love. The books are read as often as the children want to hear or read the story and the students seem to memorize the book. The youngsters hear language flow with its appropriate rhythm and intonation and see the relationship between print and oral language. Usually the book being shared is enlarged into a big book which the teacher reads. The children may have a small book just like the big book and may be following the teacher as the pointer sweeps along below the line of print in the big book or may follow the written language in their own little look-alike books. Often when a teacher has a number of sets of these books in the classroom, each set is placed in a separate learning center so that when the children become familiar with the books, they may conduct the activity themselves in small groups. The teacher may audio-tape favorite books or purchase commercial "read along" taped collections which children may have available at a listening post center. The point of these procedures is to make readers less conscious of their performance; to show them that reading should sound like language; to prove that it can be enjoyable, informative and interesting; and to make them more and more independent of the adult help being received. If the students bring appropriate experiential and conceptual background to the reading situation, this independence is likely to occur quickly.

What Are the Available Resources?

The most interesting, informed, and varied resources are, fortunately, the most available—the students. The "special education" children as well as the "academically talented" in every classroom bring a world of experiences that provide resources for the entire curriculum. By insightful observation and continuous interaction with students, a teacher can learn about their interests and discover what will motivate them to read and to learn.

As the teacher finds common concerns and interests, small groups of children may be called together for instruction. The group members might work on reading strategy lessons, discuss a book, plan a choral reading, read something of their own choosing from a special resource, write a song or play, do a science experiment, or plan a trip. The groups are formed for a purpose, lasting only as long as they are useful, interesting, and necessary for getting a job done.

In addition to the children themselves, most schools come equipped with basal reader texts, programmed reading kits, paperback books, and supplementary readers, all of which can be used in part in a comprehension-centered reading program. Audio-visual equipment such as tape recorders, record players, and projectors should be available to the children whenever they are involved in their own projects. Classroom learning centers, where individuals or small groups can work at a variety of tasks, can provide practical application of students' literacy. Here they can work on their own by reading directions (or listening to them on tapes) that tell how to use catalogues, maps, menus, recipes, brochures, newspapers, or games. In such a learning center one might find Penney's or Sears' catalogues with copies of simplified order forms developed by the teacher, or actual order blanks may be available for those readers who feel they can handle them. The children could learn to order materials necessary for projects they are working on.

Another valuable resource is a local university where teachers can take courses in the language arts, children's literature, and in the study of psycholinguistics as it applies to the reading process. Much new information has been generated in these fields in recent years and teachers must keep informed. Teachers are also helped to keep up-to-date through professional organizations concerned with language arts and reading. These organizations publish journals containing ideas for instruction, and information about language and literature. These groups also sponsor local, state, and national conferences where new ideas and recent research are disseminated.

Summing Up

Reading instruction must be student-centered, must keep language and thought intact, and must begin and end with meaning. If a program is based on these tenets, students will realize that reading is a means to an end, not an end in itself; it will entertain, inform, or in some way meet their needs, here and now.

A reading program that focuses on comprehension will make available a world of materials with all kinds of messages in them. Such programs will not tolerate artificial reading activities that frustrate readers and destroy the reading process. It will allow plenty of time for the reader and author to come together by way of written language.

The key to such a program is a teacher who understands language and language learning, who knows children's literature, and who is willing to work creatively and diligently at organizing and integrating a reading program to live with.

QUOTATIONS

"Reading children's literature's like becoming drunk with words," [my friend, John Burns] once told me. "These books are steeped in meaning." Like fragrant herbal teas that tingle your senses, I thought, as his eyes told me of books. (Rief, 1988, p. 236)

Source: Rief, L. (1988). ". . . because of Robert Frost." *Language Arts*, *65*(3), 236–237.

What is so powerful about this act of being read to? How does it appear to help children become readers? First of all, children associate reading with pleasure and love. They can cuddle up in a parent's lap and receive individual attention. (Huck, 1992, p. 521)

Source: Huck, C. S. (1992). Literacy and literature. *Language Arts*, *69*(7), 520–526.

STRATEGY: NONFICTION TEXTS AS READ-ALOUDS

Editors' Note: Fiction is often the text type of choice for many educators; yet there is an increasingly diverse and interesting selection of nonfiction texts available. Reading such texts, especially in the early grades of school, can provide young literacy learners with an understanding of these text forms that they can then bring to their own reading and writing.

▶

Why Read Nonfiction Texts Aloud?

[Nonfiction read-alouds expand] children's knowledge, thereby contributing to schema development, a critical factor in comprehension. . . . Nonfiction read-alouds sensitize children to the patterns of exposition. . . . Nonfiction read-alouds provide excellent tie-ins to various curricular areas. . . . Finally, and most importantly, reading nonfiction aloud whets children's appetites for information, thus leading to silent, independent reading of this genre. (pp. 122–123)

Selecting Nonfiction Texts

When evaluating the quality of a nonfiction book, teachers should consider the five A's: (1) the authority of the author, (2) the accuracy of text content, (3) appropriateness of the book for children, (4) the literary artistry, and (5) the appearance of the book. (p. 123)

Using Nonfiction Texts

Teachers must establish links between children's experiences and text materials . . . , particularly . . . when selecting nonfiction read-aloud books, since children are less accustomed to hearing and/or reading this genre and may have little background for some of the subjects treated therein.

Children's background knowledge for a particular topic can be assessed and activated through discussion, brainstorming, or problem-solving activities. . . .

During the reading, teachers may wish to ask or answer questions, clarify terms, or help children understand abstract concepts. They may elect to record student responses, create a chart, or involve students in webbing. . . .

After the reading children need opportunities for response . . . [such as] discussions, mock interviews, role playing, creation of models, illustrations, writing, and/or evaluating a book or creative dramatics. . . . They might also write individual or class books patterned after the book read aloud. (pp. 124–125)

Source: Moss, B. (1995). Using children's nonfiction tradebooks as read-alouds. *Language Arts, 72*(2), 122–126.

STRATEGY: THE CLOZE TECHNIQUE

Editors' Note: The Cloze technique can be used as an assessment device or to help readers think about their reading strategies.

In 1953, [Wilson] Taylor introduced the Cloze technique for use with language. Consider the sentence: The _____ came to a sudden stop when the light turned red. Most of you probably substituted *car, bus,* or *truck* to complete the sentence and provide a meaningful unit. In traditional terminology, you used *context clues*. You made the substitutions on the basis of your knowledge of the structure of the English language (syntax) and your knowledge of things that stop in response to traffic lights (semantic clues). The Cloze procedure simply extends this [omission of words in one sentence to omission of several words in a passage] so that there are several or many blank spaces. . . .

The following guidelines are suggested for using the Cloze technique as a teaching device:

1. Define your instructional objective carefully. . . . Some examples in reading might be: recognizing the referent for pronouns; correct representation for inflectional endings; appreciation of figurative language; and recognizing the main idea. . . .

2. Provide group practice exercises before asking children to complete Cloze activities independently.

3. Begin with relatively easy activities and move to more challenging ones. . . . You may want to use as few as one or two blanks per paragraph. This should depend on your purpose for using the technique. . . .

4. Discuss the children's responses with them. . . . Encourage the group of children to decide which responses are qualitatively better. . . . (pp. 317–318)

Source: Pikulski, J. J. (1976). Using the cloze technique. *Language Arts,* 53(3), 317–318, 328.

STRATEGY: READERS THEATRE INSTEAD OF ROUND ROBIN READING

Editors' Note: Round robin reading is an instructional practice that has long been used but, in recent years, has been replaced by oral reading activities that situate the purpose for oral reading in relationship to an audience. For example, readers theatre may involve dramatic reading intended to give pleasure to audience and performers alike.

———————— ✐ ————————

In "round robin" each group member has a book and is to follow along with the reader. When this occurs, the purpose of oral reading is destroyed. The remainder of the class has already obtained the "message" from silent pre-reading or reading ahead. As children follow along, the reader who has difficulty and stumbles along the way becomes tense, and anxiety increases as five to twenty children try to help the reader. In addition, boredom soon follows for listeners—both teacher and students. (pp. 975–976)

Source: Taubenheim, B., & Christensen, J. (1978). Let's shoot "Cock Robin"! Alternatives to "round robin reading." *Language Arts, 55*(8), 975–977.

———————— ✐ ————————

Readers theatre, a formalized dramatic presentation of a script by a group of readers, can be a form of interpretive dramatics more appropriate and instructionally valuable for elementary school children than acted plays. Each character is portrayed by a reader. A narrator's part fills in details of the plot or setting. Action is minimal or non-existent; emotion and characterization are portrayed by the readers' voices. (p. 331)

Script Selection

Because readers theatre is a relatively new idea . . . teachers must depend primarily on their own teacher-made scripts. A short script, about seven to ten minutes long, is usually preferable to a longer one.

Children's books are a rich source for scripts, often with little adaption. . . . Plays can be used if the story stands without action. One scene or episode, or an entire short book, can be used. (p. 335)

▶

Planning and Staging

When writing adaptations, keep the narrator's part to a minimum. Allow the audience to use their creative power to fill in the rest.

A long narrator's part may be broken up into parts for several children. Changes in speaker can be used to signal changes in setting, foreshadowing, or dramatic shifts in action. . . .

The reader's voices and expressions, rather than costumes and props, project the images portrayed in the selection, but a few carefully chosen costumes or props may add to the children's enjoyment . . . .

Include children in the planning for a readers theatre presentation. After an initial reading or two . . . , ask for their ideas about interpretation. Each child can contribute; it is a group project and every contribution is important. . . . (p. 336)

Source: Busching, B. A. (1981). Readers theatre: An education for language and life. *Language Arts, 58*(3), 330–338.

9 Learning about Phonics in a Whole Language Classroom

Penny A. Freppon

Karin L. Dahl

Editors' Text: Debates about the part phonics should play in reading instruc tion have characterized much of the literature on reading instruction for the past decade. Freppon and Dahl illustrate that the question is not whether phonics should be taught but how it should be taught. Their key principles for phonics instruction are illustrated with classroom examples.

The "Great Debate" is under way again. This time there is new information, and there are some new players. In this article we take a whole language perspective and look briefly at one of the more prominent new summaries of phonics information, *Beginning to Read: Thinking and Learning about Print* (Adams, 1990). We suggest new bases of information that need to be considered in deciding how to handle phonics effectively in beginning reading and writing instruction, and we then present a description of phonics instruction in the classroom of a "new player," a teacher with a whole language kindergarten. It is our contention that the phonics controversy this time centers not only on instructional method but also on the extent to which educators utilize data about children as language learners. We think examples of instructional events that effectively support children's learning the code are important information for the 1990s debate.

Theoretical Perspective

Our stance is based on socio-psycholinguistic theory, which holds that learning to read and write are language processes (Goodman, 1967; Smith, 1982), and on transactive theory (Rosenblatt, 1978, 1989), which grounds the learning of those language processes in each individual's interpretation of and transaction with the literacy events encountered

This essay appeared in *Language Arts* 68.3 (1991) on pages 190–197.

in daily experience. We recognize that learners interpret and make sense of instruction and that their transactional stance (Purcell-Gates & Dahl, in press) influences what they learn. We believe that instruction in school-based settings is shaped by and includes the social and cultural contexts in which it takes place (Bloome & Green, 1982; Cook-Gumperz, 1986). Thus, to understand beginning reading and writing instruction and make judgments about learning the code, we necessarily must consider the language event, the learner's perspective, and also the social context of the classroom.

Reflections on the Phonics Summary

The new phonics summary (Adams, 1990) moves away from interest in a best or most effective way to teach phonics and instead integrates information from a variety of current sources including research-based information about sound-symbol relations, skilled reading, early reading, spelling development, and instructional interventions. Although many points of difference exist between the summary and a whole language perspective, we mention here three particular points.

First, the summary emphasizes that learning the code is *the key* in learning to read. We contend that one cuing system cannot be the single most important factor in reading. The child's orchestration of knowledge about written language includes crucial information from each of the cuing systems, as well as information about the function and form of print. We also contend that multiple factors, including context, sociolinguistic elements, and the learner's own purposes and motivations, influence learning to read (Bloome & Green, 1984; Cochran-Smith, 1984; Harste, Burke, & Woodward, 1983; Matthewson, 1976; Wigfield & Asher, 1984).

Second, in discussing the aspects of instruction to be presented to children, the report seems more curriculum centered than learner centered. We argue that reading and writing are language-based behaviors and that children learn them by engaging in meaning-centered exploration with written language. Therefore, sensitivity to and support for the explorations of children in beginning reading and writing are essential parts of school-based literacy instruction (Altwerger, Edelsky, & Flores, 1987; Dyson, 1982, 1984).

Finally, we suggest that not nearly enough is known about initial reading and writing development and school-based instruction from the perspective of the learner. It is in observations of children's literacy learning in varying contexts investigated through different theoretical perspectives that we find new insights and understandings about the complexities of learning written language (Dahl, Purcell-Gates, & McIntyre, 1989; Dyson, 1989; Harste, Burke, & Woodward, 1984; McIntyre, 1990).

Therefore, educators and researchers are challenged to present school-based descriptions of children in the act of learning to read and write. To decide the issue of how phonics is learned, we need to look closely at teachers and children in the process of working with sound-symbol relations, and we need to clarify how children in various instructional environments come to understand the written language code.

A Whole Language Classroom Example

This article presents a description of phonics instruction from a whole language perspective and serves as an account of learning within that instructional context. The kindergarten on which we focus is located in a midwest urban school serving approximately 400 children. This Victorian red brick school is surrounded by a cement play area with a high chain link fence. The school has been a neighborhood landmark for many generations. Most children entering the school are relatively inexperienced with written language.

In this example we show what one kindergarten teacher does to help children understand sound-symbol relations, and in the course of our description we follow one child, Jason, through some initial reading and writing experiences. We base this discussion on a year of close observation and analysis of urban children in a whole language kindergarten (Dahl, Purcell-Gates, & McIntyre, 1989). We also draw on discussions with Jason's teacher, who is a leader among whole language advocates in her community and recognized for her success in providing instruction for children from low-income families.

Jason is typical of the learners in this classroom. Although shy, he seems interested in classroom activities and is attentive when his teacher reads aloud. Initial assessments of his written language knowledge at the beginning of kindergarten indicated that he did not grasp the intentionality of print, the alphabetic principle, or the nature of story structure. Kristin describes his learning at the beginning of the school year:

> When Jason came to school, I don't think he had ever paid attention to print or interacted with it very much. Basically, he didn't have experience with reading and writing; but he had a wonderful imagination, he was interested in stories, and he could pretend and talk really well when he played. This was a real strength,

but he wasn't at all familiar with written language; and he had
no idea of phonics.

Beginning Concepts about Written Language

At the beginning of the kindergarten year, the focus in the whole language program in Kristin's classroom is on the functionality of print as
children explore the various ways print carries meaning. Kristin describes this early instruction: "I always work from whole to part. Children need time to gain an awareness of themselves as readers and writers, and from this they develop a need for phonics in order to
communicate through written language."

Kristin continually demonstrates the functionality of print and
provides children with rich and varied daily reading and writing experiences. Kristin includes repeated readings in a wide variety of
children's literature. She chooses books recognized for their quality and
illustrations, including big books. She reads three or four stories each
morning, writes the agenda of the day, talks about words, and shows
how words look and sound. She works with writing and reading the
children's names in the context of songs and charts and uses written
language for such purposes as writing notes on the message board.

In addition, children experience reading with the teacher in small
heterogeneous groups of about five children once a week. During this
reading time Kristin reads a small predictable book, encourages talk and
predictions about story events, and has the children read to her. As one
aspect of this activity, she helps children focus on words, word identification, and sound-symbol relations.

All of the children participate daily in journal time as they write
about topics they select. Later, they discuss and share their writing. Class
writing lessons focus on thinking and talking about the intended message, word awareness, and letter awareness. All of the centers in the
classroom—the science center, writing center, book center, and dramatic
play area—include invitations to interact with print. The dramatic play
center changes frequently and features such themes as a restaurant, a
flower shop, or a zoo baby animal center. Each version of the center
contains opportunities for using written language in the course of dramatic play. For example, the center about zoo baby animals includes not
only stuffed animals, a scale and a stethoscope, and a small table with
a wooden telephone, but also some scrap paper for notations and a black
bound calendar to sign up on a "waiting list."

During the beginning weeks of kindergarten, Jason spends a good
deal of time watching his teacher and his 26 classmates. He wants to

play; but when he interacts with the other boys, he and the rest of the group often become too boisterous. Play quickly becomes running, yelling, and wrestling; and his teacher spends a good deal of time helping the children get their behavior organized for the classroom.

By October, Jason learns to "do school" fairly well. In November, sporting a new burr cut and army camouflage fatigues, he approaches the telephone and writing table in the zoo baby animals' nursery. The center already contains the maximum number of children specified for the center, and Jason wants to sign up for a turn. He hesitates, picks up a pencil, and writes two short lines of scribble across one page. When asked to tell what he is doing, he holds his pencil in midair and responds tentatively, "Well, I guess I'm making an appointment." Later in the morning when asked to tell about his writing, he says, pointing to the two lines, "I want an appointment."

The classroom environment supports many other initial experiences with print. Kristin requires children to write in journals, and she structures each activity of the day to include written language demonstrations and discussions. For example, she demonstrates the process of writing when she writes the agenda of the day by "thinking out loud" as she writes. Kristin comments:

> I provide lots of opportunities to write, and I believe journal writing, for some children, can build their confidence and ability as writers and so help them want to try writing in other contexts in the classroom. Just journal writing, just demonstrations by the teacher, just opportunities to write throughout the day in classroom centers does not do the trick. It all has to be there—integrated throughout the day.

Nudging Children toward Sound-Symbol Awareness

Once children understand the meaningfulness of print, the functions that print serves, and the nature of wordness and story, Kristin begins working toward sound-symbol awareness. She describes her approach, "I think children need a lot of time and examples and support. I do teach the code directly by sitting down with them individually when they write and also, in circle time with my demonstrations, by writing in front of them."

In individual sessions she helps children think about the words they choose. "The children generate the writing ideas first. Then I find ways to hook onto the child's ideas and work with that meaning. I might say to a learner, 'I can see this says *my* because it starts with *m*' or 'I can see this is *puppy* because it has *p* at the beginning and end.' I find the one thing that the child is trying to say and make the connection."

Kristin often says the child's intended word, slowly drawing out its sounds. Frequently, she also tells the child to say the words and asks, "What do you hear?" just after the child pronounces it. She often models listening for sounds and making connections to letters: "I want to write about dinosaurs, di-no-saurs, di-no, I hear a *D*, that starts *dinosaurs*." As she writes the letter *D* on her own paper, she adds as an aside, "Yes, *D* like in *dinosaurs* and *D* like in *David* in our class."

Jason proves to be particularly in need of these individual sessions. Kristin reports, "It was February before I saw signs of Jason beginning to understand letter-sound relations. In February I began to sit with him during journal time and nudge him along. I'd say, 'Jason, I can't read this; I don't see any sounds in your writing.' And I'd also say, 'What do you hear in that word?' and 'What else do you hear?' "

Weighing these questions, Jason begins consistently saying the words as he writes independently. He repeats the words as he writes, saying them slowly just as his teacher does when she helps him learn to listen for sounds.

In mid-February Kristin begins journal time in the usual way with a demonstration writing session during Circle Time. She tells about picking berries with her mom and sister when she was little, and after eliciting suggestions for her writing from the children, she demonstrates the writing process by writing several lines of print on chart paper and discussing the meaning, pronouncing each word, and naming the letter sounds.

When the children are dismissed to write, Jason gets his journal and goes to a nearby table. He opens his journal, looks at his letter card, and says, "Where's an *F* on here?" As he locates the *F* on his alphabet card, he begins to say the *F* sound, "Ffff," and write the letter. Another child interrupts with a request, "How do you spell 'Mom, in five days it's Valentine's Day?'" Jason thinks about it briefly, decides not to respond, and is quiet. In a few minutes he again picks up the pencil and says slowly and distinctly, "In my birthday." In the process he writes an *N* beside the *F* he had written earlier. He then announces, "I can't make an *M*." His neighbor Charlie leans over from across the table and says as he writes an *M* on Jason's paper, "You can't make an *M*?" Looking at the *M* Charlie produced, Jason continues, "In Mmmm, in my birthday," and quickly adds *BD*. He repeats, "In my Bbbb, birth, Dddd day." Then he says *E* but does not write the letter. Jason repeats "in my birthday" quickly and with conviction as his eyes track the letters just written. He looks up and says, "In my birthday someone gave me the, these shoes," and he holds up one foot, pointing to his shoe. "I just didn't want to wear them." Looking back at this writing, he repeats slowly and distinctly, "In my birthday, someone gave me these shoes. Some . . . Ssss Uuuu Mmmm . . . Ssss," and he writes the letter *C* backwards. "I'm listening to the sounds!" he announces, returning to his writing. "In, Nnnn, my birthday, Ssss, someone gave me, Thththth, Zzzz shoes." He writes *Z* for *these* and then reads it to the researcher sitting nearby. "It says, 'In my birthday someone gave me these shoes.'" Seeing that he has not written *shoes*, he begins to write the letter *S*. "I'm going to share," he adds with the last letter completed and hurries off to show his teacher.

The instruction that undergirds this writing episode appears to shape the learner's experience. Jason uses the demonstrations his teacher has provided and copies her model of "listening for sounds." The context of the event also provides support. Jason is given information by other learners and is sustained in his effort by his own substantial interest and investment in the meaning he is trying to convey. He knows that others can read his message, and he wants to share. His responses indicate that he is gaining confidence and beginning to understand how to think about sound-symbol relations. We believe that reading instruction also contributed to his understanding; however, at this point in Jason's growth his knowledge of sound-symbol relations is most evident in his writing.

Other kinds of individual nudging in this classroom take the form of helping learners find a specific starting point for their writing. Kristin helps children segment their message into distinct words. She suggests, "You want to write 'It is raining today.' That is four words. Your first word is *it*. I'll be back after you write." Kristin explains that some of the starting points she provides focus on the sounds of the initial word in the intended message.

> Sometimes they will tell me a whole story so I say things like, "Oh, you want to write about a castle? I remember you said it's about the dark castle. What does the word *dark* start with?" and I help them hear the sounds in that word. I want them to learn to hold that idea or sentence in mind and realize that it is stable.

The other significant piece of the nudging toward sound-symbol understandings takes place in group settings. Kristin models writing as she interacts with children. She notes:

> It is not all right for me as teacher to write without talking. Children need to see me thinking through the process. I model my thinking, and I see them learning to think about letters and sounds. I didn't used to do writing demonstrations this way. I used to write a lot, but I didn't verbalize what it takes to write. Then my

children didn't write, and I was very frustrated. I saw a big change in the children when I started this kind of modeling. I have learned that I can't expect my children to do what I don't do. I want to show that writers must think and make sense.

Building a Collaborative Community for Learners

As the year progresses, the children in this classroom increasingly work collaboratively. They spontaneously get books and read together on the floor each morning. Children also use some of their free choice time to experiment with written language collaboratively rather than engage in parallel play activities as they had been doing. At times the children's collaborative talk about words, sounding out words, and discussion of writing topics becomes a din; and it is difficult to distinguish one conversation from another. In the swell of these interactions, Jason continues his exploration of written language.

> On a morning in March Jason sits with several friends while his teacher distributes journals. He begins the writing session by trading pencils with other children.
>
> He then announces, "I am . . . I'm inviting you to my party . . . Devin." The name Devin is quickly copied from the front of Devin's journal.
>
> "Know what?" Jason says to Tara, "I'm inviting you and Rick. I'm inviting you and Rick to the party, you know."
>
> Turning to Toby, he says, "Will you write your name?" Toby reaches over as if to write, but instead Jason begins to write the letter *T*. "I know there is a *T* in your name."
>
> "*O*," says Toby simultaneously with Jason.
>
> Jason announces, "*Y!!*"
>
> Toby responds, "No, *B*."
>
> Jason retorts, "It ain't a *B*."
>
> Then, musing to himself, "How do you make a *Y*? Ah . . . I know how." "Now," says Jason confidently as his eyes track the print, "Toby." Jason then shows the writing to Devin and comments, "I made that kind of *Y*."
>
> "Yes, but you didn't; you forgot the *B*," says Devin.
>
> "Well," Jason replies, "I made a big *O* here, so then I can make this *O* into a *B*. Toby. That's a list of who's going to my party. I don't have enough room for Charlie. Well, I could put it right here." Jason squeezes in Charlie's name as others spell it for him.
>
> "Now you need Rick," says Tara.
>
> "I don't know how to write Rick," says Jason.
>
> Several children respond, "I do."
>
> Tara, sitting the closest, writes the letters *R I C K* on his paper. As she proceeds, Jason says excitedly, "Rick, I'm inviting you to my party and Toby, too." His eyes rest on his paper as he runs

over the list and thinks about the spelling of Rick's name. "R I C K
. . . Rick, oh why didn't I think of that!"

This writing episode shows kindergarten children collaborating
within a functional task. As learners pool their knowledge, they appear
to be as interested in their neighbor's piece as they are in their own. Their
learning is driven by the meanings and communicative purposes that
they establish, and sound-symbol relations seem to be learned in tandem with other concepts about written language.

Learners Who Don't Grasp Sound-Symbol Relations

As supportive as this context is for exploring written language, a few
of the children in this classroom still do not understand sound-symbol
relations by the end of the year. The reasons for this are as complex and
varied as the children themselves. One child, for example, spends a large
portion of her kindergarten year trying to gain acceptance socially. She
does not focus on literacy instruction until nearly the end of the year.
Another appears to be distracted by a particularly chaotic set of circumstances at home, and still another seems to follow the classroom activities but is not able to integrate new information available in her instruction with her own existing knowledge about the function and form of
written language. As we follow these learners into their whole language
first-grade classrooms, we may see a change in their understanding.
They may need more time, additional instruction, and additional experiences with print. It also is possible that instructional contexts other than
whole language may be more productive for specific learners.

We asked Kristin about the children who had not yet grasped the
alphabetic principle by the end of the year and she explained:

> Well, a few of them don't get it. I have a few children every year
> that have difficulty, but I think they get something. They use print
> in meaningful ways; they sign up on the waiting list to get into
> favorite centers. And, they internalize story patterns and struc-
> ture. They learn directionality and words, and they know that
> meaning is in the print and not the pictures. Often there is great
> oral language growth, and that transfers to such literacy learning
> and early reading behaviors as choosing books and memory read-
> ing. But some, in the kindergarten year, do not get the letter-sound
> relations through the writing and reading we do in my classroom.

If we are to understand better learners who initially do not grasp
letter-sound relations, further investigations are crucial. Research that
provides examinations of learner stance, learner ways of organizing
information, and learner interpretations of instruction may provide

explanations for these differences. Further, focus on what these children do successfully over time may provide additional explanations and suggest other factors to investigate. Clearly, this issue requires additional information.

Principles for Phonics Instruction in Whole Language

In part, our focus in this article has been on the nature of the phonics instruction in a whole language classroom. We turn now to a general summary of the principles that guide this instruction in order to describe what it consists of and how it is carried out.

- *Learner centered.* Phonics instruction in this whole language kindergarten is focused on learner needs. Rather than applying a predetermined sequence of phonics concepts, Kristin organizes and maintains a literate classroom and presents specific information as needs for instruction transpire. Thus, the instruction is developmentally appropriate for these urban learners.

- *Learned in context.* The whole language teacher's perspective holds that reading and writing are language processes and that they need to be learned in authentic language events. Phonics instruction, therefore, is contextualized in communicative acts such as writing notes or making lists.

- *Presented after foundation concepts are learned.* Phonics instruction begins when children exhibit knowledge of some foundation ideas about written language. The teacher believes that it is essential that children understand the functionality and intentionality of written language before being asked to respond to instruction about letter-sound relations. Children lacking these foundation concepts of meaningfulness cannot benefit from instruction about abstract sound-symbol relations.

- *Meaning-based.* Instruction rests on the meanings children are trying to communicate. The teacher uses children's intended meanings to provide occasions for discussing sound-symbol relations. Instruction arises from the communicative goals and purposes of the children.

- *Integrated with other written language concepts.* Learning about sound-symbol relations occurs in tandem with other concepts about the form and function of written language, rather than in isolation.

- *Learned through teacher demonstration.* The teacher shows learners how to think about letter-sound relations within the context of functional events such as constructing the agenda of the day or writing a letter. These demonstrations consist of the teacher's telling and showing her way of figuring out specific words.

- *Learned through active involvement.* The teacher invites children to become actively involved in trying to figure out how to write their intended messages. Kristin asks, "What do you hear in that word?" and encourages learners to "listen for the sounds."

- *Learned through multiple information sources.* Children learn from each other and from various print experiences. They pool their knowledge, look at print around the room, copy from each other, and ask the teacher.

Clearly, there are specifics to be taught ("What do you hear in that word?") and to be learned ("I know there is a *T* in your name . . . Toby"). And there is re-evaluation and adjustment by the teacher ("I have learned that I can't expect my children to do what I don't do"). The teaching and learning documented in this classroom example suggest that children learn about the code through direct involvement with written language, utilize the demonstrations and questioning provided by their teacher, and draw support from the social context of the classroom.

Final Perspectives and Future Directions

In this article we have looked at phonics learning and instruction through a whole language lens, describing some of the complexities that are evident. We have demonstrated the role of phonics in a whole language classroom and related a whole language perspective to the current phonics and beginning reading summary (Adams, 1990). We have shown a child learning about letter-sound relations while using written language to represent meaning, and we have seen a teacher learning from children's responses as she works to make instruction meaningful and accessible.

The future direction of the phonics controversy rests on the breadth of information that is taken into account. We agree with Dyson's contention that when we observe children's learning, the "windows" through which we look help determine what we see (Dyson, 1989). Thus, we need information from varying perspectives and information that looks at teaching and learning in all their complexities. Research that considers the influence of context, sociolinguistic elements, and the learner's responses to instruction will help clarify issues inherent in the phonics debate. First-hand classroom accounts from teachers about phonics teaching and learning will be helpful. Finally, studies investigating how the function, form, and code of written language are being taught and learned in a wide variety of classroom settings will provide information on children's orchestration of knowledge about reading and writing.

Acknowledgments

The contents of this article were developed under a grant-in-aid from the National Council of Teachers of English Research Foundation. Sincerest thanks to Kristin Schlosser, who made the work reported here possible.

STRATEGY: THINGS TO REMEMBER WHEN READING ALOUD TO CHILDREN

Editors' Note: The recommendation that teachers read to children is now a well-worn one. Apart from recommendations such as "Read books that you love" or "Be sure that you are familiar with the books you read," specific discussion of the characteristics of a "good oral reading" of a text by teachers tends to be sparse. However, more than twenty-five years ago, Linda Lamme wondered about this very topic and conducted a research project investigating the characteristics of good read-alouds.

The following items, listed in order of importance, contribute to the quality of oral reading performance by teachers:

1. *Child involvement in the story reading:* "Teachers had children chorally 'read' the refrains, or predict what would happen next, or fill in words from time to time." (p. 887)

2. *Amount of eye contact between the reader and the audience:* "Teachers who really read the text word for word did not perform as well as those who did not need to read each word, but rather, looked up at their audience frequently." (p. 887)

3. *Putting expression into the reading.*

4. *Quality of the reader's voice:* "Good oral readers tended to put variety in their voices and not read at too high or low a pitch, or too loud or soft a volume." (p. 887)

5. *Pointing to words and pictures in the book:* "Teachers who pointed things out frequently as they were reading were better overall readers than teachers who just read the story and showed the pictures in general." (p. 887)

6. *Familiarity with the story.*

▶

7. *Selection of the book*, especially in terms of choosing books with pictures that were appealing and large enough for children to see.

8. *Grouping the children so that they can see the pictures and hear the story.*

9. *Highlighting the words and language of the story:* "In the case of rhyming stories, was the rhyme apparent? Was an unusual vocabulary word glossed over or discussed? If sections were repeated, was repetition highlighted? Awareness of these language factors separated the [teachers rated as] better readers from the poorer ones." (p. 887)

Source: Lamme, L. L. (1976). Reading aloud to young children. *Language Arts, 53*(8), 886–888.

STRATEGY: PREDICTABILITY AND CHOOSING READING MATERIALS

Editors' Note: Selecting materials supportive of the reading process is particularly important for the opening moments when a child is learning to read. Predictable materials support all of the language cueing systems: prosodic (intonation), semantic (meaning), syntactic (grammatical), graphophonic (sound/visual form), and pragmatic (use of language).

The two easiest and most predictable types of reading materials are those dictated by the children themselves and those employing patterned or structured language. . . . When reading materials originate from the children's own experiences and when the language of these materials matches the children's personal language they are better able to predict what the materials are going to say. R. V. Allen (1976) explains that readers need to know four things about the material to be read: the sound of it, its meaning, its syntax, and what it looks like in print. Language experience stories eliminate all of the unknowns but the fourth. . . .

The second type of predictable materials useful in initial reading instruction is the patterned or structured language materials. Selections with repetitive structures enable children to anticipate the next line or rhyming word or episode. The children's familiarity with

▷

the repeating pattern and dependable line makes it possible for them to predict what is coming next and to sample from the visual symbols the minimum amount of information needed to confirm the prediction. . . .

One of the simplest patterns is the repetitive structure in which a certain phrase or sentence is repeated at various points in the story. Similar, but more complex, is the repetitive-cumulative structure in which a word, phrase, or sentence is repeated in each succeeding episode and with each stanza adding a new word, phrase, or sentence to the sequence, as in the well known *This Is the House That Jack Built*. The patterns provided by rhyme and rhythm are frequently used to produce predictable selections. . . .

Familiar cultural sequences can also be used advantageously to aid beginning readers in the development of predictive skills. . . . Familiar cultural sequences include the days of the week, the months of the year, the four seasons, and the basic colors. (pp. 504–506)

Source: Bridge, C. (1979). Predictable materials for beginning readers. *Language Arts, 56*(5), 503–507.

REFLECTION AND STRATEGY: SELECTING LITERATURE REFLECTIVE OF SOCIETAL DIVERSITY

Editors' Note: The increasing diversity of classrooms demands that teachers select reading materials reflecting that diversity. However, selecting literature reflective of diversity is neither simple nor undemanding, especially when a relatively homogenous teaching force is confronted with the highly heterogeneous and often unfamiliar cultures of the children in their classrooms.

Issues to Consider in Defining Cultural Groups

A major problem in defining "cultural group" is that many times cultures are linked into cultural conglomerates with an umbrella label such as "Native American," "Asian American," or "Hispanic

▶

American." Differences between the many cultures within each cultural conglomerate are substantial. . . .

Another problem in defining "cultural group" is that of excluding some cultures. For example, Jewish people feel themselves to be a distinct cultural group, yet in discussions of multicultural literature, they are often excluded. . . .

Also, the exclusion of European Americans in discussions of multicultural literature denies representation of the distinct cultures of many. . . .

With multicultural literature, evaluation of the piece must include the criteria for good literature, as well as the criteria for cultural consciousness.

Many authors discuss differences in multicultural literature written from an insider's perspective versus that of an outsider. . . . An inside perspective is one that portrays a cultural group from the point of view of one who is a member of the group. . . . An inside perspective is more likely to give an authentic view of what members of the cultural group believe to be true about themselves, whereas an outside perspective gives the view of how others see the particular group's beliefs and behaviors. . . . (p. 158)

Criteria for Selecting Quality Literature Reflective of Societal Diversity

Cultural accuracy, both of detail and of larger issues. . . .

Rich in cultural details. . . .

Authentic dialogue and relationships. . . .

In-depth treatment of cultural issues. . . .

Inclusion of members of a "minority" group for a purpose. . . . (pp. 159–160)

Source: Yokota, J. (1993). Issues in selecting multicultural children's literature. *Language Arts, 70*(3), 156–167.

REFLECTION: WHAT MAKES A HIGH-QUALITY CHILDREN'S BOOK?

Editors' Note: Different opinions exist on what makes for high-quality children's literature: The enduring underlying narrative structure? The ways in which the text provides a point of departure for personal and creative exploration? The call for reading and expressing the text's and one's own narrative? The respect the author has for the child reader? Mikkelsen explores these ideas in terms of Ezra Jack Keats's text The Snowy Day.

Thus *The Snowy Day* reveals as its governing pattern not simply a circle, the supposed pattern of children's literature and adult quest stories (home-adventure-home), as we might expect, but a spiral (home-adventure-home-adventure), of discovery, growth, and change, a metaphor of childhood and human life itself. . . . Therefore it would reveal for children, . . . on a deep subconscious level, what is deeply satisfying—a close reading of their own experience of the world and an imaginative and cognitive extension of it. . . . And perhaps this is what makes a children's book good: underlying narrative patterns of semiotic symbol, structural irony, and artistic principle that blend and merge so that readers enter the story effortlessly and participate easily in the author's created world. (p. 611)

Encountering a book that first utilizes [the reader's] . . . own experience of the world (that enables her to reduce the code systems of the author to manage the complexity of the author's world) and second, builds on her desire for more experience of the world, consequently releases her power to create (enables her to expand the code systems of the author to manage or make better sense of her own complexities and curiosities), all of which places her at the heart of the literary experience itself; discovering what it means to be human and how human it is to invent, puzzle out, and want to know more. (p. 616)

And it may be that what makes a book good, for children or adults, is this ability to call forth a strong narrative voice from readers exploring and sharing their own realities as they read—and after. (p. 618)

▶

What made a children's book good. . . was not so much what or when or how, but *why* it was written—and for whom. The missing part I almost forgot.

Nine years ago. . . , [Ezra Jack] Keats stepping down from the stage, photographers waiting across the room. But a child was waiting too.

Vinny walked directly up to the author. "I like your books," he told this shy elderly man.

Keats never hesitated. "I like you," he answered simply.

Vinny nodded. He knew. Keats had told him in the books. (p. 622)

Source: Mikkelsen, N. (1989). Remembering Ezra Jack Keats and *The Snowy Day*: What makes a children's book good? *Language Arts, 66*(6), 608–624.

10 What Miscue Analysis Reveals about Word Recognition and Repeated Reading: A View through the "Miscue Window"

Prisca Martens

Editors' Text: To some, oral readings of texts can seem contradictory—what is read correctly in one reading is not read correctly in another. The explanations for such occurrences lie in using our understandings of the reading process to help us interpret our observations. By looking at the miscues students make when reading the same text several times, Martens illustrates how our understanding of reading must go beyond word recognition models.

In 1962, Ken Goodman (1996a) decided to study reading by examining it as a language process. He asked students to read whole texts that they had not previously read and that were slightly challenging. In his analysis of these readings, Goodman discovered that the readers' unexpected responses (miscues) were neither random, capricious, nor evidence of laziness or carelessness. Instead, the unexpected responses revealed the readers were using what they knew about language and how language works to make sense of the text. Their unexpected responses were based on logical predictions using the same cues the readers used to make expected responses.

Miscues are a "window" on the reading process, a way to understand how and why readers respond to text as they do. Goodman (1994) observed that all readers, proficient to nonproficient, orchestrate cues from two bodies of knowledge in the context of their background knowledge and experience:

This essay appeared in *Language Arts* 74.8 (1997) on pages 600–609.

1. the language cue systems in the text:

    the *graphophonic system*—spelling, sound, and phonic relationships;

    the *syntactic system*—the grammar or structure of the language;

    the *semantic/pragmatic system*—the personal and social meaning in the situational context.

2. general cognitive strategies:

    readers *initiate*, making the decision to read;

    sample, selecting the most productive and useful cues based on what they know about reading, the text, and the particular situational context;

    infer, guessing information needed based on the partial information they have;

    predict, anticipating information is coming that they do not already know;

    confirm or *disconfirm*, self-monitoring their reading so they are constructing meaning;

    correct, if necessary, reconstructing the text and recovering meaning;

    terminate, deciding to stop reading.

In the 35 years since Ken Goodman first used miscue analysis, hundreds of miscue studies on readers from a broad range of cultures, ages, and abilities have consistently supported his original work (see Brown, Goodman, & Marek, 1996). Despite this vast number of miscue studies, not all reading professionals embrace the belief that miscues are part of the reading process and are evidence that readers are constructing meaning. Some believe that accuracy is a precursor to comprehension (Adams, 1990). While these reading professionals do not necessarily equate word recognition with reading, they state that good comprehension virtually never occurs with poor word recognition skills (Stanovich & Stanovich, 1995). Readers who comprehend well, they believe, decode words automatically, both quickly and accurately, leaving their attention free to focus on comprehension (Samuels, 1979). The more automatic word recognition becomes, the less readers need to rely on background knowledge and contextual information (Stanovich, 1991). As Stanovich and Stanovich (1995) claim, "The word recognition skills of the good reader are so rapid, automatic, and efficient that the skilled reader need not rely on contextual information. In fact, it is poor readers who guess from context—out of necessity because their decoding skills are so weak" (p. 92). In order to become good readers, beginning readers are encouraged to use orthographic information to identify words and not rely on context (Juel, 1995).

In this article, I will open the miscue window to examine the word recognition view of reading and its relationship to repeated readings. In repeated readings, readers read the same text a number of times until criterion goals of speed and accuracy are reached. Repeated readings do appear to make readers faster and more accurate as they read (e.g., Dowhower, 1987; Rasinski, 1990a; Samuels, 1979). Why does this happen? Is it because readers are decoding automatically? Can we learn anything about the reading process by looking at repeated readings through the miscue analysis window with miscue knowledge?

To answer these questions I will first explain repeated readings, what they are and the procedures involved. Then I will introduce Matthew, a second-grade boy, who read the same text three times, and examine some of Matthew's miscues over his successive readings to learn what miscue analysis reveals about repeated readings, fluency, and the word recognition view of reading.

Repeated Reading

Repeated reading as an instructional strategy is grounded in the belief that oral reading fluency is critical to proficient reading. Advocates have not agreed upon one precise definition of fluency (Hoffman & Isaacs, 1991; Lipson & Lang, 1991; Rasinski, 1990b), but the common thread running through various definitions is that fast and accurate word recognition in reading is necessary for comprehension. Speed is usually measured by words per minute (wpm) (Dowhower, 1994), although there is less agreement on how to count errors. Mispronunciations, substitutions, insertions, omissions, repetitions, corrections, and words supplied by the teacher after a five-second hesitation are some aspects considered (Bear, 1991; O'Shea, Sindelar, & O'Shea, 1985; Rasinski, 1990a; Weinstein & Cooke, 1992). There is also no agreement on rates to distinguish readers who are fluent from those who are not. These rates can range from 35 wpm (Bear, 1989) to 80 wpm (Downs & Morin, 1990). Researchers (e.g., Dowhower, 1987; O'Shea et al., 1985; Rasinski, 1990b; Samuels, 1979) usually measure comprehension by retellings, oral questions, and multiple choice tests. Despite the lack of agreement, advocates (e.g., Dowhower, 1994; O'Shea et al., 1985; Rasinski, 1990a; Weinstein & Cooke, 1992) believe that they can use repeated readings to teach readers to be fluent; if a reader is fluent, he/she has "a necessary dimension of proficient reading" (Zutell & Rasinski, 1991, p. 210). Within this framework, readers who on the surface are fluent and sound like they are good readers are considered good readers.

Typically in repeated reading procedures, readers must read, unassisted, a short passage of 50–300 words, with a first-reading word accuracy of at least 85 percent (Dowhower, 1994). They repeat their reading of the passage until they reach certain set criterion goals for speed and accuracy and, thus, sound "fluent." Again acceptable oral reading fluency rates vary, usually falling in the 75–145 wpm range. Second graders, for example, can be expected to read 75 wpm with 98 percent accuracy (Rasinski & Zutell, 1990) or 90 correct wpm if they are LD (Weinstein & Cooke, 1992), or 110 wpm with 90–95 percent accuracy (Howell & Lorson-Howell, 1990) or 90–100 wpm (Dowhower, 1987). When readers reach an acceptable rate of speed and accuracy on the second reading of a new passage, they are moved to a more difficult text. Students reading below 45 wpm sometimes use assisted repeated reading by reading along or listening while reading to either another reader or an audiotape (Dowhower, 1994).

Despite the popularity of repeated readings, some concerns have been expressed. One concern relates to the success of repeated reading in increasing readers' comprehension. While numerous studies (e.g., Dowhower, 1987, 1994; O'Shea et al., 1985; Rasinski, 1990a; Schreiber, 1980; Weinstein & Cooke, 1992) report success in developing fluency with repeated reading, the relationship between fluency training and increased comprehension is basically still weak (Reutzel & Hollingsworth, 1993; Stoddard, Valcante, Sindelar, O'Shea, & Algozzine, 1993). Some researchers also feel that repetition of the same passage is boring, limits the range of literature students read (thus restricting their exposure to broader vocabulary, content, and genre), and stifles the students' love of reading (Homan, Klesius, & Hite, 1993).

Matthew's Repeated Readings

Matthew, seven and a half, was selected for this examination of word recognition and repeated reading through miscue analysis because he was considered an average reader by teacher and parent evaluation and because he was willing to participate. He read the entire book *Tight Times* by Barbara Shook Hazen (1979), on three occasions, two on the same day with an hour's break between readings and the third time three weeks later. I used the entire story, rather than a short passage as is usual with repeated readings, because miscue analysis research shows that longer passages support readers' meaning construction across the text (i.e., a whole story is easier to read than a page) and readers' miscues across a text reflect their accumulating knowledge as they become familiar with the story (Menosky, 1971). I followed standard miscue analysis procedures for all three readings (Goodman, Watson, & Burke, 1987). Each session was audiotaped and played later so I could mark Matthew's unexpected responses to the text on the typescript. I explained to Matthew that he would receive no assistance at any point (i.e., he was asked to do what he does with reading difficulties when he is alone) and that when he finished reading I would ask him to share what he remembered from the story.

For each reading, I analyzed the completed marked typescript using both fluency measures and miscue analysis procedures. Since there is no standard means of calculating fluency, I used the most common methods: counting substitutions, omissions, mispronunciations, and insertions as errors but not self-corrections, repetitions, punctuation changes, and mispronounced names. I timed each reading by playing the audiotape and calculating the speed in words per minute by subtracting the errors from the total number of words in the story (697) and dividing by the elapsed time. To calculate accuracy I subtracted the number of errors from the total number of words and divided by the total number of words.

For the miscue analysis, I coded self-corrections, substitutions/ reversals, omissions, insertions, and intonation shifts changing the syntax or meaning of the text as miscues and then analyzed the readings to determine whether the miscues produced sentences that were semantically (meaning) and syntactically (grammar) acceptable. For word-for-word substitutions I also analyzed how much the miscue resembled the text. Matthew's "Meaning Construction" score showed me how concerned Matthew was with making meaning and comprehending *while* he was reading. His "Grammatical Relations" score revealed his concern with reading sentences that sounded grammatically like language. Noticeable is the difference in the number of miscues in the miscue analysis and the number of errors in the fluency calculations across the text. This difference is explained in how the miscues and errors were counted, based on what is believed and valued in each reading model.

Matthew's fluency and miscue analysis scores are listed in Table 1. The top number in each cell is his score for his reading of the entire story *Tight Times*. The middle and bottom numbers are his scores on two separate shorter portions within the whole story that I selected at natural breaking points, one towards the beginning and one farther into the story. With a couple of exceptions, Matthew's miscue analysis and fluency scores improve over the three readings.

Due to the length of the entire story as well as both portions, I will look only at selected lines and miscues from each portion over the

Table 1. Matthew's fluency and miscue analysis scores for his three readings of *Tight Times.*

Measures	Readings		
	1	2	3
Miscue Analysis			
No. of Miscues Total	104	116	106
Portion A	32	23	18
Portion B	11	17	16
Meaning Construction Total	51%	73%	80%
Portion A	38%	83%	83%
Portion B	72%	76%	94%
Grammatical Relations Total	34%	53%	73%
Portion A	25%	39%	67%
Portion B	45%	71%	100%
Retelling Total	61%	72%	72%
Portion A	45%	65%	65%
Portion B	70%	85%	70%
Fluency Scores			
No. of Errors Total	97	86	76
Portion A	24	17	11
Portion B	10	12	11
% Accuracy Total	86%	88%	89%
Portion A	80%	86%	91%
Portion B	92%	90%	91%
Total Time (minutes.seconds)	16.00	14.15	11.43
Portion A	3.17	2.22	2.10
Portion B	2.11	2.16	2.06
Words/Minute Total	38	43	54
Portion A	31	47	53
Portion B	53	50	53

Note: The entire story was 697 words; Portion A was 122 words; Portion B was 121 words.

three readings to consider Matthew's reading process. *Tight Times* is the story of a young boy who wants a dog, a wish his parents cannot grant due to the family's financial difficulties. The text was difficult for Matthew for several reasons that I came to understand only as I listened, talked with him, and analyzed the three readings. Conceptually, he had difficulty with the meaning of "tight times," even though examples were used in the story to explain that meaning. For him, shoelaces and belts could be tight but how could time be tight and what did that have to do with wanting a dog? Linguistically, the story is told by the boy in first-person narrative. Sometimes the boy is telling the story and at other times he is speaking in direct quotes. The text shifts back and forth between present and past tense verbs but has no punctuation for direct quotations. This made it difficult for Matthew to distinguish them from indirect quotations.

Portion A

In Portion A, 14 lines (122 words) in length and only 10 lines into the story, the father describes to his son what tight times are by using examples from their family life. Selected lines and miscues over the three readings will be presented, beginning in Figure 1.[1]

Matthew's Miscues

Matthew read "Dad" for *Daddy* consistently throughout the story, perhaps because he didn't feel comfortable referring to someone else's father as "Daddy." He read on in the first reading, sampling, inferring, and predicting "why we all eat more." Perhaps he was thinking "eat more potatoes or beans." But when his prediction did not work in the sentence, he disconfirmed and corrected. In his second reading, Matthew miscued on text he had read in Reading 1. At first he omitted *we* (*we* and *all* could have been considered redundant information) and read "tight times are why all it." He realized that did not make sense, disconfirmed, and read "tight times are why you eat Mr. Bilk," creating a clause in which Daddy was speaking directly to the boy, referring to him as "you." His nondeliberate omission of *all* is understandable since *all* is unnecessary with the singular "you" referring to the boy (Goodman & Gollasch, 1981). The clause made sense to him so he continued.

Matthew miscued on *Bulk* in each of the three readings, probably because he could not make sense of it as a name (some readers might pick up on the humor of a generic cereal called Mr. Bulk but Matthew didn't). In his first reading, he deliberately omitted (Goodman &

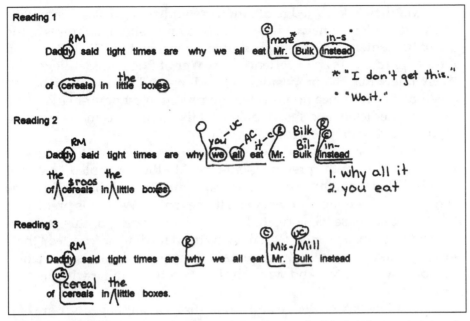

Figure 1. Matthew's three readings of a sentence in Portion A.

Gollasch, 1981) *Bulk* but, feeling more familiar and confident to take risks in the other readings, he made substitutions. In Reading 2 his concern with trying to reproduce the text was evident in the high graphic similarity between "Bilk" and *Bulk* while in Reading 3 with "Mill" he moved to a more familiar and meaningful substitution. Substituting one name for another in this instance did not disrupt Matthew's construction of meaning.

Another deliberate omission Matthew made in his first reading was *instead*, after he first attempted to read it. He omitted it two more times in the next several lines of the first reading and then, ten lines later and more experienced with the meaning and syntax of the text, he read it without hesitation and did not omit it again.

Cereals was a third deliberate omission in Matthew's first reading. Prior to this sentence, the text discussed the father and son eating breakfast. There was a picture of them at the table with a big box in front of them. Matthew's difficulties kept him too tied to the text to pick up on linguistic and visual cues of *cereals*. In his second reading, he substituted "$roos" for *cereals*. While "$roos" did not make sense, it reflected Matthew's willingness to take risks while reading. By his third reading, he predicted and read "cereal" for *cereals*, probably influenced by the one box in the illustration.

Matthew's knowledge of language and strengths as a language user were evident in his reading of the two prepositional phrases at the end of the sentence. He first substituted, then inserted, "the" in several of these phrases. As an experienced speaker of English, Matthew intuitively knew that the prepositions *of* and *in* would most likely be followed by nouns. Since nouns often are preceded by noun markers, he inferred, predicted, and inserted "the." His predictions made sense so he continued without correcting.

In his first reading of the sentence in Figure 2, two lines further on in the text from the previous sentence, Matthew sampled, inferred, and predicted "tonight" for *tight*, perhaps anticipating that Daddy was suggesting something for them to do that evening. When his prediction did not make sense, he corrected. His second reading of this part did not evidence any new miscues, but in his third reading he inserted "the," possibly predicting an indirect quote. When he realized his prediction did not fit with the text and syntax he had become familiar with, he self-corrected.

Matthew's knowledge and strengths as a language user are evident again in his readings of this sentence. In his first reading he sampled, inferred, and predicted the verb "want" for the verb *went*, reading, "Dad said tight times are why we want to," a substitution that made sense up to that point. In the published text *to* was a preposition. With his substitution of "want" for *went*, however, Matthew shifted *to* to be part of an infinitive, necessitating the nondeliberate omission of *the*. As an experienced speaker of English, he knew that it was unlikely he would say "we want to the." Since the infinitive *to* . . . required a verb, after sampling the text, Matthew inferred and predicted "sprinkle." What he read didn't make sense (he giggled, though), but he continued reading to try to regain meaning. Even though his reading was not making sense, logical and reasonable explanations for his omission of *the* and his substitution of the verb "sprinkle" for the noun *sprinkler* demonstrate that Matthew's miscues were not artifacts of chance or of his failure to recognize words, but evidence of a more complex process at work.

More experienced with the text in his second reading, Matthew predicted and read *went* followed by the beginning of the prepositional phrase *to the* which needed a noun to be complete. Curiously, he omitted *sprinkler* after having read "sprinkle" in his first reading. Matthew had had numerous experiences with sprinklers from living in Tucson, Arizona, and using them for watering (and playing). His difficulties here can probably best be explained by the grammar, rather than by his fail-

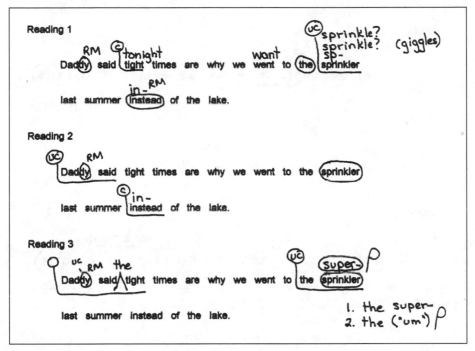

Figure 2. Matthew's three readings of a sentence in Portion A.

ure to recognize words. The sentence read *we went to the sprinkler*. But Matthew in his dialect would be more likely to say "we went *in* the sprinkler" or "we played *in* the sprinkler." The syntactic structure and meaning of the text were unfamiliar to him, making it difficult for him to predict *sprinkler*. And, if he could not predict it, he could not read and, thus, omitted it.

In his third reading, Matthew sampled, inferred, and predicted the partial "super-" for *sprinkler*. Perhaps he was predicting "supermarket" since that was a place he went *to*. But, he realized that "super-" would not make sense in a sentence about a lake, paused, and again omitted *sprinkler*.

Just prior to the sentence in Figure 3 from Portion A, Daddy explained to his son that tight times were the reason they ate lima beans on Sunday and not roast beef. The son commented that he hated lima beans and went on in this sentence to tell what he would do with his lima beans if he had a dog. In his first reading, Matthew's only miscue was "I'll" for *I'd*. Graphically, "I'll" and *I'd* are similar and they serve similar functions in a sentence, with only a slight change in meaning

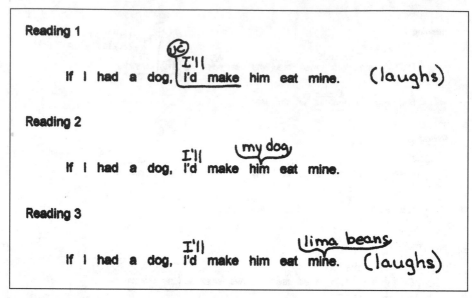

Figure 3. Matthew's three readings of a sentence in Portion A.

between "I will" and "I would." Matthew sampled, predicted, and read "I'll," possibly because it is more common and familiar to him. His laugh was an indication that he understood what he read.

Feeling more confident and willing to take risks in his other two readings of this sentence, Matthew actually made more rather than fewer miscues, miscuing on text he had read previously. He again read "I'll" for *I'd* but in his second reading predicted and substituted "my dog" for *him* and in his third reading "lima beans" for *mine*. These were substitutions he could not make unless he understood what he was reading. They reveal his focus and concern for predicting meaning rather than decoding and recognizing words. His laugh in his third reading indicated his enjoyment and comprehension. He did not correct these miscues and it would have been inefficient to do so since they made sense.

Matthew's Retellings in Portion A

Matthew's understanding and retellings were constrained by his difficulty in conceptualizing the meaning of "tight times." The initial retelling suggested that he knew the father was explaining to his son what tight times were. In successive readings and retellings, he included examples the father used but could not articulate what that phrase meant.

Matthew easily discussed parts he related to, though, such as the boy wanting a dog, not liking lima beans, and wanting to feed his lima beans to the dog.

Matthew's Strategies and Scores for Portion A

Matthew's low miscue analysis scores on his first reading reflect the difficulty he was having. His unfamiliarity with the story and his conceptual difficulty with "tight times" caused him to stay close to and work on small pieces of text, rather than conceptualize and build meaning across the whole. When he was uncertain, he made deliberate omissions (Goodman & Gollasch, 1981) and continued reading, even if the story was not making sense. Some of Matthew's comments also documented the difficulty he was experiencing.

While Matthew's conceptual and linguistic difficulties with the text continued, as he became familiar and experienced with the story, he seemed more comfortable, confident, and willing to take risks to predict and construct meaning. His fewer deliberate omissions, his fewer comments of frustration, and his willingness to attempt unfamiliar text with substitutions or nonwords indicated this. The improvement in his meaning construction, grammatical relations, and retelling scores reflected his growing competence in effectively and efficiently comprehending and understanding. (While some of the scores appear the same between the second and third readings, there were more high-quality, fully acceptable miscues than there were partially acceptable miscues in the third reading than in the second. These two scores are combined to calculate the total score reported. The scores appear the same on the surface but there was a positive qualitative change in the miscues.) Matthew's miscues over the three readings demonstrated that his improving fluency scores were not an indication that he was recognizing words faster and more accurately but that he was taking risks and predicting meaning more easily and efficiently.

Portion B

In Portion B, 12 lines (121 words) in length and 40 lines into the story, the boy finds a homeless cat in a trash can and a lady helps him get the cat out. The first of the selected sentences and miscues over the three readings is found in Figure 4.

Matthew's Miscues

In his first reading of these lines Matthew made no miscues. In his second reading, though, his experience with the story made predicting

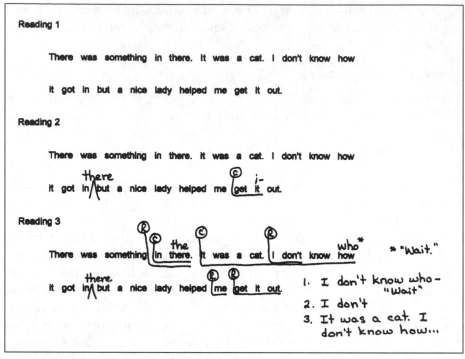

Figure 4. Matthew's three readings of a sentence in Portion B.

meaning easier for him and built his confidence as a risk taker. He inferred and predicted "there," inserting it as the object of *in* to indicate where the cat was, picking up on the phrase *in there* in the line above. This insertion created an alternate structure for the sentence that only enhanced the meaning. In his third reading, Matthew made still more miscues, continuing to evidence his strengths as a competent language user reading for meaning. He sampled, inferred, and predicted "the" for *there* to read "There was something in the." Perhaps he was predicting "in the trash can" but when he ran out of sentence, he corrected. He sampled, inferred, and predicted "I don't know who," perhaps predicting "who put the cat in the trash can." But when he realized that did not fit the sentence, he corrected. He again inserted "there."

The structure of the sentence in Figure 5 was probably unfamiliar and complex for Matthew. Since *What* sometimes signals a question, Matthew seemed to expect it to be followed by a verb. When he didn't find a verb, he abandoned *What* for "What's" to incorporate the verb he was seeking. He intoned the sentence as a statement and not a question but with a weak voice quality, probably indicating he knew he was

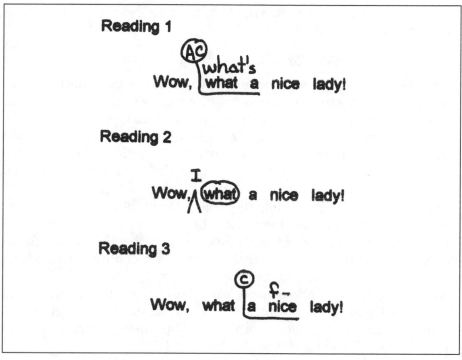

Figure 5. Matthew's three readings of a sentence in Portion B.

not making sense. He continued reading to pick up meaning across the text rather than rework the sentence. In his second reading, Matthew inserted a subject, "I," to produce "Wow, I." Perhaps he began to predict something like "Wow, I hope I can keep the cat!" But when he realized his prediction did not fit the text sentence, he paused briefly, omitted *what*, and read the rest of the sentence, intoning it as an exclamation. By his third reading, because of his experience with the text, Matthew predicted and read it easily. The text had taught him; he learned to read the text by reading it (Meek, 1988). Matthew's difficulty with this sentence was *never* with the words. He "knew" and read them on his first reading. The difficulty was with the syntax and the grammatical structure, which he had to be experienced and familiar with in order to read the sentence.

Matthew's Retellings in Portion B

In his first retelling, Matthew discussed the characters, the general plot, and the sequence of events, and he included even more details and events in his second reading. The drop in his score on the third reading may indicate what information he chose to share and not what he knew, based on his earlier retellings.

Matthew's Strategies and Scores for Portion B

As in Portion A, Matthew's unfamiliarity with the story in his first reading kept him close to the printed text. He took few risks and used his "read on" strategy even if something did not make sense. However, because he could conceptually relate to and understand the situation in this portion and because by this point he had read, constructed meaning, and tasted the author's style for 40 lines, he was more efficient and effective on his first reading. His miscue analysis and fluency scores were higher on his first reading of Portion B than they were for his first reading of Portion A and the whole story. Curiously, he made more miscues and more errors in his second reading than his first, and his speed and accuracy scores decreased. Yet his meaning construction, grammatical relations, and retelling scores all improved. His understanding was not dependent on his recognizing words more quickly and accurately. On his third reading, Matthew's meaning construction and grammatical relations scores improved, and his fluency scores improved over his second reading but not his first.

Discussion

If Matthew's fluency scores are examined over the three readings in Table 1, it appears that repeated readings do "work." For the first reading, Matthew's "fluency" was not constant across his reading of the text. His speed and accuracy varied widely for Portion A, Portion B, and the entire story. By the third reading, though, his scores improved and were much more stable with less fluctuation. In other words, someone listening to Matthew read would hear his third oral reading as fairly steady, controlled, and more proficient than his first reading.

To conclude that Matthew's improving fluency scores meant he was recognizing words more quickly and accurately in order to comprehend would be a misinterpretation of the data, however. Miscue analysis demonstrated that Matthew was tentative and unsure of himself in his first reading. He did not know what to expect and stayed close to the printed text, hesitant and unwilling to take many risks. In each successive reading, though, he became more familiar and comfortable with the story line, the syntax, and the author's style. His growing familiarity with all aspects of the story empowered him to make better predictions more easily, which propelled his speed and accuracy. His improving speed and accuracy were the *result* of his understanding, familiarity, and experience with the story; he was not reading more quickly and accurately in order to comprehend.

Matthew's miscue scores also provide evidence that his comprehension was not dependent on his improving speed and accuracy. Even though by Reading 3 Matthew's fluency scores indicated he was more "fluent," these scores did not represent an equally steady, controlled, and proficient understanding of the story across his reading. His miscue scores in Reading 3 still varied widely. Matthew's largest gains in speed and accuracy were in Portion A where his comprehension was weakest. In Portion B, he made more errors and miscues in his second reading and even read more slowly, yet his comprehension in the re-telling, meaning construction, and grammatical relations scores all improved. His increasing fluency, then, did not guarantee or represent a comparable and corresponding comprehension of the text.

Predicting Meaning or Recognizing Words?

While it is impossible to crawl into Matthew's head and read his mind to know for certain that my assumptions and analysis are truly representative of his thinking, I *can* demonstrate that his miscues were not random and haphazard. They were guided by his knowledge of language and how language works. His preoccupation with predicting meaning and making sense of the text was clearly evident in his miscues even on his first reading. There were times he went back to correct for meaning, times he didn't correct because his prediction was meaningful and correction was unnecessary, and also times he lost meaning and decided to continue reading to regain the meaning.

Matthew was not attempting to recognize individual words. In a number of instances, "knowing the words" was not the cause of Matthew's difficulty. Sometimes the difficulty was conceptual. For example, Matthew could recognize and say the words *tight times* but that did not mean he understood them. Sometimes the difficulty was with the syntax of the sentence. I am fairly confident he "knew" the word *sprinkler*, based on his reading "sprinkle" and his experiences with sprinklers. But he could not predict and read it in the phrase *went to the sprinkler*. He "knew" the words *wow, what, a, nice,* and *lady* in his first reading but could not read them as a sentence until he experienced and learned the syntactic structure they were in. Sometimes even though he "knew" the words and syntax and had read them "correctly," he miscued in a subsequent reading to construct a text parallel to the printed text that was more meaningful for him. This occurred in his substitutions of "why you eat" for *why we all eat*, "my dog" for *him*, "lima beans" for *mine*, and his insertions of "the" and "there" in syntactically and semantically acceptable places.

One Reading Process

Some may argue that Matthew miscues, has difficulty with syntax, and needs to "rely on contextual information" because he is a "poor reader." They may say that proficient readers would not have these difficulties because they recognize and decode words automatically and don't need contextual cues (Stanovich & Stanovich, 1995). Proficient readers *do* indeed make fewer miscues than less proficient readers. But as the reading of Sherry, a third-grade proficient reader, and Susan, a graduate student, will demonstrate, the fewer miscues of proficient readers are *not* because they are automatically recognizing words.

Sherry enjoys reading and often chooses to read in her free time at home and at school. In thirteen pages of *Henry and Beezus* (Cleary, 1952), Sherry made eleven miscues, including the examples shown in Figures 6 and 7.

As shown in Figure 6, Sherry sampled, inferred, and predicted an independent clause with a similar structure to the dependent clause that began the sentence. Perhaps she was predicting something like, "If I can't have a brand-new bike without a single thing wrong with it, I guess I can't have a bike." When she realized her prediction would not make sense in the text, she reread, paused, and read the rest of the sentence correctly.

In the example shown in Figure 7, Sherry sampled, inferred, and predicted "section," substituting it for *selection*. The two look similar (graphophonic cueing system) and are both nouns (syntactic cueing system). Since comic books are usually found in a particular section of a store, her miscue made sense (semantic/pragmatic cueing system) to her and she continued reading.

Miscues are not a phenomenon known only to young readers. Susan, a graduate student in Language Education, was reading *The Remains of the Day* (Ishiguro, 1989). In four pages of dense, heavy text, she made seven miscues, including the examples shown in Figures 8 and 9.

Susan's miscues shown in Figure 8 created a construction parallel to the one in the printed text and did not affect the meaning. So, she continued reading. Her insertion of "that" was probably a result of the

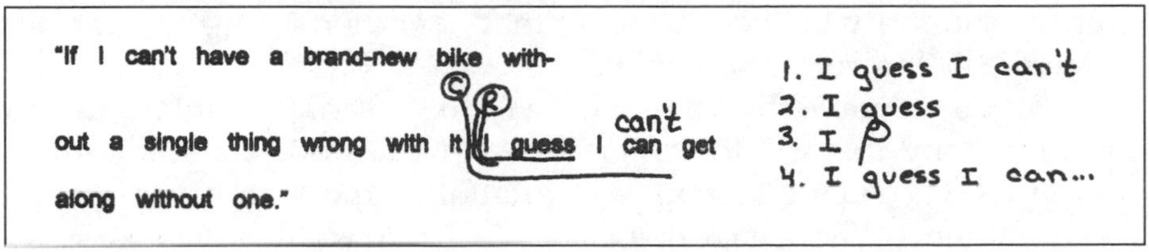

"If I can't have a brand-new bike with-out a single thing wrong with it I guess I can get along without one."

can't

1. I guess I can't
2. I guess
3. I
4. I guess I can...

Figure 6. Sherry's miscues in *Henry and Beezus* (Cleary, 1952).

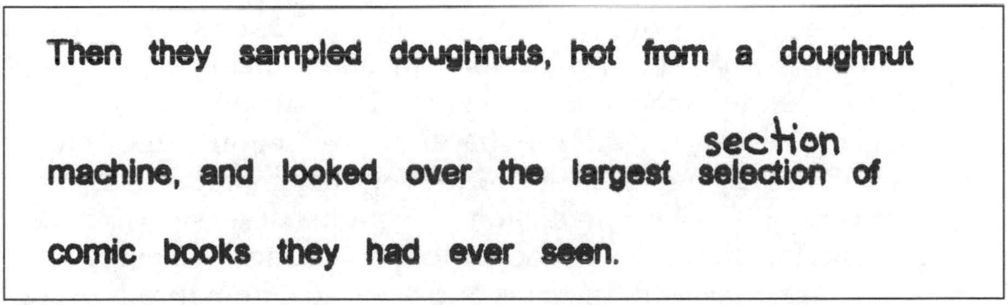

Then they sampled doughnuts, hot from a doughnut machine, and looked over the largest selection of comic books they had ever seen.

section

Figure 7. Sherry's miscues in *Henry and Beezus* (Cleary, 1952).

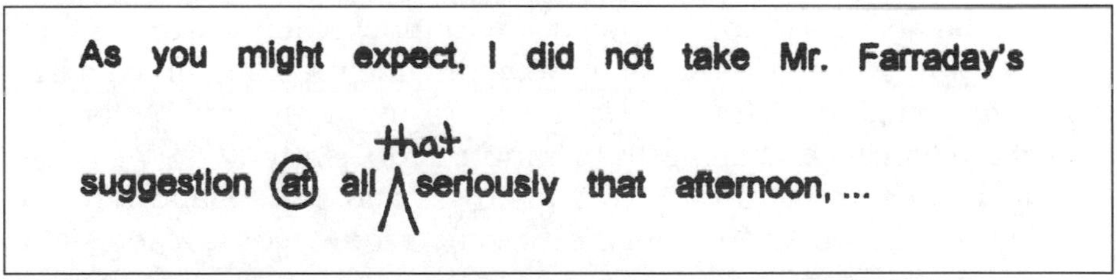

As you might expect, I did not take Mr. Farraday's suggestion (at) all seriously that afternoon, ...

that

Figure 8. Miscues by Susan in *The Remains of the Day* (Ishiguro, 1989)

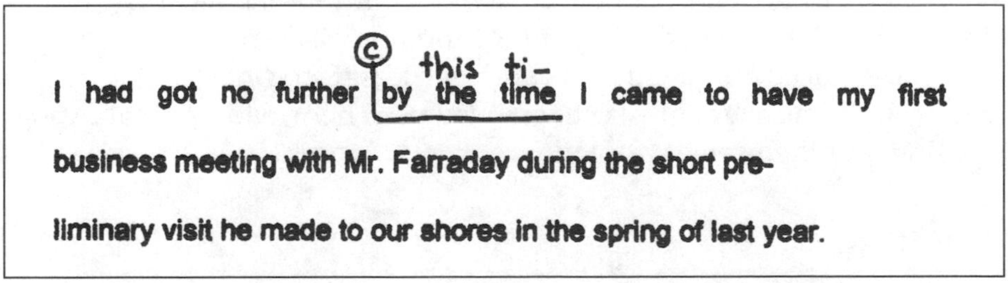

I had got no further by the time I came to have my first business meeting with Mr. Farraday during the short pre-liminary visit he made to our shores in the spring of last year.

this ti-

Figure 9. Miscues by Susan in *The Remains of the Day* (Ishiguro, 1989).

graphic similarity between *at* and "that" and her seeing *that* farther down the line in her peripheral vision.

In the example shown in Figure 9, Susan sampled, inferred, and predicted "by this ti-" for *by the time*. "This" and *the* look similar (graphophonic cueing system) and are both noun markers (syntactic cueing system). When she realized her prediction would not make sense (semantic/pragmatic cueing system), she immediately corrected.

Hundreds of miscue studies (see Brown, Goodman, & Marek, 1996) reveal that there is one reading process. Matthew, Sherry, Susan, and all other readers construct meaning as they read. They all use the semantic/pragmatic, syntactic, and graphophonic cue systems and sample, infer, predict, confirm/disconfirm, and self-correct. Matthew, Sherry, Susan, and all other readers miscue. They substitute, insert, and omit. Their miscues are evidence that they are "mining" the text for meaning. With varying levels of proficiency, they monitor their reading, correcting when their predictions do not make sense. Miscue research shows that the reading process does not change. Readers do not "graduate" from orchestrating cues in the text to automatically recognizing words. Proficient readers are experienced readers. They have read a wide variety of literature for a wide variety of purposes which has allowed them to become very familiar with a wide range of vocabulary, syntactic structures, content, background experiences, and authors' styles. They have had lots of practice with how reading works which makes reading seem effortless for them. But, their reading process isn't different from that of less proficient readers; they only have better control of the process and orchestrate it more proficiently.

The miscue window allows us to see and understand how the reading process works. Without the miscue window, we see readers who "can't read the words" as poor or nonproficient readers. With the miscue window, we see readers who are knowledgeable and capable language users and who possess a variety of strengths that we can build on to support them in becoming more proficient. Miscue analysis has enabled us to revalue reading, to see it as a transactive, constructive process focused on making meaning, and to revalue readers as competent experienced language users and learners (Goodman, 1996b). Most importantly, miscue analysis has enabled us to help readers revalue both reading and themselves as readers.

Note

1. The following are miscue analysis markings used in the text excerpts: substitutions are written above the text; omissions are circled; insertions are indicated with a caret; RM indicates a repeated miscue, meaning a miscue identical to one which occurred earlier in the story; $ indicates a nonword; ρ indicates a 5-second pause. A circle connected to a line(s) under a portion of the text marks a regression, and the letter(s) in the circle indicate(s) what occurred; C indicates the miscue was corrected; R indicates a straight repetition of the text; UC means an unsuccessful attempt was made to correct the miscue; AC means abandoned correct, that the expected response was read first and then abandoned in the regression; an empty circle indicates more than one change occurred in the regression and individual miscues are marked for the change made.

REFLECTION: PREDICTION AND READING

Editors' Note: Prediction involves the orchestration of many different aspects of linguistic and personal knowledge. At a time when the use of decodable texts moves away from understanding how varied knowledge sources contribute to reading, revisiting the nature of prediction and its role in reading can help enlarge such narrow views.

Four reasons for prediction:

1. Individual words have too many meanings. . . .
2. The spellings of words do not indicate how they should be pronounced. . . .
3. There is a limit to how much of the "visual information" of print the brain can process during reading. . . . For as long as one is trying to identify letters one after the other, reading is an impossibly slow and restricted process. . . .
4. The capacity of short-term memory (or "working memory") is limited. . . . As a consequence, it is virtually impossible to read a word more than four or five letters long a letter at a time. By the time the end is reached, the beginning will be forgotten. . . . (pp. 305–306)

My general definition of prediction is the *prior elimination of unlikely alternatives.* . . . The qualification "unlikely" in the preceding definition must be emphasized. "Prediction" in the sense in which I am using the word does not mean wild guessing, nor does it mean staking everything on a simple outcome. Rather prediction means the elimination from contention of those possibilities that are highly unlikely, and the examination first of those possibilities that are most likely. Such a procedure is highly efficient for making decisions involving language. (p. 306)

Two basic conditions must be met if a child is to be able to predict in the manner that is essential for learning to read. The first condition is that the material from which children are expected to learn to read must be potentially meaningful to them, or otherwise there is no way they will be able to predict. . . . But meaningfulness of materials and activities is not enough; children must also feel confident that they are at liberty to predict, to make use of what they already know. . . .

There are only two possibilities for a mistake made during reading, either the mistake will make a difference to the meaning, or it will not. (pp. 309–310)

One of the most formidable impediments to prediction at all levels of reading is anxiety. A child who is afraid to make a mistake is by definition anxious, and therefore unwilling to take the necessary risks for prediction. (pp. 310–311)

Source: Smith, F. (1975). The role of prediction in reading. *Language Arts, 52*(3), 305–311.

REFLECTION: ARE FICTION AND NONFICTION DISCRETE GENRES?

Editors' Note: Terms like fiction *and* nonfiction *are used as though they are not problematic categories. Dawkins provides one interpretation of how to think of these categories; however, there are many others. The key focus for teachers is to attend to the ways they talk about genres as they help students understand these text forms.*

Fiction and nonfiction are defined in typical elementary level dictionaries and instructional materials in much the same way. For example, fiction is "something made up; a story that is not fact" (*Thorndike-Barnhart Junior Dictionary,* 1968) or a "made-up story" (*Webster's New Elementary Dictionary,* 1970). From this it follows that nonfiction is "writing that describes only real people and true events" (*Exploring Literature,* Houghton Mifflin Company, 1968). These definitions, I claim, lead to faulty and useless concepts for both teachers and students. . . .

The common definitions clearly cut the world of prose into two parts, writings about imaginary or made-up events and writings about true or factual events. But they don't work very well. For example, to which group does the typical elementary level dictionary or textbook assign an Art Buchwald imaginary interview? . . . Where do they put all kinds of argumentation and persuasion, such as editorials, advertising, and propaganda? Where do they put reflective writing such as the personal essay? Are these made up? Are they factual? Are they true? (p. 127)

Instead of raising questions about the nature of truth or the meaning of reality, our definitions should raise questions about the nature and meaning of literary types. A definition that does this properly will identify the elements of the genre it is defining: *Fiction,* the general category, is writing that uses character, action, and setting to reflect a theme or to resolve a problem for the purposes of providing esthetic entertainment and meeting a psychological need. *Realistic fiction* is writing in which each of these elements—character, action, and setting—is based on a criterion or "realism." Fantasy, which may be subdivided to accommodate at least the folk tale and science fiction, is writing in which the limits of realism are exceeded by at least one of the elements. *Fable, myth, legend* and all other types of fiction are defined by their varying uses of character, action, setting, and purpose.

Nonfiction is any other kind of prose. Some kinds of nonfiction (for example, biography and the human interest story) may use character, action, setting, and problem, but they will use them for different purposes than those of fiction. There is a wide variety of nonfiction, each kind having a purpose of its own. The table below is a partial listing:

▷

Nonfiction

Type	Purpose	Example
exposition	to explain	encyclopedia
description	to describe	travelog
argument	to persuade	editorial
report (current)	to report	news story
report (past)	to report	biography
satire (light)	to make laughable	column
satire (serious)	to make absurd	profile, parody
discursive	to reflect	personal essay

(p. 128)

Source: Dawkins, J. (1977). Defining fiction and nonfiction for students. *Language Arts, 54*(2), 127–129.

REFLECTION AND STRATEGY: BOOK CENSORSHIP

Editors' Note: Censorship occurs in subtle and public ways; yet most would agree that critical, thoughtful discussion, rather than suppression, is an effective way of handling difficult ideas found in challenging texts. O'Neal provides a starting point for thinking about censorship. More elaborate and detailed suggestions can be found through the National Council of Teachers of English's SLATE group.

For Parents and Community Members

Anyone who is concerned about a particular book (or other form of media) on the shelves of schools should first read the text in question in its entirety and be prepared to state specifically the parts of the material that are objectionable. Second, one should inquire about how instructional materials are selected and used in the district. . . . Finally, parents and community members should volunteer to serve on committees dealing with book challenges, book selection and book evaluation. (p. 774)

For Administrators

If a policy for selection, evaluation, and reconsideration of instructional materials does not exist, both central office supervisors and campus administrators should request that such a policy be initiated. . . . Once the policy is in place and approved by the local board of education, central office supervisors must provide staff development . . . on the content and procedures contained in the policy. (p. 774)

For Teachers

Teachers are obligated to read all books they intend to require for instruction. . . . Teachers may wish to provide parents with book lists early in the school year and invite them to read the books themselves. When possible, students should be able to select from a group of titles, rather than be required to read one book with the entire class. Not only does this provide options for students who may be uncomfortable with a particular selection, but also the students will be able to select according to their own interests and ability levels. Finally, teachers may wish to collaborate with their school librarians when selecting materials for a classroom library. (p. 775)

Source: O'Neal, S. (1990). Leadership in the language arts: Controversial books in the classroom. *Language Arts, 67*(7), 771–775.

For a description of what happened in one school district over a call to ban books from the Goosebumps series, see: Church, S. M. (1997). When values clash: Learning from controversy. *Language Arts, 74*(7), 525–532.

REFLECTION: THE "GOODNESS" OF PULP FICTION THEN AND NOW

Editors' Note: Across the years educators have worried about the success of pulp fiction with young readers. Although these worries are often articulated without an analysis of why so many highly literate adult readers are readers of adult pulp fiction, it is also clear that the way educators have worried has both changed and stayed the same. It is interesting to think about why.

The '60s and '70s: *Nancy Drew*

The *Nancy Drew* series, which began in 1930 as an obscure pulp fiction novelette, is today [1975] the best selling juvenile series book in the United States and in France. . . .

The creator, Edward Stratemeyer . . . gave birth to sixty-eight adventure series, including the *Hardy Boys, Tom Swift,* and the *Bobbsey Twins.* . . . Harriet Stratemeyer Adams, who has written the series since 1935 when her father died, is author of all but the first three of the seventy *Nancy Drew* books and has added fourteen new series to the Stratemeyer syndicate. . . .

Responding to our comments on criticisms from educators who believe *Nancy Drew* is unrealistic and unrelated to the problems of everyday life, Mrs. Adams stated: "Children ages eight to thirteen don't care one whit about social problems. They want to be entertained." . . .

Nancy Drew lends itself to criticism in terms of limited depth of characterization and lack of realism. The action, though fast-moving and well-paced, is sustained by cardboard characters who lack scope. Stories are formula-fixes and plots are self-evident. Nevertheless children hunger for more and more of this peppery diet which, however undernourishing, seems to suit their palate. (p. 1131)

Literary attacks on *Nancy* reflect the fact that she is achievement-rather than affiliation-oriented and has not changed with the years. Her individual goals are never subordinated to group efforts, and the reading of her adventures does nothing to spur human understanding of diversity among peoples or tolerance for minorities. . . .

The poverty of literary value is somewhat offset by Nancy Drew's worth as a tool to spur non-readers in the habit of reading. (p. 1134)

Source: Wertheimer, B. S., & Sands, C. (1975). *Nancy Drew* revisited. *Language Arts, 52*(8), 1131–1134.

The '80s and Early '90s: *The Baby-Sitters Club*

"It's in—I saw it at Greenwood's! Are you going to get it? You can borrow mine, but you'll have to wait till I've finished—and my sister.".... What is this series? What is its appeal to young readers?....

Briefly, the Baby-Sitters Club does what its name implies. A varying number of girls aged between eleven and thirteen have joined together to offer a babysitting service to the town....

The strong points of the series are several. For the most part, the adventures of the girls are moderately plausible; the family upsets (death, divorce, remarriage) are neither glossed over nor exploited unmercifully. That well-known problem of getting the adults out of the way so the adventures can begin is solved, almost by definition, by the framework of babysitting....

The first-person narrative plays a useful role, especially for those readers who are just getting used to reading whole books.... The format of one book following another allows for a great deal of natural redundancy which is also helpful to inexperienced readers. ... [The author, Ann M.] Martin clearly expects a considerable measure of identification between her young readers and the comfortable suburban heroines of her books.... There are not many shades of grey in these books; she offers the conventional wisdom of the American middle class. (pp. 484–485)

What other possible reasons are there for the role played by the series book in the reading diet of so many children? One conceivable answer almost seems like a contradiction in terms: There could be a kind of intellectual satisfaction in the reading of series books which adults may often overlook.... (p. 487)

Nothing is gained by exaggerating the value of this kind of series book. Readers who never move on to anything more demanding miss out on a wide range of experience. It is also not helpful to dismiss such series reading with a passing sneer. The experience of making patterns, putting stories together, extrapolating, and confirming may be providing a crucial step towards more substantial reading. (p. 488)

Source: Mackey, M. (1990). Filling the gaps: *The Baby-Sitters Club*, the series book, and the learning reader. *Language Arts, 67*(5), 484–489.

▷

The '90s: *Goosebumps*

Designated as books for eight- to twelve-year-olds, or seven- to thirteen-year-olds, . . . Goosebumps books [by R. L. Stine] are considered mildly scary. . . . In *librarian lingo* they are subliterature, . . . and some consider the plotting to be careless and character development to be lacking. . . . In quoting a librarian . . . , Silver (1995) wrote, "If R. L. Stine wasn't writing Goosebumps, many of his readers wouldn't be reading." (Perry & Butler, 1997, pp. 454–455)

What is the lure of this particular series? . . . According to Carroll's (1990) definition of art-horror, the text must contain a monster who is "threatening" and that monster must produce "disgust or repulsion" in the reader. . . . Fourth graders said they experienced emotions and feelings similar to those described by the fictional characters. . . . The narrative is one source of the pleasure of the horror genre. (Dickson, 1998, pp. 116–117)

Part of the lure for young readers . . . is to see whether the protagonist will be successful in identifying the monster and getting help in confronting and destroying him. . . . The great lure of horror fiction comes from a combination of awe and curiosity about what is unnatural and repulsive, as well as interest in the narrative structure that is set up by the questions posed at the beginning of the story, the commonly described experience of "reading to find out what will happen." (Dickson, 1998, p. 118)

It's not so much that young people should be discouraged from reading R. L. Stine, as that they should be encouraged to seek more places for the same kinds of gratifications they get from Stine's books.

And how can we play a role in making that happen? In at least two ways, I think. Supporting children in experiencing the unfamiliar is one way. This can be done by reading alternative horror writers such as John Bellairs so that we can honestly recommend a particular book and tell them why, thereby giving them some of the language that they might begin to apply in their own reading. . . . The other way is to do what Ruth Vinz (1996) suggests. . . . I think that if, as teachers and parents, we can investigate *with* our young people their motivations for and reactions to reading horror, we might all learn from the experience. (Dickson, 1998, pp. 121–122)

▶

Sources:
Dickson, R. (1998). Horror: To gratify, not edify. *Language Arts, 76*(2), 115–122.
Perry, L. A., & Butler, R. P. (1997). Are *Goosebumps* books real literature? *Language Arts, 74*(6), 454–456.

11 Literature—SOS!

Louise M. Rosenblatt

Editors' Text: The purpose for reading is what makes our experience of a text. Drawing upon her theory of reader stance in reading, Rosenblatt challenges us to reconsider the impact of the genre of the text in reading and to think about our attitude or stance when we read. She asks us to think about public and private aspects of the meaning of texts through a discussion of aesthetic and efferent reading.

Literature-based language arts"; "the use of literature for literacy instruction"; "the contribution of the aesthetic in the teaching of mathematics"; "aesthetic response in content area studies." Such phrases are increasingly encountered in our journals. In the past, literature and the aesthetic have been neglected in our schools; now, finally, their importance is being recognized. Surely, this is a matter for rejoicing. Alas, the contrary is true: There are signs that the very efforts to rescue literature, though often excellent, may become self-defeating.

No one seems to think it necessary to explain what is meant by *literature,* or *the aesthetic.*

If one analyzes the use of these terms in their contexts, a variety of tacit assumptions seems to operate. Sometimes, all that is required is that a text already has been designated as "literature." Sometimes, the presence of story, of a narrative, is the clue. Sometimes, the presence of rhymed words, or of verse rhythms, or of metaphoric language seems sufficient to justify the claim that "literature," or at least "the aesthetic," has been operating. Sometimes, the aesthetic is attributed to the presence of emotion, as when students become excited about scientific information.

All of these elements can indeed be found in texts read as literature. Yet none of these, either singly or all together, can insure the presence of "literature." The fact is that any text, even if it contains such elements, can be the occasion for *either* a "literary" *or* a "nonliterary" reading.

After all, narrative (story) is found not only in novels but also in scientific accounts of geological change or historical accounts of political events or social life. When we speak of the "arm" of a chair, we are using a metaphor. The physicist who uses "wave" in his theory of light

This essay appeared in *Language Arts* 68.6 (1991) on pages 444–448.

is using a metaphor. As for the term *literature*—I recently received a phone call offering me "literature" about a retirement home!

The term *literature*, when it is used in contrast, say, to scientific exposition, refers to a particular mode of experience. It requires a particular kind of relation between reader and text. It requires a particular kind of reading process.

Two Ways of Reading

Take, for example, the couplet

> In fourteen hundred and ninety-two
> Columbus crossed the ocean blue.

Why are we reluctant to accept

> In fourteen hundred and ninety-three
> Columbus crossed the dark blue sea.

The point, of course, is that we want to use the verse and rhyme as a mnemonic device for the date of Columbus's arrival in America. In other words, we read the couplet in the way we read an expository essay. We pay some attention to the sound and rhythm, but our predominant interest is in acquiring information that we wish to retain after the reading has ended. I use the term *efferent* (from the Latin for "carry away") to refer to this nonliterary kind of reading.

Still, we can, if we wish, shift gears and pay attention mainly to what we are thinking and feeling as we read or speak the couplet. We can disregard the inaccuracy of the date in the second couplet and decide that it is, from an aesthetic point of view, preferable (e.g., we feel more comfortable with the order of words in "the dark blue sea"). We should then be adopting an *aesthetic* stance toward the text—reading it with attention, of course, to what the words refer to, but *mainly* to what we are experiencing, thinking, and feeling *during* the reading.

Obviously, these verses about Columbus do not provide much reward for the aesthetic stance. Yet they share with even the most valued poetry—say, Shakespeare's *Macbeth*—the potential for being read either aesthetically or efferently.

I was once asked to classify the metaphors in Shakespeare's plays. (This was supposed to reveal biographical information.) That would have meant approaching each play efferently, with my attention focused on how each metaphor should be classified—e.g., as nature, law, animal, etc. It would simply have been irrelevant to pay attention to what states of mind the metaphors were arousing in me. *That* kind of attention to what the metaphors were stirring up—associations, ideas, attitudes, sensations, or feelings—would have had to be reserved for the kind of reading that I call *aesthetic* reading.

Consider the following metaphor:

I am the captain of my soul.

If my purpose is to select the class of metaphors to which this might belong, an efferent reading of this line would be required. My mind would be carrying on an analytic, reasoning activity, in which "captain of a ship" would be seen as implied in the metaphor. Of course, I would have to reason, for someone else "captain" might produce an association with the army. I might have to classify it as naval *or* military.

In an aesthetic reading, on the other hand, I would be registering the effect on me, the states of mind produced by the idea or image of a ship's captain. If interrupted and questioned, I might report a feeling of strength, of independence, of mastery over "my soul." I would probably not explicitly analyze this feeling as resulting from the comparison implied in the metaphoric use of "captain." If asked, I could shift my attention away from the metaphoric effect and recognize this.

Adopting a Predominant Stance

It's the either-or habit of thinking that has caused the trouble. True, there are two primary ways of looking at the world. We may experience it, feel it, sense it, hear it, and have emotions about it in all its immediacy. Or we may abstract generalizations about it, analyze it, manipulate it, and theorize about it. These are not contradictory activities, however. We cannot, for example, identify the efferent with cognition and the aesthetic, or literary, with emotion.

Instead of thinking of the *text* as either literary or informational, efferent or aesthetic, we should think of it as written for a particular *predominant* attitude or stance, efferent or aesthetic, on the part of the reader. We have ignored the fact that our reading is not all-of-one-piece. We read for information, but we are also conscious of emotions about it and feel pleasure when the words we call up arouse vivid images and are rhythmic to the inner ear. Or we experience a poem but are conscious of acquiring some information about, say, Greek warfare. To confuse matters even further, we can switch stances while reading. And we can read aesthetically something written mainly to inform or read efferently something written mainly to communicate experience. Our present purpose and past experiences, as well as the text, are factors in our choice of stance.

Teachers need constantly to remind themselves that reading is always a particular event involving a particular reader at a particular time under particular circumstances. Hence, we may make different meanings when transacting with the same text at different times. And different readers may make different defensible interpretations of the same text. We need think only of the text of the Constitution or the text of *Hamlet* to document this (Rosenblatt, 1978).

The reader brings to the text a reservoir of past experiences with language and the world. If the signs on the page are linked to elements in that reservoir, these linkages rise into consciousness. The reader recognizes them as words in a language; the child is often slowly making such connections. All readers must draw on past experiences to make the new meanings produced in the transaction with the text. This experience then flows into the reservoir brought to the next reading event.

Psychologists (e.g., Bates, 1979) have pointed out that these connections between verbal signs and what they signify involve both what the words are understood to refer to (their public, dictionary meaning) and the feelings, ideas, and attitudes (their private associations) that have become linked with them through past reading or life experiences. A mixture of such public and private elements is present in all linguistic events. The differences between them result from the individual's focus of attention.

A reading event during which attention is given *primarily* to the public aspect, I call, as indicated above, *efferent* reading. If the reader focuses attention *primarily* on the private elements, I term it *aesthetic.* But each case involves both public and private aspects of meaning.

Actually, we have been talking about a continuum, not an opposition. In a sequence from 1 to 10, for example, these two numbers are not opposites or contraries but simply the end points of a continuum. In the continuum from efferent to aesthetic, these terms are end points in a changing proportion, or "mix," of elements. In any reading, at any point in the continuum, there are both cognitive and affective, publicly referential and privately associational, and abstract and concrete elements (see Figure 1). The place where any reading event falls on the continuum reflects the proportion of what, for brevity, we can call the public and private elements. In the predominantly efferent half of the continuum, the area of attention to the public elements will be greater than the area of the private. Some readings may lean more heavily on the private aspects than others and will be closer to the middle of the continuum. A book about a foreign country read for information, for example, could entail mainly concentration on abstract generalizations (Figure 1, A) or involve much attention to experiential aspects of descriptions (Figure 1, B).

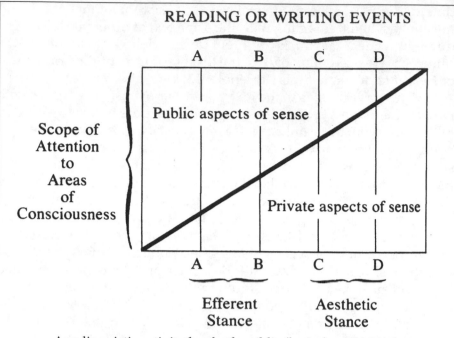

Figure 1. The efferent/aesthetic continuum (adapted from Rosenblatt, 1989).

Similarly, aesthetic readings will result when the reader's attention is focused mainly on the private, experiential aspects. But some aesthetic readings pay more attention to the public, referential, and cognitive aspects than do others. An aesthetic reading of *Encyclopedia Brown and the Case of the Mysterious Handprints* (Sobol, 1986), which invites the reader to solve a problem, will probably fall closer to the efferent side of the continuum (Figure 1, C) than will an aesthetic reading of a story such as *Charlotte's Web* (White, 1952) (Figure 1, D).

Precisely because all readings tend to have such a "mix," it becomes important for readers (and writers) to keep their main purposes clear. Beautiful and moving as the words urging us to vote for a candidate may be, it's important that we keep clear that our purpose is to get accurate information. And if we want to experience a text as a poem or a story, we need to learn to evoke experiential meaning from the text and to focus attention on that, rather than simply "the message" or "the facts." Readings that fall near the middle of the continuum especially need to keep the primary purpose, the primary focus of attention, clear.

Clarifying a Sense of Purpose

Confusion about the purpose of reading has in the past contributed to failure to teach effectively both efferent reading and aesthetic reading. Why not help youngsters early to understand that there are two ways of reading? We do not want to give them theoretical explanations, nor do we need to. We communicate such understandings by what we do, by the atmosphere and the activities we associate with the two kinds of reading, and by the kinds of questions we ask and the kinds of tests we give. Children who know that the teacher usually quizzes them on factual aspects of a reading, even if it is called "a poem" or "a story," will adopt the efferent stance and will read to register the facts that will be required after the reading. They know that they will be successful and rewarded if they recall the color of the horse or where the bunny hid, rather than if they linger over the experiences and feelings encountered. (Actually, that kind of fragmented questioning doesn't much improve efferent reading, either!)

With younger children, perhaps the best evidence of aesthetic experience is their demand to hear the story or poem again. Or they may wish to draw a picture or retell the story. Some may be moved to comment on it. I think of the three-year-old who exclaimed, "She's a mean lady!" when hearing the nursery rhyme about a certain old lady who spanked her many children "all round" and put them to bed. Certainly, evidence of "comprehension" can be gained in such indirect ways from readers of all age.

Aesthetic reading happens if students have repeatedly found that, in approaching a text called a "poem" or a "story," they can assume that they are free to pay attention to what the words call to consciousness. They can savor the images, the sounds, the smells, the actions, the associations, and the feelings that the words point to. Textbooks' and teachers' questions too often hurry the students away from the lived-through experience. After the reading, the experience should be recaptured, reflected on. It can be the subject of further aesthetic activities—drawing, dancing, miming, talking, writing, role playing, or oral interpretation. It can be discussed and analyzed efferently. Or it can yield information. But first, if it is indeed to be "literature" for these students, it must be experienced (Rosenblatt, 1983).

It is teachers who need to be clear theoretically about efferent and aesthetic reading. As they commendably seek to present more "literature" in their language arts curricula, they need to be careful not to "use" the appeal of such texts simply or mainly for the efferent purposes of teaching grammar or "skills." Also, as teachers plan to include aesthetic elements in the work in social or natural science or to utilize the interest of story in the teaching of mathematics, they need to realize that they have a responsibility not to create confusion about primary stances appropriate to different purposes.

The different purposes lead to different modes of reading and to different criteria of evaluation of the "meanings" evoked. If the emphasis is on verifiable information or practical application, not only does the mode of reading need to be efferent, but also the interpretation of the text needs to involve some public criteria of evaluation. If the purpose is literary, the important thing is that readers relate to the text, and to one another, the different experiences produced during their transactions with it.

I am decidedly in sympathy with those who, under the rubric of "whole language," speak of the importance of meaning. But I hope that they will not confuse students by using "literary works" in such a way that students read them efferently, for the primary purpose, let us say, of learning historical data. If American history is being studied, a novel about colonial life will be valuable, but only as primarily an aesthetic experience, a sharing of what it would have been like to live in those days. If the story has been read with a primarily aesthetic emphasis, one can later, of course, ask students to recall incidental information about, for example, methods of transportation. But it would often be helpful to suggest that the author of the poem or novel had acquired that information through verified historical sources.

The distinctions in purpose and stance can be incorporated into actual classroom practice without dwelling on theoretical distinctions. Even nursery school youngsters can sense the difference between looking at a picture book in order to learn the names of birds and looking at it because there is comfort in hearing a story about finding a home—e.g., in sharing a duck family's experience of finding a place to nest. Hickman (1981) tells about the boy who complained that his teacher had brought him only "story books about dinosaurs," whereas he really wanted to *know* about them.

Obviously, what is at stake is each child's total school experience —in speech, reading, and writing—with what is termed "literature," or "the aesthetic." No one episode, whether in kindergarten or in high school, will be decisive. But it will either reinforce or weaken the student's sense of the diverse possibilities of texts—and of the world. We need to look at the whole sweep of our language arts curricula, at our use of texts across the curriculum, and especially at our methods of evaluation. We need to make sure that students are cumulatively developing, in their transactions with texts, the ability to adopt the stance on the continuum appropriate to their particular personal purposes and to the situation— in short, the ability to read both efferently and aesthetically.

STRATEGY: HELPING CHILDREN UNDERSTAND NONFICTION

Editors' Note: Nonfiction can be a challenge for some children. Hess provides three strategies she uses when her children read nonfiction literature.

Establishing a Purpose for the Reading

Competent readers develop purposes before reading that help them process information in the text. Purpose setting also helps readers discern relevant from irrelevant information during reading.

Classifying Information in the Text

Classifying plays an important role in increasing students' ability to process nonfiction. . . . As students sorted their questions into groups, they generated their own text headings. . . . The students used their categories constantly during their search for answers to their questions. . . . After the students finished reading and note making, they worked individually or in pairs, cutting out and sorting their facts. (pp. 229–230)

Responding through Talk

Talk played a crucial role in developing the students' understanding of expository text. . . . Consequently, I organized the students into pairs. Each pair researched a common animal and submitted a single set of facts. (p. 231)

Source: Hess, M. L. (1991). Understanding nonfiction: Purpose, classification, response. *Language Arts, 68*(3), 228–232.

REFLECTION: DIFFERENCES IN THE GLOBAL ELEMENTS OF STORYBOOK AND INFORMATION BOOK GENRES

Editors' Note: In the table below, Pappas represents one rendering of the distinctions between storybooks and informational texts. Other schemes are possible; however, understanding the basic features of texts can assist in thinking about how to talk about them when working with children.

Storybook Genre		Information Book Genre	
Description of Global Elements	Examples from *The Owl and the Woodpecker* (Wildsmith, 1971)	Description of Global Elements	Examples from *Squirrels* (Wildsmith, 1974)
Placement—an author may introduce or "place characters" on "stage" in the story, provide time or locale information, relate what characters habitually do, or talk about certain attributes of characters, and so on. (optional)	"Once upon a time" information, as well as something about the locale—"in a forest, far away"—and about the habitual behavior of the woodpecker character—"lived in a tree in which he slept all night and worked all day"—are included.	*Topic Presentation*—the topic of the text is presented or introduced.	The topic, squirrels, is presented.
		Description of Attributes—a description of the attributes of the class or topic the book is about.	That squirrels are furry, have long bushy tails, strong back legs, two big front teeth, and so on, are described.
Initiating Event—conflict or problem of the story emerges.	The owl, who has the sleeping and working habits that are the opposite of those of the woodpecker, moves into a nearby tree. The woodpecker's daily tapping keeps the owl awake, and he becomes so bad-tempered that something has to be done.	*Characteristic Events*—characteristic or habitual or typical process/events are expressed.	How squirrels live and build homes, use their tails, have babies, what they eat, and so on, are explained.
		Category Comparison—compares or discusses different members of the class or topic that a book is about. (common, but optional)	Not realized in this book. See *The Squirrel* by Lane (1981) for a book on squirrels in which it is realized—where red and gray squirrels are compared.

Sequent Event—a recount of characters' attempts to resolve the problem or conflict.	Other animals in the forest have a meeting and decide that the owl has to leave, since the woodpecker was there first. They try one night, while the owl is out hunting, to push down his tree, but have no success.	*Final Summary*—summary statements are made about the information covered in a book.	Summarizes that if you walk in the woods, you might see squirrels jumping and frolicking on trees or hiding a store of nuts.
Final Event—resolution of the problem/conflict.	The tree is blown down by a terrible storm. However, fortunately, the owl, who had been sound asleep and was not aware that he was in danger, is saved by the woodpecker's tapping before the tree crashes to the ground.	*Afterword*—extra information about the topic is included. (optional)	Not realized in this book. See *Tunnels* by Gibbons (1984) for an example of this element—where extra specific details about tunnels are provided.
Finale—a restoration of the habitual or normal state of affairs. (optional)	The woodpecker helps the owl find a new home/tree in another part of the forest so that the owl is not disturbed by the woodpecker's tapping, and the owl and woodpecker remain "good friends all the rest of their lives."		
Moral—a moral statement or claim is made. (optional)	Not realized in this book. Can you think of a story in which it is included?		

Source: Pappas, C. C. (1991). Fostering full access to literacy by including information books. *Language Arts, 68*(6), 449–462. (This table combines two tables presented on pages 453–454 of Pappas's article.)

REFLECTION: REMEMBERING THE PICTURES IN PICTURE BOOKS

Editors' Note: Picture books offer the opportunity to explore how the visual artistic representation medium works on its own and in conjunction with text. Kiefer observed book discussions involving children of varied ages and reported that though the type of analysis children offer for illustrations may differ, children notice and think about the illustrations in books read to or by them. Such observations can provide an additional resource in exploring the meaning of books with children.

Aspects of style such as formal elements, techniques, content, and pictorial conventions represent a field of choices the artist has available to accomplish the primary purpose of making known, just as an author makes choices concerning setting, characterization, plot, theme, and language in order to convey an overall meaning. . . . Style alone is not responsible for conveying this meaning—symbols can convey meaning regardless of the style they are presented in. . . . Not only must choices be made regarding elements of design (line, shape, color, texture, and value) and principles of composition (balance, unity, variety, and rhythm) on single and succeeding pages, but illustrators can also make technical choices regarding original media, typeface, and arrangement of printed text, paper stock, cover and end pages, spatial orientation or viewpoint, and pictorial content. In addition, historical and cultural conventions of depicting represent additional choices available to the illustrator. Finally, these syntactic or literal properties may also be considered for their semantic or expressive qualities. (pp. 262–263)

Even the youngest children . . . named the elements of design using terms like "color," "line," and "shape," as they talked about the illustrations in books. When they did not actually name elements, they were aware of them, pointing to different shapes in an animal or talking about "light" pictures. . . . Five- to seven-year-olds also noticed technical choices such as layout and original media, pointing out small decorative elements facing a larger illustration, and speculating about the artist's use of paint, crayon, or pencil. . . .

▶

Younger children . . . seemed to be unsure of the artist's role as choice maker in expressing meaning. . . . The evaluative comments of these younger children were clearly linked to their own subjective responses to the book rather than objective comments about an artist's ability to express meaning. . . .

On the other hand, nine- and ten-year-olds in a third/fourth combination classroom objectively considered a fuller range of the elements and principles of design as well as technical aspects of book production. They also talked and wrote about the artist's choices of such aspects as these choices affected their own feelings about the book. (pp. 264–265)

Source: Kiefer, B. (1988). Picture books as contexts for literary, aesthetic, and real-world understandings. *Language Arts, 65*(3), 260–271.

STRATEGY: LITERATURE TALK WITH SECOND LANGUAGE LEARNERS

Editors' Note: Involving second language learners in response to literature activities can be challenging. Ferguson and Young describe two strategies used successfully by one classroom teacher.

Patterned Conversations

Maria [the teacher in this article] often selects predictable literature for her emergent readers. These repetitive stories often involve students in rich dialogues that follow patterns they can anticipate. . . .

In order to internalize the sentence structure of dialogue, students must first hear, read, and reread the story. Soon the text becomes familiar; and students "chime in" with the reading, evidencing that they are ready to dialogue using the language of the predictable text.

Teachers can facilitate the first move to dialogue by highlighting the conversation in the text. This can be accomplished by placing different colors of removable highlighting tape over the text of two or three characters' dialogue. . . .

Maria supplies props so students may dialogue as their character and lose their inhibitions in the process. . . . Then stories are read or shared by the characters using appropriate voices. (pp. 598–599)

Dialogue Improvisation

In this process, students collaborate with the teacher to create new dialogue for characters in a familiar story or to add dialogue for new characters. Having heard, read, and reread the story, students are familiar with the pattern the responses have taken and are given a boost as to how to respond. Having props available assists schematic understanding and provides an abundance of support for language. Students also draw on prior knowledge and language based on their experiences. . . .

Improvisation is a natural instructional technique to use with quality literature which has dialogue and interaction between characters. Improvisation also allows students to add new characters to the storyline. . . .

As with patterned dialogue, it is essential that the story and its language become familiar to the students by hearing, reading, and rereading the selection. The teacher plays an important part in the improvisation by providing props, prompting the improvisation, setting the stage, and demanding interaction that stimulates further language. (pp. 599–600)

Source: Ferguson, P. M., & Young, T. A. (1996). Literature talk: Dialogue improvisation and patterned conversations with second language learners. *Language Arts, 73*(8), 597–600.

12 Discussing Our Questions and Questioning Our Discussions: Growing into Literature Study

Carol Gilles with Jean Dickinson, Cheryl McBride, and Marc VanDover

Editors' Text: Literature discussion groups can involve students and teachers in a much deeper interpretive experience with texts than lists of comprehension questions can. Gilles and her colleagues present the stories of three different teachers' experiences in implementing discussion groups. Each of the teachers reflects on his or her experiences and provides suggestions that may be of assistance to others in implementing literature discussion groups in the classroom.

Many teachers have heard or read the exciting anecdotes that result from using literature discussion groups (also called literature circles or literature study) in classrooms. In these articles children are portrayed as reading, talking, and thinking about literature in sophisticated ways (Nelms, 1988, Peterson & Eeds, 1990; Pierce & Gilles, 1993; Short & Pierce, 1990; Urzúa, 1992). Yet, when these same teachers begin literature study in their own classrooms, the discussions are not always as highly developed as the "conversations" they read about. What are teachers to do when their classroom expectations aren't met?

Some teachers abandon literature study, claiming that they weren't sure it would work anyway. Others become even more directive, sure that their children aren't yet "ready" for student-led discussions about literature. A few teachers heed the challenge of Ken Goodman (1991), who asked, "If you try subtraction on Monday and it doesn't work, do you stop teaching subtraction?" If we value a proce-

---

This essay appeared in *Language Arts* 71.7 (1994) on pages 499–508.

dure, of course we keep working with it: Such teachers consider the difficulty in discussion an anomaly and use it as a point of departure for professional inquiry into their teaching procedures. They ask, What is going on here? and try to use information from their observations, the students, their colleagues, and the professional literature to help them gather and evaluate evidence in order to decide how to change the situation.

This article first describes literature discussion groups and the role of talk in them. It then examines the stories of three teachers who ran into roadblocks in literature discussion groups and turned their roadblocks into questions and inquiries. Finally, the article discusses the important insights they discovered about talk, literacy, students, and themselves as they inquired.

Literature Discussion Groups

In literature discussion groups (originated by Ralph Peterson, Mary Ann Eeds, and Karen Smith, and modified by Dorothy Watson and others), students and teachers have opportunities to use all aspects of language (reading, writing, speaking, and listening) in natural, generative ways. The strategy involves both the extensive reading of literature and intensive or close reading that leads to writing and peer discussion. Unlike basal reading groups, literature study groups are not formed to drill isolated skills. Instead, the groups are formed to explore and understand the texts and the potentials within the texts.

With literature discussion groups, talk is the keystone participants use for understanding the text and creating deeper meanings. This is not recitation-type talk in which the teacher asks a question, the student answers, and the teacher evaluates (Mehan, 1979). Instead, by talking to one another about the literature, participants verify their personal meanings and listen to others' interpretations. Barnes (1992) has called the tentative, hypothetical talk that invites modification and surmise *exploratory talk*. As students use exploratory talk to discuss complex ideas and relationships in books, they can give these relationships form and substance through interaction with another person whose interpretation might be different. Together, a group creates new meanings—meanings that no one in the group could have created alone.

In literature discussion the teacher's role moves smoothly between that of facilitator and guide (Freedman, 1993). At times the teacher is a facilitating participant, a group member who helps all students contribute. Teachers may help students be more explicit by asking, "Why do you think that?" They may slow down the conversation by saying, "I want to hear what John said again," or use their own participation as a kind of demonstration to others of what it means to be a group member. However, at other times the group needs more than a teacher-participant. As Karen Smith (1993) recalls about meeting with her students, "I wanted to have a least one group member (me) who could seize those opportunities when students began moving toward more literary ways of responding, and who could then illuminate and share their significance" (p. 9).

Thoughtful and powerful meanings are not generated and perfected in one 20-minute literature discussion. Students often ponder some of a book's issues anywhere they have a moment to think—in group discussions, on the walk home, or even at the mall. If students have not worked through the meanings for themselves, they will often bring up the topic again. If a topic such as character development has been useful in a discussion, students may use it again later as a lens to examine another book. As the group revisits topics, and books are compared and contrasted, students continue their "working on understanding" (Barnes, 1992).

These kinds of powerful "grand conversations" do not occur without hard work and change for most teachers. So, it is not unusual that many teachers find their initial attempts at literature study not eliciting what they imagined. Even teachers who have used literature with study extensively are sometimes disappointed with the discussion. The following are the stories of three teachers: Cheryl, Marc, and Jean. The stories describe their difficulties, the questions that guided their inquiries, and the new insights that emerged from their efforts.

Cheryl: How Can I Move beyond Basalizing Literature in First Grade?

Cheryl McBride has taught first graders for 15 years. Her small-town classroom is a lively place that invites children to become writers and readers. By the end of first grade, her students independently choose books to read during free time and at recreational reading times. For the last two years she has used literature study and supplemented it with basal instruction (to fulfill district guidelines).

Cheryl found that she felt pressured to teach isolated skills because her students still took the reading series tests. Yet, she wanted her students to use one another to enter into the stories and create meaning. She decided that she must first change her focus and examine her part in literature discussion. Cheryl began her inquiry in April by tape-recording the discussion that resulted from a whole-class reading of *One Hungry Monster* (O'Keefe, 1989). The class of 23 children spent a week on the book, first discussing the cover and predicting what would happen, then listening to the book read aloud, and finally returning to the book to discuss their predictions. When Cheryl listened to the tape-recorded final discussion for *One Hungry Monster*, she was surprised to find talk such as this:

> *Teacher:* What story are we reading for literature study?
>
> *All: The Hungry Monster!*
>
> *Teacher:* What else could we change the title to?
>
> *All: Ten Hungry Monsters* because they are counting to 10.
>
> *Teacher:* Who is the storyteller?
>
> *KG:* The little boy.
>
> *Others:* Monsters . . . Mom and Dad . . . brothers?
>
> *Teacher:* Could you be in this story?
>
> *All:* Yes!
>
> *Teacher:* The story starts out, "One hungry Monster underneath my bed. . . ." Let me ask again, who is the storyteller?
>
> *All:* The little boy!
>
> *Teacher:* It does not specifically say the little boy is the story-teller. But that is how you figure it out.

Listening to this tape and transcribing it, Cheryl was surprised to discover that only 17 of the 23 children answered her questions. Most of the children's answers were short and directly connected to each question. She was also surprised that one student, KG, had answered five questions, while six students had answered none. Most of all, she was surprised to see how similar her literature study was to basal instruction: She controlled the conversation, she asked the questions (nearly all literal ones), the students raised their hands to answer, and all answers were directly related to her questions. Cheryl realized that if all 23 children had responded with equal amounts of time, each child would have had only one minute! Most importantly, she observed:

> I was a slave to my structure and so were the kids. It allowed no dialogue or peer interaction. . . . My knowledge-centered questioning emphasized mechanical aspects of reading rather than the making of meaning. . . . And they hadn't visited the imaginary world of hungry monsters. Why? I had talked too much.

Cheryl decided it was time for her to make some changes. To help herself with her inquiry, she went to the literature. She read Veatch's (1978) *Reading in the Elementary School* to help her understand how to ask more open-ended questions. She also reread Peterson and Eeds's *Grand Conversations* (1990) and talked to fellow teachers. After watching a video of Karen Smith's classroom with members of a university class, she realized that the size of her group was far too large for discussion. Instead of working with all 23 children at once, she decided to reduce the group size to five to eight members and work with each of the groups for about 20 minutes apiece three times per week.

She was delighted with the results of her changes. "They talked a lot! They had fun and said that they enjoyed the time together." However, as Cheryl analyzed the discussion transcripts, she saw another pattern. She found that in her effort to ask more open-ended questions to promote higher-level thinking, she neglected the feeling, or *aesthetic*, side of the story. She was concentrating so hard on what questions she might ask next that she lost track of the flow of the conversation and didn't help group members use one another to discuss. She hadn't asked the students to clarify or explain their comments to her or one another. She found that she controlled the discussion by responding after each person's turn (about 45 percent of the time). As she recalled, "There I was at center stage, and looking at it in print was not a pretty sight!" Cheryl's inquiry was still in progress.

The next step that Cheryl took in her inquiry was to read some information about exploratory talk in her university course. Barnes (1992) has described this kind of talk as hypothetical, tentative talk that invites modification. Cheryl looked again at her transcripts and realized that if she asked all the questions, her students couldn't explore the text themselves. Cheryl had tried using a phrase, "Let's think about that," to slow down the talk and help her students revisit a topic for a longer time, but she was still not allowing enough "thinking time." As she stated, "I ultimately found I needed not only to restructure my questions but also to restructure the type of talk in my classroom. I needed to have more exploratory talk within a small-group setting and time for rethinking and moving beyond the text."

If we want students to reflect on certain topics, we must give them time to think, and that means that we can't fill up the verbal void with a new topic. Eventually Cheryl found that if she wanted her students to be listeners, then she must become a listener herself. By that phase of her inquiry, students were nearing summer vacation. Cheryl's investigation had had many twists and turns and still didn't seem to be complete. She decided that she would continue to try to improve her literature discussion groups in the fall and would implement these ideas:

1. Make sure the topics, questions, and concerns are ones in which students have interest.

2. Make sure children have opportunities to develop trust among group members so that exploratory talk and the cycles of meaning can emerge.

3. Make sure the students know they have succeeded; no checklist does that.

4. Know when to listen and when to ask questions. I must realize I have a very fluid role moving among participant, guide, and learner. I must share my whole self with the group. I now feel on a new frontier, exploring the potential of my students. I can't push them. I can't pull them over the finish line, but I can guide them by seizing teachable moments. (McBride, 1992)

What Can We Learn through Cheryl's Inquiry?

Cheryl's problem was complex and multifaceted. She found she had to consult the literature and her peers, try different experiences with her students, and then reflect on those experiences to make real changes. For Cheryl, taping the literature discussion groups and then transcribing those tapes proved very telling; she began to see a side of her own instruction that made her uncomfortable. Although in theory Cheryl believed that children could bring insights to the group and create new insights within the group, in practice she was constricting their thinking with her questions. There was no chance for them to raise real questions about their reading because she raised each new topic.

When Cheryl changed to smaller groups and more refined questions, the discussion looked much better on the surface. Her students all talked more, and many asked if they could have similar groups again. Many teachers would be satisfied and stop there, but because Cheryl was an inquirer, she went back to transcribe these "improved discussions" and examine them carefully. As she worked through the surface meanings of which students talked and what kind of questions they asked, she began to gain deeper insights: In her efforts to help children think critically, she had neglected their feelings about the book, and she was still controlling them—only in a different way. Now she was prodding them to be evaluative and analytical, but still nearly all topics came from her. Again, she returned to the professional books, her university class, and her peers to explore her new questions. Cheryl found that she would continue reflecting on her practice and refining literature study into the next school year. She has become comfortable with the fact that many questions don't have just one answer and can't be fully investigated in only one year. As we discover new solutions, we are intrigued with more complex problems, and our cycle of professional growth continues (Dix, 1993).

Marc: How Do I Help a Nonparticipating Student?

Jeff was a small, quiet seventh-grade student labeled learning disabled. Unlike most of the learning-disabled students, who are quiet in regular classes but talk in an LD setting, Jeff rarely participated in the literature discussions in his LD reading class. He seemed to read during reading time. However, during group meetings Jeff often kept quiet, paging through the book as other members spoke. He didn't ignore the discussion around him, but he never added anything to it. If he was called upon by either the teacher or another student, he refused to participate, often making excuses for his nonparticipation.

At first, Marc VanDover, Jeff's learning disabilities teacher, thought that perhaps Jeff was not comfortable with the group. He noted this as a difficulty but took a "wait and see" attitude, hoping that as Jeff became more comfortable with the members of the group and the purpose of the discussion, he would open up and begin to talk. As November neared, with little having changed, Marc began to wonder if Jeff was having difficulty with the reading. He decided to do a modified miscue procedure (Goodman, Watson, & Burke, 1987) with many of his students, including Jeff.

The modified miscue analysis profile indicated that, although Jeff made few miscues that distorted the meaning, his retelling was scanty and unspecific. He was concentrating on "sounding good" but wasn't focusing on the meaning of the story. This could have been one of the reasons that Jeff was insecure in discussion groups. If Jeff had been creating a very general meaning as he read, then hearing the discussion would have been quite helpful to him; however, he would have been able to add little to it. Marc felt that perhaps he now understood Jeff better as a reader, and he wasn't as worried that Jeff was a silent group member.

Instead, he expected and encouraged some retelling at the beginning of the groups in which Jeff was a member. Often when students are not exactly sure of the meanings that they have created, they can use the beginning of a group to retell the story collaboratively. Hurst (1988) calls this procedure "collaborative storying" and defines it as "collaboratively picking up the thread of the narrative from one to the other in a series of short, often unfinished exchanges" (p. 182). In literature study groups we find students who seem to need to retell the story first before moving into a more careful analysis of it. In this way they reexperience a portion of the text and verify the meanings that they have constructed. This kind of talk is marked by hesitations and by each member's contribution to a portion of the narrative. This process allowed Jeff to listen to those details that he might have missed in his silent reading. Occasionally the students or Marc might ask, "Where was that part?"—a question that demonstrated to Jeff that the details were in the book.

Besides expecting some collaborative storying in the groups, Marc also talked to Jeff about how to gain more meaning from the text. Sometimes he would ask Jeff to follow a certain character in the book, to see exactly what that character did. At other times he might talk to Jeff and the other students about his own process of reading, explaining what he does to help himself remember a character or a specific situation. He continued to expect Jeff to read the books and waited for Jeff to begin to talk more. Other students weren't as patient as Marc. One day, Dan, who was the volunteer leader of Jeff's group for the day, reminded Jeff:

> *Dan:* OK. Jeff, it's kind of your turn.
>
> *Jeff:* I'm done [with the book].
>
> *Dan:* I know, but you have to have a verbal turn. Did you have a journal writing for [Chapter] 13?
>
> *Jeff:* I have the book right here.
>
> *Dan:* That's not going to help. OK, Brian [go ahead] for Chapter 14. [Gilles, 1991]

Dan's tone was crisp and direct. One of the responsibilities of all group members was to complete a journal entry, an agenda, for each group meeting. That agenda helped members bring up those items that they especially wanted to discuss with others. Since Jeff wouldn't participate verbally and didn't even have a journal entry completed for the book, he was dismissed, at least by Dan. However, the influence of his peers did seem to convince Jeff to participate more, and during the next session he offered some inferences about the characters. The students accepted his insights in a nonthreatening, matter-of-fact way.

However, Jeff soon settled back into his old nonparticipatory ways—ignoring the speaker, not making eye contact, and refusing to talk. Students ignored his nonparticipation until the next book, *Snowbound* (Mazer, 1973), when Dan, once again, brought up Jeff's problem:

> *Dan:* Jeff has to say something in group.
>
> *Jeff:* I can't talk because I will spoil it for everyone else [because I'm so far ahead].
>
> *Teacher:* [To the group] What can we do?
>
> *Joshua:* Just restrict him. He never talks. Just string him up!
>
> *Tom:* [to Jeff] Why can't you talk? You have a mouth, haven't you?
>
> *Dan:* He's read the whole book, and he's not telling the whole thing because his memory is bad.
>
> *Jeff:* OK, I'm on the part [where] her dad lets the dog out, he stole his mom's car, and he's driving around town now. [Gilles, 1991]

The group continued to badger Jeff until the teacher intervened and asked the group to give written suggestions about discussions. Their suggestions led to a group discussion about these issues:

> *Talking:* The group concluded that each person needs to feel free to state his/her opinions and not feel afraid that others will respond negatively.
>
> *Ownership:* The group agreed that this was THEIR group. They decided how far to read, when to do the agenda journals, and how everyone needed to be responsible for his/her part in the group.
>
> *Functions of a Group Leader:* The group decided that group leaders were responsible for making sure that everyone had a turn to speak, that everyone could share, and that the group stayed on the subject.

The next day, a reading day, Marc asked Jeff to write in his journal instead of reading. He said, "Look, you are so far ahead that you need to write instead of reading. Every two chapters, I need an agenda from you. That will help you at group time have something to share." Jeff did write his agenda and even volunteered at the beginning of the group:

> *Jeff:* Yeah, we've talked about Chapters 1, 2, and 3. Yeah, [in Chapter 4] they were out in a field and crashed and everything. Reminds me of Christmas time, and I was driving to my grandma's house, and I hit a slick spot, and we ran into a ditch. We jumped the ditch, and it messed up our car.

Teacher: Were you driving?

Jeff: NO!

Chris: Who was driving?

Jeff: My dad. Well, [we were on] kind of a country road. We were going around the curve . . . and it was ice, and just, we couldn't really turn. We were in a Jimmy-type thing, Blazer thing, and it had a roof that came down to a lower one. I got a flat spot right here, 'cause we didn't have seat belts on 'cause we were sitting in the back. [He described everyone's injuries.] After we got off that, we got right over by Rock Bridge Elementary, and our tires blew.

Teacher: Same day?

Jeff: Yeah! And we went all over the road.

Robert: I don't want to ride with you!

Teacher: You've gotta have some shared experience with the character in the book!

Chris: That's right!

Jeff's connection between the winter accident in the book and the time his dad drove off the road in a snowstorm was well received by the other students and the teacher.

Later during the hour, Dan asked Robert if he had anything to add. Robert replied, "I'm on strike," to which Jeff retorted, "Come on, Robert, you gotta talk. I had to talk." After this incident Jeff did continue to be a contributing member of the group. He wasn't the most vocal, but he did add to the discussion, and he was valued by his peers.

What Can We Learn from Marc's Inquiry?

Marc's inquiry, unlike Cheryl's, focused more on one student than on the whole group. Marc's observation of and reflection on Jeff's behavior first caused him to believe that Jeff, like many students, needed time to feel comfortable in a group. Peterson (1992) reminds us that children do not automatically work well in a group situation. Before they will begin to share honestly, students must feel that they can trust the members of the group and that they are valued. As Marc continued to observe and reflect on Jeff, he wondered about Jeff's reading comprehension. Jeff's lack of talk could signal a lack of understanding. The miscue profile did help explain part of Jeff's lack of participation in the discussion, and Marc, for the moment, was satisfied. However, even when Jeff began reading more proficiently, he was still quiet in the group; the silent role he had adopted was hard to change. Jeff's group members became irritated by his silence, and eventually Marc, with the help of his class, convinced Jeff that his comments were needed. It isn't surprising that it took some peer group pressure finally to convince Jeff that his comments were necessary, and to ease him out of his nonparticipatory role.

Marc's inquiry, like Cheryl's, was not easily and quickly solved. Instead, like most classroom challenges, it was complex and multifaceted. Even when Jeff's reading comprehension became stronger, his pattern of silence remained a habit for him and for other members, and it was hard to change. Only when his peers became annoyed and his teacher nudged a bit was Jeff motivated to change his role in the group.

Jean: How Do I Prepare My Intermediate-Grade Students to Discuss Honestly and Thoughtfully?

Whereas Cheryl looked at her own practices and Marc investigated a particular student, Jean's investigation was a curricular inquiry. When Jean read her first article about literature study, she was sold. She felt her basal was not helping her students become lifelong readers, and she was ready to try new ideas. Jean had also been teaching long enough to know that practices recorded by one teacher in a journal article might not "fit" her students. About the same time, Jean became a member of a teacher study group of eight teachers at various grade levels from kindergarten through college. The group met once a month on Saturday mornings to celebrate their successes, analyze their classroom challenges, and discuss the professional books they had been reading. For Jean, one important aspect of the group was the questions that group members asked one another. In the group there was support and encouragement, but there also was a group curiosity about practices and strategies that various members had tried. As the group studied *From Communication to Curriculum* (Barnes, 1992), Jean connected the concepts to her students engaged in literature study. She decided that in order to be engaged in literature groups, students must think of themselves as capable and literate human beings. She developed that insight into an inquiry question: How do I help students think of themselves as literate community members? She decided to design opportunities to help her students see themselves as literate members of the classroom community.

Jean's first step was to "take stock" of what she already did to help students feel that they were part of a literate community. Jean set the tone in the classroom by offering students opportunities to choose a book, settle in, and just read. On the first day of class the students found piles and piles of paperback books around the room. Jean first invited students to browse and find some possible books that they might enjoy and then to settle into them. She often related to the children information from Karen Smith about "entertaining" a book (Short & Pierce, 1990). Smith suggests that there is a relationship between having a guest in one's home and reading a book. We give attention and care to our guests. Smith stresses that students need to give that same care and attention to the books they choose, to meet and greet the characters and pay attention to them. This helps the students enter into the book and live through it as they read. In Jean's classroom, students had quality time to entertain books before they ever began talking about them.

In order to take a closer look at the actual literature discussion, Jean taped her students' discussions. While listening to the tapes, certain patterns emerged for her. For example, she found that the discussions seemed smoother when there was a volunteer leader. Instead of acting solely on taped information, Jean went to the students to confirm her interpretation. When she asked her students about having a group leader, she found they did prefer one. As they talked, students also said that they considered sitting at a table more appropriate to literature discussion than sitting on the floor. In fact, they decided a round table was best because then everyone felt equal. Jean found that the more they talked, the more valuable insights students shared that she had never considered.

As Jean remembered how invested her students were as they talked about their likes and dislikes in the group, she decided that the best way to help them think of themselves as capable group-discussion members was to invite them into her inquiry (Dickinson, 1993). Through her professional study group, Jean had realized the power of her consciously considering talk; therefore, she also recognized the power of student's considering their own talk. She invited students to join in her inquiry and consider how talk worked in their lives. They constructed their own "talk journals" by using half sheets of blank paper on which they drew or wrote about talk in the classroom. This was a place where students reflected on how talk helped them learn, what their rules were within talk, and how the literature discussions were going. Some of the students reflected on literature study in their logs:

> *Lindsay:* I read better, when I talk inside my head about the
> book.

Briana: The best thing about lit groups is the fact that we use teamwork. Talking about the book makes the story more interesting.

Michael: We get more ideas about the book when we have someone to talk with.

These fourth graders understood the collaborative and generative nature of the literature groups, perhaps because they had been bringing talk in the classroom to a conscious level. They had asked themselves how and why they used talk and what their roles were in classroom talk. As they examined their own talk in all facets of the classroom, they discovered that talk wasn't limited to literature discussion groups but was at work in all cross-curricular endeavors. Talk helped them conduct their science experiments, understand the ways of the pioneers, and even resolve their misunderstandings with other students. Because of their emphasis on talk during the year, these children experienced education as a form of communication (Barnes, 1992, p. 14).

After the first year of her inquiry, Jean moved from a self-contained fourth-grade classroom in Missouri to a fifth-/sixth-grade combination class in a year-round school in Colorado. This was a different part of the country, a different school organization, and older learners. How would anything she had learned the year before be pertinent here? Jean decided that the question she had investigated in Missouri was quite pertinent in Colorado: How could she help these learners begin to feel part of a literate community? Because she had relied on the support that her colleagues both in the study group and at her old school had given her, Jean sought out collegial support in her new school. Collaboration with two faculty members, Leslie Leyden, her Building Resource Teacher, and Randi Allison, the Instructional Assistant, helped Jean continue to pursue her inquiry. These two faculty members knew the students and were willing to ask the "hard questions." Furthermore, they were willing to work with Jean in her classroom.

Jean also decided to do some "kidwatching," or informed observation (Goodman, 1978), to see what aspects of her curriculum seemed to be important in building a community. In order to reflect on daily occurrences, she decided to record "interesting" school events each day after school on her home computer. She began to notice that nearly every classroom event she deemed "interesting" in her fifth/sixth combination class was based on a picturebook that she had read aloud to her class. She listened and watched carefully as the students transacted with the picturebooks, noticed the kinds of books that she chose to read aloud, and even made herself a set of criteria for selecting books:

1. I have to like the book very much to choose it for my students.
2. The book must have compelling stories and illustrations.
3. I need to choose books from authors I trust.
4. If the book fits into science or social studies, all the better!

Jean shared her criteria with her students and encouraged them to draw up their own criteria for how they choose especially good books.

Jean found that as the children listened to the reading of a picturebook, they responded freely to both the text and the illustrations. They became totally involved in the story and were able to enter into it. Because most picturebooks are relatively quick to read, students listened and discussed in one sitting. Students compared an author's style or the illustrations from one book to another and talked about the merit of various characters. As the students and teacher talked about a picturebook, they began to use literary language and build a repertoire of concepts that would be useful in later literature discussions. After analyzing her notes, talking to her colleagues, asking the students, and doing some reading, Jean was certain that reading picturebooks to her students was an extremely powerful way to build a community of learners and give opportunities for students to discuss books. Using picturebooks, bringing talk to a conscious level, and setting up a literate environment were all ways that Jean found in her two-year inquiry to help her students discuss thoughtfully and honestly.

What Can We Learn from Jean's Inquiry?

The greatest lesson that we can learn from Jean's two-year, ongoing inquiry is that many inquiries never end. Just when we feel we've finally found the solution, new or refocused questions emerge; or we change grade levels, schools, or towns. Jean has learned useful ways to help her reflect on her practice: reading professional literature, conferring with colleagues, taping classroom discussions and analyzing them, and consulting her students. Jean started by reading professional books and articles and discussing those articles with colleagues that she met in university classes. When Jean joined the teacher study group, she entered a larger professional collaboration with other teachers. Eventually, she moved from looking for answers "out there" (in the professional literature, from experts, and so on) to looking in her classroom and with her students for her answers. She used her own talk journal and those of her students as data to explore and then brought the very questions that puzzled her back to the students.

Jean has developed a cycle of seeking out a new problem, thinking about it, seeking help if needed, trying a new technique, reflecting on the problem, asking the students to consider it, and then seeing how it fits into the *big picture*. For Jean and her students, the big picture begins with their appreciation of books and ease in talking about them and ends in their becoming lifelong readers and learners.

What Can We Learn by Examining the Three Teachers' Stories?

In all three stories teachers didn't abandon literature discussion groups when they were faced with problems, nor did they retreat to a more directive skill-and-drill posture. Instead, they viewed the problems as points of departure for professional inquiries (Watson, Burke, & Harste, 1989). Curricular difficulties are not simple, one-dimensional, or static problems, and that is precisely what makes them so challenging. They often involve a constellation of factors for both teachers and children. There is not one "right answer" to the question of how to encourage thoughtful group talk or how to bring reticent children into the groups. Cheryl found that she needed to examine her own talk to pursue her inquiry, but Marc found he needed to use the procedures he knew about miscue analysis to help him better understand Jeff's nonparticipatory behavior. Jean found that she needed to consult her students to answer her questions and, upon hearing their ideas, invited the students to begin their own personal inquiries into their classroom talk.

All three teachers were resourceful—they moved beyond themselves to the professional literature, university classes, their students, and their colleagues for help in exploring their questions. Teacher study groups, like the one Jean joined, provide the same kind of support for teachers that literature discussion groups provide for students—a safe but intellectually challenging harbor for inquiring and creating meanings.

The British National Oracy Project grew out of such beliefs. Volunteer teachers of all subjects from preschool through high school were encouraged to inquire about talk throughout their curricula. As they met in small study groups throughout England and Wales, they shared their classroom stories and, through their stories, gained insights into their students and the role of talk across the curriculum. Their stories are recorded in issues of *Talk: A Journal of the National Oracy Project* and in *Thinking Voices* (Norman, 1992), a volume that explains the processes these teachers used and the discoveries they made.

The work of the National Oracy Project and the stories of Cheryl, Marc, and Jean remind us that questions teachers ask demand thoughtful, systematic, and planned inquiry. Through informed observation, study, and reflection, new insights do emerge. Often these new insights cause teachers to ask more complex questions about the same topics and then search for more complex answers. Inherent in this cycle of inquiry is the element of ambiguity. We don't know for certain if we will completely answer our questions, if our inquiries will improve children's experiences with literature, or if we are even asking important questions. For some teachers, this kind of ambiguity is unsettling and stressful. Such teachers view the world as a predictable place where following their assigned curricula will result in the kind of learning that is measured by multiple-choice tests.

But, as Adrian Peetom reminds us, "Ambiguity is the aura that surrounds all complex questions" (1993). And teaching is, at its heart, a complex task full of complex questions. If we believe the best teachers are learners above all else, then ambiguity and inquiry go hand in hand. As we peel away the layers of the questions that involve the intellectual, social, physical, and spiritual aspects of literature study and children, we feel lost; we struggle to find alternate measures; and we wonder why in the world we attempted such an endeavor. At the same time, we glimpse a tough farm boy's misty eyes as he finishes *Where the Red Fern Grows* (Rawls, 1961); we marvel at the comparison the first graders are able to make between two Steven Kellogg books; and we get goose bumps when we overhear a formerly incorrigible fourth grader recommend a book to a friend on the way to recess. Questioning our literature study practices and inquiring about them isn't easy, but the rewards for children and their teachers are potentially too important not to try.

REFLECTION: READING AS A SOCIAL PROCESS

Editors' Note: Too often, reading is thought of only as a process that involves a text and a reader; however, reading theories are challenging this view. Imagine the many different examples that can be used to illustrate the points Bloome makes and consider how they make impossible the view that reading is a solitary event.

First, all reading events involve a social context. Social interaction surrounds and influences interaction with a written text. Second, reading is a cultural activity. That is, reading has social uses which are an extension of people's day-to-day cultural doings. And third, reading is a socio-cognitive process. Through learning to read and through reading itself, children learn culturally appropriate information, activities, values, and ways of thinking and problem solving. (p. 134)

Source: Bloome, D. (1985). Reading as a social process. *Language Arts*, 62(2), 134–142.

REFLECTION: KNOWING YOUR THEORETICAL PERSPECTIVE WHEN ORCHESTRATING LITERATURE DISCUSSION GROUPS

Editors' Note: When teachers lead discussion groups, they may be deliberately or unwittingly operating from a specific theoretical perspective. McGee and Tompkins illustrate through four teachers some of the perspectives that may be taken. Each perspective has its own strengths and limitations, and a teacher's choice may be bound up in thinking about how to extend the strengths of the students in her or his classroom.

Reading as an Interactive, Strategic Process

Norma pays particular attention to the students and their needs before making decisions about instruction. . . . Norma feels that reading is the best way to build a rich understanding of words and an appreciation for the care authors take in selecting words. . . . Norma attends to the word identification strategies. (pp. 406–407)

Reading as Knowledge of Literary Forms

Maria values being able to analyze literature and wants her students to capitalize on their intuitive abilities to recognize literary conventions. . . . Maria stresses the importance of literary language. (p. 408)

▶

Reading as Personal Response

Erica bases her instructional decisions on her experiences as a reflective reader and on her understanding of the reading processes that she uses. . . . Erica believes that the best instruction consists of demonstrations of actual responses, and she bases most of her mini-lessons and response activities on her own responses. . . . Erica notices and values the variety and differences in her students' responses to literature. She plans instructional activities that celebrate and build on these responses. . . . Erica also focuses on the language of a text and how that language affects readers. (p. 410)

Reading as Critical Literacy

Paul was concerned about "the stereotypical way in which the . . . character seemed to be portrayed . . .[and thinks] it is vital that all students read many books that help them see the world through different eyes." (p. 411)

Source: McGee, L. M., & Tompkins, G. E. (1995). Literature-based reading instruction: What's guiding the instruction? *Language Arts*, 72(6), 405–414.

STRATEGY: LITERATURE LOGS

Editors' Note: Response to literature may take a variety of forms: dramatic reenactment, literature discussion groups, or written response. One form of written response is the literature log. McGee provides a description of one variation of the literature log as a form of response to literature.

———— ✍ ————

Literature logs or reading logs are journals in which children write open-ended or prompted responses to literature. . . . To prompt fourth graders' literature log entries, Kelly and Farnan (1991) developed 16 reader response questions. The following are examples:

"If you could be any character in the story, who would you be?"

"Do you like this story? Why or why not?"

"Do you share any of the feelings of the characters in the story? Explain."

▶

"What do you feel is the most important word, phrase, paragraph in this story? Explain why this is important."

"What was your first reaction to the story? Describe or explain it briefly."

"How does the story make you feel? Explain."

These prompts were designed to broaden the repertoire of response options available to young readers and emphasize readers' personal interpretations and interactions with text through association and evaluation.

Teachers used the questions to prompt writing once or twice weekly through the school year. At the end of the year teachers also asked students to respond to a non-reader-response prompt: "Tell me about your book." (p. 531)

Source: McGee, L. M. (1992). Focus on research: Exploring the literature-based reading revolution. *Language Arts, 69*(7), 529–537.

For an example of the use of literature logs in a first-grade classroom, see: Wollman-Bonilla, J., & Werchadlo, B. (1995). Literature response journals in a first-grade classroom. *Language Arts, 72*(8), 562–570.

REFLECTION: PHONOLOGICAL PROCESSES

Editors' Note: The role of sound-symbol relationships in reading continues to be debated. Onset-rime is one theory that is receiving attention despite mixed research findings.

According to onset-rime theory, the psychological units of a syllable are onsets and rimes. Onsets are any consonants that precede a vowel in a syllable, and rimes are the vowel and consonants that follow it. . . . [I]n the word *beak*, for example, /b/ is the onset and /ik/ is the rime. (p. 483)

Source: Moustafa, M. (1993). Recoding in whole language reading instruction. *Language Arts, 70*(6), 483–487.

13 Joyful Noises: Creating Poems for Voices and Ears

Laura Apol
Jodi Harris

Editors' Text: Many of us, perhaps most of us, do not have good memories of reading and writing poetry in school. This is unfortunate because poetry can be an engaging genre for school-age children. Apol and Harris share a rationale for teaching poetry, along with some illustrations of poetry coming alive in an elementary classroom.

Poet William Stafford was frequently asked when it was that he first realized he wanted to become a poet, and his response has become a touchstone in talking about children and poetry. Stafford answered:

> I've thought about that, and sort of reversed it. My question is, "When did other people give up the idea of being a poet?" You know, when we are kids we make up things, we write, and for me the puzzle is not that some people are still writing, the real question is why did other people stop? (Stafford, 1978, p. 86)

Another contemporary poet, Donald Hall (1982), also traces the origins of poetic thought (what he terms the "sensual pleasures" of poetry) back to our earliest days—"both personally (back to the crib) and historically (back to the fire in front of the cave)" (p. 149). Hall termed the primitive elements that make up the sensual pleasures of poetry *Goatfoot, Milktongue,* and *Twinbird.* According to Hall, *Goatfoot* is the pleasurable thrill of rhythm and motion in poetry; *Milktongue* is oral pleasure in the texture of poetic language and in the shape and taste of poetry itself; and *Twinbird* is our pleasure with form, balance, and opposition in poetry. Like Stafford, Hall claims that all three elements—muscle pleasure, mouth pleasure, and the pleasure of match-unmatch—occur early and quite naturally in our lives.

This essay appeared in *Language Arts* 76.4 (1999) on pages 314–322.

If these poets are right and the language we enter at birth is filled with poetic possibilities, then it would seem natural for children (and adults) not simply to be comfortable, but to be passionately enthusiastic about poetry—after all, entering the world of poetry should represent a linguistic homecoming of sorts. Unfortunately, those who work with students and teachers know that poetic passion—or even comfort—is the exception rather than the rule. When the topic of poetry comes up in classrooms, both teachers' and students' facial expressions, body language, and journal responses rarely reflect joy or pleasure; often, reactions range from mild discomfort to panic to outright aversion.

Many studies have explored various causes for dislike, disinterest, ignorance, neglect, or misuse of poetry in the classroom. Teachers, researchers, and poets claim that a negative reaction to (or lack of familiarity with) poetry occurs and is perpetuated across educational levels, from preschool to graduate school, and that the best way to replace negativity and unease with passion and pleasure is to provide students of all ages with positive, meaningful, and engaging poetic encounters (Denman, 1988; Heard, 1993; Hopkins, 1987; Koch, 1970; Livingston, 1990; Nye, 1994).

In our respective roles as classroom teacher (Jodi) and poet (Laura), we have been challenged by this negativity, and in our own work have looked for ways to rekindle in students a sense of poetic passion and pleasure. This paper recounts our efforts on one such project that took place in Jodi's fifth-grade classroom in suburban Detroit, where Laura was invited in as a visiting poet.

Poetry as Dialogue: Spoken and Heard

Because the pleasures of poetry come to us early on—long before we learn to write—it seems that an important link we have to Hall's (1982) *Goatfoot, Milktongue,* and *Twinbird is* that of the spoken (oral) and heard (aural) aspects of poetic language. Poetry begins with our voices— speaking the form, creating the rhythm, shaping and tasting the words. Yet, as we progress through school, our encounters with poems are more and more often through print—words on a page that we read or we write in silence.[1]

If the root of poetry (historically and developmentally) is first and foremost oral and aural, then how do we and our students regain access to poetry that will please our ears, that will rise and fall with our voices, that will engage our muscles, our lips and our tongues?

One possibility is suggested by contemporary poet Paul Fleischman, who, in 1988, titled his Newbery award–winning collection of poems *Joyful Noise: Poems for Two Voices*—a title that highlights the aural and oral aspects of the pieces and implies that within this collection the poems are to be spoken aloud and are to be heard.

Fleischman's dialogic form of poetry is more than simply an innovative device for arranging poems on the page. His poems for two voices are nearly impossible to read silently; the poems are planned for two voices (or two groups of voices), with a set of words written for one reader or group placed on the left side of the page, a set of words written for the other reader or group placed on the right. Lines are said in the order in which they are printed down the page, and lines that are to be said together are printed directly across from one another. Sometimes both voices read the same words at the same time, sometimes they read the same words at different times, sometimes they read different words at the same time. That is the genius of Fleischman's construction: readers and listeners are required to pay careful attention to words and meanings, sound and sense, as voices weave in, out, and through.

While Fleischman's poems are created specifically to be read in dialogue, there are innumerable other poems that can be adapted for choral readings as well—poems that can be arranged and performed successfully by students of all ages. And the benefits of asking students to arrange and perform poetry in this manner are many. For example, in planning and executing choral readings, students explore multiple ways to function in community—from choosing an appropriate text to planning ways to arrange various words, lines, and stanzas, whether they are reading as a whole group in unison, using solo voices and small groups, or starting with a single voice and adding additional voices with each line. Working with text in this way—arranging a weaving of individual voices—emphasizes the poetic elements (balance, rhythm, taste, and shape of words) as they are spoken and heard. At the same time, effective choral reading asks students to examine the poem's structure in order to match the performance to the content and form of the poem. In describing the merits of choral reading, Carol Fisher (1994) writes, "As the students practice reading the poem together and experiment with different ways to read it, they are exploring its meaning, the structure, and the way each of these aspects supports the other" (p. 63).

Choral Reading: One Class's Introduction

In order to explore what we believe are the significant benefits of using choral reading to expose students to the poetic possibilities of language, we—Jodi and Laura—together created a sequence of activities for fifth graders in Jodi's classroom that would identify those students' incoming understandings of poetry, introduce them (through reading and writing) to a wide range of poetic possibilities, and include time for reflection on their own and others' poetic processes. The sequence would culminate in a project in which they read and performed Fleischman's poems, then wrote and performed their own poems for two voices.

The project began with a poetry survey that Jodi gave to her students on the second day of school. In order to get a sense of their perceptions of poetry at the outset of the project, the survey asked students to finish open-ended statements like "Poetry is . . . ," "When I think of poetry, I think of . . . ," and "I think poetry should be about . . . ." In order to get a sense of their previous experiences with poetry, Jodi also asked students to complete the phrase "I have written poems about . . ." and to indicate whether or not they wrote poetry "on their own."

The survey responses indicated that most of the students had very basic (both limited and limiting) perceptions of poetry—a finding that surprised us, given that this was a school with a strong language arts program. At the start of our project, students' perceptions of poetry fell into a few main categories. Out of twenty-six responses, nearly half of the students mentioned form when they talked about poetry; most mentioned rhyme, claiming that poems are "words that rhyme put together" and "patterns and rhyming," or that poems have "short paragraphs with many words rhymed." Many of the responses mentioned a correspondence between poetry and feelings—"Poetry helps people express themselves and their personal feelings"—and many students saw the subjects of poems falling within a few general areas as well: the natural world, people and events, and funny stories (for example, "When I think of poetry I think of happy things and nature"; "Poetry should be written about an event in someone's life"; and "Poetry is a funny work of art"). A few students refused to be pinned down about the nature or subject of poetry, responding broadly that "Poetry can be anything to anyone," and "People are entitled to write about anything."

When asked about previous experiences with poetry, six students responded that they had *never* written a poem; eight cited poetry experiences that stemmed from previous school classes, including "form" poems and poems for various "school" occasions ("I've only written a few [poems] in Ms. K's class and I don't remember what they were about"; "I wrote a haiku on Snow"; and "I have written poetry about Columbus on Columbus Day.") Some students referred to various scenes from nature (the seasons, flowers, sunsets over water, and cold winter winds) as the subjects of their poems; others related that they wrote poetry in response to events in their lives ("I wrote a poem about my mom on her birthday but I can't remember how it went" and "I have written poems about my hamster, who passed away"). One student said he'd written poems about his "thoughts of life and death," and a few listed a range of topics so wide it could only be classified as "anything and everything." One student summarized his previous experience writing poetry in this way: "I have wrote one [poem] but forget what it was about."

In answer to the statement "I write poetry on my own. _____yes _____no," fourteen students responded "no," and twelve students responded "yes." We suspect, however, that the question may not have made clear what was meant by "on my own," since two of the students who checked "yes" had previously answered that they had never written a poem, and since many later admitted to Jodi that they'd answered "yes" because they thought it was "what [she/the teacher] wanted." In addition, it is possible from the wording of the question that students may have understood "I write poetry on my own" to stand in contrast to poems authored by an entire class or a group within the context of a class. In further conversation, Jodi said that she believed that at the start of the school year only two or three of her students actually did write poems outside of class.

Our early, informal findings confirmed for us Fisher's (1994) claims that elementary students' ideas about poetry are "very incomplete and rudimentary," that the majority of students are "unsophisticated about poetry," and that "their level of sophistication stems from their minimal exposure to poetry. Further, they have encountered poetry which is almost exclusively short, rhymed humorous verse" (Fisher, 1994, p. 55).

In order to scaffold an experience that would lead students beyond a superficial encounter to a deeper understanding and appreciation of poetry, Jodi spent the early weeks of the semester introducing her students to poems and poetry of various sorts before Laura joined the class. Jodi's work with poetry was embedded within her curriculum; students read a variety of poems by a variety of authors, and they wrote poetry on a regular basis, creating group poems, class poems, poems using magnetic words, word wheels, and color poems.

In the week immediately preceding Laura's visits, Jodi got her class acquainted with the idea of choral reading. She introduced the idea of a chorus of voices that make up a choral reading, and helped the class perform a poem she had previously arranged. After the class felt comfortable with the idea of choral reading, Jodi modeled on the overhead how she goes through the process of dividing up a poem and arranging it for performance. Then she put a poem she had selected as conducive to choral reading on the overhead, and together the class divided, arranged, and performed the poem.

Later in the week, Jodi handed out folders that contained a selection of poems, asking students to form small groups, select a poem from the packet or from one of the books in the classroom or the library, arrange the poem for a choral reading, practice, then perform the reading for the class. Although this exercise followed a month-long introduction to poetry in which Jodi stressed that poetry *doesn't have to rhyme*, every poem selected by the groups was a rhymed humorous story-piece except the poem "October" by Robert Frost that one student brought from a collection he'd found at home. (Even this poem, of course, is rhymed, though much more subtly than the others, and its content is clearly meant for adults who would understand the brevity of life, the beguilement of a mild October morning, and the wish to "Slow slow! / For the grapes' sake").

After students had selected a poem, they negotiated within their groups the arrangement of the various lines and stanzas, they assigned "parts" to individual group members, they rehearsed their pieces, and they concluded by doing their choral reading for the rest of the class. When all the poems had been performed, Jodi went back to each of the seven groups and conducted a brief interview in which students explained how they made decisions about selecting the poem and arranging the performance.

In thinking about the benefits of using choral reading in the classroom, Fisher (1994) claims that "the real learning in choral reading comes from planning how to read the poem because it causes students to examine the poem's structure so that they can enhance its effect" (pp. 61–62). However, when the fifth graders in this study were asked at this point to explain why they had decided to perform the poems the way they did, their responses revealed that their examinations of the poems were limited to a superficial acknowledgement of stanza structure, with almost no attention given to more substantive issues like content or structure on a deeper line or word level. Several groups gave responses like: "We saw there were four paragraphs and said, hey, there are four people. So we each took one."

On the other hand, while the content or deep structure of the poem did not seem to have a discernible effect on the way students divided or arranged their pieces, the content *did* seem to lead to the inclusion of some interesting sound effects. For example, one group stated that "when we were working on our poem, Randi said 'and then the snake ran away' and we thought we could all go 'sssssss' because that's what a snake does."

Sometimes sound effects were communicated less overtly; several groups mentioned the oral and aural dimensions of poetry performance, saying they "just used [their] voices" in their performance. One group described planning for vocal effect in this way: "We kept playing around with how we said each paragraph until everybody sounded spooky. . . . We pretended we were talking about a real monster like Godzilla and that we would be scared." One group decided to include background "oldies" music, so they "started dancing and singing in the oldies way." Within this group, two members opted to sing backup to the rest of the group "because we thought it would be neat to have the rhythm going at the same time that [other members of the group] were singing." When Jodi asked this group whether they had noticed what the audience was doing while they were performing, they responded, "Yes, they were clapping, clicking, tapping their feet, and moving their heads. They were into it"—signifying an awareness of the level of involvement audience members experienced as a result of listening to the oral performance of the poem. *Goatfoot, Milktongue,* and *Twinbird* were beginning to find a place in class.

When Jodi asked one group why they had decided to memorize their poem, a student answered that they knew they didn't *have to* memorize it. "We just had fun with the words and were saying them over and over again, so it just happened," the student explained.

And what's good about choral reading? "You get to express the poem your way." And: "You don't have to memorize or act it out with your body, you just use your voice in different ways. This is really cool!"

Poems for Two Voices: Our Very Own Joyful Noise

By the time Laura arrived in the classroom, many of Jodi's students were feeling fairly confident about their ability to read and write poems. After some lengthy conversations about poetry in which students posed questions to Laura, and she in turn posed questions to them, and after some brief sessions writing and reading together, we were ready to move on to creating our own choral poetry—poems written expressly to be performed by multiple voices. As educators, we were convinced that students needed to be exposed to many examples of dialogic poetry before being asked to write it, since experimentation with writing makes students more appreciative of the crafting involved in the poetry they read (McClure, Harrison, & Reed, 1990). Jodi had already done a lot to prepare her students to write their own choral poetry; as a last step before writing, Laura brought multiple copies of Fleischman's *Joyful Noise* for the class to experience together.

Laura explained that this was a collection of poetry about insects that was told in those insects' own voices; then Jodi and Laura performed one of the poems. By the time the performance finished, students were eager to try reading these poems themselves. First Laura handed out copies, divided the class in half, and students together read "Water Boatmen" (one of Fleischman's simpler arrangements). After they had the hang of it (and it didn't take them long), students paired up and spread out around the room to practice. When they'd gone through the poem a couple of times, we gathered again and tried another poem, "Water Striders," as a class. After some time practicing this poem in pairs, we regathered once more to read "Fireflies," practiced in pairs, then concluded by reading "Honeybees" as a class and in pairs.

As a final exercise, each pair of students chose one of the four poems they'd practiced and polished it for a videotaped class performance. At this point, many students chose to embellish their readings of the poems by adding body motions, changes in volume and pitch, and so on. At one point a minor squabble erupted between two groups who had selected the poem "Water Striders." Each group had chosen to perform the end of the poem the same way, and there was some heated debate about where the idea had originated and who had copied whom. Though the dispute was quickly resolved, it was clear to us that students had a stake in creating interesting and imaginative renderings of the poems.

During the various stages of the activity, Laura asked the class about the characteristics of each of the selections. Students noted that the selected poems became increasingly complex, moving from "Water Boatmen" in which the two voices speak either individually or in unison, to "Fireflies," where the voices dart in and out, crisscrossing and echoing, to "Honeybees" where the very different perspectives of worker and queen bee are juxtaposed and woven through one another without any breaks. Laura asked the students to try to imagine why Fleischman would have chosen to portray these various insects in these different ways. Students were quick to notice how poetic form and content fit together—boatmen who need to row together would unite their voices for a solid "Stroke" at regular intervals throughout the poem; fireflies would flicker on-off, dart in-out, each with an individual brightness and pace; honeybees would have very different experiences and tell very different stories, depending on their roles and responsibilities in the hive.

At the end of our time together, Laura told students that they would be writing their own "poems for two voices" the next time we were together, and that in the meantime they should be "thinking like writers"—gathering ideas from their lives and their neighborhoods (Nye, 1997) that would work well in these kinds of poems. Throughout the following week, students spent time in and out of class brainstorming ideas, developing drafts, and arranging and rearranging lines (often consulting other writers for new ideas and revisions). When they'd finished their pieces, Jodi collected their poems into a book they titled *Our Very Own Joyful Noise,* and students selected partners and practiced their readings.

On Friday, we held our Joyful Noise Poetry performance, and once again we audio- and videotaped the session. One by one the writers introduced their poems and their partners. Their pride in their finished projects was unmistakable, and each poem was followed by sounds of appreciation from around the room and by rounds of spontaneous applause. The pieces themselves were, without exception, excellent examples of choral poetry—creative, deliberate, frequently clever, and often thought provoking. Students had, indeed, devoted out-of-class time to gathering ideas, and they were deliberate about choosing topics and arranging lines so that content and form complemented and enhanced one another.

After the choral readings, we reflected on the experience of writing and performing the poems. Laura opened the conversation by asking students where they had found their ideas. Dan, author of the poem "Kitty Cat," answered the question of where he got his ideas by saying, "I thought of how my cat felt when we got a new kitten that is seven years younger, and that she probably was mad and jealous, so I wrote about that and how they were the same and different."

Kitty Cat
by Dan

I'm a kitten	I'm a cat
I'm soft	I'm soft
I play	
	I rest
people pet me	
	that was before that
	brat showed up
I look out the window	
for birds	

	been there done that
my eyes are green	my eyes are green
mine glow	
	me too

Dan structured his poem so that the traits shared by the cats are spoken together, while the individual characteristics are spoken back and forth by the two voices. The final line surprises the reader by having the cat echo the kitten—perhaps reflecting the adult cat as the grown-up version of the kitten, with a kitten voice still lingering somewhere inside—while the title, "Kitty Cat," can be read as a single label or as the two voices already in tension, both kitty and cat in one poem.

Another student, Lisa, wrote the following poem about downtown Detroit, capturing the ambiguity and irony of simultaneous urban development and decay.

Detroit
by Lisa

The city of Detroit	The city of Detroit
	is very new
No it's old	
	It's both
In a way	
On my side of the	
Street, many buildings	
Stand no more	
	There are too many
	Buildings to count,
	Buildings galore
Some need more paint	
	Many are so
	Beautiful they
	Could make you
	Faint
Yes many buildings are gone,	
All my friends	
	I'm happy
I'm angry	
They're destroying	They're building
Many buildings	Many buildings
Exactly like me.	Exactly like me.

Lisa explained the origins of her subject in the following way:

> I was going to dinner in Detroit with my family over the weekend, and I was looking around at the buildings. My dad said how they are building down here again and how he is glad for Detroit, and then I looked around and saw so many run-down buildings, too. So they could be having a conversation because there were different things going on.

Several students told how their passion for hockey and for the local hockey team, the Detroit Red Wings, showed up in their poems. As one student remarked, "I love hockey. So I wrote about hockey because it is life to me." In one of the many hockey poems, Joe contrasts the rapidly changing viewpoints of an offensive and a defensive player.

Goal or Save
by Joe

Blading down the ice   Staying in the net
going for my first goal

                                        making my millionth save
I gotta get the goal   I gotta make the save
snap

                                        miss
goal

                                        whiff
boo yeah

                                        bummer
try to make the save

                                        oh I will
breakaway
snap

                                        save
rebound

                                        whiff
goal
game over   game over
yes   bummer

Shawn, author of "Greedy Selfish Brat," found his topic in his experience of family life. He said, "I thought of my brother and how sometimes he picks on me and so I thought I would write about a brother that is a brat."

Greedy Selfish Brat
by Shawn

Brat   Brat
Greedy

Brat
He cries and he cries
'til he gets what he wishes

Brat

Greedy
Selfish
Brat
When he is at school
he sure loves cheatin'

Brat

Greedy
Selfish
Brat
If the school found
out he'd sure be in trouble

Brat
He's such a
Greedy
Selfish
Brat

Selfish
Brat

He even has his mom
do the dishes
Brat

Selfish
Greedy
Brat

He's so lazy I'd give
him a beatin'

Brat
Greedy
Selfish
Brat

I'd love to be the one
to burst his bubble
He's such a
Greedy
Selfish
Brat
Brat

Shawn's piece is unusual in that his use of two "voices" is more evident in the performance than in the topic of the poem—that is, Shawn's is an example of a dialogic poem that doesn't convey two viewpoints, but rather that has a single viewpoint expressed by two voices that weave through one another in a complex, though unified, theme.

When Laura asked students how they knew how to arrange the poems on the page—where to give each of the voices a chance to speak alone and together—they were articulate about the relationship between content and form. "In my poem about aliens," one student reported, "I wanted each of us to speak in a robot voice but to say 'o-oo-ooo-o-oo' together." Marcus, author of the poem "Slithering Snakes," was particularly clear about the relationship between what he wanted to say and how it should be said. He said, "I had my snakes do the 'ssss' together because that's what snakes do and I thought it sounded cool. Then I looked for other 's' words to use for each of my snakes to say, like 'slithering' and 'sidewinding.'"

Slithering Snakes
by Marcus

S-S-S-S We're snakes slithering through the cold water	S-S-S-S
S-S-S-S	S-S-S-S we're snakes sidewinding in the hot desert
S-S-S-S we're snakes slurping our forked tongues	S-S-S-S
S-S-S-S	S-S-S-S we're snakes shedding our scaly skin
S-S-S-S	S-S-S-S

Students went on to explain several other (sometimes contradictory) reasons for deciding why voices spoke lines in unison. One student said, "In my poem 'Kitty Love,' whenever they said things that were opposite, I wanted to have them say it at the same time." Another student countered by explaining the arrangement of his poem entitled "Clouds":

> I had the clouds both say "clouds" and "beauty of the sky" because even though there are different kinds of clouds, they are all beautiful to me. So, this is to show that they are the same even though they are a little bit different if I have them say it at the same time.

Although Kayla offered little explanation about the process of writing her poem "Two Lane Highway," saying only that she'd thought of it while riding in the car, we found its dialogue comparing the number of cars traveling in each direction (in and out of the city) at various times of the day—which are always spoken in unison—to be an especially creative example of the effective wedding of content and form:

Two Lane Highway
by Kayla

Left Lane	*Right Lane*
Morning rush hour. I'm jammed with cars.	Morning rush hour. I can't see cars for miles.

Mid-morning. A car every once in a while.	Mid-morning.
	Same here.
Midday	Midday. Some cars for a quick lunch.
Some driving to the city for a half day's work.	
Mid-afternoon. Nobody	Mid-afternoon.
	Some cars getting off work early.
Afternoon rush hour.	Afternoon rush hour. I'm jammed with cars, horns always honking.
Only a few cars, maybe for a city dinner.	
Nighttime.	Nighttime. Only a small amount of cars, coming back from their city dinner.
Not many here, either. Surely, the left lane is best!	Surely, the right lane is best!

Poems for Two Voices as a Step toward Recognizing Poetic Possibilities

The observations made by the students in Jodi's class about their own choral poems are significantly different from these students' early understandings of poetry and their first experiences arranging choral readings from the poetry of others. While, initially, many of these students had limited the possible subjects of poems to nature, funny stories, thoughts and feelings, and a glib "anything and everything," at the end of their activities involving dialogic poems they demonstrated a much deeper understanding of the possibilities of poetry. These students had taken to heart the idea that poems often spring from real life, for their poems were populated with the characters, events, and observations of daily living. Through their poems, they heard and spoke in the voices of buildings they passed, roads they drove on, pets they lived with, passions they held.

Likewise, through creating and performing their own poems for two voices, students understood, on a much more meaningful level, the relationship between content and form in poetry. They played with the sounds of words and lines, shaped the slippery "s" sounds of snakes, adjusted volume and pitch to match subject and mood. They heard and created voices that could intersect, disagree, collide, unite. They knew when and why they wanted words to be positioned together, words to be spoken alone, words to be set in opposition or agreement, and their reasons were no longer limited to easy division and fairness in turn taking. They had seen how the rhythm and music of poems could move the feet, hands, heads, and bodies of members of their audience, and they had begun to understand how to pattern and position words to achieve various effects.

The activity of writing these poems was not intended to teach about alliteration, though in the end it did. It wasn't intended to teach onomatopoeia or assonance, though it did that, too. It didn't mean to address vocabulary or spelling, but it even did that. Instead, as Fisher (1994) explains,

> These explorations . . . help students learn about poetry in meaningful ways. [Students] begin to see why line breaks come as they do, which things are repeated, how poems have rhythm or beat to their pattern. They note rhymes, repeated sounds or letters, and the comparisons that are made. They begin to know intuitively the facts that make a poem a poem just as they figured out what made a story a story some years before. (p. 56)

If the language and forms of poems are birthed in our early encounters with *Goatfoot, Milktongue,* and *Twinbird,* then these fifth-grade students had been reintroduced to those elements—the pleasures of balance and form, or rhythm and motion, of taste and shape—through the oral and aural experience of poetry designed to be spoken and heard. The real purpose behind the progression of these activities was to bring poetry back to the voices and ears of these students, and to explore the poetic possibilities of language, where rhythm, sound, and form both create and reflect meaning, and where the play of words crosses from sound to image, image to sound.

These students recognized that poetry could be found everywhere in the world around them, and that the poet's job is to watch, to listen, to notice and record moments when poems occur. In a poem called "Valentine for Ernest Mann" (when spoken aloud, the name comes out "earnest man"), poet Naomi Shihab Nye explains this everyday-ness of poetry. She writes:

I'll tell a secret . . .
poems hide. In the bottoms of our shoes,
they are sleeping. They are the shadows
drifting across our ceilings the moment
before we wake up. What we have to do
is live in a way that lets us find them. (1994, p. 70)

The students in Jodi's class were learning to find poems. During Laura's final visit, a half-dozen students came up to share poetry journals they'd begun in which they were now recording observations, images, feelings, and phrases that could be turned into poems; even more students came forward to read or to offer copies of poems they'd written, unassigned, outside class. And Jodi reported that at the recent school book fair, all the copies of Fleischman's *Joyful Noise* were sold out—and she was pretty certain she knew where those copies had gone!

In a second survey taken a few weeks after their choral poetry experience, these students articulated once again what they thought of poetry, poets, and poems. This time, no one imagined that a poem had to rhyme, funny stories were mentioned as a possibility rather than a definition of poetry; and every student in the class had a considerable list of poetry credits to his or her name. Many students now felt comfortable with the process of discovering the subjects of their poems. As one student put it, "When I think of poetry, I think of all the things around me and I write about [them]."

"Poetry should be written about real things that happen in life," observed another writer. And one student claimed that his thinking about poetry had changed because he had "learned . . . how to find poems."

"Poetry is like music," one student concluded. "It is meant to make you laugh, cry, and smile. It's like having a river of words run through your head."

Note

1. The possible exception is the type of poetry that depends on a chanting, sing-song rhythm, and rhyme, which is easy to read aloud and enjoy, but which often leads students and teachers to conclude that poetry consists solely of this sort of verse and is defined primarily by its adherence to strict rhythm and rhyme. For the sake of clarity, in the remainder of this article, references to "poetry" will be to poetry that does not exhibit these overpowering characteristics.

REFLECTION: THEN AND NOW

Editors' Note: Pedagogy is notorious for its swings to and from the rhetoric endorsing particular kinds of practices, whereas, as Artley suggests, in many classrooms much has remained constant.

One needs only to walk through the exhibits at a meeting of the International Reading Association or to look through any professional journal to note the emphasis being given to phonics. Tapes, records, films, and workbooks are on the market to give instruction, practice, and self-help in the application of phonic principles. Editorials, news articles, and reports advocate a "return" (as though it were not always present) to phonics as a means of preventing reading problems. Individuals, parent groups, and even a "foundation" have been vocal in advocating the early teaching of symbol-sound relations, sound blending, and patterned words. Reading programs and textual materials have been organized on the rationale of the "phonics approach" to instruction. (p. 121)

Source: Artley, A. S. (1977). Phonics revisited. *Language Arts, 54*(2), 121–126.

STRATEGY: USING LITERATURE TO DISCUSS CULTURAL DIFFERENCES

Editors' Note: Literature can provide teachers and students the opportunity to discuss difficult issues about difference. MacPhee's example comes from a first-grade discussion on race. Literature studies can also be focused on other issues of difference, such as gender or ethnicity.

My plan was to use literature to encourage discourse among my students [31 children, all of European American heritage and from affluent families] regarding social issues to see what their attitudes were towards minorities in both historical and current situations. . . . I wanted to hear the voices of the students as they responded to the

▶

experiences described in the literature. . . . Issues and subjects that normally would be seen and understood from the students' own sociocultural perspective are examined from the perspective of others . . . .

For example, students might initially read a standard version of how Rosa Parks refused to give up her seat on the Montgomery bus, followed by an autobiographical account of the same event. . . . Although the historical account provides factual information and convinces students of the injustices of segregation and the righteousness of Parks's and other Civil Rights leaders' actions, it is the autobiographical account—Parks's own words—that establishes a context for her actions and gives her actions a specificity which, as a real-life story fraught with human emotions and decisions, challenges students' own attitudes and beliefs and adds vicariously to their own experiences. (p. 34)

Sample Response to *Jackie Robinson* (F. Sabin, 1985)

This nonfiction book not only tells the story of Jackie Robinson becoming the first black man to play Major League baseball but also of the struggles and discrimination he endured as a boy and a man. The following section of transcript is of a conversation about the part of the book where Jackie moves to California because "it would be better there."

> *Text:* There was an opportunity for black people to get a decent education in Pasadena. . . . Yet even in Pasadena, young Jackie encountered prejudice. He wasn't allowed to swim in the municipal pool with white children. He was hurt and confused by this and other prejudices.
>
> *Emily:* That's not fair. Everyone should be allowed to swim.
>
> *Adam:* I don't know what happened. Why can't he just swim? It's just not right.
>
> *Brenda:* That's not good. Jackie must have felt bad.
>
> *Connie:* I know I would have let him swim. It's a good thing that I wasn't there!
>
> *JSM:* Why wasn't Jackie allowed to swim?
>
> *Jimmy:* It says it was because he was black, but I don't think that was right. (pp. 35–36)

Student's drawing of Jackie Robinson crying.

Source: MacPhee, J. S. (1997). "That's not fair!": A white teacher reports on white first graders' responses to multicultural literature. *Language Arts, 74*(1), 33–40.

For a discussion of learning about the Holocaust through literature, see: Zack, V. (1991). "It was the worst of times": Learning about the Holocaust through literature. *Language Arts, 68*(1), 42–48

REFLECTION: THE VALUE OF TEACHING POETRY

Editors' Note: The following excerpt from an article written by poet Judith W. Steinbergh begins to explore the power of poetry for teaching metaphor and the power of metaphor to affect children's thinking.

▶

> It is a great thing, indeed, to make proper use of the poetic forms. . . . But the greatest thing by far is to be a master of metaphor. . . . [I]t is from metaphor that we can best get hold of something fresh. (Aristotle: 1952, 1.1410b)

Students' use of metaphor, I believe, reveals their individual ways of thinking about the world, offering teachers and classmates entry into each student's mind and vision. During the 28 years I have taught the reading, discussion, and writing of poetry to students in grades K–12, I have observed how poetry advances students' control over language and increases their ability to read for both meaning and literary technique. Furthermore, a growing facility with metaphor appears to offer students a powerful tool for communication of thought and feeling and a vehicle to express more abstract ideas and relationships. . . .

I want to reflect on the concept of the metaphor. Simply stated, a metaphor is any comparison that cannot be taken literally. Metaphor is rooted in the Greek *metaphora,* to transfer, to carry across, so the intention is to convey a clearer or fresher meaning by use of a figure of speech (an image where the meaning is not literal).

Metaphor is often chosen over literal description because it is concise, vivid, memorable, and, at times, the only way to express what we have to say (Ortony, 1975). Roland Bartel (1983) writes that metaphor merges two unrelated terms to form new images and concepts and claims that metaphor is an indispensable basis for all growth and progress. In literary discussions, the word "metaphor" sometimes refers to one form of figurative language, and at other times is used broadly to cover a range of figurative language. In this essay, my definition of "metaphor" encompasses *simile, personification,* and some uses of *persona* and *symbol,* along with more narrowly defined metaphors which include *renamings, comparisons of physical attributes, extended metaphor,* and *comparisons of concrete and abstract concepts.* Margaret Metzger, veteran teacher of high school English, explained that if students do not understand metaphor by sophomore year, they are lost in their literature courses (personal interview, July 1997). The ability to comprehend and use metaphor gives students of all ages a better chance to assimilate new knowledge, make meaning, communicate thoughts and feelings, and explore the imagination.

▶

Metaphor is the core and soul of poetry. It makes it possible to connect the physical world and the realm of ideas. Robert Frost (1968) wrote,

> There are many other things I have found myself saying about poetry, but the chiefest of these is that it is metaphor, saying one thing and meaning another, saying one thing in terms of another. . . . Poetry is simply made of metaphor. So also is philosophy—and science, too, for that matter. . . . Every poem is a new metaphor inside or it is nothing. (p. 24)

In poetry, students can witness how masters of metaphor shape language, thought, and feeling. Poetic metaphor brings thought and emotion to the reader in a way that can be visualized, touched, heard, tasted, and smelled.

Where do metaphors come from? "The saxophone is the sculptor of the spirit," wrote Walt Gardner in seventh grade. "Noche, llegaste oscura y desolada / Como la capa del día (Night, you came dark and desolate / like the cape of the day)," wrote Karla Figueroa in her "Ode to the Night." "I am a book telling my story," wrote Steven Geller, seventh grade. "Milkweed, a closed cocoon where hundreds of small parachutes will sail / gently across the sky to the ground / carrying a cargo of life," wrote Chris Kernin, fourth grade.

In our minds, we store the images we gather from the time we are born, vivid fragments rooted in the five senses: the smell of mother's milk, the texture of grandfather's face, the terror of trees in a night storm, the sound of sirens or dogs barking sharply in the city, the smell of scallion and garlic sizzling in a wok. At home we hear proverbs, fables, fairy tales, family stories, story books, and poems. We read and listen (Phillips, 1990). In churches, ministers describe God and heaven using familiar or exotic images. We listen and repeat. From songs and lullabies, from playground chants, street hawkers and talkers, from urban streetscapes, malls and markets, the rural patchwork of corn and wheat, images rise up through melody and pattern. All this creates our well of images; each well is entirely different. Influenced by culture, language, family traditions, class, religion, experience, landscape, and environment, we each have a substantial and growing resource of unique metaphors. Images rise up out of the darkness and depths like luminous fish. What appears does not always result from a conscious act. As we write, we dip into our wells, a process which continually provides a source of surprise and delight to ourselves and our caring community. (pp. 324–325) ▶

Source: Steinbergh, J. W. (1999). Mastering metaphor through poetry. *Language Arts, 76*(4), 324–331.

REFLECTION: WHAT IS A POEM?

Editors' Note: Reducing learning to read to a collection of skills to be applied to texts to "decode" the meaning risks draining texts of the aesthetic. Louise Rosenblatt's observation about the power of poetry is true of all literary forms.

A poem is not a ready-made object to which a reader is passively exposed. A poem is a happening, an event, in which the listener or reader draws on images and feelings and ideas stirred up by the words of the text; out of these experiences is shaped the lived-through experience. (p. 386)

Source: Rosenblatt, L. M. (1980). "What facts does this poem teach you?" *Language Arts, 57*(4), 386–394.

IV Writing about Writing

14 Composition: A Position Statement

NCTE Commission on Composition

Editors' Text: In 1975, NCTE's Commission on Composition offered a series of guiding principles for writing instruction that are still valid today.

The following are general principles which members of the NCTE Commission on Composition believe should guide teachers in planning curricula and teaching writing. It is issued as an official position statement of the Commission. The Commission welcomes comments or questions.

1. *Life in Language.* In many senses, anyone's world is his or her language. Through language we understand, interpret, enjoy, control, and in part create our worlds. The teacher of English, in awakening students to the possibilities of language, can help students to expand and enlarge their worlds, to live more fully.

2. *Need for Writing.* Writing is an important medium for self-expression, for communication, and for the discovery of meaning—its need increased rather than decreased by the development of new media for mass communication. Practice and study of writing therefore remain significant parts of the school curriculum and central parts of the English course.

3. *Positive Instruction.* Since a major value of writing is self-expression and self-realization, instruction in writing should be positive. Students should be encouraged to use language clearly, vividly, and honestly; they should not be discouraged by negative correction and proscription. They should be freed from fear and restriction so that their sensitivity and their abilities can develop.

4. *Learning by Writing.* Learning to write requires writing; writing practice should be a major emphasis of the course. Workbook exercises, drill on usage, and analysis of existing prose are not adequate substitutes for writing.

5. *Required Writing.* No formula dictates the amount of writing that should be required in a course—a paper a day or a paper

---

This statement appeared in *Elementary English* 52.2 (1975) on pages 194–196.

a week. Ideally students should be allowed to write when they want to, as much as they want to, and at their own speed. Practically, however, students need class discipline and class discussion as well as freedom, and they should be frequently encouraged and at times required to write.

6. *Classroom Writing.* Inexperienced writers especially should have an opportunity to compose in school, with help during the actual writing process in clarifying ideas, in choosing phrasing, and sometimes in dealing with mechanical problems. Writing outside the classroom, of course, should be encouraged and sometimes required.

7. *Range of Assignments.* Writing assignments should be individualized, adjusted to the age, interests, and abilities of the student. Particularly in the elementary grades but also through high school and into college, the teacher should encourage writing from personal experience, sometimes developing classroom experiences to provide material for writing. The expository essay should not be the exclusive form of composition encouraged. Especially for students who have convinced themselves that composition must be boring, a chore to be avoided whenever possible, writing various kinds of narratives, vignettes, dialogues, fables, family folklore, parodies, and the like may create interest.

8. *Alternate Techniques.* Instruction in writing techniques and rhetorical strategies should be part of the writing course, adjusted to the age and need of the students and focused on positive advice, suggestions, information, and encouragement. Instruction can include discussion of various ways in which writing can achieve its ends—in units as brief as a word or two and as long as a book—observations of procedures followed in existing prose, and constructive criticism of student writing.

9. *Composing.* Since there is adequate subject matter for direct study of writing, courses or units of English courses dedicated to composition should not be converted to courses in literature or social problems, with compositions to be written on the side.

10. *Usage.* Usage is an aspect of rhetoric; learning to predict the social effects of different dialects or different linguistic constructions is part of learning how writing can achieve its purposes. Students should be provided with information that will allow them the largest possible body of alternatives from which to choose and will help them to choose wisely. They should know, for example, that *dragged* and *drug* are both used as past tense forms, but that some listeners will react to *drug* by considering it uneducated. Or students should learn

that *we was* and *we were* are alternatives but that *we was* is not characteristic of a prestige dialect. Such information should be provided through positive instruction about how dialects develop and why variations occur—not through correction based on notions of right and wrong.

11. *Dialects.* No dialect should be presented as "right" or "pure" or "logical" or better than others. The student should be given an opportunity to learn a standard written English, but the teacher must resist the temptation to allow the cultivation of a standard written English to stifle self-expression or to overshadow emphasis on clear, forceful, interesting writing.

12. *Grammar.* The study of the structure and history of language, including English grammar, is a valuable asset to a liberal education and an important part of an English program. It should, however, be taught for its own sake, not as a substitute for composition and not with the pretense that it is taught only to improve writing.

13. *Support for Composing.* Various kinds of activities related to composition contribute to the student's ability to write—film making, debates, collecting material for notebooks, library investigation, dramatics, field trips, television and film viewing. The attractions of such activities—because of their novelty or because they seem to gain more immediate student interest—should not be allowed to supersede instruction in writing.

14. *Talking and Writing.* Students are influenced by mass media not only as consumers but also as producers. Children, for example, may find it easier to compose orally on tapes, without the labor of handwriting. The teacher can sometimes exploit this interest in oral composition as a step toward writing, but the importance of the written word remains, and practice in oral composition alone is not sufficient.

15. *Audience.* Although some writing may be intended to be private, writing implies an audience; and students should be helped to use a voice appropriate to the interests, maturity, and ability of an audience. Furthermore, since young writers are especially concerned about audience response, student writing should be read, often by classmates as well as the teacher.

16. *Grading.* The mere assignment of grades is rarely an adequate way of encouraging and improving writing; whenever possible grades should be replaced by criticism or detailed evaluation. When grades are required, the teacher should avoid basing them primarily on negative considerations—for example, the number of misspelled words or sentence fragments.

17. *Class Size.* Classes in writing should be restricted to no more than 20 students so that frequent writing, reading of papers, and discussion of written work are possible.

18. *Objectives.* Emphasis on instructional objectives or on methods of insuring accountability should not be allowed to dictate the content of the English course, particularly not to replace writing with attention to readily measurable skills—mechanics, for example. Teachers should retain responsibility for determining and expressing the objectives of their teaching: demands for accountability should never be allowed to interfere with independent thought among students.

QUOTATION

If we as teachers ache with caring it will, perhaps, be possible for us to create classroom communities within school communities in which writing matters because it's done for real reasons by real writers who "ache with caring" for a real response. (pp. 124–125)

Source: Fox, M. (1988). Notes from the battlefield: Towards a theory of why people write. *Language Arts, 65*(2), 112–125.

REFLECTION: THE EMERGENT WRITER

Editors' Note: A lot of learning occurs before children learn to write conventionally. The following lengthy excerpt from an article by Judith Newman illustrates the development of an emergent writer over several years.

Have you ever stopped to wonder what is involved in learning to be a writer? Learning to produce written language effectively is among the important achievements of a developing person, whether that person is a child at an early stage of learning to write or an adult struggling with similar aspects of the process.

Child

Until quite recently we knew very little about how children come to understand what writing is. Only in the last few years have researchers become interested in what children know about written language. We have learned, for example, that children are aware of, and make conscious efforts to use, written language at an astonishingly early age. However, rather than reporting these research findings, let me invite you to become a researcher yourself. Let's look at the writings of one child, Jane, to see what we can learn about children's development as writers.

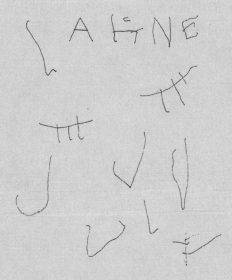

Figure 1.

The writing in Figure 1 was produced one day when I brought her a notebook of her own. She promptly got herself a pen and began writing. First she produced the ↳ in the upper left corner. Then she asked me to make an *A* for her, and she tried her own ℳ beside mine. Next she invited me to help her hold the pen and write an *N* and an *E* with her. Then she tried making two *E*s on her own. She asked me to make a *J* for her before trying several by herself. This was an important writing event for Jane. She was two years and nine months old, yet she shows just how much she already knows about written language.

She knows, for example, that some special marks are used to represent her name; she even knows what those particular marks are called. She also began writing by placing her first letter in the upper left corner of the page. This sample demonstrates how aware of the world of written language young children can be. In Jane's case that world included the wallpaper in her bedroom which had the letters of the alphabet incorporated in the design. She had repeatedly asked about these marks, hence her knowledge of letter names. She had also been read to a great deal from earliest infancy which is probably how she knew those marks were meaningful. There had been no attempt to "teach" Jane about written language; information had simply been offered in response to whatever questions she had asked.

Let's look at a writing sample produced three months later (Figure 2).

Figure 2.

The writing produced on this occasion shows considerably more control, the letters much more conventional in appearance. With the exception of a *B*, center right, all of the marks on the page are Jane's.

The writing sample in Figures 3a and 3b, produced about a month later, is very interesting. Jane was visiting my house and I had handed her paper and crayons with which to draw. Jane, however, decided she wanted to "make a book" instead. I expected her to dictate a story for me to transcribe but she took the pencil I had in my hand and proceeded to write herself. Fortunately for me she composed out loud. Here is her story:

> Mary Kate and Jane were playing outside. Then they went inside to watch T.V., they saw a scary thing—a ghost. So they hided under their covers. Then the ghost couldn't see them. The ghost felt sad and he wrecked up the place. Then the ghost finally leaved. Then the girls lived happily ever after.

When Jane finished writing her story, she asked me to type it for her. We went to the typewriter and I asked her to read her story to me. Her reading corresponded to my transcription of what she had said as she wrote. In fact, when I tried to alter the text slightly, she corrected what I was typing. She had very definite ideas about how her story should go.

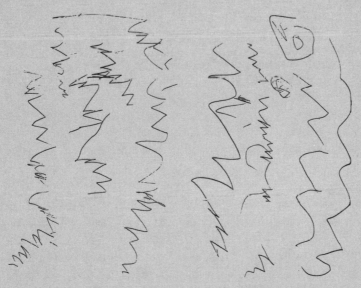

Figure 3a.   **Figure 3b.**

Let's return to what appears at first glance to be a page of scribbles. We can see how every line is horizontal, how the lines all begin at the left margin. (Each line actually represented a complete sentence as Jane composed.) And these marks functioned for Jane as meaningful text; her scribbles may not have been conventional in form but they represented a specific meaning which she was able to retrieve.

The next sample (Figure 4) was written as Jane was approaching her fourth birthday. Here we can see that writing letters of the alphabet continues to hold Jane's interest. She now has the complete sequence; most of the letters are formed conventionally and arranged horizontally from top left to bottom right.

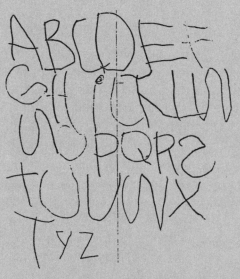

Figure 4.

About that same time (around her fourth birthday), Jane made an interesting discovery. She realized that letters could correspond to the sounds of language. Jane's older brother and I were sitting at the kitchen table writing together, and as she watched the two of us she decided to get into the act herself. We were talking about the children's favorite restaurants, and Jane started drawing a picture of a chicken (Figure 5). Then she asked "How do you write *Kentucky Fried Chicken*?" I suggested she try writing it herself. She put her hands

▷

over her face and said over and over again "tucky" each time emphasizing the "t" at the beginning of the word. Finally, she looked up and said "T" and made a *T* on the paper near the chicken's outstretched leg. Then she tried again, "tucky." Once more her hands covered her face as she said the word, this time emphasizing the "ck" part. She repeated the word several times before she lifted her head and asked whether she needed a "C" or a "K." I asked which one she thought; she replied "C" and proceeded to write a couple of them scattered around the page. Next she tackled *Fried*. Using the same procedure, hands over face and saying the word to herself several times, she was able to come up with "F" and "R" (although the *R* has its legs tied together at the bottom). *Chicken* was difficult. Jane struggled with the initial sounds, then settled for writing the "CK" in the middle and the "N" at the end.

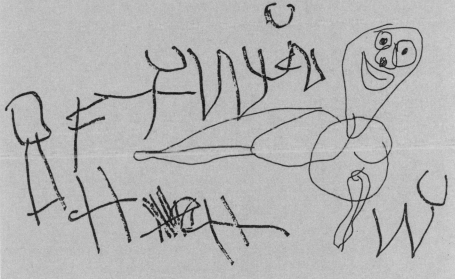

Figure 5.

There are several important observations to make about this writing episode. While Jane showed awareness previously of the linearity of writing, her concern on this occasion with identifying the letter/sound relationships overrides whatever else she knows about writing. The letters go anywhere on the page; their formation is much less controlled than before. This writing sample dispels a myth prevalent in literacy instruction. That is, that learning to read and write follows a neat, clearly specifiable sequence. Instead, we can see that Jane's struggles with a new aspect of writing can produce what appears to be a regression in her control of the process. However, let's examine Figure 6.

Ballet Championships
They were doing stuff. Ballet dancing while the music was playing.
Jane

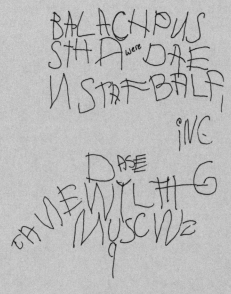

Figure 6.

At four years and ten months, Jane's developing proficiency as a writer is obvious. We can see she attends once more to writing horizontally, from left to right and top to bottom. She no longer has any difficulty forming the letters she wants although she still has to think about what letters she needs to use to represent her meaning. We can see how the conventions for "TH" and "CH" have crept in (S-T-H-A for THEY; T-H-E for THE; C-H-P-U-S for CHAMPIONS). Jane is also aware of "ING" as a unit since she uses it in D-A-S-E ING. And we can see the introduction of some lowercase letters: i (-iNG); e (THe); and u (CHPuS).

▶

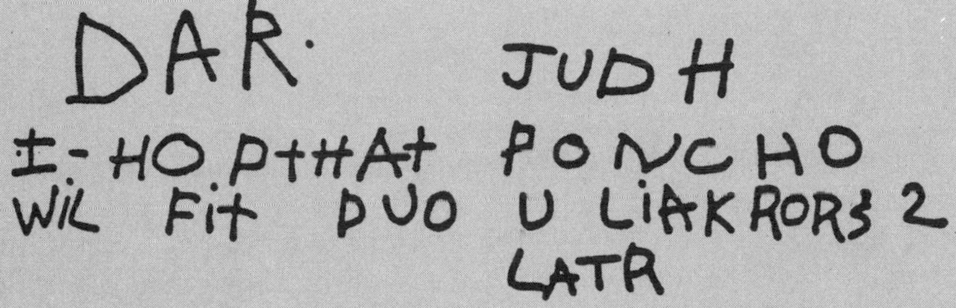

DAR· JUDH
I-HO.PtHAt PONCHO
WiL FiT DUO U LIAKRORS 2
LATR

Figure 7.

Dear Judith
I hope that poncho
will fit. Do you like Rob's two
letters.

I received this letter (Figure 7) from Jane about a month after her fifth birthday. She knew I was making a poncho for her and she is expressing her concern about whether it will fit or not. She also inquires about whether I have enjoyed her brother's letters. All in all, a proper informal letter. A number of words have been spelled conventionally, some of the letters are lowercase, and there are definite spaces between words.

Figure 8 is one last sample from Jane, now almost six years old:

Figure 8.

STOP—STOP
I WANT TO BUY
SOME ICE CREAM
PLEASE

In this sample (the third page of a book she has written), Jane has invented her own convention: words which are being said come from the drawing, hence the "Stop—Stop" written backwards, and the rest of the text written from bottom to top. The writing demonstrates the importance of invention and experimentation in a child's development as a user of written language. Jane doesn't feel inhibited by the conventions she already knows; she invents forms for herself as she tries to share her meaning.

Let's summarize what we've learned about a child's development as a writer from these few samples of Jane's writing. First, children are constantly testing hypotheses as they experiment with writing; and those hypotheses are their own, not ours. Children must be able to decide just what it is they need to explore as they try to understand what being a writer involves. Adult assistance can be helpful if offered in response to a child's questions. Our intervention can interfere, however, if we try focusing children's attention on what *we* think is important for writing.

Literacy development doesn't occur in a linear way. As children test new hypotheses, their control of previously adopted conventions often lapses. Such an abandoning of convention isn't a matter of carelessness but rather an indication of growth itself. It isn't possible to control everything in the process of writing; the new hypotheses must take precedence. That means, as children struggle with new conventions, we must accept some of the mess which trails behind.

All of Jane's writing is meaningful. Each writing effort occurred in situations where creating and sharing meaning was the focus of what was happening. Not only was meaning at the core of the exchanges, but the context was social. Jane was sharing her meaning with others who were responding with meaningful messages, often written ones, in return. Jane continued to be interested in participating in these exchanges of meaning because her efforts were accepted by those around her.

These observations have important implications for teaching children to read and write in school. This small research of ours dispels several myths which underlie much literacy instruction, such myths as:

▶

Development proceeds in an orderly sequence.

We must fragment this complex process into smaller bits in order for children to learn how to do it.

Children must be taught the skills needed for writing before they can be allowed to write themselves.

Children must practice in order to achieve accuracy before they can control the process on their own.

What Jane's writing helps us understand is that much of what we offer children as "instruction" can actually obstruct their learning. By setting the tasks, by expecting neatness and accuracy to take precedence over meaning, we interfere with the hypotheses the children must invent and test for themselves.

Jane's writing development offers some guidelines for what we should be doing in school. She helps us see that:

We need to place meaning at the forefront of learning about written language.

We need to make literacy learning an intensely social endeavor.

We need to support the children's experiments, watching for conventions as they creep into their writing.

We must participate in their learning by being writers ourselves.

It is only by creating natural language environments in which children are comfortable experimenting with written language that we can help them become writers. (pp. 860–867)

Source: Newman, J. (1983). On becoming a writer: Child and teacher. *Language Arts, 60*(7), 860–870.

15 Myths of Writing

Frank Smith

Editors' Text: Common sense has it that "writing is for the transmission of information." Frank Smith disagrees. In this often cited article, Smith challenges twenty-two misconceptions about writing, about how writing is learned, about the act of writing . . . and about who can teach writing.

Whether writing should be considered to be as natural as speech for anyone to learn and to practice may be the subject of debate. My own view is that every child who can talk has the capacity to learn to write and also to seize upon its possibilities with enthusiasm. But in any case, I think there can be little debate that writing as children are expected to learn and to practice it in many classrooms is a highly unnatural activity, reflecting (or creating) some basic misconceptions about the nature of writing and about the manner in which proficient writers usually write.

Not all teachers harbor all or even many of these misconceptions. Nevertheless, I believe they are sufficiently egregious both in school and out to warrant their exposure and examination. Many of the misconceptions constitute handicaps in their own writing as well as in their efforts to teach children how to write.

I shall present and briefly discuss a collection of twenty-one misconceptions—Smith's myths—which I acquired in the course of a recent exploration of writing (Smith 1981b). For display purposes I shall organize my collection into sets of myths about the nature of writing, about how writing is learned, and about how it is practiced, concluding with a grand myth about who is able to teach writing.

Myths about the Nature of Writing

1. *Writing is for the transmission of information.* Reality: Two major functions of writing—to create experiences and to explore ideas—are obscured if not ignored by the contemporary "information processing"

This essay appeared in *Language Arts* 58.7 (1981) on pages 792–798. It was also included in Frank Smith's *Essays into Literacy* (Heinemann, 1983). Copyright is retained by Frank Smith. Reprinted by permission.

approach to literacy (Rosenblatt 1980). Children may not have much new knowledge to convey to other people, but they will use all forms of language, including writing if they become aware of its potential to create worlds of experience and of ideas which they can explore personally, enjoy, and perhaps subsequently share with others. A danger of the information transmission myth is that it focuses attention on how texts are presented from the point of view of a reader (usually one very touchy about minor points of spelling and punctuation) rather than on what the act of writing can accomplish for the developing thought of the writer. The writer is overlooked.

2. *Writing is for communication.* Reality: Writing can of course be used for communication, but this is scarcely its only or even major value, certainly not for children. The writer is always the first reader and may often be the only one (for diaries, journals, notes, and more extended texts written for the writer's own exploratory or other purposes). Of course, children often like to *show* what they write—until they become self-conscious about their expression, neatness, punctuation, or spelling errors—but the purpose of this social act is to share their delight or to demonstrate how clever they are, rather than to communicate information. A similar personal motivation is not absent among adults who have their own written creations prominently displayed on staff room notice boards or in professional journals.

3. *Writing involves transferring thoughts from the mind to paper.* Reality: Writing can create ideas and experiences on paper which could never have existence in the mind (and possibly not in the "real world" either). Thoughts are created in the act of writing, which changes the writer just as it changes the paper on which the text is produced. Many authors have said that their books know more than they do; that they cannot recount in detail what their books contain before, while, or after they write them. Writing is not a matter of taking dictation from yourself; it is more like a conversation with a highly responsive and reflective other person. Some reasons why writing is so potent in permitting writers to form and develop ideas they might otherwise not have are considered in the following discussion of myths #4 and #5.

4. *Writing is permanent, speech ephemeral.* Reality: Speech, once uttered, can rarely be revised, no matter how much we might struggle to unsay something we wish we had not said. But writing can be reflected upon, altered, and even erased at will. This is the first great and unique potential of writing—that it gives the writer power to manipulate time. Events that occurred in the past or that may occur in the future can be

evaluated, organized, and changed. What will be read quickly can be written slowly. What may be read several times need be written only once. What will be read first can be written last. What is written first need not remain first; the order of anything that is written can be changed. Such control over time is completely beyond the scope of spoken language or of thought that remains "in the head."

5. *Writing is a linear, left-to-right process.* Reality: Writing can be done in several places and directions concurrently, and is as easily manipulated in space as it is in time. Texts can be constructed from writing done on separate pieces of paper, in notebooks, on index cards, or on chalk boards at the same time that a main draft is being produced. Words and lines can be moved around on a page just as pages themselves can be reshuffled into different sequences. Writing is a plastic art.

6. *Writing is speech plus handwriting, spelling, and punctuation.* Reality: Every kind of text has its own conventions of form and expression quite different from any kind of speech. The relevant models for writing are how other people write, not how they speak. Spelling, punctuation, capitalization, paragraphing, indentation, word dividing, neatness, and so forth are necessary aspects of the *transcription* required to make written language manifest, though what is sufficient for a writer to produce and explore written experiences and ideas is by no means as detailed or demanding as the intricacy of transcription required by a reader. The transcription aspects of writing need not in fact be done by the writer; they can be looked after by a secretary. For all writers, undue concern with transcription can interfere with *composition,* the creative and exploratory aspect of writing which is of course its major value to the writer.

7. *A writer is a special kind of person.* Reality: There is no evidence that writers are any more intelligent, sensitive, talented, dedicated, disciplined, or persevering than people who do not write. Writers come from no exclusive kind of background. Some come from large families, some from small; some from rich, others from poor; some have literate parents, others the reverse; some received family encouragement, others did not. There is only one difference between writers and people who do not write—*writers write.* This unique difference may be because writers have some rare and as yet undiscovered gene for writing, though I doubt it. An alternative is that all children are born capable of learning to write at least as well as they learn to talk, but that something goes wrong. What goes wrong could be related to some of the myths that follow.

Myths about How Writing Is Learned

8. *Learning to write precedes writing.* Reality: Both reading and writing can only be learned in the course of reading and writing. Writing may need years of practice to make it fluent and facile (for most of us this "learning to write" continues all our lives), but the fluency and facility come with writing, not with repetitive and separate exercises and drills. The only difference between children learning to write and more proficient adults is that children need more help—they can write less by themselves. They need their own writing to be done for them just as they need other people's writing to be read to them. Unless children try to write and receive help in writing, they will have no motivation for attending to "writing" exercises and instruction, they will find such instruction incomprehensible, and they will not read in ways that will help them learn to write. A disastrous consequence of the "learn now, write later" myth is that the "secretarial" transcription aspects of writing are emphasized before the learner has a chance to experience or even understand the composition aspect of being an author. Even as a means of becoming a secretary, this approach is still not an efficient way to learn.

9. *Writing is learned from instruction.* Reality: Not even such transcription skills as spelling, punctuation, or capitalization can be learned from lectures, from reading about them, or from drills. Spelling is too complex to be learned from rules or by memorizing word lists (Smith 1981a; in more detail in Smith 1981b). And the "rules" of punctuation and capitalization tend like all grammatical explanations to be circular—"Begin every sentence with a capital letter." "What is a sentence?" "Something that begins with a capital letter." Formal instruction in grammar is necessarily restricted to conventional niceties like subject-verb agreement, which do not constitute a comprehensive or even comprehensible system for enabling anyone to get thoughts on paper. The easiest way to learn to write is to see something you would like to say (or would like to be able to say) being written.

10. *Writing is learned by writing.* Reality: No one writes enough, especially at school, to have enough mistakes corrected to learn to write by trial and error. Not even the transcription aspects of writing could be learned in this way, let alone all the subtleties of style and expression. The only source of knowledge sufficiently rich and reliable for learning about written language is the writing already done by others. In other words, one learns to write by reading. The act of writing is criti-

cal as a *basis* for learning to write from reading; the desire to write ourselves provides an incentive and direction for learning about writing
from reading. But the writing that anyone does must be vastly complemented by reading if it is to achieve anything like the creative and communicative power that written language offers.

11. *Most classrooms are reasonable places in which to expect children
to learn to write.* Reality: Most professional writers could not write with
the physical and psychological constraints under which many children
are expected to learn to write in school. Children who attempted to behave the way most adults find it necessary to behave while writing
would probably not be permitted to stay in the classroom. Much of this
discrepancy can be attributed to the following myths (unless the myths
themselves have been created to justify the conditions existing in many
classrooms).

Myths about the Act of Writing

12. *You must have something to say in order to write.* Reality: You often need
to write in order to have anything to say. Thought comes with writing,
and writing may never come if it is postponed until we are satisfied that
we have something to say. Like every other reference to "writing" in
this article, this assertion of "write first, see what you had to say later"
applies to all manifestations of written language, to letters and memo-
randa as well as to short stories and novels, to poems, plays, and film
scripts as well as to diaries, journals, term papers, research reports, and
notes for ourselves and for others.

13. *Writing should be easy.* Reality: Writing is often hard work; it
requires concentration, physical effort, and a tolerance for frustration
and disappointment. The fact that writing is a demanding activity
should not discourage anyone from writing, especially children. Many
satisfying activities require physical effort and are not necessarily easy,
especially in the learning. Children are not strangers to the idea that
worthwhile ends may require effort and concentration, which they frequently display in their "play." Only work which seems to have no point
or productive outcome is aversive.

14. *Writing should be tight the first time.* Reality: Something all experienced writers know that seems to have been concealed from many
teachers is that writing generally requires many drafts and revisions to
get ideas into a form that satisfies the writer, and that a separate editorial polishing is required to make the text appropriate for a different
reader. Part of the power of writing is that it does not have to be right
the first time, that drafts can usually be modified or even thrown away.

In a few situations, usually contrived ones like examinations, writing may have to be right the first time. But ability to write in this way requires special practice and is the result of considerable experience. Only through freedom to write provisionally most of the time can the facility be developed of producing first drafts in a form reasonably presentable to a reader.

15. *Writing can be done to order.* Reality: Once again, every experienced writer knows that writing is often most reluctant to come when it is most urgently required, yet quite likely to begin to flow on inconvenient or impossible occasions. Writing to order is not an ability that develops independently of writing in a more spontaneous and unpredictable manner, nor should it be expected to take priority over such writing.

16. *A fixed period of "prewriting" can or should be distinguishable before any writing act.* Reality: The fact that it is difficult to write to order or to be right the first time does not entail that a fixed period of "prewriting time" exists that should be allocated before writing can be expected to occur. On the one hand, much of what is written involves a whole lifetime of preparation—of experiencing, reading, reflecting, and arguing. It is only from a transcription point of view that an author can say that work began on a particular text at a particular time, even if that was the time when a decision to write was made or formal research begun. And many relevant ideas for what we might propose to write come to us when we are not thinking specifically about what we propose to write, perhaps when we "daydream" or when we are supposed to be thinking about something else. On the other hand, writing itself can be prewriting. As we draft one part of a text, we reflect upon what we might write next or upon what we have written already. The act of writing does not break itself down into neatly identifiable and manageable "steps," rather it is a part of all our existence.

17. *Writing is a sedentary activity.* Reality: Little of the reflective or preparatory aspects of writing can or need be performed at a desk, and even the transcription of writing is sometimes more comfortably performed standing up or against a wall. The traditional notion of the writer quietly working at the desk is romantic and unrealistic.

18. *Writing is a silent activity.* Reality: Writing frequently involves making noise, not only to exchange ideas (or feelings) with other people, but to give vent to expressions of exhilaration or frustration. As with myths #15 and #17, the image of a writer attentive to his muse in garret or cell (the stereotype is usually sexual as well as behavioral) is sentimentalized and unrealistic.

19. *Writing is a solitary activity.* Reality: Writing in general often requires other people to stimulate discussion, to provide spellings, to listen to choice phrases, and even just for companionship in an activity which can be so personal and unpredictable that it creates considerable stress. And especially when writing is being learned there is often a great need for and advantage in people working together on a letter, poem, or story. The ability to write alone comes with experience, and is not always easy or necessary.

20. *Writing is a tidy activity.* Reality: Truly creative (or difficult) writing spreads itself all over the writing surface and all over the floor. Writing is messy; it can involve scissors, paste, transparent tape, paper clips, staplers, pens and papers of many colors, and more than one working surface (not all necessarily horizontal).

21. *Writing should be the same for everyone.* Reality: All writers have idiosyncrasies. Some write best in the morning, some in the evening; some with pen or pencil, some with typewriter or tape recorder; some only in silence, others only in company; some systematically, others irregularly. Most writers have very strong preferences about writing with a particular kind of instrument on a particular kind of paper in particular locations at particular times with particular kinds of physical and psychological support, holding to these supports with a tenacity verging on superstition. But then superstition is a characteristic of all high-risk occupations. Steeplejacks and astronauts have their rabbits' feet. Writers put themselves on the line and undertake enterprises without knowing what the outcome will be. Inconvenient though it might often be, writing behavior may have to be idiosyncratic if it is to be engaged in at all.

The Grand Myth about Who Can Teach Writing

22. *People who do not themselves enjoy and practice writing can teach children how to write.* Reality: Anyone who hopes to teach children how to write must (1) demonstrate what writing does, and (2) demonstrate how to do it. A "teacher" who dislikes or fears writing will demonstrate that writing is to be disliked or feared, just as a teacher who is only seen writing comments on children's work, reports for parents, or notes and exercises for classroom activities will demonstrate that writing is simply for administrative and classroom purposes. Children will learn what they are taught (Smith 1981a), and a teacher who perceives writing as a tedious chore with trivial applications will teach just those things.

For most of the myths I have collected I have not attempted to present a means for their eradication. My general feeling (or hope) is that recognition of the myth should be sufficient for most teachers to avoid falling victim to it. But for the myth of who can teach writing I want to offer a practical suggestion.

The assertion is that children will learn to write and to enjoy writing only in the presence of teachers (or other adults) who themselves write and enjoy writing. If some teachers do not have these necessary characteristics, then more might be done to bring people who do have them into the classroom, not just the professional like local authors and journalists but anyone who enjoys writing letters, poetry, or short stories (just as athletic coaches and assistants do not need to be professional athletes themselves, though they are expected to understand and enjoy the sport).

But an additional and even more desirable solution would be for all teachers to learn to become at least moderately keen and competent writers. And for this they should not themselves turn to the exercises and "how to do it" books any more than they should try to educate their own pupils in this way. Teachers should learn the way children should learn, in the mutual effort of writing with a purpose—the primary initial purpose being one's own joy and satisfaction with what is written—and in the delight of reading widely from a writer's perspective. The easiest way for teachers to learn these things in order to teach children in this way is to learn them *with* children, to share the writing activities with the children themselves. In this way, teachers and children alike should be best able to avoid the tyranny of all the myths of writing, and in the process discover that writing is a natural, attainable, enjoyable, and highly productive way of spending one's time.

REFLECTION: RESEARCH ON REVISION

Editors' Note: Here we've excerpted at length some findings from research on revision that Don Graves shared with Language Arts *readers over twenty years ago.*

———— ❧ ————

1. Children revise in other media forms such as block building, drawing, and painting before they revise in writing. Children who demonstrate an overall learning stance toward revision in

▶

one area are more likely to demonstrate it in another such as writing.

2. When children try a new approach to writing, other areas in which they have been competent may suffer temporarily.

3. Beginning writers do not revise. Getting the new step down is enough. (When Sarah introduced a logical construction, she did not revise it even though it did not make sense to her.)

4. Early writing is often impressionistic. Children put words down for a certain feeling. Feelings are revised only if the child senses the feeling is not accurate. (Sarah "sprinkles" in "It is good. I love you." after her work is completed.)

5. Invented spellings go through stages of development along with the child. They fall into different classifications—first inventions, words in transition, stable inventions, sight words. Words that are more stable, as in stable inventions and sight words, are more likely to be revised.

6. Toward the end of the primary years many children reach a point of equilibrium when handwriting and spelling problems are behind them and messages flow easily onto the paper. Children do not revise these messages.

7. Eight-year-old children find it easier to revise topics about personal experiences than about the experiences of others. They find it easier to recall their own experiences than the experiences of others.

8. Revision begins when children choose their own topics. Children who quickly arrive at a number of topics, who learn to exclude some topics and write on others, are learning to revise.

9. Children who can quickly list personal topics for writing, and write a series of leads about the same subjects, demonstrate a strong capacity for revision.

10. Peer audiences have an effect on children's revision and their use of new approaches to the writing process.

11. Teachers can play a significant role in releasing a child's potential for revision. . . .

12. When children no longer erase, but cross out, draw lines and arrows for new information arrangements, or change their hand-

▶

writing to a scrawl, they indicate a changed view toward words. Words, for these children, are now temporary, malleable, or clay-like. The words can be changed until they evolve toward the right meaning for these children.

13. Children who write rapidly are more likely to revise in larger units and sustain a single composition for a longer period of time than those who write slowly. (Andrea writes at fifteen words per minute, does three or four drafts over a three-week period, whereas Brian writes at five to six words per minute, does two drafts over a one-week period.) (pp. 318–319)

Source: Graves, D. H. (1979). Research update: What children show us abut revision. *Language Arts, 56*(3), 312–319.

REFLECTION: LOOKING FOR REVISION

Editors' Note: When Kay Hink looked at the writing her students did, she worried that her students weren't doing much revision. When she looked more carefully, she came to the following conclusions:

Unlike some descriptions of the writing process, writing does not come in nice tidy packages where the student takes a piece of writing through multiple drafts with obvious revisions. Much of the revision goes on behind the scenes, and changes are made when one child talks to another. This type of revision may only be apparent if looked for closely or if the writer is asked to tell what was done with a piece of writing. (p. 251)

Source: Hink, K. E. (1985). Let's stop worrying about revision. *Language Arts, 62*(3), 249–254.

16 Finding the "Right Measure" of Explanation for Young Latina/o Writers

Liliana Barro Zecker

Christine C. Pappas

Sarah Cohen

Editors' Text: Dennis Searle's question, "Who's building whose building?" (see Chapter 3), raises another question about the appropriate level of support teachers should provide for their students. Zecker, Pappas, and Cohen consider how teachers decide what to make explicit for Latina and Latino learners and how to strike the right balance between teacher support and students' ownership of their learning.

Learning has been compared to an apprenticeship in which the more experienced members of a social group share their expertise with novice learners to support their progress into more advanced levels of performance or understanding (Bruner, 1983; Vygotsky, 1978). However, the exact form that this sharing takes, or should take, is still puzzling to many educators. How much expertise is to be shared, when, and how? What are the best ways to build on learners' previous experiences so that they can construct new knowledge? Deciding what to make explicit for learners and finding the right balance between giving specific assistance and letting learners reshape knowledge through discovery is no easy task (Edwards & Mercer, 1987).

Apprenticeship in Literacy Learning: Two Dimensions of the Challenge

A major problem in supporting apprenticeship in literacy learning stems from the fact that reading and writing are mental processes, silent and not obvious in many ways. Wells and Chang-Wells (1992) have argued

---

This essay appeared in *Language Arts* 76.1 (1998) on pages 49–56.

that there are many possible ways for readers and writers to relate to texts but it is a certain kind of engagement with text—which they call "epistemic"—that fosters truly literate ways of thinking. Epistemic modes of engagements are ones in which "meaning is treated as tentative, provisional, and open to alternative interpretations and revision" (Wells, 1990, p. 369). Thus, teachers of young children face the challenge of modeling the idea that meaning can be transformed and reformulated.

Classroom talk, what is said and how it is said, can then be considered *oral text* and as such it is a most effective vehicle to make explicit to young children the covert aspects of literate thinking. In other words, classroom talk provides an opportunity for teachers to model epistemic kinds of engagement with text.

But, as they support young writers in their apprenticeship, teachers face the challenge of having to balance the focus on meaning with the focus on form, since young children are also attempting to tackle the complex conventions of written language as a coded medium of communication. In recent years, literacy instruction has taken a more constructivist or collaborative tone, one that is more inclusive of students' interests and previous experiences (Hiebert, 1991; Willinsky, 1990). Within this framework, the mechanics of writing—punctuation, capitalization, spelling, etc.—are not taught in isolation via drill activities but, rather, in the context of students' needs as they *use* literacy to communicate. But teachers who have attempted to adopt this philosophy have often found it hard to decide *what* should be learned at different grade levels. Many tensions arise as teachers try to integrate form (i.e., written language as a code to be learned) and meaning (i.e., the ideas to be communicated). As a result, instruction in specific skills can sometimes become casual and random (McIntyre, 1995a, 1995b). Many questions still remain about how teachers can most effectively incorporate skill instruction in the context of meaning-centered approaches (Atwell, 1991; Labbo, Hoffman, & Roser, 1995; McIntyre, 1995b). This issue is particularly relevant as teachers prepare to teach the growing number of linguistically diverse students in American schools. It has been argued that these students need explicit and systematic instruction in the Standard English code in order to have access to better socioeconomic opportunities (Delpit, 1995; Reyes, 1991).

Sarah as a Teacher-Researcher

This article describes a second-grade teacher-researcher's efforts to foster her Latina/o students' growth in writing. Sarah, for whom Spanish was a second language, was teaching for the first time in a bilingual classroom in a Midwestern inner-city public school. All of her students were Spanish-speaking children, mostly from Mexican families who had recently immigrated to the United States. Sarah's reading and writing instruction was conducted predominantly in Spanish since her students had varying but, in general, very limited command of English.

Sarah participated in a school-university collaborative research project that explored teachers' self-selected inquiries on how to implement changes that would make their literacy curricula more effective and student centered. University researchers and teacher-researchers met weekly as a group to discuss the teachers' successes and struggles. Videotapes and field notes collected by university researchers were shared with teacher-researchers, individually and as a group. These ongoing discussions provided opportunities for the teachers to examine and reflect on the observations of their classroom work related to their inquiries (see Pappas, 1997, and Pappas & Zecker, in press a & b, for more details about the larger collaborative school-university project in which Sarah's inquiry was embedded).

"¡Pero yo no escribo!": The Impetus of Sarah's Inquiry

At the beginning of the school year, Sarah had been surprised and saddened by the children's reluctance to engage in writing activities. When, soon after classes started, Sarah encouraged one of her students to write a story to accompany her picture, the girl simply responded, "¡Pero yo no escribo!" ("But I don't write!"). Having experienced a first-grade year during which writing had been limited to the completion of phonics worksheets and handwriting exercises, the children did not see themselves as writers or believe they could become writers. Thus, the focus of Sarah's inquiry was to find possible ways to scaffold her students' development as writers. She set out to present a variety of possible writing invitations for them so that they could experience writing for communication. As the school year progressed, the ways in which she tried to make explicit for her students many of the not-so-obvious what's, why's, and how's of written language and authorship became especially salient.

Two facets of the challenge to support an appropriate apprenticeship in writing were present in Sarah's inquiry: she struggled to balance meaning and mechanics and made efforts to provide opportunities for her students to engage with texts epistemically. In this article, we focus on the latter as we reflect on Sarah's strategies—sometimes successful, sometimes not—to make the tacit aspects of writing explicit to her students via classroom talk. In two areas especially—fostering revision and making genre distinctions—Sarah tried to find the "right measure" of explanation so her students might begin to see how meanings can be tentative and transformed.

Note that, due to space restrictions, only some examples include both the original Spanish and its English translation. The other talk samples in the paper are translations only.

Invitations to Write and Revise

Sarah started by setting up a variety of opportunities for her students to write, share, and reflect on texts. She had whole-class, teacher-led minilessons and student-sharing activities similar to "author's chair" sessions (Calkins, 1994; Graves, 1994; Graves & Hansen, 1983). She also set up a system that enabled her to have individual writing conferences with her students. Within these various routines, she frequently "put into words" the many tacit aspects of writing.

Because her students did not see themselves as writers, Sarah was careful to articulate in detail for them the rationale and goals of their writing engagements. For example, she explained to Felipe, a student who joined the class later during the school year that "the journal is where we put our thoughts, what we did during the day, on the weekend, how you feel, what your family is like. You can make drawings about what you have written. If you have questions, you can ask your classmates, okay?" When introducing readers' logs, Sarah explained, "Write your name and the date. You have to write the title of the book that you read. Then I want you to write about what the story was about, if it was a story, what happened? If it was a science book, about nature, what did you learn?" Thus, Sarah talked about the communicative functions of these two kinds of writing, making explicit for the children their content as well as their form.

Sarah approached the teaching of the mechanics or surface aspects of writing from the same perspective. She included detailed explanations about spelling, punctuation, and capitalization rules during group and individual conferences. Sometimes, she would conduct whole-class spelling lessons, explaining to the students, *"Estas son palabras que usan mucho y que escriben mal"* ("These are words that you use a lot and you often misspell."). In that sense, Sarah was able to achieve some balance in her teaching as she was able to address both the message and the medium of written language in the context of her students' own writing.

Talking the Talk of Revision

Sarah paid special attention to the revision process as she felt it was important for the children to experience ways in which they could transform their writing and thus their thinking. As she explained the goals of whole-group conferences, she said:

> We are going to give our comments, suggestions, questions . . . and we are going to talk as a group . . . [about] how those comments can be used to change the story, to develop the story . . . the stories that the authors write. You are the authors already . . . listening and giving suggestions, asking questions on the story. Later, we are going to think together about how the person who reads the story . . . can improve it, or how she or he can develop her or his story. What happens is that, often, we write a story and we think that it is already finished, but sometimes it is missing details in some parts, or it could be developed much more.

Often, Sarah capitalized on the students' comments to help them reflect on the role of audience feedback from the author's vantage point. For example, at the end of October, after Raúl had shared his Halloween story with his classmates and responded to some of their questions, Sarah closed the session by saying: "These questions, they make me think, Raúl, that sometimes it is good to give more details. The audience wants more information. Maybe next time you can give more details." Thus, in promoting revision, Sarah was helping students to understand that initial meanings can be reexamined and retold.

Sometimes, Sarah modeled through talk the possible ways in which students could incorporate changes in their stories. During one of these sessions, Lorena volunteered to read one of her stories to the class. Sarah explained she would write the audience questions on the board as a way to provide Lorena with assistance during the revision to follow. Lorena read a story about Julia, a girl who liked to draw, color, and make books. Julia had a friend who also liked to engage in drawing, coloring, and book making. After finishing her reading in front of the group, Lorena answered questions from her peers using short, succinct responses and not elaborating on details. Afterward, Sarah explained how Lorena could use the feedback to revise her story. She modeled some possible changes for Lorena to consider. Note: In the transcripts below, the symbol (***) indicates speech that was indecipherable.

Example 1

> *Sarah:* Estas preguntas pueden ayudar. ¿Okay? Te preguntaron, "¿Por qué le gustaron los cuentos a la niña?" y "¿Por qué le

gustaban los dibujos?" Eso es una cosa que no está en el cuento. Podrías poner estos detalles en tu cuento. Parece que a la gente que lea tu cuento le gustaría saber mas sobre la niña. ¿Me entiendes, Lorena?

Lorena: Sí, entiendo.

Sarah: Y si pones esos detalles, sería mas completa. ¿Entiendes? También te preguntaron, "¿Por qué los coloreó, los cuentos y los libros?" Y si lo hacía sola o con su amiga. Si su amiga la ayudaba. ¿Okay? Parece que tus compañeros, Lorena, están diciendo que quieren saber mas; podrías darnos un ejemplo. Podras darnos una escena entre la niña y su amiga haciéndolo . . . lo que hacían. ¿Entiendes? Eso es diferente que decir, "A la niña le gustaban los dibujos." Podrías decirnos, umm, "Una niña, Julia, y su amiga un día estaban haciendo unos dibujos. Julia hacía eso y . . . después dijo su amiga, ¿Por qué no ponemos el color rosa en el conejo en el cuento?"

Boy 1: (***)

Sarah: Uh-huh. Puedes darnos una perspectiva sobre cómo se portan las niñas. ¿Entiendes?

Lorena: [Nods.]

Sarah: Hay otras cosas que podrías decir sobre la niña. ¿Cómo es su vida? A parte de que le gustaba hacer dibujos y cuentos, podrías decirnos si va a la escuela, si sale, cómo es su familia, cosas así. ¿Verdad? ¿Okay? Entonces, si tu crees que te gustaría hacer el cuento mas grande, cambiar un poquito, contesta algunas preguntas que te hicieron tus compañeros. ¿Okay? Esas preguntas, Lorena. [As she is pointing to the board.]

Translation

Sarah: These questions can help, okay? They ask you, "Why did the girl like stories?" and "Why did she like the pictures?" That is something that is not in the story. You could put those details in the story. It seems as if the people that read your story would like to know more about the girl. Do you understand me?

Lorena: Yes, I understand.

Sarah: And if you put in those details, it would be more complete, do you understand? They also asked you, "Why did she color the stories and the books?" And if she did it alone or with her friend. If her friend helped her, okay? It seems that your classmates, Lorena, are saying that they want to know more; you could give us an example. You could give us a scene between the girl and her friend doing that . . .

what they did. Do you understand? That is different from saying, "The girl liked pictures." You could tell us, umm, "A girl, Julia, and her friend, one day were drawing pictures. Julia was doing that and . . . then her friend said, Why don't we color the bunny in the story pink?"

Boy 1: (***)

Sarah: Uh-huh. You can give us a perspective about how the girls behave. Do you understand?

Lorena: [Nods.]

Sarah: There are other things that you can say about the girl. What's her life like? Besides liking to make drawings and stories, you could tell us if she goes to school, if she goes out, what her family is like, things like that, right? Okay? Then, if you think that you would like to make the story bigger, change a little, answer some of the questions that your classmates asked you, okay? Those questions, Lorena. [*As she is pointing to the board.*]

(Field notes, 11/02/94)

Sarah used the questions asked by Lorena's classmates to provide her with specific examples of how to incorporate more information into her story and then orally "revised" Lorena's story to model for her a possible new final product. She was using classroom talk as "text," as the canvas on which to make explicit the need to treat written texts as tentative and provisional, always having the potential for revision. But when Sarah later reminded Lorena to use the audience response to revise her story, Lorena looked puzzled and her response consisted of copying from the board all the questions that Sarah had written. For her, that was revision.

Thus, Sarah experienced difficulty in "handing over" her expertise in revision. As other teacher-researchers have discovered, Sarah realized that, more often than not, students seemed to talk the talk of revision but did not actually revise their writing (Calkins, 1994; Labbo et al., 1995). Students in Sarah's class, like other young writers, seemed to write for the here and now. Despite her efforts, they seemed to translate revision strategies into very concrete operations, writing more for the sake of the activity than for the creation of a final product that would consider the needs of the audience (Calkins, 1994). Near the end of the school year, Sarah encouraged Raúl to use Pablo's feedback to improve his story, reminding him to "take notes" on Pablo's comments so that "you can remember what he tells you." Later Raúl approached Sarah and asked: "And now, what do I do with this? He gave me all this." He showed Sarah his "notes" which were parts of his story copied verbatim on a new piece of paper. As Sarah mentioned that the notes could help him revise his story, Raúl responded: "But I already copied all the parts he liked!" Frequently, during whole-class conferences, Sarah highlighted that praising the good parts of a story was very important. Apparently, Raúl had focused only on that part of the discussion, and his "revised" product consisted of the audience's favorite parts copied unchanged from his original story.

Despite Sarah's explanations and other attempts to scaffold the revision process more explicitly, some of her students never realized these new ideas in their final products. However, the mismatch between what is "talked about" and what "gets written down" is not atypical (Calkins, 1994; Pappas, Kiefer, & Levstik, 1994). Sarah found that it was hard to find what she called the "right measure" of explanation and keep individual children's focus of interest and understanding. At times, it seemed as if she might have unintentionally made writing too complex by *forcing* writing into being too much of a process (Labbo et al., 1995). Beginning writers need time to incorporate flexible revising strategies into their repertoires (Calkins, 1994). They use oral language as a bridge to many aspects of literacy learning (Dyson, 1986; Gundlach, 1982) and talking the talk of revision may be sufficient as an initial, emergent step into more conventional authorship.

Explaining Genre Distinctions

As the year progressed, Sarah's students began to participate more actively in the discussions around their writing. In example 2, Sarah uses Felipe's writing to launch a discussion about the differences between fiction and nonfiction.

Example 2

> *[Sarah is standing in front of the class, addressing the students while holding Felipe's piece.]*
>
> 1 *Sarah:* Felipe no está haciendo exactamente un cuento.
>
> 2 *Boy 1:* (***)
>
> 3 *Sarah:* Está escribiendo algo—algo que no es ficción; es sobre la ciudad de Chicago.
>
> 4 *Boy 2:* ¿Cómo?
>
> 5 *Sarah:* ¿Mande? ¿Cómo? Dice cómo es Chicago . . . es lo que está escribiendo. Eso no es un cuento; no es ficción.
>
> 6 *Boy 1:* Yo no quiero hacer eso.

[Sarah is interrupted by students telling her what they are writing about. There is lots of overlapping talk.]

7 Sarah: Umm, lo que estoy diciendo es que no tiene que ser un cuento. Si quieren hacer . . . escribir otra cosa, otro tipo de cosa, cómo son los animales, las plantas . . . otra cosa que no es—que no sea ficción. Kara, tú pronto vas a Puerto Rico. Podrías escribir cómo es Puerto Rico; hacer no exactamente un cuento sino una descripción, como hemos estado haciendo descripciones sobre monstruos, sobre tu persona, sobre tu casa; podrías hacer otro tipo de descripción sobre otra cosa, animales, o lugares, lo que sea. . . .

[Children talk about the "cuentos" they have written.]

8 Sarah: ¿Mario? ¿Entienden la diferencia entre ficción . . .

9 Boy 2: *[Completing Sarah's sentence.]* Y cuentos?

10 Sarah: Cuentos y cosas que no son cuentos, que no son ficción. ¿Qué entiendes, Vicente?

11 Vicente: Que no debo hacer cosas de ficción.

12 Sarah: No, no . . . no que no debes sino que—no que no tienes que hacer cosas de ficción. Puedes hacer cosas de ficción pero también puedes si quieres hacer cosas que no son ficción. ¿Qué es ficción, Alma? ¿Qué es ficción, Raúl? ¿Franco?

13 Franco: Como de eso de . . . de brujas.

14 Sarah: Okay, brujas sí, si escribes sobre brujas generalmente . . . generalmente es ficción. ¿Por qué? *[Addressing the class.]*

15 Boy 3: Porque es mentira . . .

16 Sarah: Mentira . . . o también se puede decir que no exactamente es mentira sino que no es real. ¿Okay? Una cosa que . . .

[There is an interruption as a child yells at Mario and Sarah needs to spend some time asking them to quiet down. Then she goes back to her discussion.]

17 Sarah: Una cosa que escribes sobre algo que no es real es, es como ficción. ¿Entiendes?

18 Franco: ¿Como básquetbol?

19 Sarah: ¿Mande?

20 Franco: ¿Como básquetbol?

21 Sarah: ¿Como básquetbol? Bueno, puedes hacer un cuento de ficción sobre básquetbol pero . . .

22 Children: (***)

23 Sarah: Un cuento, por ejemplo, de ficción es como diciendo

cosas que no, que realmente no han pasado. ¿Okay?
Inventado una historia.

24 *Children:* (***)

25 *Boy 1:* (***) cuento de básquetbol (***)

26 *Sarah:* ¡Claro! Un cuento sobre cualquier cosa, de básquetbol,
de pescados, todas esas cosas son reales. Solamente cuando
hacen cuentos, usan esas cosas para inventar una historia.
¿Entiendes, Vicente?

27 *Vicente:* Sí.

28 *Sarah:* ¿Bien? ¿Sí? ¿Pablo? *[He is raising his hand.]*

29 *Pablo:* ¿Cómo un pescado que juega básquetbol?

30 *Sarah:* ¿Cómo qué?

31 *Pablo:* ¿Un pescado que juega básquetbol?

32 *Sarah:* Bueno, eso sería como muy, muy irreal, como fantasía.
Ficción no tiene que ser fantasía. Ficción puede ser un niño
jugando básquetbol; o un hombre, o una mujer jugando
básquetbol. . . . Ficción no tiene que ser fantasía, Pablo.
¿Okay? Solamente la diferencia entre ficción y fantasía es
que—si no es ficción, tiene que haber pasado . . . haber
pasado en la vida . . . umm, por ejemplo, una descripción
sobre la vida de Michael Jordan es una historia sobre su
vida, es real. ¿Okay? Pero si tú quieres escribir un cuento
sobre . . .

33 *Boy 1:* ¿Michael Jordan?

34 *Sarah:* Sobre tu—siendo una estrella de básquetbol, no sería
real . . .

35 *Children:* (***)

36 *Sarah:* Sería algo que estás creando en tu imaginación.

37 *Pablo:* (***) pero (***) puede ser real.

38 *Sarah:* Puede ser en el futuro. *[Turning to Franco.]* Franco, me
molesta que estés haciendo ruido! *[Returning to the class.]*
Puede ser real en el futuro pero ahorita no es real. ¿Okay?
Es algo que estás imaginando, Pablo, para escribir como un
cuento. ¿Okay? ¿Felipe?

39 *Felipe:* Maestra, lo que escribí ¿Qué es? *[Pointing to his piece,
which Sarah is holding up.]*

40 *Sarah:* ¿Esto? Lo que estás escribiendo, algo sobre Chicago,
de cómo es Chicago en tus ojos, verdad? ¿Es algo real o
irreal?

41 *Children:* Algo . . . real.

42 *Sarah:* Real? Sí . . . es algo muy real . . . estás haciendo como
un librito explicando cómo es la ciudad . . .

43 *Felipe: [Interrupting]* Como (***).

44 *Sarah:* No estás inventando una ciudad. ¿Verdad? Entonces es real, no es ficción. ¿De acuerdo? *[To the entire class]* ¿Otras preguntas?

Translation

[Sarah is standing in front of the class, addressing the students while holding Felipe's piece.]

1 *Sarah:* Felipe is not writing a story, exactly.

2 *Boy 1:* (***)

3 *Sarah:* He is writing something—something that is not fiction; it's about the city of Chicago.

4 *Boy 2:* What?

5 *Sarah:* Pardon? What? He tells what Chicago is like . . . that's what he is writing. That's not a story; it's not fiction.

6 *Boy 2:* I don't want to do that.

[Sarah is interrupted by students telling her what they are writing about. There is lots of overlapping talk.]

7 *Sarah:* Umm, what I'm saying is that it does not need to be a story. If you want to do . . . write something else, other type of thing, what are animals like, plants . . . something else that is not—that would not be fiction. Kara, you are going to Puerto Rico soon. You could write about what Puerto Rico is like; write not exactly a story but a description, like we have been doing descriptions about monsters, about yourself, about your house; you could do a description about something else, animals, or other places, whatever. . . .

[Children talk about the stories they have written.]

8 *Sarah:* Mario? Do you understand the difference between fiction . . .

9 *Boy 2: [Completing Sarah's sentence.]* And stories?

10 *Sarah:* Stories and things that are not stories, that are not fiction. What did you understand, Vicente?

11 *Vicente:* That I should not do fiction things.

12 *Sarah:* No, no . . . not that you shouldn't, but—it's not that you shouldn't do fictional things. You can do fiction things, but also, if you want, you can do things that are not fiction. What's fiction, Alma? What's fiction, Raúl? Franco?

13 *Franco:* Like that about . . . about witches.

14 *Sarah:* Okay, witches yes, if you write about witches, in general . . . in general it's fiction. Why? *[Addressing the class.]*

15 *Boy 3:* Because it's a lie . . .

16 *Sarah:* A lie . . . or we can also say that it is not exactly a lie but it is not real, okay? Something that . . .

[There is an interruption as a child yells at Mario and Sarah needs to spend some time asking them to quiet down. Then she goes back to her discussion.]

17 *Sarah:* Something that you write about something that is not real, it's like fiction. Do you understand?

18 *Franco:* Like basketball?

19 *Sarah:* Pardon?

20 *Franco:* Like basketball?

21 *Sarah:* Like basketball? Well, you can make a fiction story about basketball but . . .

22 *Children:* (***)

23 *Sarah:* A fiction story, for example, it's like saying things that, that have not really happened, okay? Making up, a story.

24 *Children:* (***)

25 *Boy 1:* (***) basketball story (***).

26 *Sarah:* Right! A story about anything, about basketball, about fish, all those are real things. It's only that when you write stories, you use those things to make up a story. Do you understand what I am saying?

27 *Vicente:* Yes.

28 *Sarah:* Good. Yes? Pablo? *[He is raising his hand.]*

29 *Pablo:* Like a fish that plays basketball?

30 *Sarah:* Like what?

31 *Pablo:* A fish that plays basketball?

32 *Sarah:* Well, that would be like very, very unreal, like fantasy. Fiction does not have to be fantasy. Fiction can be a boy playing basketball; or a man, or a woman playing basketball. Fiction does not have to be fantasy, Pablo, okay? It's only that the difference between fiction and fantasy is that— if it's not fiction, it has to have happened . . . have happened in real life. . . . Umm, for example, a description on Michael Jordan's life is a *story* about his life, it's real, okay? But if you want to write a story about . . .

33 *Boy 1:* Michael Jordan?

34 *Sarah:* About you . . . being a basketball star, that wouldn't be real . . .

35 *Children:* (***)

36 *Sarah:* It would be something that you are creating in your
   imagination.

37 *Pablo:* (***) but (***) it can be real.

38 *Sarah:* It can be in the future. *[Turning to Franco.]* Franco, it
   bothers me that you are making noise! *[Returning to the
   class.]* It can be real in the future but now it is not real, okay?
   It is something that you are imagining, Pablo, to write as a
   story, okay? Felipe?

39 *Felipe:* Teacher, that what I wrote, what is it? *[Pointing to his
   piece, which Sarah is holding up.]*

40 *Sarah:* This? What you are writing, something about Chicago, about what Chicago is like in your eyes, true? Is it
   something real or unreal?

41 *Children:* Something . . . real.

42 *Sarah:* Real? Yes . . . it's something very real . . . you're
   making like a flyer explaining what the city is like . . .

43 *Felipe:* *[Interrupting]* Like (***).

44 *Sarah:* You are not making up a city, true? Then it's real, it's
   not fiction. All right? *[To the entire class.]* Other questions?

(Field notes, 06/02/95)

The above conversation shows how Sarah would respond to the
children's initiations by using their comments to extend their budding
understandings (Wells, 1986; Wells & Chang-Wells, 1992). Sarah used
Felipe's text on Chicago (lines 3 and 5) and other students' ideas about
writing on basketball, Michael Jordan, and witches to be explicit about
the distinction between fictional and informational writing. She built
upon their prior work on "descriptions" and provided other possible
informational topics, such as Puerto Rico for Kara (line 7). In her responses, Sarah provided additional information that clarified some of
the children's current ideas, as was the case when she told them about
the difference between fantasy and realistic fiction (line 30), or when
she explained that writing about witches is generally considered a work
of fiction (line 14). The students eagerly participated, venturing possible
answers even when, as illustrated by Felipe's remark near the end of
the discussion (line 39), they were not fully sure of how Sarah's explanations applied to their own writing.

But collaborative classroom discussions, because they are not
scripted, can become more complicated than teachers have anticipated,
precisely because they are spontaneous. When Sarah responds to Pablo's
comment about a fish playing basketball (line 31), she moves into an

apparent unplanned discussion of the differences between fiction and fantasy. Her explanation becomes somewhat tangled when she talks about what could happen in *real life,* and what is *very, very unreal* (line 32). The discussion might have also been confounded by Sarah's use of the word "story" to describe both nonfiction and fiction: ". . . a description of Michael Jordan's life is a *story* about his life, it's real. . . . But, if you want to write a *story* about . . . you being a basketball star, that wouldn't be real" (lines 32 and 34).

Nevertheless, example 2 shows how much classroom talk was co-constructed. Jointly, Sarah and the students examined a set of very implicit ideas that writers often apply as they compose different kinds of texts. Sarah was able to build upon the students' genre conceptions, however partial they were, by helping them consider new aspects of the fiction/nonfiction differentiation. She was successful in helping her students see the potential and possibilities of making meaning.

Summary

Sarah's inquiry shows how difficult it can be to realize the apprenticeship perspective in literacy learning. Finding the right measure of explanation is not always easy. Meeting students at their developmental levels to provide the right amount of assistance at the right time is a complex, multifaceted endeavor. Not all attempted scaffolds work, and they need to be constantly readjusted if they are to be truly collaborative. Bringing the writing process into practice in the reality of the classroom requires constant retooling (Lensmire, 1994; Sudol & Sudol, 1991, 1995). And, certain aspects of written language learning can be made explicit more easily than others. But Sarah's teaching also illustrates the power of classroom talk as a tool for literacy instruction. It demonstrates that it is possible to include skill instruction in the context of a meaning-centered approach to the teaching of literacy.

All children are likely to benefit from instructional strategies like the ones that Sarah used to promote epistemic literacy engagements. The teaching described here, however, is quite different from what is usually provided for low-socioeconomic and ethnic-minority children. Too frequently, students' existing knowledge bases are not valued or considered in their literacy instruction (Moll & González, 1994), and, as a result, they experience unchallenging, rote learning (Bartolomé, 1994). Sarah's students certainly had the cognitive and the linguistic resources to become literate, to understand, and to use writing meaningfully.

STRATEGY: A LOOK AT WRITING CONFERENCES

Editors' Note: In this excerpt, Don Graves offers general guidance for thinking about writing conferences.

The Writing Conference

The focal point for developing self-critical powers in the young writer is the writing conference. The conference, depending on the developmental level of the child, may be as often as every five days, or every ten days. The reactive writer needs more frequent interviews and is often helped best while he is actually engaged in the first two phases of the writing process. Sometimes the teacher may be able to be of assistance when the child has just finished writing, through questions and reactions during the postcomposing phase. Conferences usually do not last more than five to ten minutes and are easily scheduled when children are engaged in other self-directed activities.

How are writing conferences conducted with children? The teacher elicits information from children, rather than issues directives about errors on their papers. This is done for two reasons. First, children need to hear themselves offering opinions. They gain a sense of voice by first hearing themselves express ideas and opinions orally. This is particularly true if the teacher is a good listener who actively enables children to express their thoughts. Secondly, the teacher needs to gain a sense of children's logical thinking and interests. This can only come from the words of the children. Greg's statement, "The teacher likes the words, not the pictures, but I like the pictures," provided valuable insights into Greg's composing priorities.

What factors in the writing process need to be considered during conferences with the young writer? The following are examples of questions and procedures used in child conferences:

Factor	Conference Procedure
Voice	"You seem to know a lot about fashion. How did you decide what outfit your doll would wear? . . . How was that made? I didn't know that you knew this much about clothes. Are there some clothes you especially like to wear for different times . . .

▶

	like parties . . . going to school . . . to visit someone special?"
A Need for More Specifics	"What happened after the man won the race? Good. I would be interested in reading what happened."
	"You say he had an accident in the race. What happened to the car? What did the front fender and headlight look like after it hit the guard rail? Here are some words you just used in telling me about the accident. Would you like to use them?"
	"I am going to close my eyes. Can you tell me some words that will help me get a picture of what that racing car looks like?"
Language and Organization	"Which word do you like best? Do you have some words here you have never used before?"
	"Is there a sentence here that seems to say what you wanted to say more than any other?"
	"Do you think this sentence ought to come after this one? Read it out loud and tell me what you think."
	"You have two thoughts in this sentence. Read it out loud and tell me where the first one ends."
Progress and Change	"Let's look in your folder here. Do you see any changes between this paper you wrote last December and the one you have just completed? Where do you feel you have improved? What are some of the things that haven't improved, yet you still wish were better? Do you think your handwriting has improved?"
Audience Sense	"Which paper do you think is your best? I agree. Do you think it is good enough to go into the class collection? Do you want it to go there? Are there some things you would change in this paper, to make it your *very best*? Who are some of the people in this room who would be interested in reading this? Would you like to share it with them? Will they be able to read it?"

These questions will respond to a range of child differences to help both the reactive and the reflective writer. The teacher will need to be sensitive to the degree of abstraction and amount of reflectiveness contained in each question, the children's interest in their own work,

▶

and sensitivity to their own changes as writers. The questions are intended to develop children's senses of authority and voice, as well as to provide questions they will ask when writing alone.

When children are involved in individual conferences from the beginning, led to discover strengths and weaknesses in their own communication, it is not long before they begin to tell *us* what is needed to make their writing a stronger communication. When this point has been reached, we know the issue of dependency has been removed; indeed, the entire writing welfare issue has been put behind us. We know the writing process is where it belongs in the first place, in the hands of the child. (pp. 649–651)

Source: Graves, D. H. (1976). Let's get rid of the welfare mess in the teaching of writing. *Language Arts, 53*(6), 645–651.

REFLECTION: WRITING INSTRUCTION MUST BE EMBEDDED IN SOCIAL CONTEXTS

Editors' Note: This excerpt from Piazza and Tomlinson reinforces a major finding of Anne Haas Dyson's research: Writing is a fundamentally social act; therefore, writing instruction needs to be embedded in social contexts.

———————— ✎ ————————

Children who engage in social interactions during drafting learn fundamental principles of how writing works. Through face-to-face interactions, they come to understand that writing serves many functions, that writing is aimed at, and therefore must be sensitive to, a speech community (audience), and that relationships exist between speaking and writing. (p. 155)

Source: Piazza, C. L., & Tomlinson, C. M. (1985). A concert of writers. *Language Arts, 62*(2), 150–158.

REFLECTION: THE MEANING OF "DECONTEXTUALIZED" WRITING EXERCISES

Editors' Note: Fu and Townsend suggest that decontextualized drills are based both on behaviorist assumptions about learning and on assumptions about the abilities of learners.

———❧———

Language is an act of creative construction, and when we remove personal purpose and meaning from its expression, we lose language itself. Writing is creative when it has real purpose to the writer and when it draws on a child's inner resources and imagination. . . . Though we need to help students to learn how to present information clearly and in a logical sequence, an expository-writing assignment could be more challenging, drawing on students' personal interests and curiosity. . . . Decontextualized exercises demonstrate a lack of confidence in children's literacy abilities (and may even make school tasks tremendously difficult for some students), yet these kinds of activities persist despite research that has consistently documented children's extraordinary genius in learning to use language for a wide variety of purposes *before* entering school. (p. 409)

Source: Fu, D., & Townsend, J. S. (1999). "Serious" learning: Language lost. *Language Arts, 76*(5), 404–411.

17 The Writer's Toolbox: Five Tools for Active Revision Instruction

Laura Harper

Editors' Text: The best writers may be those people who are willing to struggle with a text over a period of time. These people recognize that the key to good writing is revision. Laura Harper offers a set of "tools" to help teachers of writing teach students about revision.

> Revision is body work, overhaul
> Ratcheting straight the frame
> Replacing whole systems and panels
> Rummaging heaps of the maimed.
> With blowtorch and old rubber hammer
> Pound and pull, bend, use your 'bar
> Salvage takes sweat but it pays well
> (Though never rule out a new car.)
> —Dethier, 1994, p. 43

I used to think of my classroom as a workshop. I set it up so that my seventh graders had the tools they needed to get their jobs done. Instead of the hammers, nails, and drills of a traditional workshop, I provided a trunk full of writing supplies—paper, markers, reference books, and stationery. Instead of blueprints, lumber, and scrap metal, I organized a file cabinet holding brainstorming lists and drafts and writing logs. Instead of being filled with the sounds of grinding and hammering, this workshop was filled with pencils scratching, fingers typing, and students conferring. "Functional," I thought as I looked around the room. I was proud that my students had all the tools they needed for effective writing.

Yet, two years after setting up the writing workshop, I had a nagging feeling that some of the most important "tools" for writing were missing. Yes, my students had choices. They had time. Certainly, they had the physical tools they needed. Yet, their final drafts and the steps

---

This essay appeared in *Language Arts* 74.3 (1997) on pages 193–200.

they took to write them suggested that they lacked some basic tools. My students didn't know *how* to revise.

Revision seems like a natural process in books such as Nancie Atwell's (1987) *In the Middle* and Linda Rief's (1992) *Seeking Diversity*. These books suggest that, if you ask good questions during conferences and provide plenty of time for writing, students will be able to re-see their drafts and, thus, revise. I discovered, however, that student conference partners didn't hear or couldn't articulate the weaknesses in each others' writings. If a partner did find something that needed work, the writer most often would simply add or delete a couple of words and pronounce the revision a success. After years of just being told "Revise!" without further explanation, my students had become furtive recopiers, adding a few words here and there and using neater handwriting to revise their drafts.

In addition, my students' revision difficulties were compounded by other language factors. Two-thirds of them came from limited English backgrounds—the majority speaking Spanish as a first language, with most of the other students from Native American homes. Most of my students lived in poverty, with three-fourths receiving free or reduced lunches. In addition, with parents working seasonally in agriculture, many of my students were migrant, spending time each year traveling south to Mexico and back. As a result, they wrote and read significantly below grade level. They had limited vocabularies and ways of expressing themselves in English. They had almost no natural "ear" for how English should sound.

Try only to explain your *own* revision process, and it quickly becomes clear why it is a difficult thing to teach, even to the most able students. Revision is, according to Donald Murray (1978), "one of the writing skills least researched, least examined, least understood, and— usually—least taught" (p. 85). My students, like the inexperienced writers studied by Nancy Sommers (1980), "understood the revision process as a rewording activity" (p. 381). In addition to their limited English backgrounds, they "lacked . . . a set of strategies to help them identify the 'something larger' that they sensed was wrong" in their writing (p. 383). My students needed toolboxes full of strategies, or "tools," with which to pound, saw, drill, and otherwise rebuild their writing.

What should a Writer's Toolbox do for writers? Well, consider what makes toolboxes so valuable to carpenters or mechanics. First, toolboxes keep tools immediately accessible. Carpenters or mechanics can grab their hammers or wrenches instantly and put them to quick use. A Writer's Toolbox must do the same. I wanted my students to have quick access to revision options and not waste time in needless mental blocks or endless rewordings. Second, toolboxes provide carpenters and mechanics with flexibility. They have a range of tools from which to choose, tools appropriate to each job. Likewise, I wanted our toolboxes to contain a range of choices, or techniques, to expand my students' flexibility in making revisions.

Fortunately, I found a source for these tools. During our reading workshop time, I read Barry Lane's (1993) *After the End,* and I was eager to try some of his revision ideas with my students. I gave each of them a five-by-eight-inch manila envelope that would serve as a "toolbox" and stay in each student's writing folder. During the following six weeks, we filled the toolboxes with five of Lane's revision "tools": Questions, Snapshots, Thoughtshots, Exploding a Moment, and Making a Scene.

Questions

When I became engaged to be married, my students cross-examined me for all the details. I took this to be the perfect way to introduce our first tool, or revising technique, called Questions. I stood at the front of the room and said, "Last month, my boyfriend asked me to marry him." I paused and looked around the room. "Any questions?"

"Where were you?" yelled Erin, probably surprised by the opportunity to quiz me about my life outside of school.

"How did he ask?" asked Jamie, followed by giggles from classmates.

"How did you feel?" called Melanie, with more giggles.

I quickly scrawled the questions on the board until I was out of room. When I finished, one curious student ventured, "Are you really going to answer these?"

I stalled. Before I would answer their questions, I said I wanted them to try Questions themselves. I asked them to pair up, read aloud the drafts of writing they were currently working on, and then write down any questions they had as they listened. There was only one rule: No yes/no questions allowed. One student, Monica, was asked by her partner how she felt when she realized that her house had been robbed. Andrew's partner asked him to tell more about the setting of his story, a favorite swimming hole. Elena's partner asked what made Elena's aunt, who had recently passed away, so special. Then, the students selected the most appealing questions about their drafts and freewrote on them.

In her first draft, Elena listed a few of the things she and her aunt liked doing together. She said that her aunt "had a baby boy named Anthony," and went on to write: "When my brothers would fall asleep, after playing with Anthony and his toys, Angie and I would go in the kitchen and make cookies."

After our Questions session, Elena decided to describe a specific time when she helped her aunt take care of Anthony:

> As I was pushing Anthony in his rocker, his short brown hair blew in the breeze. He was laughing and clapping his hands. "Mama!" he called. As I walked to put him down, he hugged me with his hands. They looked like his mother's. I put his socks on and his pants. His chubby legs moved around in the air.

The Questions technique not only allowed Elena to add a few paragraphs in response to her partner's questions, but more importantly, it prompted her to rethink her story. Her first draft, which had been a rather impersonal expository piece explaining her sadness at her aunt's death, evolved into a narrative that vividly portrayed their close relationship.

While revising, Elena experienced what Murray (1978) refers to as "a process of discovery." He asserts that "writers much of the time don't know what they are going to write . . . [and they] use language as a tool of exploration to see beyond what they know" (p. 90). The Questions technique reinforces this idea, especially for students writing in non-native languages. It slows the writing process so that new angles and memories can be expressed bit by bit. It also can be used to push drafts in new directions as new discoveries are made.

I wanted my students to have some way to keep this revision technique handy, just as carpenters keep their tools ready for quick access. I knew that, for middle schoolers, simply putting the technique in their notes wouldn't be enough. The "tool" would grow rusty with disuse and would eventually be lost. They, like the twelfth graders observed by Janet Emig (1971), needed a way to "translate an abstract directive . . . into a set of behaviors" (p. 99). Since most of my students were non-native users of English, creating "scaffolding," or temporary structures for building language skills, was especially important in the development of their English (Boyle & Peregoy, 1990). I wanted them to have something tangible—like a manipulative in mathematics—so they could remember the steps of the technique and begin to use them on their own. We needed to make actual Questions "tools" to put inside our toolboxes. To that end, we brainstormed about the technique's basic steps and then wrote them on index cards. Each student put a Questions index card, or tool, in his or her Writer's Toolbox, or manila envelope, which then went into his or her writing folder.

Finally, to save time for me as well as to make the technique easier for my students to use, I wanted us to have a shorthand with which we could communicate about our revisions. I wanted us, for example, to be able to jot notes to each other recommending that certain tools be used in certain places. As Lane (1993) notes, "though each writer's process is different, a shared language helps writers . . . to gain control" of the writing process. To that end, we created a symbol for the Questions technique, a fat question mark with a circle around it. Instead of writing a lengthy comment such as, "Try having a conference on this passage to see if you can get some more information," we could simply draw the fat question mark symbol on a draft. The writer would know at a glance to try a Questions conference. Peer conferences and teacher conferences, both crucial in helping non-native English speakers gain confidence in their writing (Mendoca & Johnson, 1994; Zhang, 1995), became more focused. Having created and practiced using our first tool, we were ready to move on.

Snapshots

I wish I had a nickel for every time I scrawled "Describe" or "Explain" or "Give more detail" next to an imprecise sentence in my students' writing. To double my earnings, I wish I had a nickel for every time my students, having read my scrawled comments, simply added a word or two, believing they had done what I had asked. Sentences such as "I walked into my bedroom" actually became worse after complying with my margin comments, turning into "I walked into my big, blue, full, messy bedroom." Although it is true that my students *did* need to do better jobs describing, explaining, and giving more detail, my suggestions did not help them discover the kinds of details that would bring their stories to life.

Information is critical to the revision process. During revision, writers need ways to "gather new information or to return to their inventory of information and draw on it" (Murray, 1978, p. 93). They need ways to re-enter their stories and actually "see characters walking or hear characters speaking" (Murray, 1978, p. 90). Like William Faulkner, they must be able to "trot along behind [their characters] with paper and pencil" (Murray, 1978, p. 101).

The Snapshot, our second revision tool, allows writers to do these things. It forces them to focus on close, physical detail and move from describing "preconceived thoughts and feelings to an objective reality that's both more mysterious and compelling" (Lane, 1993, p. 37). In other words, Snapshots provide a structure for the very thing we incessantly implore our students to do: Show, don't tell.

By way of introducing my students to the tool, we first looked for some good descriptions by authors we were reading, from Gary Soto to Gary Paulsen. I offered an excerpt from *Little House in the Big Woods* (Wilder, 1989), which I had found in Lane's (1993) description of Snapshots:

> Ma kissed them both, and tucked the covers in around them. They lay there awhile, looking at Ma's smooth, parted hair and her hands busy with sewing in the lamplight. Her needle made little clicking sounds against her thimble and then the thread went softly, swish! through the pretty calico that Pa had traded furs for. (p. 33)

I asked my students to notice how Wilder, as she describes Ma's sewing, is freezing the action and painting "boxes within boxes" of descriptions (Lane, 1993, p. 33). I wanted to give them a visual representation of how Wilder had accomplished this. In a box the size of a Polaroid snapshot, we drew the scene described, including the lamp, Ma, and the kids in bed. Then, in a second box the same size, I drew a "zoomed in" picture of the same scene, but with only Ma, letting her figure fill the entire frame. As a result, she was larger, and it was possible to see details of her hair and her sewing. Last, in a third box the same size, I drew only Ma's hands, zooming in on the details of the needle and thimble, and even the design of the calico fabric, so that they became clearer.

Students practiced by taking Snapshots of nearby classmates. They either wrote a description of what they saw or drew a picture from which they were then able to write. After taking Snapshots, they were ready to try them in their current drafts. Students paired up and began looking for places in their partners' writing where they had trouble visualizing what was going on. The partners marked three or four of these places with our symbol for Snapshots, a small outline of a camera.

During one Snapshot conference, Amber's partner told her to add a Snapshot to a scene in which Amber is getting a new punk haircut. Amber had written in her original draft: "The chair rumpled as I wiggled. The razor buzzed along my neck. I could feel the hair falling, and I didn't exactly want it to anymore." She began by unlocking more of the memories she had of this scene and finding places for them in her story. First, she drew a picture of the scene at the exact moment the haircut began, with the action frozen. In a box on her paper, she sketched herself nervously seated in a barber's chair. Then, she wrote a paragraph describing what she saw and what the picture helped her remember. Under the drawing, she described the scene:

> I sat there squirming, the blue plastic of the chair crumpled and cracked under me. The tightness of all the clips and hair ties made my head throb. I could hear the razor buzzing. I couldn't believe I was doing this.

Next, Amber picked a part of the picture she thought would be interesting to zoom in on. She chose her head as it was being shaved on one side. In another box, she drew a second picture, one that zoomed in on her head so that it nearly filled the entire box. Then, Amber wrote a second paragraph, describing what she could see in her second drawing. Under this box, she wrote what she saw:

> I felt my hair falling to my shoulders, then to the floor. The razor vibrated behind my right ear, making me giggle. I tried as hard a I could not to move. I didn't want her to cut me.

Finally, Amber zoomed in one last time. She selected the part of her second picture that was the most interesting to her, and, with the action frozen, zoomed in on it in a third picture. She took an almost microscopic perspective, sketching the bristly hairs that remained on her head. Under this third box, she described the memories that the drawing triggered:

> The tiny bristles left behind itched, but I didn't dare scratch them. The beautician still had the left side to shave. As the razor pulled away from my head, I scrunched my neck back. The bristles jabbed into my skin, and I felt a tear come to my eye. What if she messed it all up? It would be impossible to grow back.

Through the Snapshot technique, Amber discovered things about her story that she thought she had forgotten. Instead of being commanded to "Describe more" or "Be more specific," she was given a strategy by which to recreate the experience. Having been given a strategy instead of an abstract comment, she elaborated more on physical sensations, such as the "tightness of all the clips and hair ties," as well as on her own emotional state. Amber *showed* what it was like to be getting this drastic haircut, instead of only *telling* about it. Like Robert Frost, she experienced the "surprise of remembering something I didn't know I knew" (as quoted in Murray, 1978, p. 101).

After completing our Snapshots and finding places for them in our drafts, we made our Snapshot tool. We brainstormed about the basic steps of drawing and then writing the Snapshot. Whenever we are reading a draft and have trouble picturing a character or a setting in our minds, we simply draw a small camera in that spot, confident that the writer will know how to fix the problem. This symbol is probably our most frequently used.

Thoughtshots

Helping students create vivid descriptions of the concrete stuff of their stories is challenging. However, this challenge pales in comparison to the difficulty my students had in portraying the internal landscapes of their characters. They struggle with describing how their characters feel and what their characters think. At best, my students resort to simply telling. They write statements like "He felt confused" or "She was mad" or "I couldn't wait." At worst, they leave out their characters' thoughts and feelings completely, resulting in stories populated with unthinking robots. Indeed, characters in middle school students' writing often "exist merely to serve the plot" with no attention given to their "internal reflection" (Graves, 1994, pp. 288–289). No wonder realistic characters are so rare in their writing. Thoughtshots, our third tool, give writers ways to move inside their characters and show what their characters are feeling.

To get a better understanding of how professional authors move inside their characters, my students and I turned to our novels. We flipped through examples from our independent reading as well as from books like *Walk Two Moons* (Creech, 1994), *Fallen Angels* (Myers, 1988), and *Catherine, Called Birdy* (Cushman, 1994). We listed three basic things that authors do to portray the internal reflections of their characters: (1) characters have flashbacks, triggering their memories of related events or causes; (2) characters have what we called "flashforwards," predicting the outcomes of their actions and anticipating what people will say and think; and (3) characters have what we called "brain arguments," debating with themselves about what is going on and what they should do about it.

Once again, I asked my students to read their current drafts aloud to their partners and look for three or four places where they would like to know what the characters were thinking. Then, the students set to work, choosing one such place and giving characters flashbacks, flashforwards, and brain arguments.

Maria's story was about an incident that happened while she babysat her brother. He decided to fry the legs of a frog he had caught in the backyard, a tense situation for any babysitter. Her first draft contained only one line of thoughts or feelings: "I was bored." Maria's partner suggested that she write a Thoughtshot to describe what it was like when her parents came home. Maria began with a flashforward:

> I heard the rattling of a car engine coming closer to our house. Could it be my parents? I thought. I could picture my mom's face in my mind when she sees that we have two frogs in the kitchen. I know she'll throw away the pans and dishes we used. I hope they know it was all my brother's fault.

Then, she added a flashback:

> I remember when my brother and I had made my mom a mud cake for her birthday. She had thought it was real chocolate, probably because we had put real candles on it. It wasn't long before she found out it was mud, after all. Why don't I ever say anything against my brother's ideas?

Last, Maria wrote a brain argument, showing the way she argued with herself about what to do to stay out of trouble:

> I started feeling the sweat on my hands when the door shut. "Quick, in my room," my brother whispered. "Should I stay where I am or hide with my brother?" I asked myself. Why should I leave if I didn't do anything bad? I'm getting out of here. Before I knew it, I was in my brother's room leaning against the door.

By adding Thoughtshots to her story, Maria not only lets her readers know what her characters are thinking but also does some rather sophisticated characterization. From these brief paragraphs, we get both a history of this brother-sister relationship as well as a glimpse of Maria's desire to be seen as "good." This characterization was something Maria did with little difficulty once she was given a strategy, essentially a set of behaviors, rather than an abstract command to "develop these characters."

To keep this strategy easily accessible, we discussed and wrote the steps for writing Thoughtshots on index cards and put them in our toolboxes. We then decided on the thought bubble as our symbol, our shorthand way of saying, "I'd like to know what this character is thinking right here. Let me inside!"

Exploding a Moment

"Time to the writer is like play dough in the hands of a toddler" (Lane, 1993, p. 65). Writers are in control of time in their stories, and they can shape it according to their purposes. Yet, my students were not able to stretch out the exciting moments of their stories. They rushed through climactic events—motorcycle crashes, high-dive plunges, and romantic advances—in a matter of one or two sentences. Their stories more than lacked suspense. Major life events in their stories were almost laughable because of the cursory treatment they received. Exploding a Moment makes writers the masters of time in their stories. It links together Snapshots and Thoughtshots by using action, thus allowing writers to stretch the exciting seconds of their stories into what seems like hours, creating suspense for the reader to savor.

I brought my kitchen timer to school when I introduced the Exploding a Moment tool. I read aloud an excerpt from *The Chosen* (Potok, 1967), one paragraph at a time, getting students to time the length of each one. We then looked at what actually happened in each paragraph—a wind-up, a pitch, a return throw from the catcher, a second pitch, and, finally, a hit. While the entire action in *real time* probably took less than two minutes, the *story time* took twice as long.

The students identified the exciting moments, including the time preceding, during, or subsequent to the exciting moments, in their own drafts. Salvador picked the moment when he was being chased by a dog; Israel, the few seconds before he gave a girl a Valentine present; and Felicia, the instant when she knew she was locked in the trunk of a car. They estimated how long these exciting moments lasted in real time. Then, they read the exciting moments in their drafts to determine the story time. Most students found that, instead of making their exciting moments last as long as they did in real life, they actually were cutting them to less than one-tenth the actual time. The students inserted the symbol for the Exploding a Moment technique—a stick of dynamite—into these scenes.

Felicia was writing a story about a time, during an especially aggressive game of hide-and-seek, when she had gotten locked in the trunk of a car. In an early draft, she told the story in an abbreviated way: "I was playing hide and seek, and I thought I would hide in the trunk of a white car." However, by Exploding a Moment, she broke this moment down into smaller actions. She realized there were actually four events that she had been lumping together: One, she climbed into the trunk; two, she pulled the trunk almost closed; three, her brother pushed the trunk closed; and, four, Felicia kicked and screamed to be let out. Now, Felicia wanted to explode the moment by using these four actions as the main ideas for three paragraphs and by adding Snapshots and Thoughtshots to each one.

In her first paragraph, Felicia paced herself and described only her first action: her entry into the trunk. She blended with this single action some fragments of Snapshots and Thoughtshots:

> I crawled into the trunk, onto the hard but padded floor. I looked
> to see if he was there. I glanced back at the door. As soon as I saw
> him coming, my face pinched into a worried frown. I slowly lay
> down. I grabbed the steel white rim of the trunk and pulled on it
> until it reached the tip top of the lock. I could see a little, just
> enough to peak. It looked like a line of light between the trunk
> door and the car.

Already, Felicia had created more suspense, taking the reader inside the
trunk with her. She then showed, in slow motion, the next action, again
blended with mini-Snapshots and Thoughtshots:

> "Where is he?" I asked myself. I could no longer see through the
> small opening of light that had come into the trunk. It was com-
> pletely silent. No one was to be seen. I looked out, raising the
> trunk lid a little. He sneaked around, looked right at me, eyeball
> to eyeball, and slammed the door shut. I pushed. I kept on push-
> ing. It was locked!

Finally, Felicia moved to the final action, her response, which was made
more vivid by including her thoughts and some physical details:

> I panicked. "Open this trunk right now!" I said. I kicked at the
> door. How could he open it, though? I asked myself. He didn't
> have the keys. I started to feel sweat roll down my body. I kicked
> and kicked and kicked. What could I do? All I could do was wait.
> I felt bruises forming, and my legs started to sting. It was dark,
> and I just lay there. I was burned out with no energy left. It was
> all silent.

This passage of Felicia's story, which originally could be skimmed over,
if not skipped entirely, was expanded into three suspenseful paragraphs.

Exploding a Moment allows students to tell important parts of
their stories in slow motion, and, in the process, it helps them remember. "One unexplored skill which might help our understanding of . . .
revision," suggests Murray (1978), "is the writer's use of memory" (p.
95). He theorizes that writing actually "unlocks information stored in
the brain" (p. 95). Exploding a Moment allows us to access information
locked in the brain, resulting in both more descriptive writing on the
part of the author and more suspenseful entertainment for the reader.

Making a Scene

At the root level, revision means "to re-see." According to Sommers
(1980), inexperienced writers frequently have an "inability to 're-view'
their work again . . . with different eyes" (p. 382). Furthermore, non-

native English speakers, with which my classroom was filled, need additional help remembering that their drafts are temporary, that they can make extensive changes to their writing without focusing on conventions (Diamond & Moore, 1995). Our fifth revision tool, Making a Scene, works as a diagnostic tool that helps students see their writing through new eyes. Like a mechanic's lift, this tool allows students to take a better look at their writing and see if it is balanced.

Many students only use one element of narrative writing: action. Their stories read like laundry lists of things their characters did. Few student writers and conference partners know when a piece of writing needs more dialogue or description or internal reflection to flesh out the action in the story. The Making a Scene tool helps students evaluate their drafts for the four main ingredients of narrative writing—action, dialogue, Snapshots, and Thoughtshots—and allows them to see where and how often they used each type. We began by designating one marker color for each main ingredient in narrative writing: blue for action, yellow for dialogue, red for Snapshots (here being used to include almost any physical description), and purple for Thoughtshots (or internal description). The students then traded drafts and underlined every line in one of the four colors. Some drafts were almost completely underlined in blue; others had no yellow; others had huge blocks of red; but only a few drafts had a rainbow of colors. In case the colors didn't get the message across boldly enough, we also tallied the percentages of each type of writing in the drafts. Suddenly, my students could "re-see" their drafts.

Monica, writing about the robbery of her house, saw that she needed to add more dialogue and action to her story. Nearly two-thirds of her story was Snapshots; 17 percent was Thoughtshots; 14 percent action; and a mere 2 percent dialogue. Angelica's story about her family's recent move was overloaded with action at the expense of physical detail: 44 percent of her story was action; 22 percent Thoughtshots; 18 percent dialogue; and only 6 percent Snapshots. Even students who had balanced the elements of their writing more proportionally could "see" areas of their drafts where they could better blend the elements, mixing thoughts with descriptions, combining dialogue with action. With the evidence in front of them, my students had reasons to revise and saw possibilities for doing so. Furthermore, Making a Scene helps students as they draft new stories. They realize the importance of drawing from all four elements of narrative writing in order to create balanced scenes.

Our symbol for Making a Scene is the black and white board that a movie director clicks shut when crying, "Action!" Placed in our toolbox, it became our fifth tool for revising.

Conclusion

Like the toolboxes of any skilled craftsperson, the Writer's Toolboxes give my students a set of easily accessible options for getting their jobs done. As a result, my room works more like my vision of a real writing workshop. However, I still have a few nagging questions. First of all, what other tools might be added to my students' toolboxes? For example, what tools work well in other genres, such as expository or persuasive writing? What tools might work better with students with other language backgrounds? Second, I wonder what methods are most effective in teaching these revision techniques. Is it important, as one group of students advised me, to perform all of these techniques on one piece of writing? Would it be more effective to scatter these throughout the year? Third, and most importantly, what effect does the toolbox have on related areas of the reading and writing workshop? How do these tools change students' approaches to conferencing, to reading, to prewriting, and to drafting? My sense, as I listen to writing conferences and book groups, is that these tools, with frequent use, become internalized and improve my students' abilities as conference partners, readers, and drafters.

Despite the inevitable need for fine-tuning, the Writer's Toolbox—by increasing choices and by creating a common language—strengthens my students' ownership over their writing. Tait, a reluctant reviser at the beginning of the school year, came to this conclusion after our Writer's Toolbox unit: "I used to think revision was just a waste of time, but now I've seen what revising can do to a story." Brian, a student instantly frustrated by comments like "Describe more," also came to understand the purpose of revising: "My ideas about revision have really changed. Now, I can do more to help my writing, to make it better. At the beginning of the year, I didn't understand it. Now I do." In fact, when questioned in an anonymous survey, all of my students said they would definitely use these revision techniques in the future. By giving them a way to talk about, to make decisions about, and eventually to perform revisions, the Writer's Toolbox transformed my students from recopiers to writers more in control of their craft. After all, that is what a writing workshop is all about.

REFLECTION: COMPLICATING OWNERSHIP

Editors' Note: Most language arts researchers and theorists stress the importance of ownership in learning to write. But all students may not be equally capable of taking ownership of their writing.

Students who do not perceive themselves as being competent writers, who cannot successfully control the many cognitive and physical demands of most writing tasks, may be unwilling, or even unable, to take ownership of their writing tasks. (p. 417)

Source: Spaulding, C. L. (1989). Understanding ownership and the unmotivated writer. *Language Arts, 66*(4), 414–422.

REFLECTION: THE PROBLEM OF "CHOICE"

Editors' Note: Kamler raises the question, How "free" are free-choice activities, given the ideological contexts in which we are all immersed?

A number of studies have suggested . . . that so-called free choice in the curriculum actually encourages pupils to choose according to sex stereotype (Marland, 1983). From an early age, children engage with gender ideology in taken-for-granted ways of speaking and interacting in the culture (Hasan, 1986); they encounter gender stereotypes at home, at school, in their picture books, nursery rhymes, television programs, and reading programs. Children's choices are never really free because their gender constrains them from some practices and pressures them to engage in others (Clark, 1989). (p. 95)

Source: Kamler, B. (1993). Constructing gender in the process writing classroom. *Language Arts, 70*(2), 95–103.

REFLECTION: WRITING FOR A VARIETY OF PURPOSES

Editors' Note: Zecker discusses ways in which different purposes for writing challenge young writers to approach writing differently.

———— ❧ ————

Emergent Knowledge of Written Language and Its Different Dimensions

When faced with the request to write different types of texts, children apply their emergent knowledge about written language differently. It seems that the various characteristics of a given genre are likely to influence, to some extent, the emergent writing systems used by young authors. Children's written responses vary and are, at least in part, task-dependent (Sulzby, 1985; Sulzby, Barnhart, & Hieshima, 1989). Young writers are flexible and resourceful symbol-system users who, in the process of becoming conventional written-language users, adapt to the different demands of the tasks they face. There was a considerable mismatch between the perceptual/symbolic aspects that were observable in these young writers' products and their knowledge of the psychosocial aspects of different kinds of genres, as evidenced in the readings of their own compositions.

The literacy behaviors of these children support the idea that young children possess knowledge about a variety of text types from early on (Newkirk, 1989; Pontecorvo, Orsolini, Burge, & Resnick, 1996). They also challenge the entrenched belief that most early writing is—or should be—narrative or story-like in nature. They raise questions about the generalized notion that the story is the most adequate—or primary—type of genre when working with beginning readers and writers (Newkirk, 1989; Pappas, 1993). In fact, from the text types included in this study, the story, as it is conventionally defined, was the one text that appeared to be the least *mastered* among the kindergartners and first graders. Children's lists and personal letters were more developed and complete in terms of their content and style characteristics.

These kindergartners' and first graders' knowledge about the communicative intent of text seemed to be better developed and more stable than their knowledge of the graphic and symbolic aspects of

▶

written language. It is possible that knowledge about the psychosocial aspects of written language (namely, its format and communicative function) develops more rapidly and is generally more advanced than knowledge about its graphic/symbolic characteristics. Finally, these children's early literacy performance highlights the often overlooked value of using children's readings of their own texts as a way to explore their emergent knowledge of written language. Young authors' readings of their own compositions are better windows to their emergent understandings of the functional aspects of written language than are their written products considered in isolation. (pp. 488–489)

Source: Zecker, L. B. (1999). Different texts, different emergent writing forms. *Language Arts, 76*(6), 483–490.

18 The Courage to Write: Child Meaning Making in a Contested World

Anne Haas Dyson

Editors' Text: Anne Haas Dyson's research has made it clear that children's writing is embedded in sociocultural contexts and, therefore, does sociocultural work. By helping us think about what writing does, she helps us think about the creation of optimal environments for fostering children's writing development.

> Kristin has asked her urban third-grade class to think about the important criteria for a "good" story. Lynn suggests that "it should be original, not like, you know, *X-Men*." But Tina disagrees; in her view, "you *can* [write a good story about these comic and cartoon superheroes]" but "only if you have enough courage in yourself."

Out of context, this might seem like an odd statement. Surely it takes more courage to do as Lynn suggests, to write something at least relatively "original," rather than to retell superhero stories unabashedly. In the context of Tina's classroom, however, her comments are sensible. In this article, I explore this sense and, more broadly, the ways in which Tina's experiences make concrete new perspectives on authorship, originality, and the responsibility of the "good" writer.

During the last 20 years, we have marveled at young writers' remarkable powers of "meaning making"—the processes of invention and crafting through which they render inner meanings visible in graphic form. The driving force of children's writing, we have emphasized, is the intention to communicate the stuff of their own lives. Thus, a child who says, "I have nothing to write" may be directed inward, to write "what you know," as the common advice goes (or, on the other hand, "what you want to figure out," to reflect on). Over time, children become more "responsible," more able to craft their information and, thereby, make those driving intentions clear to others (Graves & Hansen, 1983).

This essay appeared in *Language Arts* 72.5 (1995) on pages 324–333.

These visions of child writing are not out of date—but they are not enough. Many urban classrooms, like Tina's, are places where, to use Renato Rosaldo's (1989) phrase, teachers and children continually cross "border zones" (p. 207) of gender, class, race, and ethnicity, among other such zones. This heterogeneity is a tremendous resource and a tremendous challenge for teachers—*and* for children, who must also learn to participate in and help build a fair world that can contain them all. Constructing such a world requires superheroes of a special kind; and it also requires new perspectives on authorship and authorial responsibility, perspectives that stress rewriting what is taken as given and, to use Tina's words, having courage.

Thus, before taking readers further into Tina's classroom world, I provide a theoretical backdrop for that world by considering new perspectives on child writing and child culture, and the possibilities for critical action in children's worlds.

Writing in the Common Culture of Childhood

The Responsible Author

In the view of the language and social philosopher Bakhtin, meaning only exists in the meeting of voices when we, as authors, both address and respond to the voices of others. Thus, our intentions do not come from turning inward, but from turning outward, from listening to the voices around us and from being moved to speak. And the paradox of the matter, the challenge, is that we must use others' voices, others' words, to say what we want to say.

As Bakhtin (1981) explained, we do not learn words from dictionaries; we learn them from "other people's mouths, in other people's contexts" (p. 294). When we enter into those contexts ourselves, as speakers or writers, we are expected to appropriate certain words, given the prevailing ideology or assumptions about our social place as children or adults, students or teachers, women or men—as people of varied roles, status, and disposition. Violating such expectations can be a mark of ignorance . . . or, as Tina will illustrate, of courage.

Bakhtin's "dialogism" sees speech and writing as appropriated from, and as a response to, others. Such a view emphasizes that language is not a transparent medium, a window to the soul, but rather a medium through which the self is constructed.

All writing is rewriting. Originality comes from "shak[ing] loose familiar structures of meaning," from looking at the taken-for-granted in new ways (Williamson, 1981/1982, p. 81). The "responsibility" of authors is to answer preceding texts with their own and, more broadly, to contribute to the ongoing social dialogue in a particular referent community.

Child Culture/Common Culture

In the community of Tina's class, it was with the texts of commercial culture (e.g., *The X-Men* [Lee, 1963]) that Bakhtinian concepts of authorship and responsibility emerged most clearly. Such media stories pervade child culture in our society and, when not specifically banned by teachers, they frequently pervade young children's "free" school writing as well. In Tina's classroom, the children made extensive, but by no means exclusive, use of media stories during the daily "free writing time" (the most open-ended of the diverse literacy activities in this language- and literature-rich classroom). Moreover, Kristin, Tina's teacher, used an optional practice called "Author's Theater," in which children could choose classmates to act out their stories. This practice may have further encouraged the children to bring their peer play life into the official school world.

As in other classrooms, the boys played with, and wrote about, television and video superheroes, like ninjas (both the human and mutant turtle variety) and X-Men, a team of mutant humans, both women and men, with great powers; in contrast, the girls wrote about friends and families, real and imagined (see, for example, Gilbert, 1994; Nicolopoulou, Scales, & Weintraub, 1994). In fact, media stories are designed to appeal to just this sort of divided gender world, a world that is complexly interwoven with issues of race and class (Kline, 1993). Commercial marketing strategists urge a dualistic vision of gender roles, that is, a vision structured by opposing characteristics. For the boys, best-selling products emphasize physical action and technological dazzle; for the girls, physical beauty and soft feelings.

The influence of such marketing strategies on the lives of children is a serious cause of much concern (Kline, 1993). Nonetheless, children's intense interest in these stories makes them worthy objects of study. Moreover, children's use of these stories allows much insight into their lives and, moreover, into the nature of meaning making itself.

As cultural theorists point out, much of common or popular culture is produced in the social use of commercial culture. The latter—be it television, film, or music, for example—is not reified; it is not set apart for study in the schools or museums. Commercial culture is widely available and thus widely appropriated by diverse peoples, including the young, who use it as play material for expressing, and exploring identity. The meanings provided by commercial culture are not simply reproduced, but, rather, they are "selected, reselected, highlighted, and recomposed" to make some statement about the place of the individual in the social world (Willis, 1990, p. 21).

In Tina's class, the fact that popular media stories were common knowledge and common property contributed to the liveliness of the discussions they inspired. These stories were brought into the official school world through the "cultural forum" (Bruner, 1986) provided by Author's Theater. As participants in that forum, the children did not simply react to the clarity of others' texts, but to the choices others had made in representing these stories. That is, they pointed out how "fun" and how "fair" the texts were, from their points of view.

Some of Tina's peers, like Sammy, used popular media stories primarily as tools for affiliation; they reproduced the "fun" parts of such stories (Dyson, 1994, 1995). However, for Tina herself, passionate and intellectual engagement in writing came from *transforming*—shifting the meanings of—stories so that they included her. But this, as she said, took some courage.

The Setting and the Data

The following case study of Tina is based on an ethnographic project at her urban K–3 school. The school served primarily two neighborhoods: one, an African American, low-income and working-class community (where Tina lived) and the other, an integrated, but primarily European American, working- and middle-class community. The project took place primarily in Kristin's classroom; she had begun teaching second grade in March of that school year, and she kept her class through their third-grade year. The case presented here draws primarily on the children's experiences during their third-grade year, when I visited their school approximately two hours weekly from January through mid-June.

The goal of the project was to examine the interplay between the social and ideological dynamics of classroom life and the particulars of individual children's writing processes and products (for methodological details, see Dyson, 1995). To understand these dynamics, I used an ethnographic analysis of all 28 class members' audiotaped discussions of gender, race, and power (i.e., I asked myself who raised these issues, when, and for what evident reason). I also engaged in ongoing informal interviews with the children and their teacher and case study analysis of the writing and talking of focal children. Focal children were those who played key roles in contesting or defending the ideological status quo of the children's stories.

Finally, I studied all "freewriting" products written during the children's third-grade year. In analyzing that writing, I was most interested in how children marked human relations. Among possible relations were parent/child, spouses, lovers, equals (friends or teammates), enemies, and perpetrator/victim/rescuer. Most revealing were the kinds of actions that energized those relations, including nurturing, romancing (especially kissing and marrying), joint or oppositional physical forcing ("kicking butt," as Tina said), or rescuing. The boys' extensive narrative use of superheroes led to stories filled with physical force; in contrast, the girls made relatively greater use of familial or friendship scenes, with minimal references to physical force. (For example, 51.4 percent of the boys' third-grade products involved physical fights; only 6.5 percent of the girls' did so; 41 percent of the girls' entries involved experiences at school and home, but only 6 percent of the boys' did.)

The dualistic worlds constructed by the children—and the ways in which the boys' worlds in particular excluded girls—led to animated and increasingly complex class discussions about Author's Theater presentations, particularly with regard to "fairness" and "power." In Tina's case especially, ways of developing texts (e.g., the characters she included, her specifications of characters' qualities and of plot actions) were dialogically linked to those ongoing discussions. Tina had something important to say in the ongoing social dialogue, and she said it, in part, through writing—or, more accurately, rewriting.

The Rewriting of Tina

A tiny child with (not-always-worn) large glasses, Tina was a complex character, one who voiced a strong sense of identity as an African American, as a caring person who "love[d] the world," and as a "tough" kid. "She thinks just because I'm small [that] I can't beat her up," said Tina one day in the midst of a verbal (or rather chillingly silent) fight with her good friend Makeda. "But I'll show her," she finished. Still, before too long, she and Makeda were once again playing mommy and baby, with Tina as the nurturing mommy buying food for child Makeda (who "was really bossy when it comes to food"). Tina joked and talked tough with the boys as well, though; and she was very knowledgeable about video games and superhero stories—in part because of her two teenage brothers.

In her valuing of both nurturing and being tough and in her sense of her own physical possibilities and vulnerabilities, Tina defied simplistic, dualistic gender relations in ways characteristic of many urban, working-class girls (see, for example, Anyon, 1984; Connell, Ashenden, Kessler, & Dowsett, 1982; Fordham, 1994; Miller, 1982). Indeed, her intense involvement in the daily writing time was, from the beginning of the project, directly related to this conflict—to her desire for rewriting stories that seemed to exclude her from role and relational possibilities important to her.

When Kristin became her teacher in the spring of her second-grade year, Tina responded to the newly initiated writing time with brief texts (approximately 35 words) about her love for family and friends and for doing fun things. She named her journal "The Peace Book." However, she and her best friend Holly also campaigned regularly for parts in the boys' superhero stories; they wanted to be the females rescued in ninja stories (roles given primarily to middle-class White girls), *and* they wanted to be the powerful female X-Men Storm (who can control the weather) and Rogue (who can fly through the air and can absorb the powers of others with a single touch). Indeed, in defiance of the boys' reluctance to write female roles in their X-Men stories, the two girls wrote their own, the only female-authored superhero stories in the second-grade class. (For an analysis of the children's second-grade year, see Dyson, 1994.)

In the third grade, though, Tina was without her best friend and fellow activist; Holly had moved. When I began observing in Kristin's room in the third grade, I found a Tina who seemed to have decided to write "girl" stories. In the following three-part story about Tina, I illustrate three ways in which she responded to the ongoing social dialogue in her classroom about human relations: appropriation, inversion, and, finally, reconstruction of available roles, of the expected words, in the story worlds of her classroom.

Appropriating Available Roles: On Being a Girl

On my first day in the third grade, I noticed that Tina had written "X-Men" on the back of her journal, and, above those letters, the words "no no." No more X-Men. "Too boyish," she had told her teacher. Underneath this negation, she had drawn pictures of Aladdin and Princess Jasmine, the romantic pair from a popular animated fantasy movie.

Tina was the *only* girl in her class who, by this January date, had written superhero stories. But now she seemed to be playing with more traditional gender roles and relations. She even wrote a superhero story from the perspective of a female victim. In its exaggeration, it seemed a parody, a revoicing of a victim's plea infused with a sharp directive to the "boy." (Spelling and punctuation of Tina's stories have been corrected for ease of reading.)

> Batman is going to save us girls.
> Hurry, Batman, hurry.
> We are about to die.
> Penguins came, too. . . .
> Batman, wrap them up, kill them.
> Hurry, boy, hurry.

In fact, during Author's Theater, when Tina played the role of victim in fairy tales (e.g., Snow White) or superhero stories, she consistently exaggerated the role for dramatic effect—and she also consistently made the children laugh. As the girlfriend Emily in Sammy's ninja story, for example, she raised the pitch of her own voice. And, when Emily's bike was stolen by the tough boys, she boohooed with enthusiasm and, in a pathetic voice, called for help from the three ninjas—Rocky and his brothers TumTum and Colt. She did complain, however, that the role was "boring"—that she had nothing to do. "Even if a person has a little part," she told Sammy, "make it so they're not just sitting there doing nothing, 'cause that's boring."

Tina also appropriated and exaggerated romantic encounters for performative purposes, using stories like *Aladdin* (Musker & Clements, 1992). In the movie, Aladdin, a street boy, falls in love with a princess; outwits an evil sorcerer; and, with the help of a genie in a lamp, wins that princess's love. In her written version of this story, Tina highlighted the opening scene of the movie, in which a nurturing Aladdin befriends small children by giving them bread. But, when she brought this piece to Author's Theater, Tina improvised a romantic encounter for dramatic, and humorous, effect. In her performed and oral version of the story, Aladdin and Princess Jasmine get caught kissing, marry, and then, with help from a genie who grants them five wishes, "eight days later, they have 5 children."

In this period of appropriation and play with romance and rescue, Tina did continue to seek roles as an X-Man in the boys' stories. Indeed, in the third grade, Tina's efforts at transforming traditional gender storylines dated from the very class discussion that opened this article. It was that discussion, and the support of her teacher Kristin, that moved the third-grade Tina to be responsible, that is, to respond to the conversation with action through texts.

The discussion began when Kristin asked the children to look over their writing folders and choose a "good story," one worthy of revision, editing, and publication. As we reenter this discussion, after Lynn's comment on originality and Tina's on courage, Tina is elaborating on the kind of media story she thinks would be good:

> *Tina:* It should be more about the girls winning instead of the boys.
>
> *Kristin:* So, should every story have the girls winning instead of the boys?
>
> *Tina:* No, not *all*, just some. Just some of 'em, not all of 'em. Because in every story the boys always have to win, and that's really not fair to the girls.
>
> *Victor:* Not *fair* to the *girls*? Not *fair* to the *boys*. (Victor has a disgusted look on his face and grumbles inaudibly after he finishes.)
>
> (Kristin intervenes to keep the peace and, also, to bring the children back to the task at hand.)
>
> *Kristin:* It seems to me what you're talking about . . . [is] that the story should in *some* way be original. It should be a little bit different. You should put some of your own ideas into it. And one idea might be to have the girls win instead of the boys. Would that be fair to say?
>
> *Tina:* Yeah, 'cause in *most* stories, like X-Men and all that—
>
> (Victor interrupts.)
>
> *Victor:* There's girls in there, too!
>
> *Tina:* I know, but the boys are always doing things for the girls, and it seems like the girls are weak.
>
> *Victor:* Look at Storm! Look at Rogue! [Storm and Rogue are two female members of the X-Men super-heroes team.] (Victor has his face right up in Tina's face, but she is not blinking.)
>
> (Animated and incomprehensible conversations erupt, quite heated, among all the children, and Kristin reiterates that the concerns are "not necessarily [about] what happens on *The X-Men* [television cartoon], but [about] what you choose to write about.")

Kristin had tried to clarify the tension between Victor and Tina—a tension which, in fact, is a central one undergirding the field of cultural studies (Storey, 1993): the tension between what is offered and what is taken. The meanings provided by commercial culture are not simply reproduced by consumers, but re-created. In essence, Kristin was saying, "There are about as many powerful female X-Men as male X-Men in the cartoons and videos, yes. But those females have nonexistent or minor roles in the boys' stories." Indeed, in the third grade, child-composed X-Men stories included 104 references to male characters, but only 24 references to females; moreover, female roles in narrative action were quite limited.

The class discussion ended and composing time began, but neither Tina nor Victor was finished with the conversation. Victor's mind was on the media stories; he muttered over and over that "they" just didn't know about the X-Men; it was well known among the children that Kristin didn't even have a TV! But Tina's mind was on her classmates; during composing time, she asked the boys at her writing table, "Is a girl gonna win? 'Cause you guys—Why don't you guys let a girl win? I make you a deal. If you write a story with a girl winning, I'll make a story with a boy winning."

In fact, like Victor, that very day Tina chose for publication—for her "good" story—an X-Men piece she had written. Tina's featured the female character Storm, and she approached it with great seriousness and no evident parody. In the story, Storm rescues the X-Men's male leader, Professor X, who is, unfortunately, possessed by a demon; at the same time, Storm saves the life of another male character, Gambit, whom the deranged Professor X is attacking. And yet, at the edges of Tina's text is symbolic material that echoes earlier stories, stories about everyday life and "loving" its pleasures:

> Once the X-Men were
> taking a walk in the park.
> They love to walk in the park.
> So when they got done
> they went home to eat pizza from Pizza Hut.
> They love pizza from Pizza Hut.
> So they went to Professor X. Gambit was going to him,
> and Professor X shot at him. Storm came and pulled him out
> of his chair, and turned him upside down, and shook him and
>   shook him. Then
> the bad guy came out and he died. The end of this one.

Inverting Available Roles: On Being—and Not Being—Emily

In her stories about victims and heroines, including Storm, Tina was composing within the relations provided by the media stories; she was selecting appealing roles and exaggerating more "boring" ones for performative fun. However, a few weeks after the initial tense encounter with Victor, Tina wrote a story that not only appropriated but also inverted given gender relations (Babcock, 1993). She wrote this story after the class returned to the "fairness" discussion.

The discussion resurfaced the day Victor brought *his* "good" X-Men story to Author's Theater. It was a long story (approximately 163 words), requiring 9 characters; among them was one girl, Rogue, played by Tina. Unfortunately, Rogue had but one action, or, more accurately, one line: At the end of a long battle, in which the male characters engaged in an intricately detailed fight scene, Rogue said to the escaping bad guy Magneto, "You are not going to get away, Magneto." But he did.

After the performance, Tina immediately asked why her part was so small. "I didn't have time," said Victor; otherwise, he implied, her part would have been much larger. Victor's explanation was met by an unusual reaction: All of the girls, across lines of race and of class, objected to this excuse, which, like Rogue, seemed quite weak.

> *Melissa:* I think you kinda meant to do that because, um, she was before a lot of people [i.e., other characters came into the action after Rogue], and um . . . all she got to do was say a couple of words.

> ....

> *Lynn:* Well, next time you should write more because the males were like fighting, the other boys get to, so the girls should. . . . You had a little time to write some more. You could have left out one of the male actors.

> *Victor:* All right, all right.

> ....

> *Adam:* But [Rogue's] so powerful.

> (Bryant concurs, but Kristin poses a question.)

> *Kristin:* So, in Victor's play, did she have any effect on the bad guys?

> *Bryant:* Well . . .

> (Kristin, in fact, has often discussed with the children the concept of being "powerful," a topic that began with the superhero stories but carried over into social studies and literature. For example, the class has discussed the power of speech and, moreover, the power of internal determination and the way in which it may defeat the power of physical force, as in the civil rights movement. But, in the context of *this* story, she asks, is talking powerful? In the world Victor has made, could "a male X-person show his strength without actually getting in a physical fight [i.e., by talking]?")

Victor: Yeah, like Jean Gray.

(Giggles break out, since Jean Gray is a female, and soon there are many references to funny movies in which men dress like women. Eddie Murphy, Martin Lawrence, and Robin Williams, among other actors, have played roles that exaggerate stereotypical female qualities for laughs—just as, in fact, Tina herself has done. Indeed, Tina is laughing now, and then makes a comment that excludes Victor from possibilities.)

Tina: I think it wouldn't look as funny if a girl played a boy's part, but it would look funny if a boy played a girl part, like [the TV show] *Martin.*

Victor: Why is that?

....

Victor: Tina, I gotta question for *you.* Just a while back you said, "Girls don't look funny in boys' clothes, but boys look funny in girls' clothes." Well, I mean, what's the difference? Just look at me. Just look at Aloyse dressing like you. Would that be funny?

(There is much laughter, but Victor is very serious. And, after all, all three children are wearing t-shirts and jeans.)

Victor was working within a kind of story that, at its heart, is about physical power—a traditional male possession. Other definitions of power are not so important in this narrative context. In helping the children clarify their ideas about power and gender—and in directing their attention to narrative logic—Kristin was not trying to teach the children *what* to think, but *to* think. "It's 'only a story,'" she told the children, "but stories have the power to create things, to change things." Stories include or exclude; they influence people's imaginative possibilities:

—as Victor seemed to acknowledge when, on his own initiative, he rewrote his piece. In the revision, Rogue engaged in physical action, and no one yelled a warning at Magneto; instead the warning became a defiant parting shot from the gloating bad guy: "You will not get me, X-Men!"

—and as Tina seemed to acknowledge, too, for soon after that discussion she began an intense period of writing stories that not only appropriated female roles but also transformed them. For example, in her first ninja story, "Emily," the title character herself displays physical power. Tina inverted the expected gender relations but stayed within the basic relational structure of the story: physically abusive perpetrators, victim, physically powerful rescuer. Still, once again, there were potential signs of "difference" (Derrida, 1978), signifiers of other kinds of power, of other relational roles seemingly ignored but, nonetheless, there in the background details of her texts. The major adult figure in "Emily" is not, as in the media's martial arts stories, a wise grandfather who teaches karate, but a "nice" mother, a nurturing one who loves and protects kids, male and female:

> Once there was a girl named Emily. She was tough. Her and her boyfriend was eating pizza. They love to eat pizza. So one day they were going to school. They love school. Emily's mother walks them to school. She was nice. She loves little kids. Kids love her. Then they went into the room. Bad boys, they love to beat up kids. . . . School is over now. Rocky, Emily, TumTum, and Colt. Colt was going away. Emily found him. The bad boys had him. Emily can whip some butt. So she did. So they all ran away. She is tough. So they walk home again. The end.

Reconstructing Available Roles: The Coming of Venus Tina

In the last weeks of school, Tina wrote two particularly long stories in which she did more than appropriate available roles and invert dominant relations. Within a story of romance and another of rescue, she reconstructed these relations, making new selections from available possibilities by negating, extending, foregrounding, and recombining them in new ways (for a discussion of such a concept of originality, see Rosaldo, Lavie, & Narayan, 1993).

These reconstructed stories had roles in both family and school relations. They were written in large part after school at her kitchen table, Tina reported. And yet, both were deliberately linked to ongoing class dialogues. The deliberateness was suggested by Tina's manipulations of details, of relations and actions, and by her interactions with her peers about her texts.

The title characters of the first story, "Asia and Mike," were named for her siblings: Asia was her baby sister, who "kept messing with me when I was writing, so I put her in it"; Mike was her teenage brother. The story was her only written text that foregrounds a romantic encounter. And she was *serious* about this encounter, unlike her playful dramatization of Jasmine and Aladdin's romance. When her classmates acted out this story in Author's Theater, Tina became quite distressed at their improvisations, which she usually very much enjoyed. She wanted all concerned to attend not to the actors' funny lines, but to her text, a text in which she had taken great care to make her gender roles "fair":

> (Tina has called her actors to the rug. Makeda is Asia; Demario is Mike; Rhonda and Edward are the parents. [Her text is in boldface where it details gender relations.])

Tina: Ready? (begins reading)

            "Once there was girl and her name was Asia."

            (to Makeda, who has begun to crawl around the floor)

            You're not a baby! You're a big girl. So stand up.

            (again reading)

            "She was bad to her mom

            and her dad.

            Her mom was always good to her.

            So was her daddy."

Edward: (acting) Say! I buy you a Barbie Doll.

Rhonda: (acting) Come on and I'll take you to the hair-dresser
            to get your hair done (much laughter from the
            audience).

Tina: Ok, ok! FREEZE! SEE? Where am I?

(Tina is irritated. "Freeze" is the order given by authors/
directors when they feel the actors are out of line. Her "SEE?"
implies that their silliness has made her lose her exact place in
her text—which usually does not matter; she *usually* does not
read her texts, but improvises on them.)

            "And her mom name was Mary.

            And her daddy name was Tom.

            And they love her."

(Edward says nothing, but Rhonda says, "I love my darling
girl, but she needs to get her hair combed." The audience
laughs; Tina sighs and keeps going.)

Tina: **"The mom was going to work**

            and Asia daddy was going to work also.

            The mom work at Taco Bell.

            And Asia dad work at Burger King."

Edward: (acting) What you want? Well, we outa that, man.
            Get you something else.

Tina: WILL YOU *SHUT UP* AND *LISTEN* TO WHAT I'M
            SAYING?! (returns to reading)

            "And Asia mom was 33

            and Asia dad was 33

            and Asia was 15

            And she work at a Christmas tree lot.

She love to give people trees.

Once there was this boy.

His name was Mike

and he was nice and quiet.

He was 15 too.

He love Asia

and Asia love him too.

The next day

Asia mother was coming home from North Oakland

and she saw Asia's daddy

because he worked there

and Asia's mom saw Mike and Asia kissing."

(Demario, playing Mike, says, "I gotta go. I gotta go. I forgot I
got football [practice]." Tina keeps reading.)

Tina: **"Asia mom kicked Asia in the butt**

And Asia daddy came home and did the same

thing. Kicked her butt.

Asia and Mike ran away

and got married

and had no kids

and die May 32, 1996

at Asia 96

Mike 96 also.

The end."

In the children's acting, there was an undercurrent of gender stereotypes, of dualistic difference; and, indeed, many children, including
Tina, relied on these stereotypes for improvisation when acting. But
Tina's text explicitly marked equality of male and female action. Although Asia's mom was mentioned first, she and her similarly aged
husband both worked, and both loved and disciplined their daughter.
Asia and her similarly aged boyfriend loved each other; they ran away
and married; they even died on the same date, at exactly the same age
("at Asia 96, Mike 96 also"). Moreover, Tina's text explicitly negated
common narrative expectations: "Asia and Mike . . . [though married]
had no kids."

Indeed, both actors and audience members were impressed that
her piece "had a lot of details," as Makeda said. After head nodding all

around, Jonathan elaborated: "It described the names, the jobs, and a lot about their personalities"—personalities, I would add, that are complex, that are sometimes loving and sometimes not. But Tina's details were not just evidence of crafting, of clarifying her intention; in the context of the history of the class and of dominant societal storylines (Gilbert, 1994), the details made a point, offering new visions of relational possibilities in the ongoing conversation about gender.

Tina's last extended text provides a fitting end to my own narrative of this child writer. The text was written during a class unit on the superheroes of ancient Greece, a unit generated by the children's enthusiastic response to Kristin's reading of Greek myths. These stories emphasize physical force, as well as magical transformation, and they also foreground female beauty, a beauty represented in all the children's books with golden hair and fair skin. Tina's Venus story began, in fact, when she and her friends Makeda and Lena were drawing their chosen goddesses: Venus for Tina and Makeda, Persephone for Lena.

Sitting side by side, Tina and Makeda drew Venus fair-haired and White. Lena, also at their table, made her goddess Black. But, Lena was sure, it was "wrong." "People from Greece are not Black," she said.

"Yes, they can be," countered Tina.

When Makeda reiterated that her Venus was White, Tina commented, "Well, maybe she's White to you, but not to me"—a typical Tina response to exclusion from a narrative world.

Tina (and later Makeda) redrew Venus, this time as a Black goddess. Moreover, Tina wrote the piece excerpted below, in which Venus Tina saves the world for both boys and girls:

> Once there was a boy and girl in the park, and two men was walking by the park, and the men saw the two kids. So the two men started to run after them. And the kids ran. One man chased the girl; the other ran after the boy. The boy's name was Aloyse [a classmate], and the [girl's] name was Asia [her sister]. So when Venus Tina heard about this, she was mad. So she came down . . . and picked the kids up on her magical flying horse named Makeda. It was a girl horse, and she took the two kids . . . in the sky. There was a big park on a cloud. There was a lot of kids play[ing] on flying horses. It was kids from [Tina's] school. . . . Then she took them home. They said what about those two mean men. Venus Tina made them nice. And on earth was fun again. She made parks safe for us kids of the world. By Tina. Love, Tina.

In Tina's story of perpetrators and victims and of a grand rescue, the heroine is Venus, a Black Venus named after herself. And this Venus Tina rides a magical flying horse, a female horse, one named after her friend Makeda. The world of mortals, however, is terrorized by the more traditional "mean men," who terrorize equally a girl and a boy. And Venus Tina saves them both. Moreover, she does not "kick butt," like the appropriated Storm or the inverted Emily; in keeping with the goddess role, she transforms them. She makes them nice. "And on earth was fun again."

Both "Venus Tina" and "Asia and Mike" were "original," as Lynn had desired in the opening anecdote. But they were not a window to the "true" Tina, the essential core. Rather, they were responses by a dynamic and growing Tina, a responsible Tina, who was playing with the symbolic material around her.

On Courage and the Teaching of Writing

This article has featured the dramas of Tina, a child who linked writing with courage. In observing her actions and reactions in the classroom community, I too, as an adult observer, thought Tina's writing took courage, for it was writing that was clearly rewriting—shifting the constructed world and the possibilities of the constructed self in notable ways.

The story of Tina and her classmates makes concrete new theoretical visions of authorship and, by implication, new pedagogical visions of writing, learning, and teaching. In these new visions, the motivation to write comes from the need to respond, to participate in the ongoing dialogue.

Current sociocultural visions portray learning to write as learning to use the medium to interact with others in appropriate ways (see, for example, Gutierrez, 1993; Heath, 1983; Moll & Whitmore, 1993; Vygotsky, 1978). A dialogic perspective extends this view, emphasizing that children are not unproblematically "growing into the intellectual life of those around them" (Vygotsky, 1978, p. 77). Rather, they are also growing into, or in some way against, the existent social order through which that life is enacted (Dyson, 1995). For Tina, social conflicts—not only social interactions—helped make salient new kinds of writing choices, newly imagined ways of depicting human relationships.

These visions of authorship and of development suggest the importance of a thematically substantive language arts curriculum, one concerned not just with individual crafting, but with collective conversations about ideas that matter (see also Applebee, 1993; Dyson, 1993). In storywriting, the rich conversations are about the human condition, about good and evil (and ambiguousness), about power and love of varied sorts. Grand ideas, rooted in daily concerns, interweave—and are interwoven in—people's use of the arts, whether the popular or the classic, in the classroom or on the playground.

In Tina's class, the starting point of those conversations was not teacher-led critical discussions, but child-initiated and teacher-supported objections to unfair play, to exclusion from imaginative possibilities. For example, Tina raised the issue of race when she felt excluded from being a "goddess," and the issue of gender when excluded from being a "good guy." With the assistance of Kristin, the children compared their symbolic worlds and discussed ways of constructing and reconstructing those worlds. In this way, social conflicts became matters of textual choice (Hall, 1981) and critical literacy (Edelsky, 1991; Freire, 1970; Greene, 1988).

Amidst such conversations, Tina appropriated, inverted, and reconstructed symbolic material. She built symbolic worlds in which central characters were worthy of being saved and capable of saving others, in which they were often beautiful and strong but sometimes rebellious and bad. Her worlds suggested complex possibilities, possibilities born of feeling, naming, and then rewriting. And Tina was not only developing her own texts. She was a key player in the classroom collective; she "talked back" (hooks, 1990), raising issues that reverberated in the class and caused others to rethink—not in grand moments of collective classroom revolution, but in small moments of shifting positions. For example, Victor appropriated a tough Rogue, effective in the logic of the world he had made, and Makeda reproduced Venus with a difference.

In a recent and highly readable discussion of language, culture, and identity, Michael Agar (1994) explains that when we are exposed to information, to details, that are other than what we expect and, moreover, when those details challenge our sense of self, it can be hard to open up to their possibilities. Imagining different worlds, he writes, requires "a kind of courage," a kind that allows us to risk humiliation and embarrassment. But, if we do open up, we can change. "The old 'self,' the one in your heart and mind and soul, mutates as it comes into relationships with others. The self stretches to comprehend them all" (p. 28). Thus, we become like X-Men, superheroes of a special kind.

For children to display this sort of courage requires teachers of courage, teachers, like Kristin, who are not afraid of children's worlds and children's concerns, who are interested in their ideas and, also, in challenging and extending those ideas. Those with such courage, whatever their age, may be rewarded by a life that is not of "being," as Agar

(1994) writes, but of "becoming. You turn into a sailor and immigrant for as long as you live" (p. 28), a participant in the continual process of reinventing, rewriting, one's world.

Acknowledgments

Support for this work was provided by the Educational Research and Development Center Program (grant number R 117G 10036 for the National Center for the Study of Writing) as administered by the Office of Educational Research and Improvement (OERI), U.S. Department of Education. The findings and opinions expressed in this report do not reflect the position or policies of the OERI, or the U.S. Department of Education. I would like to thank the fine graduate students who contributed to this project: Elizabeth Scarboro, Wanda Brooks, Michael Ford, and Gwen Larsen.

STRATEGY: WRITING FICTION

Editors' Note: In this excerpt, Taberski offers a set of strategies for helping young children write fiction.

Choose Topics You Care About

Topic selection is a crucial element in good writing. Writing is often facilitated when the writer cares deeply about what he or she is writing. When this quality is present it can elevate the writer's energy level and make the piece more powerful. It can also evoke feelings in the reader. . . .

Use Literature as a Resource

. . . Literature is an invaluable tool to help children write better fiction. During the months that I conducted my research, I enveloped the children with quality literature by reading to them daily. Among the books I read were picture books since these stories were closest to the ones the children could approximate in their writing. As I did this, it was very natural to discuss the qualities that made these books so special and endearing. I also involved the children in a daily reading workshop. During this workshop the children read for forty-five minutes each day. . . . Children need to know what good literature looks and sounds like. . . .

▶

Every Story Is about Change

As the children and I read and "talked books," we discussed how the main character of the story had changed or solved his or her problem. The children soon learned that this change is a crucial element in fiction and looked for it in the stories they read. . . .

Fiction Writers Draw on Personal Experiences

. . . Whenever I read to the children, I pointed out how the author might have used some personal experiences when writing the book . . . .

Research Is Essential in Fiction Writing

Authors are students of their topics. Since realistic fiction, and especially fantasy, must be believable, fiction writers must often research their topics to create a world that is credible to the reader. (pp. 587–591)

Source: Taberski, S. (1987). From fake to fiction: Young children learn about writing fiction. *Language Arts, 64*(6), 586–596.

STRATEGY: JOURNAL WRITING

Editors' Note: Journal writing is a popular strategy for increasing students' writing fluency. As Hipple makes clear, journal writing can even be used productively in kindergarten classrooms.

How did my kindergartners "write" in their journals? They wrote in a variety of ways, most of which involved drawings. These drawings were often accompanied by printed texts—scribbles, random letters, numerals, or even words—depending on the maturity of the writers. It was important to me and to our success that the children saw themselves as writers, that they viewed their drawings as forms of writing, that the focus remained on the communication of thoughts rather than on the production of pleasing visual images. Therefore, we never used the word "drawing" in connection with journal activities. Instead, children "wrote" in journals and later dictated what they had written to an adult, regardless of their capabilities in actual printing. (p. 255)

Source: Hipple, M. L. (1985). Journal writing in kindergarten. *Language Arts*, 62(3), 255–261.

REFLECTION: WRITING SCIENCE FICTION

Editors' Note: The basic goal of writing instruction is to help students learn to write for a variety of purposes in a range of social contexts. Expanding the purposes for which students write may also help them find their voices as writers.

———————

It is often difficult to make definite statements about children's writing, or anyone's writing for that matter. What does stand out for me after my study of Noah's fourth-grade writings is the strength of his science fiction as compared with his other work. Writing science fiction helped Noah to find his voice, a voice that holds within it a tremendous capacity for humor, as well as a capacity for entertaining a number of complex concepts simultaneously. His science fiction serves as a reflection of his thinking, revealing both his questions and his hypotheses on how the world works. And for Noah, the joy of science fiction may be that no one is saying he has to answer the questions he raises. For others . . . other types of fiction can serve a similar function. I suspect in all fiction writing, the permission to create a world where the outcome of events is in the author's control enhances his or her sense of power, something most children do not experience in many areas of their lives. (p. 361)

Source: Marks, D. (1985). When children write science fiction. *Language Arts*, 62(4), 355–361.

19 Another Story: Putting Graves, Calkins, and Atwell into Practice and Perspective

David Sudol

Peg Sudol

Editors' Text: Sudol and Sudol offer a glimpse of one teacher's efforts to implement a writing workshop in her classroom. What makes this story especially interesting is its emphasis on "the messy reality" of life in classrooms. A sequel to this article (see, Sudol & Sudol, 1995) explores the implementation of writers' workshop over time.

Peg has been an elementary school teacher for the past 17 years. For most of that time she taught little writing. Why? It wasn't required. Instead she taught "English"—parts of speech, complete sentences, capitalization, punctuation—the basic stuff of English books. The closest she came to writing was teaching kids to identify topic sentences. Once in a while she assigned creative writing ("Write a story"), but the main focus of her language arts instruction was reading; writing was a blur in the margin.

When we moved to Arizona in 1985, she found writing was still not important. However, during her second year, the language arts curriculum was revised; and by state mandate the teaching of writing was now required. Suddenly, at the fifth-grade level she was responsible for 15 objectives. She had to teach writing processes—prewriting, drafting, revising, and editing. The following year she struggled to fulfill these requirements. Still stressing grammar and usage, she tried to plug in writing wherever she could make it fit. She also began looking for help. At the time David was taking a graduate course on written language acquisition and was hearing a lot about the revolution in elementary school writing. He recommended that Peg read Graves's *Writing: Teachers*

This essay appeared in *Language Arts* 68.4 (1991) on pages 292–300.

and Children at Work (1983), Calkins's *The Art of Teaching Writing* (1986), and Atwell's *In the Middle: Writing, Reading, and Learning with Adolescents* (1987). According to David's professor and several elementary teachers in the class, these were the main texts, the handbooks of the new pedagogy.

During the spring of 1988, Peg read Graves and began to incorporate several of his ideas. For example, instead of assigning topics and requiring a single draft, she taught lessons on invention and revision. She had mixed results. On the one hand, she was frustrated because she couldn't devote enough time to teaching writing—a process approach took longer than she'd anticipated. On the other hand, she was pleasantly surprised to see her students excited and enthusiastic. In the past, on those rare occasions when she assigned writing, the students moaned and groaned, worrying about length, complaining about having to copy over. She realized she had to make a change; it was no longer possible to teach grammar and usage in lieu of writing. Not only did the new curriculum demand changes, but also her own reading and classroom experience convinced her there must be a better way. Hence, she made a decision to give up the skill-and-drill approach and commit herself to writers' workshop.

Preparations

But before the year ended she encountered a problem that Graves, Calkins, and Atwell don't mention—the reluctant administrator. Peg could not throw away her English book; she had to get her principal's permission, no easy task. His philosophy of teaching was fundamentally different from the holistic workshop approach. He believed lessons should be skills-oriented and that skills should be taught separately, using the text. To him, writers' workshop lacked structure; it smacked of a freewheeling, open classroom, which he disfavored.

Peg explained that she was not satisfied teaching writing from the text; the skills approach didn't work. She wanted to teach the language concepts and writing sections of the curriculum in a writers' workshop, not using the text at all. He was reluctant, to say the least, but granted her permission because he knew she was a good teacher and because he trusted her. She had worked for him for three years; he had observed and been impressed with a revision lesson she had taught. In short, he wouldn't allow everyone to do this but was confident she could make it work. He warned her, however, to cover everything in the curriculum because that's what she was accountable for.

In contrast, Graves, Calkins, and Atwell seem to present teachers as free agents who can operate independently of administrative or curricular constraints. Only Atwell discusses changing the curriculum, but she had the freedom to develop her own curriculum and the luxury of a supportive principal. Peg's experience points out that it's not always so easy. She wondered if her situation were unique but decided it couldn't be; surely her principal wasn't the only one with reservations about writers' workshop. In effect, her case highlights the realities of getting started. Had she less experience or persuasive skill, she might have been denied the chance. Her workshop could have been derailed before it got on track.

During the summer Peg began preparing in earnest. She reread Graves carefully, then moved on to Calkins and Atwell. They state that they are not guidebooks that explain step-by-step methods, but they nevertheless offer plenty of advice. Peg evaluated each book in terms of how useful it would be. She found Graves to be an excellent starting point. He inspired her. Further, he laid the theoretical and methodological foundation on which to build her workshop. But when she finished his book, she felt overwhelmed and thought, "How in the world am I ever going to do this?" It's not that Peg expected him to write a teacher's manual like the one accompanying her basal reader; but, lacking confidence, she needed more than the brief discussions he provided.

When she turned to Calkins, her initial reaction was, "Haven't I already read this?" Indeed, Peg found Calkins little more than Graves revisited and, consequently, didn't read closely. She was also bothered by the way Calkins tried to cover everything in 300 pages. Whereas Graves focused on teaching writing, Calkins discussed writing at different grade levels, reading-writing connections, writing across the curriculum, and various modes of writing. Although a minor point, Peg was also irritated by Calkins's style. "Too many sentimental stories," she complained. "How are they going to help me?"

She then read Nancie Atwell and once again found the same things Graves and Calkins had said. The big difference was that Atwell was an actual classroom teacher writing about her own experiences. Whereas Graves and Calkins had reported from the outside perspective of researchers, Atwell was sharing an inside view. Everything she talked about was grounded in the context of her own eighth-grade classroom. Further, when she explained how to "survive day one" (to use Graves's phrase), she did so in detail, supplying a transcript (script) that any teacher could use. If Graves and Calkins had laid the foundation, Atwell gave Peg a blueprint, plans she could use to construct her workshop. Atwell explained how to set up the classroom, how to structure the workshop, how to manage conferences, and how to evaluate writing. Finally, Peg could see how the parts fit together. As a result, though she consulted Graves and Calkins throughout the year, Atwell became her primary source.

Concerns and Doubts

By summer's end, Peg had read the books, taken copious notes, and made extensive preparations to begin in the fall. She also expressed some concerns. Although Graves, Calkins, and Atwell inspired her, she had a nagging suspicion that something wasn't quite right. They never discussed failures: Their workshops ran so smoothly; everyone achieved such success. She also noticed that problems, though mentioned, were quickly glossed over or easily solved. She'd been teaching too long to believe these stories; they sounded too good to be true.

Logistically, Peg worried about how she was going to find the time to do writers' workshop. Atwell says, "Writers need time—regular, frequent chunks of time they can count on, anticipate, and plan for" (p. 55). Graves says, "Teachers find time for writing by taking it" and recommends at least four 45- to 50-minute periods per week (p. 90). Calkins urges "an hour a day, every day" (p. 25). But that's easier said than done. Peg needed solid blocks of time for reading and math in the morning. As an experienced self-contained classroom teacher, she knew these were the only solid blocks she could get. Where was she going to find another guaranteed 45 minutes every day for writing?

More problematic, Peg was troubled by a fundamental difference between her curriculum, which requires students to do certain types of writing, and Graves's, Calkins's, and Atwell's insistence that students write whatever they please. Indeed, a workshop basic is authentic self-sponsored writing. Yet Peg was bound by her curriculum and accountable to her principal to teach a personal-experience narrative, a short story or play, a poem, a report, a communication (directions), and a summary. Further, her students had to meet specific criteria. In the short story, for instance, they had to include a beginning, middle, and end; describe a main character and setting; and develop conflict in the plot. Peg realized these were writing exercises and was disturbed by their a-rhetorical nature, but there was no getting around them. Hence, even before starting, she questioned whether or not she could do the workshop correctly. Again she wondered if her situation was unique or if Graves, Calkins, and Atwell were unrealistic in demanding so much time and freedom of choice.

At the beginning of the 1988–89 school year, Peg still felt overwhelmed. Realizing it was impossible to plan out the whole year in advance, suffering reservations and doubts, she was still committed to doing writers' workshop. So she decided simply to start, to work, and to learn along the way, surviving one day at a time.

Persistent Problems

After intense negotiating with the other fifth-grade teacher and the remedial teacher, Peg was able to schedule a daily 45-minute period for the workshop. Unfortunately, it wasn't the best time for writing—right after lunch, before afternoon recess. Returning from the cafeteria, the kids were sluggish; before recess they'd get antsy. Moreover, because this was the only other block of time not reserved for reading or math, everything extra happened then. Whenever there was an assembly, it was scheduled during the workshop. When the school resource officer came to teach a drug awareness program, he could be there only during the workshop. The only time the ESL teacher could work with the non-English-speaking students was during the workshop. And these problems cropped up over and over all year long. Peg would get a week when the kids could spend five consecutive days writing; then the following week the workshop would be canceled three times. The consequences of these interruptions were numerous. Continuity was lost because there wasn't a daily flow of writing. If the kids missed several days in a row, they would forget where they were, lose excitement and interest, get stuck, and have trouble getting back on track. The craft that Graves, Calkins, and Atwell say comes only with daily writing was hard to develop.

Another problem Peg could never entirely solve was ownership—choice of topics and genres. She was required to teach certain writing types. How could she do that and still allow the children some freedom of choice? She considered a couple of possibilities. One was to announce at the start of the workshop, "All right, group, these are the types of writing you have to do this year. Make sure you get them done." But that was impractical. Knowing each type of writing required specific criteria that required instruction, she'd have to teach the criteria 32 times to 32 different children—an exhausting prospect, an inefficient use of time, and a management nightmare. So she scrapped that plan. Instead she had everyone do the same type of writing at the same time, but she let them choose their own topics.

Additionally, she tried to make the writing types relevant by scheduling them in conjunction with something happening in the community or at school. For instance, in October a local newspaper announced a contest, open to all ages, for scary Halloween stories. She said to her class, "Look, we have to write short stories. Would you be interested in entering this contest, with the possibility that your stories may be published in the paper?" They enthusiastically said yes. Basically, she tried to make the assignments rhetorically genuine by showing her students there was a reason to write other than fulfilling curriculum requirements. Even though the kids weren't completely free, she hoped this was an acceptable compromise.

Actually, Peg thought these writing restraints might be better than giving students free rein. She understood the need for self-expression, but she thought Graves, Calkins, and Atwell over-emphasized it. Even though they discuss different types of writing and encourage students to write for various purposes and audiences, they nonetheless seem to prefer the personal and expressive. Most of their examples of student writing are narratives or poems. In fact, modeling his own composing process, Graves lists these topics: "When I Got Mad When I Was in Sixth Grade," "My First Air Raid," and "My First Fight" (p. 45). Peg wanted her students to have practice in many modes. She was afraid that, if given the chance, a student might spend the entire year writing about a trip to California or about Teenage Mutant Ninja Turtles. That might be fun, it might even be developmentally appropriate; but it's like eating Twinkies for breakfast, lunch, and supper. She wanted to make sure her students had a balanced diet.

Ironically, Peg encountered an unexpected problem with the personal narrative. Letting her kids write about what they know best—themselves—she was confident they would do well, and most did. One little girl, Amy, painfully quiet and shy, wrote a delightful story about going fishing with her Uncle Todd. She was so proud of her piece that she volunteered to read it to the class. On the other hand, Peg had three children who would not—could not—write their narratives. Two were Hispanic; one was Native American. Although she did not know for certain and was reluctant to stereotype, she believed the issue was cultural. She'd had sufficient experience with minority students to know that many will not speak openly about their personal lives to outsiders. Indeed, she believed that requiring these kids to write personal narratives was a violation of privacy, a cultural intrusion.

Another problem Peg had to deal with was deadlines. Graves, Calkins, and Atwell rightly point out that writers don't all work at the same pace, so why should we expect students to? A basic fact of writers' workshop is kids working at various stages on their pieces. Teachers must accommodate these differences. Unlike her concerns about ownership, Peg was confident she could let students work at their own pace and originally planned to set no deadlines. If some finished before others, they could write whatever they wished. When it was time to move on, they could file away their "work-in-progress" and come back to it later. But this plan didn't work because without deadlines the students procrastinated, fiddled around, and failed to make progress. Even during conferences Peg couldn't motivate them to complete their writing. They took a month to do what she knew they could do in two weeks. Although everyone enjoyed writers' workshop—they said it was their favorite time of day—they didn't produce. Consequently, she had to impose deadlines.

Furthermore, this failure to complete work made Peg question her students' commitment to writing. They weren't as into the workshop as she expected them to be. It wasn't just the procrastination. On any given day, 5 of her 32 students would be off task. They'd go to a corner for a peer conference and talk about everything but their writing. They'd wander the room bothering other kids who were working hard. They wouldn't pay attention in teacher conferences. They manipulated other students to do the work for them. They'd miss deadlines. When Peg compared her kids to the ones Graves, Calkins, and Atwell describe, she realized they weren't the same. All year she asked herself why.

She worried that the required writing types were putting kids off. As Calkins says, "Noise can mean that there is a lack of commitment to writing. Perhaps students are writing on topics they don't care about" (p. 216). Maybe she wasn't making the assignments relevant enough. She questioned her procedures. Graves and Atwell stress that a workshop must have well-established routines that everyone understands and follows. It must run like a precision machine. But that wasn't a problem because her workshop was very well organized. In fact, when she decided to do writers' workshop, she wasn't worried about rules and regulations because she is an excellent classroom manager.

Then she began to doubt Graves's contention that "Children want to write" (p. 3). Most maybe, but not all. She suspected that he, Calkins, and Atwell had a romantic, idealized view of children. Or, more likely, they weren't considering all the reasons why a child wouldn't write. Perhaps their explanations were incomplete. For instance, one student, Brian, continually caused problems. Peg tried everything in the book to get him to write, but he refused. Plus, she had to watch him constantly to make sure he didn't keep others from doing their writing. In short, he disrupted the atmosphere of the workshop, and there was a dramatic improvement whenever he was absent. Ultimately, Peg couldn't blame writers' workshop, the required writing types, the imposed deadlines, or the procedures: The boy had emotional problems caused by trouble at home. She was convinced that these overriding problems so controlled him that he could not commit himself to anything at school—not writing, not reading, not math. And Brian wasn't the only one with outside problems: One student's parents were getting divorced, another's grandfather had died, and others were experimenting with drugs. Once again, Peg thought Graves, Calkins, and Atwell had ignored these issues, glossed over them, or offered simplistic solutions. Their workshops seemed unreal—the kids were too normal. She knew from experience that no class is ever so uniform; she had a Brian every year.

Workshop Specifics

Peg structured her workshop as Atwell and Calkins recommend: a 10-minute minilesson, 30 minutes of writing and conferencing, and 5 minutes of group sharing. Like them, she used minilessons for a variety of purposes. During the first few weeks, she taught procedural lessons to establish workshop guidelines. For the remainder of the year, she taught discourse criteria, process strategies, and editing skills.

Generally, her minilessons followed a pattern for each type of writing. First, she did a minilesson to generate criteria. Although certain that Graves, Calkins, and Atwell would frown upon such direct instruction, she nonetheless had to teach the criteria that the curriculum required. Instead of telling students what to do, however, she guided them to discover criteria for themselves. For instance, when teaching directions, she had them tell her how to make a peanut butter and jelly sandwich, which she actually made. The kids had a wonderful time telling Mrs. Sudol what to do. More importantly, working through the process—which wasn't as easy as they'd expected—they learned that good directions must include materials, steps, proper sequence, time-order words, and concrete details. The point is that they, not the teacher, determined the criteria, based on their experience. And these criteria guided them in drafting and revising. Peg used similar activities for all the writing types and concluded that the criteria minilesson was an effective, efficient way to teach elements of discourse.

Next, she modeled writing processes. Graves says children don't know how writers compose; they think "the words flow, arrive 'Shazam!' on the page" (p. 43). He argues that teachers must show students that writing is not a magical or mysterious process. Taking his lead, Peg did modeling minilessons on prewriting, drafting, revising, and editing. For each writing type she demonstrated her process on the board, asking for student input. Watching Peg, the students could see that composing involved a lot more than producing one perfect draft. Further, just as Graves claims, Peg's kids picked up what they needed, internalizing her techniques, so that by the end of the year she didn't have to model as often. For example, initially, students had a terrible time generating topics, so Peg did lots of minilessons demonstrating how to brainstorm, list, map, and cluster. By the last assignment, finding a topic was no longer an issue.

Finally, she used minilessons to teach editing skills. In the past, she had taught skills from the English book, in isolation, explaining how to correct problems, assigning workbook pages, then giving objective tests. In the workshop, however, she taught skills only when her students needed them. For instance, when she noticed many children having trouble with run-on sentences, she did several minilessons. Asking permission, she put student papers on the overhead projector, and the entire class worked on locating and correcting the run-ons. After these sessions, the problem was virtually solved.

Overall, Peg found minilessons to be valuable, one of the most successful components of the workshop and an excellent way to teach students what they needed to become good writers. Moreover, because these lessons addressed specific needs and were related to actual writing, the learning was always contextual and genuine. Graves, Calkins, and Atwell were absolutely right; after teaching minilessons, Peg could never return to the English book.

Her experience with conferencing wasn't as satisfying or successful. She conducted two types of conferences: (1) daily check-in conferences, during which she'd circulate around the room looking at drafts, asking and answering questions about content, organization, process, and revision; and (2) formal conferences, which she'd do after a student had finished a draft and wanted more extensive comments before writing a final version. Her main problem with the daily check-in conferences was that she couldn't do as many as she wanted. Following Atwell's advice, she walked in a zigzag pattern through the classroom trying to see as many people as possible. Peg tried to keep these conferences short—Atwell says "just a quick minute or two" (p. 94)—but she couldn't. When she left early, the kids weren't satisfied; they didn't think she'd really conferred with them. Moreover, she thought Atwell's advice to look the student in the eye and never read the draft was imprudent. Unlike Atwell, Peg didn't believe reading drafts would take away ownership; on the contrary, she felt that refusing to read was an insult. She was worried about sending these tacit messages: "You're not important enough to spend time with; your words aren't worth looking at." Reading was a way of showing interest in their work; unfortunately, reading slowed her down, and all year she lagged behind, never building up enough speed to catch up.

Atwell also warns against making judgments about writing, but Peg also found that difficult because the kids begged for her opinion. They continually asked if something was good or bad; and if she withheld judgment, they were upset. Following Graves, Calkins, and Atwell, she asked questions, letting the children lead. But that also took time, and once again she got behind and had to put other kids off. One partial good to come from the backlog was that students learned to rely more on each other for help and did peer conferences. These often worked well; kids gave and received assistance. But they sometimes deteriorated into gossip.

Peg held formal conferences whenever someone completed a draft. The night before, she would read and make comments on the paper; the following day, she would talk with the student for 5 or 10 minutes. Everyone thoroughly enjoyed these conferences; a student had her undivided attention and felt special. Further, Peg knew these conferences were valuable because she was able to teach intensively in the "zone of proximal development" (Vygotsky, 1978), concentrating on those areas where a student most needed help. Sadly, these conferences did take more time than she expected. If a child was making progress, she couldn't say, "Time's up. Next." Also, she was plagued by distractions; Brian and the four others off task that day invariably caused static and interference.

Overall, Peg couldn't deny the benefits of conferences; but again, she thought Graves, Calkins, and Atwell had not been realistic. They made conferencing seem a lot easier than she found it. She wondered if her slowness came from a lack of experience and expertise. Maybe she would speed up with more practice. But she never believed the quick content conferences Atwell recommends could be effective. To do a good job, she had to spend more time with students, asking questions, listening, reading their writing, and talking about ways to improve it.

The one component of Peg's workshop that utterly failed was group sharing—the five-minute meeting at the end of each session. Calkins calls these share meetings "a vehicle for helping children become good writing teachers" (p. 126). Atwell used them "to bring closure to the workshop, and to find out what other writers in the workshop are up to" (p. 85). They are not a show-and-tell time but an occasion to engage in serious dialogue about writing. Peg thought this activity made perfect sense and was sure it would work. But it didn't, primarily because of space and time constraints. Whereas Atwell had her students push back the desks to make a clearing on the carpet and sit in a circle on the floor, Peg had a tiny classroom, no carpet, and 32 kids staring at the clock waiting for afternoon recess. They didn't want to share; they wanted out. Consequently, her workshop never became a close discourse community.

Peg wasn't particularly successful with publishing, either. Graves, Calkins, and Atwell urge teachers to publish student writing. Atwell says it's "crucial" (p. 98). Graves says it's "an important mode of literary enfranchisement for each child in the classroom" (p. 55). He even prints detailed directions and diagrams explaining how to make a book (pp. 59–62). Graves stresses publishing because "writing is a public act, meant to be shared with many audiences" (p. 54). It's also inherently joyful, something students love to do. Further, they learn firsthand what it means to be an author. Peg agreed completely, but she didn't do much publishing because, to be frank, it was too much work. She was putting so much time into the workshop and the six other subjects she was teaching that publication became a low priority. The prospect of gathering materials and making books was more than she could face. Graves recommends finding parent volunteers to help out, but in Peg's school volunteers were in short supply. Students kept their finished pieces in permanent folders, they shared their work, but that was about it.

She did, however, publish twice. In September, after her students wrote directions, she assembled them into a book. After Christmas, a first-grade teacher asked if Peg's class would like to write stories for her children. Even though this wasn't a required assignment, Peg's students agreed it was worthwhile and decided to do patterned-story picture books. They wrote and illustrated the stories; she bound the books. Afterwards, fifth graders read to first graders, first graders read to fifth graders, and everyone had a grand time. In fact, Peg's kids enjoyed the experience so much they asked to read to the kindergarten class. Then they donated the books to the school library for anyone to check out. Clearly, this was a positive experience. Peg saw dramatically the effects of writing for an audience. Her students became highly conscious of appropriate subject matter and word choice. Several even interviewed the first-grade teacher for advice. They were also meticulous about spelling, mechanics, and punctuation because they wanted their books to be perfect. In retrospect, Peg believes she overreacted to the difficulty of publishing—it didn't have to be that much work, and it was definitely worth the effort.

More problematic was evaluating student writing. After reading Graves, Calkins, and Atwell, Peg wasn't sure what to do. She felt they didn't want to deal with the hard issue of grades. In fact, Calkins barely mentions evaluation. Graves, although more thorough, stresses record keeping, using the writing folder to keep track of topics, completed assignments, and skills. Rather than grading writing, he recommends charting development over time, preferring teacher observations noted in an anecdotal record. Atwell, as usual, is more specific, but she too emphasizes development. She awarded first-quarter grades based on "growth over time in the basic activities in which writers engage" (p. 120). From then on she gave grades based solely on how well students fulfilled self-selected goals discussed in evaluation conferences.

Once again, Peg's problem was district requirements. She had to evaluate every piece of writing and on report cards include not only a letter grade but also a percentage. Could she devise a system that would incorporate Graves's and Atwell's ideas but still give her quantitative results? She developed a two-part evaluation form using a five-point scale. Because she asked students to work through all stages of the writing process, she gave points for prewriting, drafting, revising, and editing. But the bulk of the grade was based on writing-type criteria which the students had generated themselves in minilessons. Although not totally satisfied, Peg felt this wasn't an artificial method of evaluation; and, given district requirements, it was adequate. At least her students understood how their writing was evaluated and why they received the grades they did.

Actually, Peg disagreed with Atwell's refusal to "grade individual pieces of writing" and to "impose 'objective' standards for 'good' writing" (p. 114). According to Atwell, writing "isn't one ability but a combination of many—experimenting, planning, choosing, questioning, anticipating, organizing, reading, listening, reviewing, editing, and on and on" (pp. 113–114). This may be true, but the goal of writing is a finished product—as Graves says, something to be published and shared. Though the process should be acknowledged, it's the product that ultimately counts. When a writer submits a manuscript for publication, editors don't evaluate brainstorming. They don't care how many hours were spent at the word processor. The decision to accept or reject is based on the quality of the writing, how well it meets "objective" standards. Peg felt Atwell's refusal to grade was a cop-out, not an accurate reflection of writing in the real world, a disservice to students.

Reflections

At the end of the year, Peg evaluated her workshop. On balance, she thought it was a worthwhile experience and was glad she'd done it. In the main, her children enjoyed the writing. (Now they moaned and groaned whenever the workshop was canceled.) They wrote more than any previous students, and the quality of their writing was better. One student, Jason, complained at first that he had nothing to write about and for a month wrote nothing. Peg worked with him, classmates helped out, and—unlike Brian—he eventually came around. By March, Peg never had to do topic searches with him. He wrote fluently and prolifically in school and at home. He even started a personal journal. Jason was a workshop success right out of Graves, Calkins, and Atwell.

In June, when Peg received the Iowa Test of Basic Skills scores, she was eager—and anxious—to see how her students performed on English skills. Happily, they did as well as last year's class and somewhat better than the other fifth grade, who did not have a writers' workshop. Peg showed her principal hard evidence that she could teach language concepts in workshop without the English book.

Yet, she wasn't completely happy. Persistent problems with time and student commitment plagued her all year. And she never could overcome her initial diffidence and insecurity: She always worried that she wasn't doing the workshop right. In May she visited the workshop of a fifth-grade teacher in another school. Observing this woman and talking with her afterwards, Peg was relieved to discover she had similar problems and successes. Comparing experiences was invaluable.

Indeed, the purpose of telling Peg's story is not to discredit Graves, Calkins, and Atwell, but to compare her experience with theirs. For teachers who tried a writers' workshop but quit when it didn't work, or for those too overwhelmed to start, Peg's story may help put Graves, Calkins, and Atwell into practice by keeping them in perspective.

Another Story about "Another Story": Comment from William Teale, *Language Arts* Editor for This Article

Two reviewers examine each *Language Arts* manuscript that goes out for review. Occasionally reviewers come to completely opposite conclusions in their recommendations about the suitability of a manuscript for publication in *LA*. The article by David Sudol and Peg Sudol that you just read was a manuscript that stirred just such a difference of opinion. I was intrigued by the reviewers' responses to this piece because I thought each offered such a different and yet valid perspective on Peg's struggles to implement a writing workshop in her fifth-grade classroom.

I got permission from the reviewers to reproduce their comments here. I have included them because I believe that the issues raised in the Sudol and Sudol article are ones that many language arts educators are struggling with, and I feel that the field needs much more discussion about them. Perhaps these comments will provide additional food for thought in the exchanges that go on among readers in their schools and colleges. Perhaps they will provoke more contributions for the pages of *LA*. In any case, the issues about the roles of teachers and students in a writing workshop raised by this article need to be talked about more among language arts educators. I invite you to join the interchange.

Reviewer 1: This piece appealed to me because it reflects many of the common experiences and concerns articulated by teachers who are in the process of exploring Writing Workshop. The author's "compare/ contrast" of the work of Graves, Calkins, and Atwell is particularly effective in relation to Peg's own thoughts and classroom experiences. Peg is presented as a professional educator who capably examined the work of others and then, just as capably, explored it within the context of her own classroom. The struggles reported are real. The conflict between recommendations for success and the reality of district requirements, gaining administrative support, scheduling problems, and the time factor are objectively reported here. I found this piece to be refreshingly analytical in terms of identifying problems, as well as recognizing successes. I respect Peg's improvisations, solutions, and her efforts toward making Writing Workshop "work" for her and her students. In my opinion, this piece could serve as the focus for good faculty meeting and study group discussions. I would be interested to read a subsequent article should Peg network with others to continue to explore Writing Workshop.

Reviewer 2: My overall reaction to this article was its negativism. While there were attempts to provide and suggest solutions to the problems encountered, the negative dominated. There are scores of teachers who would read this in *LA* and quote it for *not* getting into writing. (I am an elementary administrator and speak from experience.) There is no mention of integrating reading and writing, so I wonder why this research is never discussed because it is such a good way to solve so many of the problems mentioned—time, criteria, evaluation, and so forth. While the sources used (Graves, Calkins, Atwell) are excellent, they are becoming dated. I wonder at the wisdom of relying on sources that are nearing ten years old and at the same time omitting recent works. There is newer information out there for teachers to read and use. Yes, there are problems in changing and implementing, but the *LA* audience needs to read more positive approaches backed up with the research and study on reading *and* writing.

STRATEGY: DEVIN'S DAYBOOK

Editors' Note: Here Winston and Low use Devin's daybook to illustrate a particular kind of writing that encouraged third grader Devin.

―――――✑―――――

The Daybook

Devin carried his daybook with him everywhere. He wrote in it almost daily, at school and at home. Keeping a daybook clinched his conception of himself as a writer. He came to writing workshop three times a week, for forty-five-minute periods, and he kept me posted (though I never asked him) on the number of pages he wrote each day. He did not offer to share any of his entries with me or with his classmates until just before Thanksgiving in late November. I waited, without saying a word. I trusted him.

A few days before Thanksgiving vacation Devin said he wanted to show me what he was doing in his daybook. He asked if we could get together at lunch so he could go over it with me. "You see," he said, "there's some stuff in it about people—my opinions on them—and I don't think it's fair to let anyone see that. So I can't let you have the book to look at by yourself."

He turned to the back of the book first, to show me how he was preparing an index ("So I can find things when the book's done"). The index was based on key words that he's printed in the top left or right hand corner of each completed page in the daybook. The key word for the first few entries was "Profile."

"I got the idea of writing about people from *Harriet the Spy* by Louise Fitzhugh. When I started, I thought I might put only profiles in and nothing else. It starts with a couple of people I thought were most important. Really nice, or mean, or made a lasting impression on me. And people who were visiting, who I might never see again." I pointed out that in some cases there was more than one profile for a given person. "Sometimes I find out more about them and change my opinion," he said. The profiles tended to follow a similar format, usually including information on physical appearance, personality, race, grade, age, courage, passion. "For instance," Devin said, "are they black or white, do they wear glasses, have freckles? What makes the person special? How fast do they normally walk? Are they in a hurry all the time? Are they really tough guys? I rate them on a scale of 1 to 20. 20's the tough-

▶

est. And their passion can be a lot of things—a toy, or they like boating—it's whatever they're most enthusiastic about."

Next, Devin showed me an entry marked "Pen Pal." He had joined a student letter exchange mentioned in *The Young Writer's Handbook* (Tchudi, 1987). A third entry, marked "Dreams," referred to a dream in a Walt Disney movie.

A Red Robot diagram came next. "My brother's toy," Devin explained. The last entry he showed me was a description of an elaborate game he and a friend had made up, with strike teams and careful records of games won, lost, and tied.

I thanked him for sharing his daybook with me, and asked if he wanted to share any of it with his classmates in group-share time. He said he'd think about it and let me know.

In December, on Parents' Visiting Day, Devin decided to share one of his daybook entries:

> Opinion or "My First dictonarys"
>
> by Devin low
>
> Why are there so many "My First dictonarys"?
> Who are they refering to when they say "my" in a My First dictionary? Why dont they say "your First dictionary? And most familys have an oxford in the house so its probably your 2nd dictionary. or maybe your 3rd. or maybe its the 8th in your collection! Howcome some have simple words like ~~~~ and others have complex words like rhodendron, philospher, potasium, and preliminary
>
> If you have ohswers to these Questions write to:
>
> Meaders Digest in Linda's center.
>
> at, dad, yesterday, "my First dictionary?"

(pp. 36–38)

Source: Winston, L., & Low, D. (1990). Devin's daybook. *Language Arts,* *67 (1)*, 35–46.

REFLECTION: THE POWER OF DIALOGUE JOURNALS

Editors' Note: As Roderick and Berman discuss in the following excerpt, journal writing can be a powerful kind of writing, encouraging students to write for a range of communicative intentions.

―――――✥―――――

How We Used Language

We discovered the following language functions in both our journals.

1. *Hunching/questioning*: Tentative, questioning, conditional expression; guessing at outcomes, hypothesizing (e.g., "I would hunch the experience would be very helpful to the foreign students.").

2. *Describing/elaborating*: Stating what is, was, or will be: telling course of actions, delineating a situation, extending ideas, subject, or area; making reference to outside sources (e.g., "There was an interesting article on this topic in *JTE* some months ago.").

3. *Chaining*: Sustaining the dialogue by referring to a prior entry or picking up on an idea expressed earlier (e.g., "Yes, I think that activity contributes to personalizing the course.").

4. *Reflecting on self*: Expressing feelings, hopes, plans, aspirations, intent, preference; more definite in tone than item 1 (e.g., "I ended with a question, and now I have many questions.").

5. *Suggesting*: Proposing to the other person a course of action, what could or should be done in a declarative, definitive mode (e.g., "I'm convinced we should be dealing with concerns like the teachable moment.").

6. *Logistics*: Make definite reference to the practice of dialogue journal writing, such as critiquing or raising questions about the procedure (e.g., "I think we should discuss some possible ways of responding to entries.").

The first four functions accounted for the bulk of our journal entries. These functions suggest we focused more on pondering ourselves as teachers as well as sustaining a conversational mode than on making suggestions to each other or dealing with the logistics of dialogue journal writing. However, neither of us used the same set

▷

of functions predominantly and consistently, and our use of the functions shifted depending on whether we were initiating or responding to journal entries (although when writing we were not always consciously aware of our role). Furthermore, we both did not use the same functions when playing the initiator and responder roles. Consciously or not, we probably perceived our roles as initiator and responder quite differently, although we both described and explained more when initiating and chained more (to maintain the conversation) when responding. (pp. 687–688)

Source: Roderick, J. A., & Berman, L. M. (1984). Dialoguing about dialogue journals. *Language Arts, 61*(7), 686–692.

20 Informational Books: Models for Student Report Writing

Evelyn B. Freeman

Editors' text: One persistent criticism of the writing process as it is enacted in classrooms in the overemphasis on writing fiction. Evelyn Freeman offers some guidance for helping students learn report writing.

Streams paved with gold! Glittering nuggets loose on the ground, scattered everywhere! No machinery needed. A pick, shovel, pocketknife, even a kitchen spoon will do. Free for the taking, no government restrictions. Stake a claim, collect the loot, carry home a fortune. (Blumberg, 1989, p. 1)

On a sunny October morning, a van pulls up in front of a ranch-style house in an American suburb. Out jump a young man and woman dressed in black tailcoats and top hats. They are both professional chimney sweeps, and are wearing the costume that has been the trademark of chimney sweeps for almost four hundred years. (Giblin, 1982, p. 1)

These beginning paragraphs from *The Great American Gold Rush* by Rhoda Blumberg and *Chimney Sweeps* by James Cross Giblin pique the reader's interest and convey the authors' enthusiasm for their topics. These fine informational books provide models for children in writing their own works of nonfiction.

Although narrative writing has enjoyed a major place in the elementary writing program, informative writing has been relegated to a lesser position. Britton, Burgess, Martin, McLeod, and Rosen (1975) describe informative writing as a subcategory of transactional writing in which language is used to "record and report, to classify and compare, to infer and deduce and hypothesize, to ask and answer questions, to assert, to explain, and to evaluate" (p. 94). In elementary schools informative writing has generally been equated with the report.

This essay appeared in *Language Arts* 68.6 (1991) on pages 470–473.

Many students cling to stereotypes about the report—an exercise too often associated with paraphrasing from the encyclopedia. As Atwell (1990) points out:

> Report writing per se isn't the problem. . . . [T]he problem with school reports lies in our methods of assigning them. We need to put the emphasis where it belongs—on meaning—and show students how to investigate questions and communicate their findings, how to go beyond plagiarism to genuine expertise and a "coming to know." (p. xiv)

Report writing, therefore, involves children in the process of gathering, organizing, and synthesizing information about a topic. When this topic is self-selected on the basis of student interest, the report can be a vehicle for students to explore a topic in depth and share their knowledge with others.

This article presents a basic framework for guiding children in report writing using children's informational books as models in the process. Various aspects of report writing are discussed, and specific book titles are described as they relate to these aspects. Since each elementary classroom is unique, teachers will adapt ideas in this article to respond to the particular needs and interests of their students.

Exploring the Topic

Writing informatively requires a process of investigation prior to putting pen to paper. If we consider the various steps in writing a report, we see how informational books support this process and serve as models for children.

First, a student selects a topic to investigate. Graves (1989) suggests that students list things they know about, discuss their list with peers, and then choose a topic to research. We find that many noted authors of nonfiction for children specialize in particular areas of interest: Leonard Everett Fisher usually writes about historic occupations and locations; Patricia Lauber focuses on science; and Brent Ashabranner explores social issues and cultural differences.

Once students identify a topic to investigate, they locate resources and collect data. To begin this process, students may web their topic, brainstorming possible subcategories and related ideas. Or they may formulate questions that they hope to answer in their investigation. One way to get an overview of a topic is to consult a picture book. Graves (1989) encourages the use of picture books "as a good place for children to begin to explore their subject. Authors of picture books . . . have chosen essential information underlying basic concepts" (p. 90). For example, *People* by Peter Spier (1980) provides a wonderful introduction to culture with detailed illustrations framed around the universals of culture and the different ways those universals are realized. Downs Matthews's *Polar Bear Cubs* traces with color photographs the lives of two bear cubs from their birth to when they can "live alone in the Arctic" (Matthews, 1989, unpaged) two years later. Children get a first lesson in sign language by visiting the zoo with a group of children in *Handtalk Zoo* by George Ancona and Mary Beth Miller (1989). The picture books of Gail Gibbons provide a wonderful introduction to a wide variety of topics, such as kites, newspapers, milk, and skyscrapers.

Writers of nonfiction consult diverse sources to obtain information. By reviewing informational books, students become aware that researching a report requires far more than reading one encyclopedia entry. One type of source is first-hand experience or personal observation. Kathryn Lasky participated in the making of maple syrup to write the Newbery Honor Book *Sugaring Time* (1983). George Ancona and Joan Anderson traveled to Massachusetts, Georgia, and Iowa to follow the daily lives of three farm families for their book *The American Family Farm* (1989). To write *The Riddle of the Rosetta Stone,* James Cross Giblin (1990) visited the Egyptian galleries of the Metropolitan Museum of Art, the Brooklyn Museum, the Cleveland Museum of Art, and the Museum of Fine Arts in Boston.

Primary source material provides valuable information in writing a report. Milton Meltzer's books are known for their reliance on primary sources such as letters, speeches, and court testimony. Primary source material was used by Peter and Connie Roop, whose book, *I, Columbus: My Journal* (1990), is based on the diary of Christopher Columbus. Personal interviews with young people comprise the focus for *A Tree Still Stands: Jewish Youth in Eastern Europe Today* by Yale Strom (1990). Interviews also provide the basis for *Operation Grizzly Bear* by Marian Calabro (1989), which documents the 12-year study of the grizzly bears of Yellowstone National Park by Frank and John Craighead.

In addition to interviews, first-hand experience, and primary sources, writers of nonfiction also consult a variety of secondary sources. Rhoda Blumberg lists more than 20 secondary sources as references for *The Great American Gold Rush* (1989). These sources include magazine articles as well as books. Similarly, the four-page bibliography for *Panama Canal, Gateway to the World* by Judith St. George (1989) consists of books, newspaper and magazine articles, government documents, brochures, and the written proceedings of meetings.

Children, therefore, are provided examples in these and other informational books of the variety of sources consulted to collect facts for a report. This wide range of sources enables the writer to see a broader perspective of the topic, one not limited to a singular point of view.

Writing the Report

Once sources have been collected, children record their information in some way. Taking notes can be done in a variety of formats such as note cards, learning logs, individual pieces of paper, computer entries, or writing answers to the questions generated by the students. Students should be guided to consider key words and phrases and put down main ideas and supporting details. Copying directly from the book should be avoided unless students think they may want to use a direct quote from the source in writing.

After the information has been gathered, it must be organized in some way. Students make decisions about which facts to use. They may want to consider those that are most interesting to them and necessary to understand the topic. If they have discovered contradictory evidence in their sources, they must decide how to handle the discrepancy. After students have determined what information to include, they can again consult informational books that provide examples of various types of organization and structure. The alphabet format has been used by many authors to convey information around a given theme. The Caldecott Award–winning *Ashanti to Zulu* by Margaret Musgrove (1976) describes 26 different African tribes. *Illuminations* by Jonathan Hunt (1989) provides a wealth of material about the Middle Ages on each page.

Another way to organize information is by chronology, as exemplified by Aliki's *The King's Day: Louis XIV of France* (1989), which follows a typical day in the life of Louis XIV from morning to night. Chronology is also frequently used as in *Volcano: The Eruption and Healing of Mount St. Helens* by Patricia Lauber (1986), which traces the eruption of the volcano on March 20, 1980, to the possible future of the mountain 100 years from now. The passage of time in years provides the framework for *A Long Hard Journey: The Story of the Pullman Porter* by Patricia and Fredrick McKissack (1989), which takes the reader from 1829 to 1979.

Still another way to organize the material is conceptually. Students may return to their webs to review the subcategories of their topic. Rhoda Blumberg (1989) uses this structure in *The Great American Gold Rush*, which includes chapters on "Women," "Foreigners," and "Law and Order." Russell Freedman's *Immigrant Kids* (1980) presents a detailed account of the lives of immigrant children in American cities between 1880 and the early 1900s. The book is organized into chapters that feature different facets of the children's lives: "At Home," "At School," "At Play," "At Work."

Many children may prefer to relate their information using a more narrative-like structure. An example of the story format in an informational book is *Growing Up Amish* by Richard Ammon (1989). It begins like a piece of fiction:

> A small light shines in the barn as Anna throws back the covers. Daat (Dad) has already stoked the wood stove downstairs in the kitchen so it isn't such a frosty surprise when she swings her feet onto the cold linoleum floor. "Schtef uff," ("Get up") Anna says to her sister, snuggled under her heavy quilt, trying to deny morning. (p. 1)

Another example of a story structure is *Totem Pole* by Diane Hoyt-Goldsmith (1990), told in the first person by David, a Tsimshian Indian boy.

Atwell (1990) points out that there are many ways to report knowledge and suggests a variety of genres that the writing may take. For instance, students may construct a pop-up book. Models for nonfiction pop-up books do exist, such as *Leonardo da Vinci* by Alice and Martin Provensen (1984). Another format is the how-to book, in "which students pass on specialized knowledge related to a unit of study" (p. 164). Perl's *The Great Ancestor Hunt: The Fun of Finding Out Who You Are* (1989) provides a good model for this type of book. Students may present their information in the format of an annotated catalogue such as in *Book of Eagles* by Helen Sattler (1989), which provides a glossary of the different kinds of eagles. Information about a topic can be written in poetry form, as in *The Steamboat in the Cornfield* by John Hartford (1986). Atwell also suggests that children write math concept books. *If You Made a Million* by David Schwartz (1989), with humorous illustrations by Steven Kellogg, would be such a book.

The student will need to make other decisions about his or her writing. Should I include headings and subheadings? Do I need an index and table of contents? Should I include a glossary? Should I organize the report into chapters? Should I include illustrations or diagrams? Will the tone of my writing be serious or humorous? After the student has completed the writing, he or she may share it in some meaningful and interesting way with the entire class.

Graves (1989) notes that "the purpose of the report is to help children enjoy the process of discovering information on the way to learning some of the tools that will help them sustain more complex reports" (p. 101). Further, the

> object of the whole report process is to help students find a territory of information they know something about, and then enjoy the process of learning still more by listening to their reading and to the texts they compose. The report should become a natural part of children's lives and a tool for important learning. (p. 103)

Nonfiction children's books can serve as positive models to children in understanding the process of report writing.

STRATEGY: WRITING IN A PENPAL PROGRAM

Editors' Note: One of the challenges of learning to write is anticipating the needs of readers who may be separated from the writer by time and space. In this excerpt, Berrill and Gall discuss how penpal programs offer young writers the opportunity to write for distant readers.

Writing Apprenticeship

When penpal letters are read on the carpet, everything that is written is read. This means that the reader begins by reading the date and the salutation. The children thus hear 22 letters in a matter of a few days, each of which begins with a slight variation on ways in which the date and salutation can be written. It takes them very little time, indeed, to learn that they begin the writing of their own letters with date and salutation. The same thing is true of endings, where most penpals close with a variation of the phrase "Your penpal," followed by their name. The predictability of the language and genre forms quickly enculturates the children, and enables them to predict what is going to be said in at least part of the letter, whether they are reading a letter from their penpal or writing their own. Pappas and Pettegrew (1998) refer to these contextual regularities of genre as providing a strong foundation for personal agency. Certainly, that seems to be true here.

Molly explicitly encourages the dialogic nature of letter writing by referring to the older penpals' questions and content as things the children can answer in their responses. For instance, in one carpet session the following interchanges took place:

[Molly is reading Kayla's letter with her.]

Molly: [Reading] "What is your favorite thing to do in the
   snow? [She looks at Kayla.] There's a question you have
   to answer back."

* * *

[Reading Amy's letter with her.]

Molly: [Reading] "This year because [Remembrance Day]
   landed on a Saturday, I guess the schools couldn't do
   anything. [Molly looks at Amy.] We did something. You'll
   have to tell her."

* * *

[Reading Ben's letter from Mark who has written about a
popular television show, *Hockey Night in Canada,* and about
his favorite commentator, Don Cherry.]

Molly: [Reading] "I like Don Cherry the best. Who do you
   like?" [Molly turns to Ben.] Do you know who Don
   Cherry is? Maybe you'll have to ask him who Don
   Cherry is when you write to him."

In hearing these explicit suggestions, not only do the children learn
that they are supposed to answer questions in a general sense, but
Molly draws the child's attention, and that of the whole community
sitting on the carpet, to particular questions. When Molly senses that
the child may not understand a question, she mediates the communication by giving additional prompts regarding possible things the
child might write. As well, the children learn that a question can be
answered with another question. This modeling occurs for the whole
community.

Through the public nature of these interchanges, the emergent
writers see and hear a variety of writing strategies and how these
strategies can be applied to particular writing situations. The children
are thus enculturated into the genre in a way that enables them to
experience both the typification of the genre as well as the variation
possible within the genre. Neither of these things would happen in
nearly the same way if each child read only her or his own letter, nor
if they were given writing ideas only about their own writing context.

As well as giving writing instruction regarding ways of responding to specific questions or comments in their penpals' letters,
Molly also uses time on the carpet to give information about appro-

▶

priate content. One way in which she does this is that before the children leave the carpet to go to their desks and tables to work on their own letters, she reviews with the children things they have done in school that they could write about. The children know that, in addition to answering their penpal's questions, they are supposed to "write something about ourselves or tell some news," as one child put it.

These particular examples give only a sampling of the kind of sociocognitive activities and negotiation that occur on the carpet. This sociocognitive knowledge construction, enculturation, and mediation includes procedural knowledge and skill development in relation to letter reading and writing as well as knowledge about the culture of reading and writing letters. Time on the carpet is particularly valuable in these regards because children see and hear many examples of the typified actions of the activities. This both reinforces the recurrent and predictable aspects of letters and shows the range of acceptable variability within the activity, the plasticity of the genre as it were. (pp. 473–474)

Source: Berrill, D. P., & Gall, M. (1999). On the carpet: Emergent writer/readers' letter sharing in a penpal program, *Language Arts*, 76(6), 470–478.

STRATEGIES: FROM AUTHOR STUDY TO MINI-LESSONS FOR NONFICTION

Editors' Note: A variety of mini-lessons can spring from one source. The author study in Duthie's first-grade classroom became the source of numerous mini-lessons, only some of which are listed below. Similar lessons might arise from the study of a fiction writer or from a theme unit.

Author Study

Throughout the year, I had used author study to illustrate style and perspective, as well as the concept that writing is produced by a real person. . . . I based my author study selection on the age and interests of my students and chose to begin the exploration of nonfiction with a study of Gail Gibbons. . . . Each day for about a week, I read

▶

one of her books, and we observed and listed the techniques she used to convey the information. Because Gail Gibbons writes on many topics, the Gibbons author study brought us to the issue of research and a research mini-lesson. (pp. 588–589)

Research Mini-Lesson

After reading Gail Gibbons's *Whales* (1989), I found that my first-grade children already knew that nonfiction writers have to seek information, to research. In a whole-group mini-lesson, I asked, "How do you think Gail Gibbons got the information about whales?" Some of their responses included:

> She probably went to Florida to watch whales. . . .
>
> She probably read about whales in books.
>
> Maybe she asked a sea captain. . . .

We listed ways to get information on nonfiction topics. Although the children knew how to obtain information before I taught the mini-lesson, their learning that all nonfiction writers research or write from personal experience seemed to give them a better understanding of nonfiction as a genre. I concluded the mini-lesson with a brainstorming session on topics familiar to the children. I told them to think about a writing topic they might like to choose. (p. 589)

Contrasting Presentations

After about a week of the Gail Gibbons author study, I decided to switch from the author study to the technique of using several books with very different presentations on the same topic as a focus for mini-lessons. In planning, I selected books that offered different presentations of the same topic. The children observed the variation in style, illustration and technique. . . . In discussions, I would often ask the children why a writer chose a particular technique and what other techniques might the writer have chosen. (pp. 589–590)

A "Permission" [to Read Selectively] Mini-Lesson

I introduced the idea that, often, when reading nonfiction, the reader does not have to read the whole book. Rather, readers can seek out specific information on their interests. The table of contents and indexes help us to do this. (pp. 590–591)

Source: Duthie, C. (1994). Nonfiction: A genre study for the primary classroom. *Language Arts, 71*(8), 588–595.

STRATEGY: HELPING YOUNG WRITERS IMPROVE THEIR STORY BEGINNINGS

Editors' Note: Sometimes drawing students' attention to the wonderful demonstrations of writing found in children's books can be a resource for a wide variety of writing mini-lessons. This excerpt from Lunsford provides an example of using children's storybooks to help improve the leads of stories.

As I glanced through the stack of writer's workshop folders, I noticed that nearly half of the students' stories began with "Hello, my name is . . .," and the other half began with "This is a . . . ." I went to my shelf, grabbed an armful of my favorite books, some chart paper, and some markers. What follows is a [partial] transcript of the heart of the mini-lesson that evolved the next morning when the students and I met on the carpet with our writing folders. . . .

> [Mrs. L. begins with a discussion of what she was writing and mentions that she liked her story but for the beginning and thought about a children's book dealing with a similar topic. Some of the children make comments about the beginning of the story.]
>
> *Mrs. L.:* Good! I have some of our favorite books here. Let's look at them to see how these writers got started. Yesterday, some of you were working on make-believe stories. *The Frog Prince Continued* by Jon Scieszka (1991) doesn't begin with "Once upon a time" but with "Well, let's just say they lived sort of happily for a long time."
>
> *Eve:* That makes it different.
>
> *Mrs. L.:* Yes! Let's try this one. "Swish! Swash! Splash! Swoosh! Strange sounds come from the house on East 88th Street."
>
> *Jessie:* That's the beginning of *Funny, Funny Lyle* (Waber, 1987).

▶

Mrs. L.: Right! What do you think about this beginning?

Jessie: I want to know what's making the swishes and swashes.

Mrs. L.: The beginning of a story should do just that. You know from books you read that if the first page doesn't excite you, it's hard to keep reading. Who wrote a beginning that they would like to share?

At read-aloud time that afternoon we created a chart where we recorded the first sentences of the books we shared together. Our list grew longer and longer, reflecting the many styles of story beginnings . . . . Each time we added a sentence to our list, we briefly discussed how the words made us want to read more. In time, I began to notice changes in the children's story leads. (pp. 43–44)

Source: Lunsford, S. H. (1997). "And they wrote happily ever after": Literature-based mini-lessons in writing. *Language Arts*, 74(1), 42–48.

21 Developing a Spelling Conscience

Jan Turbill

Editors' Text: Jan Turbill draws on a series of case studies and instructional projects to illustrate the importance of proofreading in developing a "spelling conscience" and, ultimately, learning to spell.

> Spelling is easy — it is getting it right that's the hard part.
>> (11-year-old Guilda, as cited in
>> Bean & Bouffler, 1987, p. 70)

Guilda's insightful comment highlighted for me the vital role that proofreading seems to play in the spelling process. But what do we know about the proofreading process? Just what does "getting it right" entail?

In a time when many standardized tests are using a proofreading task to test students' spelling ability, isn't it time we understood more about proofreading and its links to spelling? A focus on proofreading, I will argue, serves to operationalize the connections between reading, writing, spelling, and phonics development.

I will argue that spelling is best *learned* if the way it's *taught* is congruent with what we have discovered about learning, about language, and about the role that spelling plays in our culture. I want to present some research findings, which span several years, and which strongly suggest that we have not understood the role that proofreading actually plays in the learning-to-spell process. Nor have we understood that proofreading is a special kind of reading that needs to be explicitly taught, so that students, in turn, can understand how it differs from other kinds of reading, such as reading for meaning, skim reading, and critical reading. Proofreading, I will argue, requires readers to *read like a speller* (Smith, 1982). Basically, I want to argue that proofreading might be the missing link between spelling and phonics and effective reading and writing.

The data that have led me to this conclusion emerged from a series of case studies I conducted over several years and include taped

---

This essay appeared in *Language Arts* 77.3 (2000) on pages 209–217.

interviews, transcripts, and retrospective journal notes. In what follows, I outline briefly what emerged from each of these studies, and how, cumulatively, these case studies led me to generate a possible theoretical link between proofreading, reading, writing, and spelling, and phonics.

Case Study 1: Sally's Story

Sally was a young woman who had just commenced a course at a vocational college. She feared she would not succeed because she was, as she put it, a hopeless speller. She walked in to the Education Center in which I worked at the time to ask for help. She asked for a spelling book with lists of words that she could take and memorize. My notes of that meeting indicate that I was reluctant to give her what she asked for because it seemed that she had already spent years at school trying to learn to spell through rote memorization of lists of words. When I pointed this out she pleaded, "So what will help me?"

Over coffee, I shared with her what being a speller involved. We did a short activity that helped her see that there are various spelling strategies people use to spell (Bean & Bouffler, 1987, 1997). I talked about the role that reading plays in learning to spell and, of course, the role writing plays (Graves, 1981; Smith, 1982, 1985; Wilde, 1990, 1992). We then discussed the proofreading process. She agreed to try some new strategies. She agreed to buy a small notebook in which she would jot down a few of the words each day that caused her trouble in her course. Then, when she was reading materials for her course or reading magazines on the train, she would look for these words in the text; perhaps even underline them when she found them.

She seemed to understand that the idea was to look carefully at how others spelled the words that were causing her trouble. Finally, she agreed that she would add the conventional spellings of her trouble-words, as well as others she saw that interested her from her reading, into the back of her notebook. I also suggested that she look carefully at the advertisements in magazines and note how words were often deliberately misspelled to grab the reader's attention. Before Sally left the Center, we did some of these activities together as a demonstration of what I meant.

Sally appeared again some months later. She told me that she came back in order to tell me how much her spelling had improved and to thank me for being such a great teacher. I responded by pointing out that she was doing all the work, and all that I did was to help her understand what spelling involved and how it fitted within the reading/

writing processes. I pointed out to her that she had become a very careful proofreader of her own and others' work (she was even finding typographical errors in the magazine articles she was reading). She indicated that she was now far more confident in her spelling ability.

That was the last time Sally and I met. I did learn that she had easily passed her course.

Sally's case interested me and caused me to wonder about the connections between spelling development and the proofreading process.

Case Study 2: Andrew's Story

Andrew is my nephew and, between the ages of 5 and 10, he spent a great deal of time with me and was my guinea pig during those writing process days in the '80s (Butler & Turbill, 1984; Cambourne & Turbill, 1987; Graves, 1981; Turbill 1983).

By the age of 20, Andrew was a prolific reader and writer—yet, by his own admission, he was a terrible speller. His first drafts were full of errors. and he had great trouble in deciding what was conventional and what was not. He would often send me copies of the narratives he wrote, requesting a telephone conference. His narratives were excellent stories but so filled with spelling errors that my attention was often diverted from the message. This caused me great concern. I felt that I might have been responsible for his poor spelling by inadvertently giving him the message during his formative years that spelling was not important.

Some years later, he stayed with me in order to finish the final report for an honors degree in science. As usual, he asked me to read his paragraphs and chapters to check the logic and flow. I noted that while he seemed to be able to spell the specialist technical terms conventionally, he had misspelled many comparatively simple words. For instance, he confused the use of "their" and "there," often spelling the latter, "thear." I asked him why he thought this happened. He admitted that he seemed to learn the technical words easily because, as he said, "I had to look at them very carefully as I read in order to work out their meaning." He also commented that when he was writing the technical terms, he had trained himself to check to see if they were correct because he knew "the spell checker didn't always have these scientific words in it."

My journal notes indicate that it was during this discussion that I made this connection: Here was a 20-year-old reader/writer with no understanding of the connections between the reading and writing processes, in particular the spelling connection. It was at this point that we began to discuss how I thought spelling was learned. I explained that we learn much of our knowledge of how to spell words by seeing them as we read. He seemed to miss the point I was trying to make, for he argued, "I read a lot. Shouldn't I therefore be a great speller?"

I pointed out to Andrew that his ability to spell the scientific words demonstrated that he *could* be a great speller. I explained that when he read for meaning, his eyes sampled only parts of words—just enough for him to work out the word's meaning; his eyes didn't look at the letters and letter patterns in sequence. However, when he read to get the visual spelling pattern of the scientific words under control, it seems that he deliberately slowed his reading down, and looked at the letters and patterns of letters in sequence. He admitted that in attempting to write these words he had been forced to return continually to the original written text he was reading in order to check them. It seemed from this conversation that Andrew was using a different form of reading to both check and then write the technical terms. I began to wonder whether this was akin to what Smith (1982) called "reading like a writer." In Andrew's case, he knew that he would most likely need to write the technical words he was reading, so he engaged in the demonstrations of the letter patterns on the page in such a way that he would be able to spell them at a later time. Andrew was "reading like a speller." What was the relationship between this process of reading-as-a-speller and the proofreading task that we have tended to ask students to carry out only in final drafts of writing? These were the questions that were being raised by our discussions.

This case study concluded in much the same way as did Sally's. My notes indicate that we decided that Andrew should try to do the same with all the words he consistently misspelled. And he did. He became consciously aware of these words. He looked for them as he read and he wrote them in a personal list. It took just a few weeks before he had control over most of the words he needed to use. Like Sally, Andrew had become an efficient proofreader. The portfolio of Andrew's writing that I keep (I am at heart a doting aunt) indicates that the change has been both significant and permanent. The pieces he now e-mails me (and they are all examples of one-draft writing) show very few spelling errors. It seems that the conventional spelling patterns of words that he would have typically misspelled had been internalized so that he can now retrieve them automatically. Furthermore, when he now encounters a word he can't spell, he has a strategy for learning it. Like Sally, he has become an astute proofreader of his own and others' writing.

Pulling Some Threads Together: Clarifying the Research Problem

These case studies forced me to think more deeply about the issues inherent in learning to spell. I knew for example, that Andrew had experienced a strong phonics-first program in his early years at school and an intensive, direct instruction spelling program, heavily oriented toward lists and rote memorization during his middle school years. As well, he was an avid writer and reader.

Both his and Sally's case studies made me more conscious of the reading/writing connection and the role that spelling played in this connection. Each made me think more and more about proofreading and its importance in the spelling process, particularly in the getting-it-right process, which, after all, seems to be what really counts with both teachers and students.

These case studies, together with other data I've collected since, led me to ask why, with the plethora of research into spelling, with the number of recent books written to help teachers teach spelling (Bean & Bouffler, 1997; Gentry, 1997; Pinnell, Fountas, & Giacobbe,1998; Snowball & Bolton, 1999 to name a few), we still seem to have made little headway. In fact, there is some rather alarming evidence that today's children do not appear to be spelling as effectively as their predecessors (Westwood, 1994).

Findings such as these puzzled me when I knew that today's children were engaged in more sustained reading and writing than ever before. Especially when we are supposed to know so much more about the learning and teaching of spelling. Or do we?

Three questions began to form in my mind:

1. What is the relationship between the proofreading process and spelling knowledge?
2. What skills and knowledge do we need and use to be effective proofreaders?
3. What happens in classrooms where proofreading is taught alongside spelling?

These key questions helped frame several research projects which I subsequently carried out over the next few years. One project focused on identifying the skills and knowledge that effective proofreaders use. The second project focused on the implications for practice when these skills and understandings were incorporated into the reading/writing curriculum of a grade 2 class. In what follows, I will describe what emerged from these projects. First however, I need to make explicit the presuppositions I held at the time about spelling, and about the teaching and learning of spelling.

Presuppositions Underpinning the Projects

There were many basic assumptions about spelling and the teaching of spelling that I held as I began these projects; assumptions that are strongly supported in the literature on spelling (Bean & Bouffler, 1987, 1997; Gentry, 1978, 1981; Gentry & Gillet, 1993; Henderson & Templeton, 1986; Wilde, 1990, 1992; Zutell, 1990). These include the following:

- Spelling is a language process governed by the same subsystems as reading and writing—namely the semantic, syntactic, and graphophonic systems.
- Spelling serves writing.
- Spelling is primarily learned through reading (i.e., reading provides demonstrations of the spellings of words).
- Learning to spell is a developmental process.
- There are certain orthographic patterns that are consistent within English spelling.
- Being able to spell conventionally is regarded as a desirable attainment (or, conversely, there is a social stigma attached to poor spelling).
- Spellers use a range of strategies to spell words, including phonics (or sounding out) and visual memory.
- Spelling needs to be explicitly taught.

While there is a great deal written in the literature on most aspects of spelling, there seems little written about proofreading and the role it plays in the teaching and learning of spelling. In fact, when I reviewed the literature, I found only one reference which actually supported my hunch, namely that the process of proofreading is not a common feature of many classrooms. Hall (1984, as cited in Madraso, 1993) goes as far as claiming that "most teachers expect students to proofread but few teach it or in fact were taught specific proofreading skills themselves" (p. 32).

Working Definitions

It became apparent that before I could begin these projects I needed a working definition of the term proofreading. Bean and Bouffler (1987) define proofreading as "the scanning of a written text for surface errors, focusing on grammar, punctuation and spelling in order to detect de-

Error	Corrected word	Skills, knowledge I used to identify word
peicemeal	piecemeal	• looked wrong • checked out rule, "i before e" etc. • read on to see if word used elsewhere
stowtly	stoutly	• looked wrong • more I looked, more I wasn't sure because "ow" as in "cow" sounds the same • reread

Figure 1. Sample of grid used by participants.

viations from the standard" (p. 66). I decided to begin with this as my working definition.

Project 1

The focus question of this project was: What skills, knowledge, and strategies do people need to know and use when they proofread; that is, to identify words that deviate from the standard and to write the standard form?

To examine this question, I prepared a simple instrument that would enable me to tap into the skills, knowledge, and understandings that were activated when proficient readers are asked to proofread a text. I had the first page of an interesting article from an academic journal electronically scanned so that it was easy for me to create 12 spelling errors without changing the format of the text. The 12 words were chosen deliberately. For instance, one was "peicemeal." This word was chosen because of the "ie" rule and because the word was used again at the end of the text. Another was "managment." Deleting the "e" from the middle of a word, it was thought, would make it more difficult for the reader to "see" the error. Also, the spelling of the word "judgment" is acceptable with or without the "e."

Participants were given a response sheet in the form of the grid shown in Figure 1 in which to write their responses and reflections.

The instrument was administered to more than 200 participants, all of whom were teachers. They were given 10 minutes to proofread the text individually and underline any errors they found. They were then asked to work with a colleague and reflect on the skills, knowledge, and strategies they used to first identify the words that deviated from the standard, and then to fill in the standard form. On completion of this procedure, the groups collaboratively analyzed and summarized their responses. I then used their summaries to generate a set of principles about "what proofreading means for our classroom teaching."

Results of Project 1

The analysis of these data indicated that proofreading required participants to carry out two broad tasks. These were to identify the misspelled word and then to use a range of strategies for changing that word so that it met the conventions of spelling.

With respect to being able to identify the misspelled words, participants indicated that they first needed to be able to read. If one could not read, they argued, one would not be able to identify the word as right or wrong. But they also agreed that they needed to be strategic readers. That is, they were aware that they used reading strategies such as skimming through the whole text to gain the meaning before coming back and rereading the text carefully. They were conscious that they were reading a text from an academic journal and thus some words could be "jargon" words, spelled in a particular way. They read ahead as well as reread to check if the word they thought was wrong was written somewhere else in the text, or that they had the correct meaning for the word and thus the spelling (e.g., the use of words such as "to," "two," "too," and "there," "their," "they're"), and so on.

Participants indicated that they had developed a good eye for identifying misspellings (they'd become, as one person indicated, "spelling detectives"). This meant that during the proofreading process, they needed to slow down their reading of the text, quite consciously and deliberately, so that each word was scanned carefully.

Having confidence in themselves as spellers seemed to be another important aspect in the proofreading process. Some participants viewed themselves to be "good" spellers and thus made their decisions about which words were incorrect confidently. Those who perceived themselves to be "poor" spellers indicated that they began to feel anxious as to whether they had identified all the incorrect spellings, and began to seek reassurance from people around them. Others indicated that the more they searched for incorrect words the more uncertain they became about their choices, and they began to feel uncomfortable about sharing with others.

Participants agreed that an understanding of the writing process was vital during proofreading as this meant that a reader knew that there is a time for draft writing and a time for polished, published writing. This understanding led to knowing why and when proofreading should be done. They indicated that, although it seems obvious, it is important that writers understand that they write texts for readers to read. Furthermore, writers need to know and use the conventional, accepted ways for writing (spelling) words or they risk being labeled a poor speller, and, by implication, a poor writer, and possibly a poor student.

Critical to the proofreading process was having a range of proof-reading strategies that can be used to assist in checking writing. Participants identified many personal strategies they used as proofreaders. These included fixing one's focus on each word, reading aloud and looking at the words as one reads, using a pencil to physically touch each word in order to slow down one's reading of the words, placing a ruler or piece of paper under a line of text, or reading one line at a time beginning from the bottom of the page and so on.

Finally, it was agreed that once misspellings were identified, it was important to have a range of spelling strategies to be able to locate their conventional spellings. Participants indicated a range of strategies such as writing the word several times to see which one "looked" right, sounding out the word and the syllables in the word, referring to spelling rules they knew, checking in books where they knew the word was written, using dictionaries and spell checkers, and, most importantly, asking others.

Comment on Results of Project 1

The general principles that emerged from this project were:

1. The "getting-it-right" aspect of spelling (the proofreading process) is a highly complex process that draws on reading, writing, spelling (i.e., encoding), and phonics (i.e., decoding) skills and knowledge.

2. Proofreading seems to be a powerful tool that integrates reading, writing, spelling, and phonic knowledge in the minds of the users.

3. Society values conventional spelling above all and these values are reflected in the attitudes and perceptions we have of ourselves as spellers.

Given these findings, I began to ask myself: Should we be focusing more on proofreading as a classroom instructional strategy? What were the implications of the above for classroom practice? These questions became the focus of the next project.

Project 2

Project 2 took place in a grade 2 classroom of 28 mixed-ability children. Mark, the teacher, had participated in Project 1 because he had become frustrated with his current spelling curriculum. While he felt that the children in his class were learning to spell words, he was concerned that there was little transfer to their first-draft writing. He was particularly frustrated that the children showed little effort or ability in proofreading their writing, even though he felt that he had set up the expectation that they should.

Mark asked if I would work in his classroom in a project aimed at improving the teaching of proofreading in his classroom. I agreed to work with Mark in a co-researching relationship (Cambourne & Turbill, 1991), a relationship in which each recognized the other's expertise and what the other had to offer the project. From the beginning, the project would belong to both of us, and we would make all major decisions together.

We decided to focus on the many ways proofreading could become part of Mark's reading/writing curriculum and to monitor carefully the children's responses to his modified instruction. Mark's task, therefore, was to introduce various strategies (described below) into his reading/writing curriculum. My task was to observe Mark's classroom as he introduced these strategies into his reading/writing block and to interview the children to ascertain what they were learning from these strategies.

Mark had indicated that he already modeled for his students how to proofread. However, as a result of his experiences in Project 1, he recognized that he needed to make explicit for himself and me what he was doing in the name of spelling and proofreading and why he was doing these things. He began to realize that only then would he be in a position of being able to make explicit to his students the strategies he used as a proofreader and the many decisions that he made during the proofreading of a text. Such explicitness, he believed, would also enable him to be more systematic about his planning and instruction.

Together, Mark and I formulated three principles that he would use to guide and frame his teaching. These were to:

- make explicit wherever possible the covert, invisible processes that underpinned effective reading and writing and spelling
- help his students understand what he meant by reading-like-a-writer and how this in turn entailed reading-like-a-speller
- demonstrate often how to read one's writing with a reader's critical eye (i.e., to be able to change one's stance from that of the writer of a text to that of the reader)

These decisions enabled Mark to establish a class ethos that led children to understand when and why they needed to proofread their writing as well as the ramifications of not doing so. He increased the incidence of modeled writing, specifically focusing on the writing process, when it was important to spell conventionally, and when it was all right to draft-spell. During modeled writing, he used a "think-aloud" strategy as he attempted to spell words, thus demonstrating a wide range of strategies, including using words on the many charts around the room, using books he had been reading, and using a dictionary and the spell-checker on the computer.

Mark focused students' attention on spelling patterns, syllables, the use of prefixes and suffixes, word derivatives, and so on, whenever the opportunity arose. He modeled proofreading, both with groups and individuals, specifically focusing on identifying unconventionally spelled words and how to fix them.

He introduced "peer proofreading" (Turbill, Butler, & Cambourne, 1999) as a class activity. Peer proofreading entails selecting one child's unedited draft (with permission), making copies for all students, and then using an overhead transparency to demonstrate the proofreading process on the first few lines of this draft, finally asking the students to work in pairs to proofread their version of the text. On completion, Mark would return to the overhead and ask the class to complete the overhead together.

Each child was given a spelling journal. These were made by Mark. The photocopied pages (one for each week) were set out with the top half used by students to "have a go" at spellings they were trying to use. In the bottom left-hand section, the students recorded the words that they believed they had learned that week. And in the bottom right-hand section, they recorded words that were causing them trouble and needed to be learned. Mark found that these journals also provided valuable information about each student's spelling growth.

Many opportunities were provided for word study activities (see Bear, Invernizzi, Templeton, & Johnson, 1996; Pinnell et al., 1998; NSW Department of Education's *Teaching Spelling K–6*, 1998; Snowball & Bolton, 1999, to name a few). These included word sorts, have-a-go cards, developing charts of like words, adding prefixes and suffixes, and so on. As well, Mark introduced various word games. These included hangman, Scrabble, Boggle, crosswords, and Snap. Class and group work were placed in prominent positions on the walls and Mark constantly modeled how these could be used as spelling resources. He brought into the classroom a range of dictionaries and taught children how to use them.

Finally, Mark provided many reading and writing opportunities in which children could practice their spelling and the proofreading of their spelling. He would leave messages on the board with deliberate misspellings and encourage his students to be word detectives. Students who discovered the "typos," as he called them, were given the task to "fix" the words and thus score a point for their class team.

During the 10 weeks of this project, I collected observational data, interviews, and work samples from several case study students. Nicole was one of these students. She was an interesting child who made significant gains during the time of the project.

Case Study: Nicole's Story

Nicole was an eight-year-old second grader whom I observed and interviewed in Mark's class as she developed as a reader, writer, and speller. When we began the project, Nicole's reading and spelling were below grade average, but she loved to write. Her spelling was often so unconventional she was unable to reread what she had written by the next day.

The following is a first draft of a report written by Nicole:

the rads

rads are wit black dran and ossoss of cules thay Et ~~vegetarian~~ vegetables mostlliy kares. Thay are mosliy fad in dotes or farway pases some rads liv with peple in the city The baby radt folos ther ~~mum~~ mumthers The radts barow into the growd with ther sharp kcoos to make the ~~hom~~ nests they have a tanll to cam in and aut thay are protected from llal cids of wiyd emos.

A translation of the above is this:

The Rabbits

Rabbits are white, black, brown, and all sorts of colors. They eat ~~vegetarian~~ vegetables mostly carrots. They are mostly found in bushes or faraway places. Some rabbits live with people in the city. The baby rabbit follows their ~~mum~~ mothers. The rabbits burrow into the ground with their sharp claws to make their ~~home~~ nests. They have a tunnel to come in and out. They are protected from all kinds of wild animals.

When Nicole brought the piece to me, she struggled to read her written text. An analysis of Nicole's text indicated that she was able to spell most of the high frequency words, such as "are," "and," "of." Other words she attempted to sound out. There were some words, like "black," "vegetables," "protected," that she had spelled correctly. When asked how she was able to write these, she commented that she had copied them from various charts around the room. A further analysis indicated that she sometimes had two ways of spelling the same word. In this text, these were "they" and "thay" for "they," "mostlliy" and "mosliy" for "mostly," and "rads" and "radts" for "rabbits." When this was pointed out to Nicole, she looked amazed and said, "I thought that I was supposed to do that."

It seemed that Nicole has taken literally the encouragement given by well-meaning teachers to invent her spellings, to guess, or have-a-go at the spellings of words.

Somehow, Nicole had picked up the message that invented spelling meant having-a-go at the same word as many ways as she could. Because she did not read very well, Nicole, it seemed, relied on her phonemic awareness and her understanding of the sound/symbol relationships of the words. She sounded out almost every word. She was an expert at phonemic and orthographic segmentation and analysis. For instance, she had written "like" in a previous piece as "lyk," "lik," "licke," "liek" (as in "lie -k"). The first breakthrough therefore came for Nicole when she began to understand that she did not have to invent every word she wrote.

Mark's constant, systematic, and explicit demonstrations that there was a conventional way to spell a word, and that words could be found in books that she read, on charts on the wall, or in dictionaries, began to have an impact on Nicole. She first began to understand that the words she read could be used for her spelling when she wrote and that, if she needed to check the spelling of these words, she could return to where she had read the word (the proofreading process at work). She also began to understand that the knowledge of sounds that she used to write unknown words could be used to work out unknown words in her reading. This in turn helped her to develop more and more word-attack skills. Thus, the more she read, the more she began to engage in the visual patterns of words and the more conventional her spellings became in her writing.

The next major breakthrough came when Nicole was helped to understand the writing process. She began to realize that there was a place for her many invented spellings, but there was also a time when she needed to read over her work and begin to identify which words were conventional and which were not. She learned that her readers had rights too. Thus, she needed to read her writing with a reader's eye. She could only begin to do this after she had begun to look at the words she read with a writer's eye. And so one thing fed on another and Nicole began to make rapid progress. Her reading improved greatly and, alongside it, a love for reading began to grow. The more she read, the more she could draw on for her own writing, not only for spelling but also punctuation and ideas for her writing. And so it went on.

Nicole began to develop a spelling conscience. She worked hard at "fixing" her writing so that people could read it and so that people didn't think she was "dumb and couldn't spell." She learned to use strategies such as writing the word several times until it looked right, asking people, checking words in books, and using a dictionary. She happily used her own spelling journal and dictionary, filling it with words that she wanted to record as well as with strategies and mnemonics she could use to remember her trouble words. For instance, "'i-g-h-t' is in 'night' and 'fight' and 'might'—am I right?" She became a spelling detective. She noticed words: different spellings of words that sounded the same, little words within long words, and so on. She became an astute proofreader.

An Emerging Theory

Figure 2 summarizes what has emerged from all these studies:

Proofreading is a far more complex process than we have previously realized. It is not a simple strategy that can be taught and learned easily The process of proofreading involves the orchestration of many other skills and strategies.

The ability to proofread requires a person not only to be a reader but also to understand the reading process in such a way as to know when to slow down one's reading and consciously focus on the letter clusters in a word. A person needs also to understand that the conventional spellings of words are there in the texts that one reads.

Proofreading also requires a person to be a writer and to understand the writing process. When one understands the writing process, one begins to understand when it is appropriate to draft-spell and when it is appropriate to check that spellings are conventional. Most importantly, a person needs to understand the role that society plays in dictating the need for "getting spelling right" at particular times in the writing.

Critical in all the case studies cited in this paper is the conscious awareness of what readers and writers do with letters and letter clusters that go to create words and texts. Moreover, readers have at their disposal, in the texts they read, all the information about letters, letter clusters, and words that they as writers need in order to spell the words in the texts they compose. Such understandings about the connections between reading and writing, about how one supports and feeds off the

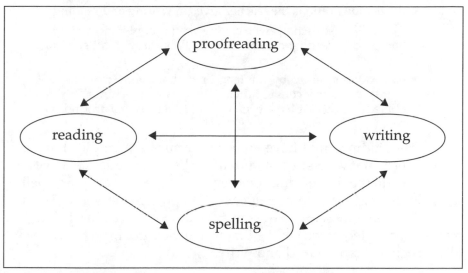

Figure 2. The relationship between the proofreading process and reading, writing, and spelling.

other, contributes greatly to the ability to produce conventional spellings in the first place. More importantly, it contributes to one's ability to change one's stance from a writer of the text to a reader of the text and proofread one's writing so that "getting it right" is made easier.

A knowledge of conventional spellings of words is the outcome of this orchestration, one in which proofreading is pivotal and not simply an end piece.

This model has some potentially important implications for classrooms. One is the potential importance of proofreading and proofreading instruction. Another is that proofreading needs to be more than an occasional activity. Another is that the proofreading process needs to be introduced into the reading/writing curriculum in the very early grades. Finally, there are potential theoretical implications related to the role which proofreading might play in spelling development. My data seem to suggest that the process of proofreading relies on the skills and understandings used in both reading and writing. This in turn suggests that proofreading should be an integral part of learning to read, write, and spell. It involves a complexity of overlapping factors, including:

- a classroom culture that emphasizes the social purposes of standard spelling
- the language the teacher uses to make explicit the many invisible and often intuitive decisions made during the proofreading process

- the demonstrations the teacher gives in writing and reading
- the explicit instruction given during writing conferences, shared and guided reading activities, as well as through all spelling activities
- expectations set up by the teacher that students would spell words they knew conventionally in first-draft writing. This included words that have been explicitly referenced around the room.

The findings that have emerged from these studies have convinced me that if we want our students to be effective spellers, we need to develop in them a spelling conscience. In order to develop a spelling conscience, they need to become effective proofreaders. Proofreading should be seen, therefore, not simply as a set of procedural skills, but rather as an integral part of the literacy curriculum from the time children begin to learn to read and write.

REFLECTION: THE RELATIONSHIP BETWEEN READING AND SPELLING

Editors' Note: Hughes and Searle draw on their research to clarify the relationship between reading and spelling development.

————✎————

Our longitudinal study of children's spelling development confirmed what has been well documented: that learning to read and subsequent engagement in reading are closely related to successful spelling development (Hughes & Searle, 1997). Yet, as all teachers can attest, it is possible to be an effective and active reader and not be a good speller. While it may be a *necessary* condition, reading does not appear to be a sufficient condition for the development of good spelling. (p. 203)

Source: Hughes, M., and Searle, D. (2000). Spelling and "the second 'R'." *Language Arts, 77*(3), 203–208.

REFLECTION: SPELLING *IS* IMPORTANT

Editors' Note: This excerpt from one of our editorials as Language Arts *editors emphasizes the importance of spelling while cautioning against too much emphasis on spelling accuracy.*

Progressive writing practices built upon the work of Graves, Murray, Calkins, Macrorie, and Atwell, among others, attempt to put writing conventions in perspective. From this perspective, spelling *is* important. Poor spellers jeopardize the rhetorical effect of their writing . . . . Readers whose attention is focused on spelling will always find it more difficult to attend to the writer's intentions. But, although spelling is important to effective writing, it must be considered as a means to an end and not an end in itself. Dull, vapid writing devoid of the writer's voice, no matter how well spelled and punctuated, will have little communicative effect beyond demonstrating the writer's mastery of the conventions. (p. 201)

Source: Murphy, S., & Dudley-Marling, C. (2000). Editors' Pages. *Language Arts, 77*(3), 200–201.

REFLECTION: SPELLING LISTS

Editors' Note: In this excerpt from a letter to the editors of Language Arts, *Tim Rasinski argues for a place for spelling lists in spelling instruction.*

I . . . think that many words are learned through informal conversation and interaction about reading and writing. And I don't think a lock-step method of direct instruction using a mandated set of spelling words and methods is the way to go. However, I do believe that a thoughtfully developed list of words taught through informed, varied, engaging and direct instruction by an enthusiastic teacher can have a significant and positive impact on children's development as readers and writers. (p.88)

Source: Rasinski, T. (2000). Letter to the editor. *Language Arts, 78*(1), 87–88.

22 What We Learned from Josh: Sorting Out Word Sorting

Mary Jo Fresch

Editors' text: Word sorting . . . sorting words . . . what do children make of this classroom practice? Mary Jo Fresch examines the space that lies between the teacher's hopes for this instructional strategy and the students' engagement with it.

Peek inside Aileen Wheaton's third-grade classroom about nine years ago. The children were preparing their papers to take the Friday spelling test. As Aileen walked by Michael's desk, she noticed he had not just numbered his paper. His sheet looked like this:

1. __ate
2. __ate
3. __ate
4. __ate
5. __ate

This teacher-student conversation followed:

Aileen: Michael, what are you doing?

Michael: Getting ready for the spelling test. When you give me the word, I'm going to plug in the first letter!

The student's reaction to this conversation was a huge smile of pride. He was going to get 100 percent on this test! The teacher's reaction was a cringe and a silent pledge to change her spelling instruction. Thus began a collaboration between a classroom teacher (Aileen Wheaton) and a university professor/researcher (Mary Jo Fresch, Michael's mother) who discovered that they shared concerns about spelling instruction. Like many schools around us, our district no longer purchased a basal speller. The planning was left up to each teacher. Little professional

---

This essay appeared in *Language Arts* 77.3 (2000) on pages 232–240.

development was provided to develop alternative instructional plans. Aileen had tried word families and words from thematic units. Our concerns were the low level of challenge for those students who already knew the word families, and the high reliance on memorization for the thematic words. Together, we focused on finding a way to design student-centered instruction that would make a difference in developing spelling knowledge. Years later, we would meet Josh, who challenged us to remember four things:

- Our understanding of how children learn must guide instruction.
- Children's analysis of words is in "the eye of the beholder." That is, how they focus on words and what they hear and see relies on their current operating knowledge of the English language.
- We should never assume that we understand how children think. We have to be observers and listeners.
- When we consider using a particular activity, we must analyze its benefits and drawbacks for individual children. We can no longer simply embrace an activity and assume it will work. We must constantly reflect on the instruction we choose.

Our Hunt for Instructional Guidance

Our pursuit began by examining what was already "out there." In many elementary schools in our area (a large, Midwestern university town), instruction had become less explicit and was woven into children's daily reading and writing. Many argue that embedding spelling instruction within a writing workshop approach gives children authentic reasons to learn to spell (Rhodes & Shanklin, 1993; Wilde, 1990). Yet others would argue for inclusion of specific spelling instruction as a major element in any language arts program (Adams, 1990). Some area teachers purchased instructional programs that required children to memorize high-frequency words. These programs suggested specific grade-level words children must "master." Many teachers we spoke to complained of "re-inventing the wheel" each week by scouring thematic unit readings for a word list. For example, during the study of the Revolutionary War, a list might include such words as *minuteman, massacre, continental, Congress, declaration, independence, intolerable,* and *colonies*. Such lists had little carryover to student writing because the words were theme-specific and not generally used in the children's everyday writing.

What became evident to us was that our philosophy of how children learn to spell was being challenged. We needed to articulate our beliefs about how children learn to spell, and then use that to guide our planning. The experience with Michael, in contrast to our experiences with children who could not easily learn the words declared as "this week's spelling list," made us question the traditional memorization model. Yet, we wondered what other approach would help individual spellers. Therefore, we sought to explore how children learn about the English language.

We found research which suggested that the most promising organization for instruction was to be found in a developmental approach for studying words. This approach uses various activities to assist children in bridging their current understanding about language with new learning about orthography. The research suggested that if children were reading at different levels, their word knowledge would differ, and this had to be taken into account when learning to spell (Henderson, 1990).

This developmental approach to teaching spelling was based on the work done by Read (1971), Henderson (1990), and Beers (1980). Developmental stages in learning to spell were identified. The stages are described as preliterate/phonetic, letter name, within word, syllable juncture, and derivational constancy. Each descriptor conveys the general features of language the learner is using when spelling. Table 1 presents the basic characteristics of spellers at each stage of development. The stages are considered a continuum, with varying degrees of understanding at each level. This important theory has been grounded in examining children's writing and has been supported and replicated by many researchers (Bear, 1991; Gentry, 1981; Temple, Nathan, & Burris, 1982).

The proponents of this theory suggest word sorting as one activity to move children along in developing their understandings because the focus is on "active, thoughtful problem solving" (Zutell, 1996, p. 107). Word sorting provides hands-on opportunities for children to work through the complexities of the language (Bear, Templeton, Invernizzi, & Johnston, 1996; Gillet & Kita, 1980; Invernizzi et al., 1994; Sulzby, 1980; Templeton et al., 1994; Zutell, 1996). Children study words for similarities and differences. They formulate tentative hypotheses about spelling patterns as they group words into categories (Beers, 1980). For instance, a child may be given words such as *sleeping, dreaming, hopping, grabbing, riding,* and *writing* to "discover" the rule for adding the "ing" ending to a root word. Once the child has categorized the words by "in common" patterns, a rule is generated and discussed with other children and the teacher. The activity of sorting encourages word analysis, which in turn can be helpful in other reading and writing activities (Gillet & Kita, 1980). Therefore, we began designing a sorting component to Aileen's instructional planning.

Realizing the Cart Was before the Horse

As we read the many ways to organize and create word sorts, we realized the need to know which words, for which sorts, for which children. In other words, how would we know which sorts would be most beneficial to individual learners? Because we were examining how children learn, simply employing the same activity for all children did not seem appropriate. We would be putting the activity "cart" before the individual-needs "horse." How could we design the activity to best match each child's current operating knowledge of the English language?

Table 1. Characteristics of stages of developmental spelling knowledge.

Preliterate/Prephonetic
• scribbles • imitates reading and writing • is aware of print
Preliterate/Phonetic
• learns alphabet • strings letters to represent words
Letter Name
• develops sight vocabulary in reading and writing • uses obvious strategies to spell, such as letter name to represent sound or word • often exchanges short vowel for closest long (*a* for short *e*; *e* for short *i*) • makes common sound/letter errors—affrications (*jriv* for *drive*), nasal (*bop* for *bump*) • uses exaggerated sounding (*palena* for *plane*)
Within Word
• develops growing sight vocabulary in reading and writing • correctly uses short vowels • marks long vowels (sometimes incorrectly) • uses -*d* for past tense, adds -*ing* • understands words have two elements—beginning consonant pattern and a vowel plus ending • begins to internalize rules • may overgeneralize application of rules
Syllable Juncture
• begins to correctly double consonant • invents at the juncture or schwa position • spellings show orthographic awareness available for word attack during reading
Derivational Constancy
• reads efficiently and fluently • attends *less* to words as processing of print quickens

To design the most appropriate word sorts, we needed to assess each child's needs. This would provide information about where each child was in terms of understandings about spelling. This led us on a search for an assessment tool. We found the *Qualitative Inventory of Word Knowledge* (*QIWK*) (Schlagal, 1992). This spelling inventory consists of eight lists of progressively more difficult words. The words are selected for their particular word features (such as *r*-controlled vowels or doubling a consonant before adding an ending) at various levels of word-knowledge development. Children's attempts are analyzed for error patterns and indications of developing understandings. Tests are analyzed qualitatively as well as quantitatively (testing stops when children score 50 percent or below). Once we had administered the *QIWK* to every child, we felt we had a "compass" that we could use to guide the particular word sorts we would create.

Questioning Our Practice

For several years, we were quite excited about the results of children sorting words. Each week, a particular spelling pattern was chosen, based on September *QIWK* results and analysis of the children's ongoing writing. Words were selected using Henderson's (1990) *Teaching Spelling*. Henderson's lists, grouped by similar spelling patterns (long "a" spellings, short "o" spellings, consonant digraphs, etc.) had suggested words for grades 1 through 6. Using this as a guide, we could select words at or below third grade. These words were pretested. Children who correctly spelled words on the pretest worked with Aileen to select other words to learn that fit the spelling pattern for that week. These words were above, at, or below grade level, allowing us to target individual needs. The children worked with their word selections to sort and discover the "rule" that each particular spelling pattern followed (such as the way the long "a" sound can be spelled, or how to add plural endings to words). The children were engaged in exploring words (Fresch & Wheaton, 1997). We especially liked the community feeling of everyone focusing on the same spelling pattern, while working with words that matched both their reading level and current understanding of how words are spelled. When the children sorted their words for the week, we noticed that some children could sort alone, quickly establishing the pattern and generalizing the rules of the language. Other children needed more support from Aileen. While the sorting was designed to put the children "in charge," Aileen often needed to provide more guidance to certain students.

Aileen then switched grade levels, moving to fifth grade. Again, we used the *QIWK* to establish baseline information about the children. During the second year of fifth-grade teaching, Aileen had some of the same students she had had in third grade. This gave us the opportunity to observe the long-range effects of the sorting activity. Once again, there were children who could sort and generalize the rules of the language, while other children needed guidance and support in order to complete the sorts. Some of the same children who needed help in third grade still needed help in fifth grade. Occasionally, we wondered how some children had arrived at their particular categories. This led us to question how we could improve the sorting activity. Aileen set the stage when she said, "I want to know what they are thinking when they sort." Thus began our study, during which we asked children to think aloud as they sorted words.

The Fifth-Grade Sorters

There were 24 children in Aileen's inclusion class the year we investigated how children thought as they sorted words. The students included six with Attention Deficit Disorder (ADD), two Learning Disabled (LD) students, four Developmentally Handicapped (DH) students, one English-as-a-second-language (ESL) user, and four gifted learners. Using the *Gates-MacGinitie Reading Tests* (MacGinitie & MacGinitic, 1989), grade-level reading scores were obtained, ranging from 3.2 to 10.

The children had been sorting from September to April when we asked them to think aloud. Each child was taken to a separate room and asked by a research assistant to read a set of cards. Any words the child did not know were taken out of the stack. The first sort included the words *night, bright, flight, right, twice, wise, nine, smile, prize, fly, try,* and *style*. The aim was to watch the children as they heard the long "i" sound, noting the various ways that it could be spelled. A video camera recorded the children's hands and voices as they moved the cards into categories. They were told to "put your brain in your throat and tell us what you are thinking." The research assistant modeled this type of thinking aloud. Each child spoke out loud about what they were noticing concerning the words and why they were establishing certain categories. This way, we learned quite a bit about how the children analyzed words; we also learned the power of the think-aloud.

Many of the children needing additional support for sorting only attended to one attribute of the collection of words. That is, they only sorted by visual elements, or they only sorted by auditory elements.

Taylor, who remained a within-word speller throughout the year, attended to the arrangement of letters, without ever noticing the common sound of long "i":

> *Taylor:* I'm going to lay them all out so I can see all my different choices, to see what I can see, what categories I might be able to put them into. I see a few "i's". So I'm going to go "ight" [*right*], "ight" [*night*], "ight" [*flight*], "ight" [*bright*]. . . . OK, then we have uh, "i-consonant-e," these two are "i-consonant-e" [*wise, smile*, adds *twice* and *prize*], here's "y" on the end [*try, fly*], "i-consonant-e" [*nine*] and "y" and this one [*style*] could be an oddball.

> *Research assistant:* I understand that Mrs. Wheaton asks you to write down your generalizations. Can you tell us what your generalization is?

> *Taylor:* OK, I sorted my words and I discovered there are three different ways my words are spelled. I have "ight" over here, "i-consonant-e" over here and then I have "y" on the end and then I have an oddball here.

Mark, a syllable-juncture speller, had a very similar approach, but he established his categories for different reasons:

> *Mark:* [holds pack of cards] That [*fly*] has a "y" on the end so we can call that a category [puts *night* next to it], and "silent e's" on the end [*nine*] and *smile* and *bright* has the "g-h," and *wise* and *try* has "y" on the end, and *prize* has "silent e," and *style* would probably go here because "silent e," and *twice* would also go there, and *flight* would go there [with the "g-h-t" words] and so would *right*. We have three categories.

> *Research assistant:* I understand when you are finished, Mrs. Wheaton asks you to write down a generalization. Would you tell me your generalization?

> *Mark:* OK, I made three categories. This one I made because it ends in "y," and this one because it had a "g-h" in the middle, and this one because it had a "silent e" on the end.

Both boys had a category with *try* and *fly*, another category with *nine*, *prize*, *twice*, *wise*, and *smile*, and a third category with *night, right, bright*, and *flight*. Taylor chose to call *style* an oddball (a word that did not fit any existing category) and Mark chose to include it in his "silent e" category. While the completed sorts looked similar, each boy had used different visual information to create his categories. By simply looking at the finished categories, we could have assumed that the boys were using three spelling patterns of the long "i" sound to sort the words. The think-aloud suggested that different information was in operation for both boys. This information seemed to be linked to their particular developmental stage.

Sean, a within-word speller, gave us yet another view by establishing two categories for the same words.

> *Sean: Bright, right* that's an "i-g-h" so it would go with *bright.*
> *Prize,* that's "i-consonant-silent-e" and *twice* [puts with
> *prize*], yeah, *fly* and *try,* it has a long "i" sound so we'll put
> those here [puts with *prize*]. *Style* that's a "i," *prize* has a long
> "i" too. *Twice* is a long "i" [puts with *prize*], and "i-g-h"
> [*flight*] and "i-g-h" [*night*]. *Wise* is a long "i," *nine* is a long
> "i" sound [puts with *prize*].

> *Research assistant:* OK, are you finished sorting? You have two
> categories. Will you tell me about each of your categories
> and why you put each word where you did?

> *Sean:* I put all of these because they have a long "i" sound and I
> put all of these because they have a long "i" and they are
> spelled "i-g-h."

Sean approached the task by hearing the long "i" sound and discovered two ways to categorize that sound/spelling pattern. Brian, however, gave a different perspective on hearing sounds. He had begun the year as a letter-name speller, and had moved to the within-word stage by the time the sorting activity was done. He created five categories that seemed more based on their rhyming principles than spelling patterns:

> *Brian:* I'm going to put this in . . . *right.* Because it has the sound
> of a "t." I'm not sure about that yet [*style*]. *Try,* I'm going to
> put that with *right,* oh no, I'm not sure about that. *Prize.* The
> "z," I'm going to put that in the "s" pile. I'm not sure about
> that. *Flight,* that has the same sound as *right. Smile* [puts
> with *style*], they both start with "s" and they both sound the
> same. That's *style* and *smile. Try.* I'm going to put that in the
> "y" section [along with *fly*]. *Twice,* I'm not sure about that
> one. . . . *Wise* and *prize,* I'll put that in the, uh, the . . . "s"
> category cause the "z" sounds like an "s" and the "s"
> sounds like a "z." *Nine* . . . hmmm . . . I'll try that . . . [moves
> aside with *twice*]. *Bright, right, flight* and *bright. Night,* I'll put
> that in *right, flight,* and *bright.* [Studies *twice* and *nine*] I'll put
> that [*twice*] with *prize* and *wise* because the "c" sounds like
> an "s," 'cause *twice. Nine* . . . hmmmmm . . . *nine* . . .
> hmmmmm . . . I'm not sure about that one.

> *Research assistant:* What does Mrs. Wheaton tell you when you
> are not sure about something?

> *Brian:* Put it in the oddball section.

> *Research assistant:* OK, want to leave that in the oddball section?

Brian: Yeah.

Research assistant: You want to tell me again why you put the
words together like you did?

Brian: Well, I put all these words together by how they sound.
Because *style* and *smile* sound the same, and *prize* and *wise*
sound the same, but this one [*twice*] doesn't sound the same,
but the "c" sounds like an "s" and a "z." Right, *flight*, *bright*,
and *night* sound the same, that's a category. And *fly* and *try*
sound the same, too.

Once again, by listening to the think-aloud, we heard Brian's decision-
making path. This gave us insights into what information he focused
on when seeing and hearing each word.

Some students were able to use both visual and auditory information when sorting. Lorraine, a derivational-constancy speller
throughout the year, demonstrated her ability to attend to both features
of the words:

Lorraine: Well, I'm just going to look at them all and see if I see a
strategy. And the strategy I see is a long "i". . . . Some long
"i's" I can see are made with a "y" [*try, fly, style*], and those
are the ones, and some are "i's" by itself, like *wise, nine,
prize, twice,* and *smile.* And then others are "ight," like *night,
bright, flight,* and *right,* and they all have the same long "i"
sound.

Research assistant: OK, tell me one more time about your
categories.

Lorraine: These are the "i" sound made by the "y," these are the
"i" by itself, and also, I just noticed that the "e" on the end
of them probably makes the "i" long. And then these are the
"ight," where the "g-h-t" makes the "i" long.

Enter Josh

Josh was the student that convinced us that every activity, no matter
how student-centered we believe it to be, needs careful planning to make
it worthwhile. The children had been completing word sorts each week,
but only through listening to the think-alouds were we given a view of
their decision-making path. Josh was focusing on completely different
parts of the word than were Lorraine or Brian. Josh, a syllable-juncture
speller, ended up with four categories (1) *smile, wise, style, twice;* (2) *bright,
right, night, nine;* (3) *try, prize, fly;* and (4) *flight* (oddball):

Josh: We're going to do a sort within a sort . . . and it's just
basically you sort about by the sound and also by the
spelling. So . . . *twice,* let's see, *twice, style . . . style,* "sss." I'm

putting this one here [*style* with *twice*] because it's probably a "c" category and it's probably the "sss" sound, is the category type, like the name, this one here, *ni-i . . . night*; *st-i . . . style*; *n-i-ght . . . st-i. . . .* I take that back, it's probably in the "t" category with the "t" sound. But it could also probably be the "c" sound, so I'm going to put that there, and that there [*night* by itself], they are both going to be in the same category, same sound and same category. I'm going to put this one here because it doesn't have the "c" sound, but it does have the "t." So, I'm going to put that one here. *N-ine, n-ine, n-ine*, um, *n-ine*, let's see. This one, I'm going to, um, I'm going to put this one here [with *night*] because it doesn't show the same as the "t," but it does show the "n." OK. Right, this is probably going to have to go here. It has the same sound spelling, it basically has the same, except this letter is an "n" and this is an "r." *W-ise.* I'm going to put this here, because it shows the "s" and has the "sss" sound. This one [*flight*] is going to have to go here because it's the "t," got the "t" sound, but it could also probably go here, so it's in between. *Smile. Style. Smile.* I'm going to put this here because it's about the same as *style*, *smile* and *style* are about the same. *Try, try, right, try, night, try.* This is probably in a category all its own. It's about the same as these [*night, right*] but not exactly, not spelling-*wise*. *Prize, right, prize, style, prize, wise*, um, I'm going to put it in this one too [*try*], because they both have "r" and they both have the same sound, you know? *Bright, right, try, bright, right*, I'm going to put this here because it has the "t" sound with it and it's spelled "g-h-t," so it's there. *Fly, smile, fly, try, fly, prize, fly, flight*. I'm going to put this here because it's the same as *try, prize*, and *fly* about, because they all have the "i" sound.

Research assistant: How does Mrs. Wheaton tell you to express when you are finished with your sort?

Josh: Usually, we'll write a generalization.

Research assistant: Can you tell me your generalization?

Josh: These are generalized, these words are generalized using they can also be spelled within a sort by the "i" sound, the "g-h-t," "i-l," "r," and um, um, and some of the oddballs, which are like *try, prize*, and *fly*. So, the generalization is probably "i," "i," "g-h-t," "r," "g-h-t," *nine*.

Without doubt, Josh caused us to pause the longest as we watched the videotapes. What attracted his eye was completely different from that of any of the other students. We realized that many of the children, while looking at the same words, saw different features of the words. We looked back at the results of the QIWK and saw a link between children's developmental knowledge of spelling and their approach to the word-sorting task. This is displayed in Table 2.

To test our hypotheses, we had each child complete a second think-aloud using another set of words: *doctor, October, monster, gather, attack, panic, patches,* and *shovel.* We chose multisyllabic words with short "o" or short "a." *Shovel* was added because it did not fit with the short "o" words, but had visual similarity. Returning to Taylor, categories were established for the "o-r" at the end, the "k" sound at the end, and "e" as the second-to-last letter. Mark has "o-r" at the end, "e-r" at the end, "k" sound at the end, and two oddballs [*shovel, patches*]. Sean has an "e-r" category, two sounds of "c," and endings of consonant-vowel-consonant [*shovel, patches, doctor*]. Brian also had an "e-r" category, then completes his sort by making an "a-t" category [*patches, attack*] and leaving the rest as oddballs. Lorraine repeats her ability to attend to several features at one time:

> *Lorraine:* Um . . . I just going to spread out the words and see if I see a generalization. And . . . I think I see a short vowel. I'm not sure yet, I have to check. *Monster* . . . that has a short vowel . . . *panic* . . . *doctor.* . . *October.* . . *gather.* . . *attack* . . . *patches* and *shovel.* They all have a short vowel so I'm going to divide them into categories. These are short vowel "a" . . . *attack* . . . *patches* . . . *gather.* . . *panic* . . . and these are short "o's" . . . *monster.* . . *doctor.* . . *October.* . . and this [*shovel*] is not. This would be probably a short "e," or it could be in a "u" because *sho* . . . *vel.*

Table 2. Student's developmental stage and approach for sorting.

Student	Developmental Stage at Time of Sorting	Approach for Sorting
Taylor	Within Word	Visual categories of end letters
Mark	Syllable Juncture	Visual categories of middle and end letter combinations
Sean	Within Word	Auditory category and Visual category
Brian	Early Within Word	Auditory, rhyming categories ("s" and "ight")
Lorraine	Derivational Constancy	Auditory with spelling pattern (Visual) categories
Josh	Syllable Juncture	Auditory ("s," "t," "r," "i") with Visual categories of specific letters

Josh, once again, took us on an unusual journey as we followed his decision-making path. He completed his sort with five categories, four of which had only one word in them:

> *Josh:* OK, *attack, attack, shovel.* Well I'm going to start out right here because there isn't a strategy yet. *Shovel, shovel.* We're going to put this over here because of the "e-l." What's the strategy? I don't have the strategy yet, so I'm going to put it in that category [*attack*], so I'll put it in another category [*shovel*]. I'm going to put that [*doctor*] in another category because it doesn't go with either one of those. *October,* this one is going to go here because it has the same sound strategy as *doctor* and it also rhymes. It's got the "k" sound in it. *Gather, attack, doctor, shovel, gather, shovel, gather.* This one's kinda strange because it's not either one of these. So I'm going to put it over there [*gather*]. *Monster, gather,* I'm going to put this one over here because it has the "er" sound in it [with *gather*]. *Panic, attack, shovel, panic, attack, doctor, shovel, gather,* uh, this is tough [sets *panic* aside]. This one is really strange. I'm going to put it [*shovel*] over here because it doesn't go with any one of these. *Patches, attack, doctor, shovel, gather, panic.* This one's in a category all it's own [*patches*].

> *Research assistant:* OK then, you want to tell me about each one of your categories?

> *Josh:* This one [*patches*] probably has an "e-s" and this one [*attack*] has the "c-k" ending. This one [*doctor*] has the "o-r," the "er" sound. Wait a second, I want to make one change, put this over here [moves *doctor* out of "er" category]. This one [*shovel*] has the "el" sound and this one [**gather**, *October, monster*] has the "er" sound and this one [*panic*] has the "k" sound.

While his categories were based in sound, he did not seem aware that he had one-word categories. Josh taught us that, although we can all "look" at the same words, we can "see" and "hear" different things. We discovered stronger evidence that our hypotheses about the relationship between developmental word knowledge and how the sorts were completed would be useful for instructional planning. These general patterns are summarized in Table 3.

We realized that in order to make the sorts most beneficial, some of the students, such as those in the letter-name and within-word stages, would need more support. Such learners would need key words to guide their sorts, or they would need additional discussions about how to analyze the words for common features. Our philosophy of how children learn to spell was firmly in place during this close examination of our current practice. Children approach the task of looking at and learning about words in a variety of ways, depending on their developmental stage of knowledge. This information would guide future instruction in new ways.

What We Learned: Guides for Instruction

What we learned from children like Josh assisted us in refining an activity we believed to be particularly useful in developing word knowledge.

- Our understanding of how children learn must guide our instruction. We believe children develop knowledge about the English language through active exploration of words, not through mere memorization. Therefore, our instruction needs to assess where they are, followed by activities that will move them forward in knowledge. The research that provided a developmental framework guides the creation of appropriate instruction.

- Children's analysis of words is in "the eye of the beholder." We came to understand that the way children focus on words and what they hear and see relies on their current operating knowledge of the English language. The sorting became a demonstration of their knowledge, and the think-aloud provided information about how the children were analyzing the words. Our job was to discern what knowledge children were using and help them expand the way they examined words. We could no longer simply use an activity without discovering how individual children use it in their learning.

Table 3. Relationship of developmental stage of fifth-grade sorters and how sorts were completed.

Developmental Stage (as identified through the *QIWK*)	Number of Students	Approach for Sorting
Letter Name through Within Word	9	Reliance on one element—either completely auditory or completely visual
Within Word, moving to Syllable Juncture	3	Visual information, with auditory "checking"
Syllable Juncture	9	Auditory information with visual "checking"
Derivational Constancy	3	Auditory information with visual "checking"

- We should have never assumed that we understood how children think; we had to be observers and listeners. We found the think-aloud gave us insights into student thinking. While some children may arrive at the same categories, their journey to create them and their reasons for doing so may vary greatly. We were surprised by the path many of them took to establish their categories. The activity of sorting is not receptive: It is an active display of how children think about words. Some of the children in the early stages of spelling development gave procedural information as they spoke. We became aware of the conceptual knowledge that was or was not in operation while the children sorted. We found the think-aloud to be a powerful indicator of what was guiding children's thinking as we watched and listened.

- When we consider using a particular activity, we must analyze its benefits and drawbacks for individual children. We could no longer simply embrace an activity and assume it would work. We must constantly reflect on the instruction we choose. While the word sorts continue to be a weekly activity, some children work alone and others work with buddies. Many of the children are challenged to find what a set of words have in common: some children are given key words to match the remainder of their list to; and some children work directly under Aileen's guidance.

We now focus on "word study": purposefully analyzing words in terms of relationships and patterns. In the end, we all work together to investigate the English language.

Exit Josh

Children like Josh keep us asking questions and seeking answers. We asked Josh, just as we did all 24 children, to watch the video of his sorting. As the first sort began, the following conversation took place:

> *Mary Jo:* What you see in front of you is the TV and in there is the tape of the very first word sort you did for us. I'm going to have you watch the tape and while you're watching it, just tell us whatever you're thinking about. Do you think you would keep the sort the way you had it, or any other ideas that you have about it. OK? So you get to watch yourself, well your hands anyway. All right? Here we go. What's the matter? You're shaking your head. You thinking?

> *Josh:* Yeah.

> *Mary Jo:* What are you thinking?

> *Josh:* I should have washed my hands before I did this.

Thank you, Josh, for teaching us to never assume.

Acknowledgments

The Ohio State University Seed Grant #221783 supported this research. The author would like to thank Aileen Wheaton for her support and continued assistance in the author's spelling research.

STRATEGY: KNOWING WHEN TO INTERVENE

Editors' Note: This excerpt from O'Flahavan and Blassberg offers some advice to teachers uncertain of when to provide support for young children's spelling development.

―――――❦―――――

Embedded Spelling Instruction Occurs within a Generative Cycle of Contextualized Assessment, Teaching, and Learning

Contextualized assessments of students' orthographic theories lead naturally into socially constructed orthographic generalizations. These assessments enable instructional decisions that are closely aligned with students' developing literacy abilities (Lucas, 1988a, 1988b; Valencia, McGinley, & Pearson, 1988). While reading provides students optimal exposure to new and correct spellings (Henderson, 1990), students' writing serves the teacher best as insight into students' generalizations about sound-symbol correspondence.

Young children's writing is often a rich combination of conventionally and inventively spelled words. Some invented spellings are better approximations of conventional spellings than others. It would be folly to have students create lists of words they can spell conventionally with some constancy; likewise, it would also be a waste of instructional time to teach students the words they represent only cryptically (e.g., *G* for *girl*). A more sensible approach suggests that words or spelling patterns chosen for the basis of instruction by the teacher from students' writing need to conform to four conditions:

1. The word or spelling pattern must be an approximation of the conventional spelling.

2. The student must recognize this as so (i.e., the student must be confident that the word is not spelled conventionally).

3. All phonemes must be represented sufficiently through symbol use (e.g., *OHVORE* for over).

▶

4. The student plays a role in choosing words or patterns for further study. Selected patterns then become the content of instructional activities that engage students in constructing generalizations and word families which illustrate the generalizations.

Embedded approaches enable teachers and students to negotiate the scope and sequence of the spelling curriculum as students produce and respond to environmental print and make known which words they think they need to learn next. Traditional approaches, on the other hand, predetermine the scope and sequence of abstract generalizations for all children and treat learning explicitly, providing procedures for learning generalizations and practicing their application. However, unlike an embedded approach, normative orientations to spelling instruction may be the most indirect means through which to evoke individual change. Instruction must be dovetailed into the ongoing literate and orthographic development of the individual (Wilde, 1990).

Tailoring spelling instruction to individual development in the context of ongoing literacy activity requires the recognition of what to teach and when to attend to it. Consider Wesley's story . . . as an example. Wesley, a second grader, tells his story using 16 words. If we include the reversal in *and*, 6 of the words are spelled conventionally. According to our criteria above, 5 words are candidates for spelling instruction (*CAM, OHVORE, HUOS, SICKR, FOTBALL*). These words can serve as the genesis for word families in mini-lesson settings, as we illustrate later. Once an assessment is made, the teacher solicits from Wesley which of these words he would like to study further. These words become part of an ongoing record for Wesley, as well as a class record that also includes words students voiced an interest in learning more about. These archives help the teacher design learning activities that are social and constructivistic.

Just as the botanist studies and classifies physical phenomena, teachers who embed their spelling instruction in the total language program invite students to view the words they read and compose as linguistic, cultural, and historical phenomena to be selected, studied, and classified. Driven by their subjective perspectives on orthographic generalizations, students make otherwise internalized theories public in direct ways such as decoding attempts, invented spellings, and small group discussion of novel spelling patterns encountered in reading. The kaleidoscope of public renderings, coupled with reflective activities and responsive teacher guidance, establishes a dialogue between students through which individual change becomes possible (Vygotsky, 1978).

While the variation of social activity is unlimited we see the social construction of word families as a powerful tool in spelling instruction. Developing these families is a theory-driven enterprise, especially when families take on the following characteristics:

1. Families illustrate specific orthographic generalizations.
2. Families are composed of words that are in the realm of students' oral language use.
3. Families are flexible in composition (i.e., some words fall within more than one family).

(pp. 414–415)

Source: O'Flahavan, J., & Blassberg, R. (1992). Toward an embedded model of spelling instruction for emergent literates. *Language Arts, 69*(6), 409–417.

STRATEGY: CREATING AN ENVIRONMENT FOR LEARNING TO SPELL

Editors' Note: Drawing on psycholinguistic perspectives on children's spelling, Jerry Zutell offers some advice about teaching spelling for teachers and parents.

Some Psycholinguistic Perspectives on Children's Spelling

1. Children need opportunities for and encouragement to explore thought and structure through their own writing. . . .Thus, creating and examining their own written products provides children with the opportunity to consciously reflect upon both their content and how that content is expressed through the structures of written language. The spelling system is, of course, one of those structures. To the degree that children recognize their writings as genuine communicative acts, learning about words will be viewed as a necessary aspect of facilitating communication. To the degree that it contributes to

cognitive development and self-reflection, honest writing provides situations in which word knowledge can be expressed, examined, and evaluated.

In contrast, a spelling program based solely on a weekly spelling list-test format provides little opportunity for conceptualization. In many such programs children interpret the spelling task as one of rote memorization. The results are inefficient processing, boredom or frustration, the development of a strong dislike for writing in general, and a lack of carry-over from the teaching-testing situation to their own written products (e.g., class compositions, essay examinations, term papers).

2. Children need to be read to, as well as given the opportunity and encouragement for both wide reading and investigation of specific self-generated topics. In order to promote such activities the classroom environment should include a wide range of available reading materials—books, magazines, reference works—and objects, materials, and situations which act as stimuli for further exploration. Furthermore, and most important, such activities should be integral, planned parts of the overall language arts program for every child. Too often they are regarded as enrichment activities, done only when all other "essential" schoolwork has been completed, and therefore they are reserved for special occasions or for only the brighter, quicker children. The point is that they are fundamental to the language and reading growth of all children.

In terms of spelling, extensive reading provides children with a greater reservoir of written words and meanings which can then serve as a data base for generating and testing rules and for recognizing relationships among words. Both Zutell (1975) and Beers et al. (1977) report that the less children use and know about a given word, the more primitive their spelling strategies. Reading and being read to can provide children with this essential word knowledge. In addition, if, as I have argued, letter sounds alone provide insufficient information about how words are spelled, then it stands to reason that children need the opportunity to see words in print in meaningful contexts in order to note structural, syntactic and semantic similarities and differences. Reading, vocabulary development and spelling are interrelated and mutually facilitating components of a complete language arts program.

3. The environment should include a variety of word study activities through which children have the opportunity to consciously explore and manipulate the various structural, syntactic and semantic relationships present in written language. Systematic word study should be based on tasks which emphasize comparing, contrasting and categorizing words according to a variety of salient features including root words, word origins, similarities in structural patterns, etc. Such activities can be supplemented with a selection of less controlled word games—crossword puzzles, scrambled letters, word webs and the many commercial word games available.

Such a program must, of course, be individualized—based on the needs and abilities of each child. Children's writing can provide samples of their spelling strategies, which can provide the informed and observing teacher with vital information about what the child already knows about words and consequently which activities would be most effective in helping to expand that knowledge. (pp. 847–849)

Source: Zutell, J. (1978). Some psycholinguistic perspectives on children's spelling. *Language Arts, 55 (7)*, 844–850.

STRATEGY: AN INTEGRATED APPROACH TO SPELLING INSTRUCTION

Editors' Note: Bartch considers the role of mini-lessons and teacher modeling in supporting students' spelling development.

Mini-Lessons

Spelling strategies became the focus of my spelling program. During our weekly spelling time, I began with a mini-lesson. I taught one strategy in each mini-lesson. The spelling strategies included:

> **Word bank:** The children kept a personal 3 x 5 spelling box with corrected words that they had misspelled in their written work. They used this as their personal dictionary.

> **Dictionary/thesaurus:** The children were taught how to use a basic picture dictionary and thesaurus.

> **Printed resources:** If the weekly spelling sentences written by the children focused on the topic of maps, then I had literature

▶

and nonfiction books on maps available to use as references. The children could then find the spellings of words that were map terms in the social studies text, nonfiction books, and literature related to maps.

Word wall: I used the basic sight words and made a list for a wall display, to which the children also added words.

Environment: I encouraged the children to use the environmental print in the classroom to help in the spelling of a word.

Spelling rules: I examined the children's written work for common spelling rule errors such as the use of *are/our, their/they're,* contractions, and *-ed* endings. These spelling rules I taught children, along with other selected rules from a spelling text. Example rules that I included were silent letters, *qu* spellings, *wr* spellings, and *'s.* I also concentrated on the four that have been found to be fairly consistent (Wilde, 1990):

1. *ie/ei*
2. dropping *-e* and adding *-ing*
3. changing *y* to *i* and adding *-es*
4. doubling consonant

Have a Go: We explored how to write a word three different ways and circled the correct spelling. This is a helpful strategy for visual learners.

Stretch: Some words can be articulated slowly according to how they sound. Examples: *go, at, also, rodeo.*

Other areas: I also looked at the weekly spelling sentences to determine problem areas. If a majority of the children needed help capitalizing the names of cities and states, then that became the focus of my mini-lesson. When I observed the children having difficulty with digraphs (*ch, th, sh, wh*), we spent time looking at examples from the children's work and exploring other words that began the same way. Then lists of words beginning with digraphs were posted in the room on a reference chart.

Teacher Modeling

Early in the week, we had a lesson during which I modeled how to write a paragraph while the children observed. We discussed letter formation, spacing, basic sentence structure, invented spelling, and strategies for spelling. Then I asked each child to write a few sentences about a focused topic, and I varied the focused topic so they would

▶

discover new words. Topics included responses to literature, writing about a science experiment or about an art project, an evaluation of a field trip, or sentences about their families. Some children wrote only one sentence while others (who needed to challenge themselves) wrote more. Children were encouraged to use invented spelling that emphasized their knowledge of sounds along with spelling strategies.

To give them extra support, I wrote the number of misspelled words on the top of each paper. At the end of the week, the children's papers were returned, and they were told to locate the misspelled words. They drew a line through each misspelled word. Then they corrected only five (Wilde, 1992) of these words, using the spelling strategies that had been taught during spelling mini-lessons. I circulated around the room, checking their proofreading skills while helping individual children rely on their knowledge of letters and sounds. After they had corrected five words using strategies, they wrote their strategies on a small Post-it note and attached it to their paper. Then I was able to determine whether they had used the word wall, dictionary, "have a go," or some other strategy. They gave the paper to me to check for the correct spelling of these five words. After I had taught the strategies mentioned previously and had the children use each one, I encouraged them to use the strategy that worked for them. Some children benefited from the use of the dictionary, while others were more successful with "have a go." (pp. 405–406)

Source: Bartch, J. (1992). An alternative to spelling: An integrated approach. *Language Arts, 69*(6), 404–408.

V Literacy Intersections: Multilinguality, Home, and Assessment

23 Educating African American Learners at Risk: Finding a Better Way

Dorothy S. Strickland

Editors' Text: Dorothy Strickland revisits many of the principles articulated in preceding chapters as she outlines a better way for educating African American learners who are at risk. She challenges us to give African American learners the classrooms they deserve and considers, among other things, the role of basic skills in that process.

E ven before they enter school, at least one-third of the nation's children are at risk for school failure. The deck is stacked against them, not because of anything they have done or failed to do. Most of these youngsters live in poverty, and they are members of a minority group. A large proportion of them are African American. The fact that they are poor is the key reason they are at risk for failure. Indeed, children from middle-class black families academically outperform poor children, regardless of ethnicity (Hodgkinson, 1991). Although education cannot solve all the societal problems that poor, African American children face, it remains an important and powerful weapon against poverty and crime. It is becoming increasingly obvious that whether or not these children become literate has a profound effect on all our lives. For these children, the successful application of what is known about the teaching and learning of literacy is of critical importance. In this article, I bring that knowledge together with my very deep concern for a group of children who are in desperate need of our help.

This essay appeared in *Language Arts* 71.5 (1994) on pages 328–336. It was based on an article that appeared in the Virginia State Reading Association journal *Reading in Virginia* (Volume 17) in 1992.

New Trends in Literacy Instruction

Throughout the United States, teachers and administrators are thoughtfully reexamining the assumptions underlying their literacy programs. Dramatic changes have taken place in many individual classrooms and schools. In some cases massive reforms have been initiated across entire school districts. The changes appear under the heading of various holistic and process-oriented terms such as literature-based curriculum, integrated language arts, language across the curriculum, whole language, and emergent literacy (Allen & Mason, 1989; Cazden, 1992b; Edelsky, Altwerger, & Flores, 1991; Hiebert, 1991). Among the changes in evidence are:

- *Increased attention to writing and its relationship to reading.* Students in these classrooms write every day. The writing does not stem from a series of teacher-based assignments to be collected, corrected, and returned. Rather, it is grounded in the ongoing activities of the classroom and the interests of individual students. Students are helped to see their writing through the entire process of prewriting, drafting, revising, editing, and publishing (Farnan, Lapp, & Flood, 1992; Jensen, 1993; Shanahan, 1990).

- *Greater use of tradebooks or library books rather than the more traditional reliance on textbooks.* Children in these classrooms read and are read to every day. Sharing and responding to literature are fundamental to all aspects of the curriculum. The reading aloud continues long after children are fluent, independent readers. Textbooks remain important as *one* of many resources for learning literacy and learning through literacy. Response to literature takes many forms: personal reflection, group discussions, writing, art, and drama may act as a means of reformulating children's understanding and interpretations of texts. Poems, stories, and informational texts are discussed in terms of their content, their literary qualities, and the art of writing. Students are encouraged to apply what they learn about the author's craft to their own writing (Cullinan, 1992; Huck, 1992; Norton, 1992).

- *Greater student choice in what they read and write in the classroom.* Teachers encourage children to share in the decision making regarding choice of topics to write about and materials to read. Making thoughtful selections and decisions is considered to be a valuable part of students' literacy development (Calkins, 1986; Cambourne, 1988; Wells, 1986).

- *Greater integration of oral language and literacy across all subjects in the curriculum.* Literacy learning is viewed as a key element of every aspect of the curriculum. Reading, writing, speaking,

listening, and reasoning are integral to every subject throughout the day (Lipson, Valencia, Wixson, & Peters, 1993; Pappas,
Ouler, Barry, & Rassel, 1993).

Dissenting Voices

These ideas and their applications are continually gaining acceptance
and applicability where mainstream, "typical" learners predominate.
There is disagreement, however, about how these principles and practices might relate to more diverse populations. Some educators have
expressed their concern about the effect of holistic practices on the reading and writing achievement of learners considered to be at risk for
school failure, particularly when those learners are black.

Lisa Delpit (1988), a prominent African American educator, has
complained about the lack of a display of power and authority in process-oriented classrooms: "The teacher has denied them access to herself as the source of knowledge necessary to learn the forms they need
to succeed"(p. 288). She stresses the need for teachers to be explicit, "both
with what you're trying to communicate and why that information is
important to the task at hand" (Teale, 1991, p. 541), particularly when
they are teaching across cultures, as is often the case in schools where
African American children are prevalent.

Others have questioned the value of holistic approaches to any
learners considered to be at risk for failure in school. When questioned
by the *Washington Post* regarding practices associated with young
children's emergent literacy and the whole language approach, Jeanne
Chall of Harvard University responded: "The new approach is particularly harmful for below-average children or children at risk of failure
because of poverty or learning problems" (1991, p. A16). More recently,
Chall expressed similar concerns, directing them specifically at what she
perceives to be a lack of appropriate phonics instruction in programs
that engage in holistic approaches. Once again, she is concerned for
"especially those who are at risk" (Willis, 1993, p. 8).

Still others express concern about the change process itself. Walter
MacGinitie (1991) warns that advocates of holistic approaches are
doomed to repeat the failures of the past if they are not more specific in
their descriptions of what they propose. "Those who seriously wish to
improve education must do more than describe a classroom atmosphere;
they must describe how that atmosphere can be achieved and maintained and how people function within it" (p. 57).

Each of these individuals is a highly respected scholar whose
words require serious consideration. Perhaps even more importantly,

their concerns are shared by many well-intentioned, caring parents and teachers of African American children. Unfortunately, when these views are expressed by those less well informed or less well intentioned, two very fundamental but faulty assumptions often underlie them. One is rooted in learning; the other, in teaching.

First, there is widespread belief, whether tacit or explicit, that African American children are inherently less capable than most other learners. Indeed, many black children are a risk for failure. But, the risk is neither inevitable nor inherent (Heath, 1983; Shepard, 1991). Second, the traditional view of "teacher as source of knowledge and power" remains highly prevalent, not only among the general public, but among many educators as well. Effective teachers are far more than repositories and dispensers of information. Their primary goal is to help children become independent learners. They share power in order to empower. Even Delpit (1988) concedes that, "The teacher cannot be the only expert in the classroom. To deny students their own expert knowledge is to disempower them" (p. 288).

Effective teachers also regard the direct instruction of strategies (with their attendant underlying skills) as fundamental to the "new" approaches outlined above. At the same time, however, they reject instruction that relies heavily on merely transmitting, "explicitly," a body of information from a single viewpoint or relaying only one way to solve a problem or address an issue. While such instruction may be explicit and clear, it risks denying the strengths that diverse views and cultural frameworks bring to the classroom. Moreover, effective teachers take care not to reduce explicit teaching merely to "telling." They know that modeling and demonstrating are key to being explicit (Duffy, Roehler, & Rackliffe, 1986).

Still, it behooves those of us who espouse new approaches to heed MacGinitie's admonition to be clear about what we advocate and to relate new practice to the many traditional practices that should be preserved. Indeed, Chall's concerns may be well founded in classrooms where basic principles of holistic education are not well understood and only in evidence at a superficial level. Fortunately, there is a growing body of literature, written not only by university theorists and researchers but also by classroom teachers and teacher-researchers, in which classroom environments and practices are explicitly described and related to theory (see Atwell, 1987; Chew, 1991; Feeley, Strickland, & Wepner, 1991; Routman, 1991, among others).

It is not surprising that some are skeptical about the new approaches to helping children learn literacy. For many educators, shifting to a new paradigm or to a new way of thinking is difficult under any circumstances. It may be virtually impossible when old ideas are tenaciously held, regardless of new evidence. For others, the reservations are guided by a healthy and informed skepticism. Their expressions of concern should be welcomed and reflected upon by all those working to help African American children become literate. They serve as a reminder of the constant need to reexamine our changing beliefs and practice.

Basic Skills: Pros and Cons

In the past, the educational problems of at-risk African American children have received a great deal of attention. The Johnson era brought about widespread attempts at school reform. Most of the resulting efforts were characterized by highly structured, isolated skills instruction in reading, with little or no attention given at all to instruction in writing. In schools where low student achievement was persistent, the emphasis was placed on increasing test scores in reading and math; and, for the most part, that focus remains today (Strickland & Ascher, 1992).

Oddly enough, the initiation of these "basic skills" reforms had a positive side. Applied skillfully, the conventional ways of responding to the educationally disadvantaged did improve student performance on standardized tests. This was especially true in the elementary grades. It demonstrated that when schools rallied around a common purpose, were goal oriented, and were given explicit help to achieve those goals, students would learn what was taught. For some, it may have been the first real evidence that these students were capable of learning. This proved to be a morale builder for students and teachers alike. When administrators and teachers saw their efforts pay off, they felt good about themselves and their clients—the students they served. And, the community also felt a sense of pride (Knapp & Turbull, 1990).

There was also an ominous and negative side to this, however. As the definition of what it means to be literate in our society becomes more demanding and more complex, the constraints of this type of teaching become increasingly evident. Teaching to low-level, basic skills apparently places an unintended ceiling on learning. Those rising test scores, the pride of a school district, begin to level off, and children actually appear to stop learning. In an effort to increase test scores at any cost, many schools may spend excessive amounts of time and effort aligning curriculum to test and valuable instructional time teaching directly to the test. Focusing so much attention on tests and so little on true instructional reform tends to yield benefits that are both limited and temporary (Darling-Hammond, 1993b; Shepard, 1991).

The really important message in all this, however, lies well beyond what the test scores reveal. When students are repeatedly served a diet of low-level, impoverished basics, they accumulate a kind of knowledge that is neither empowering nor self-improving. Students may conscientiously take in the information dispensed to them, and they may spout it back on cue. But, they are frequently left not knowing how to use that information, how to learn on their own, to think for themselves, solve problems, and critique their own work and the work of others.

A Better Way

Fortunately, some promising instructional alternatives exist. Building on the work of previous researchers, contemporary investigators have broken fresh ground to create new paradigms for the way we view children's literacy development and the way adults can best help them learn. Much of what has been learned applies to all children regardless of race or socioeconomic level. Several major principles seem to stand out regardless of the learner variables present. Whether the learners be high achieving or at risk, inner city poor or affluent suburban, second language or native speakers, certain learner characteristics are maintained:

■ **Literacy Learning Starts Early and Continues throughout Life**
(Goodman & Goodman, 1979; Harste, Woodward, & Burke, 1984; Teale & Sulzby, 1986). African American children deserve early literacy programs that are framed from an emergent literacy perspective. Such programs would capitalize on the fact that, like all other children, African American children enter school eager to learn and to please the responsive adults around them. They are aware of the print in their environment: their names, the names of siblings, the logos and slogans from fast food restaurants, and various other signs representing environmental print.

Recommendations

1. Avoid readiness tests that screen children out. Implement instructional strategies and systematic observational techniques that allow children to demonstrate what they do know. Use what is learned to build their linguistic awareness and expand their knowledge about the world.

2. Create learning environments that give children confidence that they can learn and let them know *by your actions* that you believe they can learn.

3. Initiate family literacy programs in which adults and children approach literacy learning as a cooperative social experience. At the very least, such programs would make books and other materials available to parents for reading to and with their children.

4. Seek out information from parents about their perceptions of their children as learners and their educational goals and concerns as a family. Let parents know you value whatever literacy experiences they give to their children. View home and school as making different but interdependent contributions to the child's total education.

5. Start coordinated school and social service intervention programs early and make them ongoing. The purpose should be to prevent failure and promote accelerated achievement rather than merely to remediate problems.

6. Treat instruction in phonics as an important part of beginning reading and writing, but not a precursor to it. View phonics for what it is—one of several enablers (including word meanings and sentence structures) to success in literacy. Nothing more! Nothing less! Allow neither students nor their parents to think they are receiving instruction in reading when they are merely receiving instruction in phonics. Emphasize sound/symbol relationships during the reading of interesting, predictable texts and during writing through children's own attempts at spelling.

■ **Literacy Learning Is Used to Make Meanings out of Our World** (Donaldson, 1978; Smith, 1982; Wells, 1986). African American children deserve literacy programs that stress the construction of meaning right from the start. As with every other aspect of their learning, these young children are attempting to make sense of the world around them. Print is simply one of the many curiosities in the world about which they are eager to learn.

Recommendations

1. Take care to see to it that the tasks students are given make sense to them. Keep in mind that low-level, rote tasks tend to make less sense than tasks that require reasoning and reflective thought (Resnick, 1987b).

2. Select instructional materials that employ whole texts, including a wide variety of fiction and nonfiction. Avoid meaningless drills on isolated skills delivered in the form of workbooks and worksheets.

3. Integrate instruction in the language arts so that students connect learning how to spell with proofreading a composition, expanding their vocabularies with comprehending stories and informational books, authoring and responding with what they do as writers and readers, and so on.

4. Foster inquiry-based curricula, in which individuals and groups of children pose questions and seek to answer them. Allow the teaching of literacy to be largely driven by needs arising from the content and questions that children are curious about—for example, learning how to conduct a good interview during the study of personal health in order to learn what nurses do. Even when content foci are preset by a fixed curriculum, independence and motivation can be fostered by allowing children to pose their own questions within the sphere of the content they are required to study.

- **Literacy Learning Takes Place through Active Involvement and Use** (Lindfors, 1987; Wells, 1986). African American children deserve literacy programs that recognize that knowledge is not merely an accumulation of assorted facts absorbed like a sponge. Knowledge is constructed by active minds and grounded in life experience.

Recommendations

1. Plan instructional activities that involve children in a high degree of critical thinking and problem solving. For example, postreading activities based on student-generated questions and observations related to key ideas in a text are more likely to stimulate active response and involvement than those that simply require students to answer a preset list of teacher-generated questions.

2. Help students use talk as a means of mediating what they are attempting to understand. Engage students in literature study groups, collaborative group discussions, partner activities, and research groups. Rather than attempting to keep students quiet, plan activities where talk is channeled and used along with reading and writing as a tool for learning.

3. Employ collaborative group learning strategies and peer teaching methods to promote active learners. Approaches that emphasize the fact that everyone in the classroom is both a teacher and a learner help increase student involvement and tend to promote active learning.

4. Keep instruction as close to the point of use as possible. Expand the definition of direct instruction to go beyond conveying information to an entire group of students in a pre-ordered way. Include the demonstration of strategies for individuals and groups of students that they actually need in order to com-

plete a given task. Both the how and the why of a strategy are made explicit when the need is clearly understood.

■ **Literacy Learning Is Influenced by One's Language and Cultural Background**
African American children deserve literacy programs that build on and expand their language and culture with a view toward helping them understand and value their heritage and respect the heritage of others. They deserve teachers and administrators who value diversity and recognize its presence in every child (Au, 1993).

Recommendations

1. Never use a child's dialect, language, or culture as a basis for making judgments regarding intellect or capability. Competence is not tied to a particular language, dialect, or culture.

2. Learn as much as you can about students' language and cultural backgrounds. Avoid making sweeping generalizations based on skin color or surnames. There is a high degree of variability within every cultural group. Learn as much as you can; then keep an open mind.

3. Give students literature that reflects a wide diversity of cultures. Take special care to see to it that African American children are familiar with literature by and about African Americans as well as with the writers and illustrators themselves.

4. Encourage Standard English through exposure to a variety of oral and written texts and oral language activities. Keep in mind that while competence in Standard English is a worthy goal for all children, it must not mean a rejection or replacement of one language and culture with another. Rather, it should be viewed as language expansion and enrichment of the students' home language to include Standard English, giving them the opportunity and the *choice* to communicate with a broader speech community (Galda, Cullinan, & Strickland, 1993).

■ **Literacy Learning Is Influenced by Social Context**
(Cazden, 1992b; Moll, 1990; Scribner & Cole, 1981). African American children deserve opportunities to learn in contexts that reflect what is known about the social nature of literacy and literacy learning. This requires administrators and teachers who know how to establish supportive and responsive contexts for learning. According to Darling-Hammond (1993a), "the problems of equity are constrained by the availability of talented teachers, by the knowledge and capacities those teachers possess, and by the school conditions that define how that knowledge can be used" (p. 754).

Recommendations

1. Foster a sense of community and interconnectedness within each classroom and throughout each school. Keep schools and classes small enough, or divide them into manageable units, so that individual students feel known and recognized as participants in a community, and closer student-teacher relationships are more likely to develop.

2. Avoid long-term ability grouping and tracking. These deny equitable access to learning opportunities (Epstein, 1985; Oakes, 1985). Seek alternatives such as flexible grouping practices, which may include some short-term ability grouping and cooperative learning instructional methods that treat diversity as a valued resource.

3. Create large, uninterrupted blocks of time for language arts instruction, during which no children leave the classroom for special activities. Short time periods lead to a one-size-fits-all instruction, in which every student is assigned precisely the same tasks and given the same amount of instructional support and time to complete them. Large time frames foster integrated learning and allow for differentiated instruction, thus fostering true educational equity.

4. Give incentives to attract the very best teachers available and provide ongoing professional development focused on empowering teachers to make instructional decisions. Emphasize classroom observation—how to assess what students are learning and use it to plan accordingly.

5. Encourage ongoing professional development such as teacher networks that operate as voluntary support groups. Professional networks allow teachers to organize their own staff development efforts so that ideas close to the classroom may be discussed in a risk-free atmosphere of mutual support. Avoid placing all resources in one-shot staff development days, and be wary of intensive "training" programs on narrowly construed, highly prescriptive models of instruction.

Conclusion

For most educators, the ideas offered here are neither new nor revolutionary. In fact, some would argue that these suggestions are appropriate for any child, regardless of ethnicity, socioeconomic status, or intellect. And, that is precisely the point. We now know enough about the learning and teaching of language and literacy to offer some basic principles to guide instructional decision making for the education of every child. Perhaps the greatest value of these principles and recommendations is that they are learner centered and thus adapt to and support all learners, no matter who they are.

Teachers who work with large numbers of African American children in situations where failure is chronic may wonder how these ideas will help them deal with diversity. Having placed so much emphasis on how their students are different from others, they may be confused by the suggestion that there are "universal" principles of learning and teaching from which all children may benefit. They want advice specific to the needs of the children they teach. This is highly understandable. Yet, these teachers should know that the ideas offered here are not meant to suggest a one-size-fits-all curriculum. They in no way negate the fact that there are great differences among the children we teach. Respecting and building on these differences is an important part of what good teachers do. The differences we face in schools, however, go far beyond those distinctions commonly made *between* various ethnic groups. There are important differences among children *within* ethnic groups and linguistic communities, even among those who live at the poverty level. These include children's interests, experiential backgrounds, abilities, and motivation. These differences may be overlooked by teachers who come to the teaching situation with preconceived ideas about how certain children learn and behave. Moreover, when the curriculum fails to value each learner's unique background, there is a risk that important individual characteristics may never be revealed as potential building blocks for instruction.

Dawn Harris Martine, a second-grade teacher in Harlem, once told me that she could trace at least a dozen different national origins among her group of 26 children. More than half her students had very recent roots in several countries in Africa, the Caribbean, and Central America, as well as various parts of the United States. Yet, she said, to most people they simply look like any other group of African American kids. To Dawn, the differences were very important and helped shape the curriculum and the ways in which she interacted with each child.

What then should teachers know that is specific to these youngsters? Teachers who work with these children should enter the classroom informed as much as possible about the broader population from which these children come—both from reading the relevant literature and from first-hand experiences with others who belong to that population. They should also learn as much as they can about the immediate community and the families of these children. They should use what they learn as a framework for understanding who and where their learners are. At the same time, they should use the principles described here to develop a literacy curriculum that is both rigorous and learner centered. Most importantly, they should avoid assigning preconceived characteristics and attributes to any child, bearing in mind the need to suspend judgment and respect each as an individual.

Irving Harris (1993), a philanthropist and child advocate, recounts a parable about some people picnicking beside a river. Suddenly, they see an enormous number of babies being carried down the river by the current. Their first impulse is to jump in and pull out as many of the babies as possible. But they keep coming, and the rescuers can't save them all. Finally, someone is smart enough to run up the river to see who is pushing them in (p. 30).

As teachers of the language arts, we sometimes feel like those rescuers—attempting to "save the children" despite overwhelming forces beyond our control. Indeed, the responsibility for helping African American students, or any other students who are at risk for educational failure, is not ours alone. The problems are serious and demand the attention of everyone—the home, the school, and the community.

Nevertheless, there is a great deal that we *can* do. We can work as individuals and within professional and civic organizations to effect social policy change; and we can work with students and their parents to achieve better mutual support between home and school. Most importantly, we can take advantage of a growing body of research that suggests better educational policy and more comprehensive and meaningful approaches to raising the academic achievement of African American students. The knowledge is available. It is time we demonstrated the commitment to seek a better way.

QUOTATIONS

The two major trends in education—toward centralized control and toward school-site management—enact the deepest tension in our democracy: how to maintain a common identity as a country while respecting and using the richness of our diversity. (p. 49)

The issue isn't whether we want standards. Rather, it is how we define education. The pursuit and capture of trivia is one way; becoming literate is another. (p. 49)

Source: Harman, S. (1991). National tests, national standards, national curriculum. *Language Arts, 68*(1), 49–50.

REFLECTION: CALL TO ACTION ON STANDARDIZED TESTING

Editors' Note: Though written some time ago, Farrell's call to reach out to the media and the public on the misinformation associated with standardized testing holds considerable currency in today's educational climate.

❧

What is now needed is a well-financed campaign through newspapers and journal articles, workshops, and institutes to educate the public to these elementary truths:

- Testing and evaluation or assessment are not synonymous . . . .

- Standardized norm-referenced tests may have little or nothing to do with the content and quality of the English language-arts program in a particular school. . . .

- Ability to read and commitment to reading are not the same . . . .

- Eighth-grade reading ability is a construct, not a reality. . . .

- The teaching of reading, writing, speaking, and listening is a responsibility to be shared by all teachers and by parents. . . .

- Tests which are not diagnostic are educational dead ends. . . .

- Schools and teachers are not responsible for social conditions that militate against learning. (pp. 488–489)

Source: Farrell, E. (1977). The vice/vise of standardized testing: National depreciation by quantification. *Language Arts, 54*(5), 486–490.

REFLECTION: CRITIQUE OF STANDARDIZED TESTING

Editors' Note: The critique of standardized testing comes from many sources. Here is a small sampling of comments that makes one wonder why these instruments continue to play a role in education.

❧

[Standardized] tests have three big problems:

▶

Firstly, they never measure well at the earliest stages of learning (onset ages) nor at the point where most children are competent.

Secondly, they do not allow the study of the processes which contribute to better learning, and one can only guess at how to go about interventions which might bring about improvements.

Thirdly, they have to be made up of items that are relatively simple and quantifiable, involving perfected responding, and ignoring the partial successes of children in the process of learning. (pp. 289–290)

Source: Clay, M. M. (1990). Research currents: What is and what might be in evaluation. *Language Arts, 67*(3), 288–298.

One of the commonest arguments against standardized assessment is the argument of *context*. It has frequently been shown that pupils' performance in assessment tasks that are lacking in interest or purpose, when the mind and intentions are not engaged, is likely to be poorer than when they are involved in an interesting, perhaps self-chosen, piece of work, where the context is supportive. . . .

Secondly, most standard assessment is *biased*. It is recognized that boys and girls perform differently in tests, and that some aspects of test design have differential effects on girls' and boys' performance. There is considerable evidence, for instance, that boys do better than girls in multiple-choice questions compared to 'free response' questions. . . .

Thirdly, standardized assessment . . . offers little in the way of information which will help the *teaching and learning process.* Most standardized tests produce a single score, which tells teachers nothing about a child's strengths and needs, provides no diagnostic information, and is less informative than what the teacher knows already from observation. . . .

Finally, there is now a fundamental dissatisfaction with conventional measures of children's language, because of what we have come to know about language and literacy development. Most reading tests are based on old-fashioned theories of reading. (pp. 249–251)

Source: Barrs, M. (1990). "The Primary Language Record": Reflection of issues in evaluation. *Language Arts, 67*(3), 244–253.

▶

The most important condition for learning how to perform a skilled act is the opportunity to do it. Beginners will necessarily execute any skill more awkwardly than an expert, but the only way to gain the proficiency that comes with experience is to practice the skill. In the case of reading, this means that no amount of workbook exercises designed to inculcate knowledge will substitute for practice in making one's way through the paragraphs and pages of books. . . . The necessity for practice in learning how to read may seem like a common sense requirement, but the manuals accompanying widely used tests rarely if ever discuss this need. (pp. 303–304)

To the extent that tests reward attention to surface details and literal meaning, they correspondingly penalize attempts to bring outside knowledge into play in answering questions. . . . Many such errors were made on a passage concerning Bud and a pup. The relevant lines from the passage and the test question appear below:

> Bud had fun. He fed the pup. The pup ate a bun.
> Question: What did the pup eat?

Some children read *bone* for *bun* and answered the question accordingly. Others read *bun* correctly but still answered that the pup ate a bone. Still others said the pup ate 'some food.' When pressed on the matter, some didn't know exactly what a bun meant in the context; others couldn't imagine such a thing being fed to a dog. According to the test manual, neither 'a bone' nor 'some food' qualify as correct answers for the comprehension score. (p. 307)

Source: Bussis, A. M., & Chittenden, E. A. (1987). Research currents: What the reading tests neglect. *Language Arts, 64*(3), 302–308.

24 Guiding Bilingual Students "through" the Literacy Process

Stephen B. Kucer

Editors' text: Literacy learning for bilingual students is complicated by the conventions of both their languages. Yet, many of the same general strategies used for monolingual students can be used for bilingual students. Kucer maps out how he and a classroom teacher introduced literacy strategies to students, as well as the changes in strategy use that resulted across the year.

I recently had the good fortune to spend a year in a third-grade bilingual (Spanish and English) classroom in which the students were being formally transitioned into English literacy. During this year the teacher, Cecilia Silva, and I explored a variety of ways to help the children become independent readers and writers (Kucer, 1990). We wanted the students to be both efficient and effective users of written language, able to comprehend and compose without constant teacher assistance.

In order to become independently literate, the students needed to develop various strategies to use when they encountered "blocks" during reading and writing. "Blocks" are those times when a student, for various reasons, experiences difficulty in understanding what is being read or in putting ideas into a written form (Kucer, 1993). Such encounters are not unique to bilingual students; at times all readers and writers, regardless of language background, experience blocks. More independent readers and writers, however, have access to a number of strategies for overcoming or working through these blocks.

Unfortunately, many Spanish-speaking students are introduced to only a limited number of strategies when being taught to read and write in their home language (Au, 1993; Flores, Cousin, & Díaz, 1991). Given the relatively consistent relationship between letters and sounds in Spanish, as compared to the more varied letter-sound relationships in English, the graphophonic system is frequently emphasized in early

This essay appeared in *Language Arts* 72.1 (1995) on pages 20–29.

literacy programs. As students transition into English literacy, this emphasis on the graphophonic system may continue. However, just as a carpenter uses more than a single tool to build a house, we know that good readers and writers use more than graphophonics to build a meaningful story. Able readers and writers use and orchestrate various cognitive strategies to work their way through print (Flower & Hayes, 1981; Goodman, 1985; Rummelhart, 1985). They rely on graphic, syntactic, and semantic information to predict, confirm, and integrate meaning. They monitor their involvement with written language by asking such questions as, "Does what I am reading or writing make sense?"; "Am I meeting my purposes by reading or writing this text?"; and "What should I do when I encounter difficulties in my reading or writing?"

Cecilia and I wanted the students to have a box full of tools (strategies) to use when they encountered blocks in their reading and writing. Not to give the students knowledge of these additional strategies, we reasoned, would be like asking a carpenter to build a house with only a hammer. Although a hammer is a necessary tool in home building, it is not sufficient. In this article, I present and discuss a series of instructional lessons ("strategy wall charts") that were developed to provide the students with various tools to work their way through literacy blocks as they read and wrote in English. I begin with a general overview of the students and the literacy curriculum. This overview is followed by a discussion of the strategy wall charts, how they were generated, and how conferences were used to demonstrate and mediate strategy development. I conclude with a look at the patterns of internalization that occurred when the students attempted to use the various strategies; I also look at those curricular activities that either promoted or inhibited such internalization.

The Setting: Students and Curriculum

The students in the third-grade class were Mexican American, bilingual in Spanish and English, and literate in Spanish. Linguistically, most had entered kindergarten speaking predominantly Spanish and were in Spanish literacy programs until the second grade. In the second semester of the second grade, they were formally transitioned into English literacy. However, because this transition had been difficult for the children, they were once again placed in a transition program in the third grade.

Until the third grade, both the Spanish and English literacy programs experienced by the children were fairly traditional in nature. To a large extent, a basal reader, speller, and grammar book "framed" the instruction. Sound-symbol correspondences and vocabulary were explicitly taught in an isolated manner, as were spelling words, punctuation, capitalization, and penmanship. Because the school's bilingual students had historically progressed at a slower pace than English monolingual students within this traditional program, the principal supported a shift to a holistic curriculum in the third grade.

The third-grade teacher, Cecilia Silva, was originally from Colombia and bilingual and biliterate in Spanish and English. She had been a bilingual teacher for 11 years. I was a participant-observer in the class three mornings per week; I watched, talked with the children, and recorded field notes, but I never engaged in any direct instruction. However, I did work with Cecilia "behind the scenes" to develop the literacy curriculum.

Informal literacy assessments (interviews, oral readings, spelling and writing samples, and observations) conducted at the beginning of the school year indicated that the children used a limited range of strategies when reading and writing. For example, students focused on the sound-symbol relationships of written language and rarely demonstrated the ability to use contextual clues when they encountered unknown words. Reading miscues tended to be substitutions that graphophonically resembled the target word (for example, *they* substituted for *the)* or omissions (for example, skipping *broken)*. Both types of miscues, however, usually distorted the meaning of what was being read. Additionally, during the discussion of particular reading selections, the students had difficulty responding to what they had read. They were able to retell specific events or facts from the readings (for example, Ira taking a teddy bear when he slept at a friend's house) but less able to respond to such issues as the theme, links to other books they had read, or what they liked or disliked.

The students also appeared to lack experience with writing as a process, that is, in the use of conferences to move a written piece from a rough draft to a final publication. They rarely used such techniques as brainstorming when experiencing writer's block, and their written stories often lacked development and organization. To a certain extent, the frequency of writer's block and lack of developed stories appeared to be due to the students' concern with conventional spelling. Many students were unwilling to continue writing until each word was spelled correctly. Consequently, students often forgot what they wanted to say or were unwilling to expand their stories because such expansion might involve more difficulties with spelling.

Based on these informal assessments, it was clear to the teacher and me that the students needed to acquire additional strategies to work their way through written language more effectively. Instructional support for such strategy development was embedded within a four-part curriculum: themes, teacher reading, free reading, and free writing. The themes engaged the children in integrated activities related to a particular topic under study, such as "Getting to Know about You, Me, and Others." Thematic activities were designed to help students develop conceptual knowledge about the topic and to promote literacy development. Embedded within the themes were a number of learning events that tended to get repeated throughout the year, regardless of the theme under study. On a regular basis, students experienced choral and paired reading, expert/research groups, learning logs, reading/writing conferences, predictable books, and cloze activities. Lessons involved art, music, and math, as well as oral and written language. Materials came from the sciences, social sciences, and literature and represented a range of discourse types (narrative, expository, poetic, dramatic) and resources (books, magazines, filmstrips, records, movies). When available, materials in both Spanish and English were included in the curriculum.

During teacher reading, Cecilia read aloud short stories, trade books, and articles related to the theme. Cecilia used this activity not only to expose the children to the sounds and content of quality literature but also to make visible her metacognitive reading behaviors. She frequently verbalized her thoughts about and responses to the content of the reading and encouraged the children to do so as well. Cecilia also shared particular process behaviors. For instance, if she read a sentence that did not make sense to her, she would reread the sentence and discuss with the children why she had done so. Or, if she changed words in the text as she read and still maintained the author's meaning, she would highlight this behavior, noting that this is something good readers frequently do.

Following teacher reading, students engaged in free reading. Throughout the room were plastic tubs of paperback books and magazines on different topics, representing various discourse modes, and written in English and Spanish. The children selected their own reading material and were provided opportunities to share and to respond to what they and others were reading.

Free writing, in contrast to theme writing that focused on the topic under study, required students to select their own topics and to determine which texts to publish. Choosing texts to be published usually involved the children in two conferences. The first focused on the ideas in the text: In small groups the students and Cecilia discussed the ideas and organization of the drafts and made suggestions for revisions. In the second, or editing conference, students and Cecilia revised surface-level errors such as punctuation, capitalization, and spelling. Following the editing conferences, Cecilia corrected any remaining errors and either typed the stories or had students recopy them. The stories were then illustrated, front and back covers were made, and the books were bound.

Strategy Wall Charts: Instructional Support for Literacy Development

Although the curriculum did not engage students in the manipulation of, or practice with, isolated skills, Cecilia and I felt there needed to be embedded within the curriculum specific instructional activities to support student development of additional literacy strategies. We were not comfortable thinking that students would spontaneously discover and systematically apply new strategies without specific curricular mediation. However, we wanted such mediation to occur within the context of whole texts being read or written for authentic purposes.

These two concerns led to the development, in collaboration with the students, of a series of strategy wall charts. Each chart had a heading related to one of the four literacy blocks frequently experienced by the students: reading strategies, reader response strategies, spelling strategies, and writing strategies. The wall charts were introduced to the students over a two-month period, with Cecilia beginning the introduction of each chart by asking, "What can you do when . . . ?" and recording student responses. For example, students were asked what they could do when they encountered "something" they did not know or understand during reading. Students brainstormed various strategies, and Cecilia listed those on the corresponding chart. Throughout the year, these charts were reviewed with the students, and new strategies were added. Eventually, Cecilia typed the problems and solutions on 8 1/2" by 11" paper and gave copies to each student for easy reference. Students were encouraged to use these charts when reading and writing. Table 1 illustrates how the charts appeared at the end of the academic year.

Using Conferences to Demonstrate and Mediate Strategy Development

Cecilia and I were aware that simply telling or discussing alternate reading and writing strategies with the students might have little impact.

Table 1. Strategy wall charts.

When reading and you come to "something" that you do not recognize, know, or understand, you can:	When reading and you have a hard time "getting into" or engaging with what you are reading, you can ask yourself:
1. Stop reading → think about it → make a guess → read on to see if the guess makes sense.	1. What is my purpose for reading this text?
2. Stop reading → reread the previous sentence(s) or paragraph(s) → make a guess → continue reading to see if the guess makes sense.	2. What am I learning from reading this text?
3. Skip it → read on to get more information → return and make a guess → continue reading to see if the guess makes sense.	3. Why did the author write this text? What was the author trying to teach me?
4. Skip it → read on to see if what you do not understand is important to know → return and make a guess if it fits with the rest of the text.	4. What parts do I like best? What parts are my favorite? Why do I like these particular parts?
5. Put something in that makes sense → read on to see if it fits with the rest of the text.	5. What parts do I like the least? Why do I dislike these parts?
6. Stop reading → look at the pictures, charts, graphs, etc. → make a guess → read on to see if the guess makes sense.	6. Does this text remind me of other texts I have read? How is this text both similar and dissimilar to other texts?
7. Sound it out (focus on initial and final letters, consonants, known words within the word, meaningful word parts) → read on to see if the guess makes sense.	7. What would I change in this text if I had written it? What might the author have done to make this text better, more understandable, more interesting?
8. Stop reading → talk with a friend about what you do not understand → return and continue reading.	8. Are there things/parts in the text that I am not understanding? What can I do to better understand these things/parts?
9. Stop reading → talk with a friend about what you do not understand.	
10. Read the text with a friend.	
11. Stop reading.	
Reading Strategies	*Reader Response Strategies*

continued on next page

Table 1 continued

When writing and you come to a place where you do not know what to write next or you have difficulty expressing an idea, you can: 1. Brainstorm possible ideas and jot them down on paper. 2. Reread what you have written so far. 3. Skip to a part where you know what you will write about. Come back to the problem later. 4. Write it as best you can and return later to make it better. 5. Write it several different ways and choose the one that you like the best. 6. Write whatever comes into your mind. 7. Talk about it/conference with a friend. 8. Read other texts to get some new ideas. 9. Stop writing for a while and come back to it later.	When writing and you come to a word that you do not know how to spell, you can: 1. Sound it out. 2. Think of "small words" that are in the word and write these first. 3. Write the word several different ways and choose the one that looks the best. 4. Write the letters that you know are in the word. 5. Make a line for the word. 6. Ask a friend. 7. Look in the dictionary.
Writing Strategies	***Spelling Strategies***

Students needed to see the strategies highlighted and demonstrated within meaningful contexts and to have support as they attempted to use the strategies themselves. Cecilia engaged the students in two kinds of conferences in order to provide such demonstrations and mediations: problem/solution conferences and response conferences. These conferences usually consisted of no more than four to seven students and were initially led by the teacher.

In problem/solution conferences, students were asked to bring something currently being read or written and to share a problem they were experiencing. Typically, these conferences focused on (1) a particular book that a group of students had selected to read within the thematic unit, (2) something being written as part of the thematic unit, (3) a book being read during free reading, or (4) a draft being written during free writing.

As each problem was shared, Cecilia and the other students in the group discussed and "tried out" various solutions to the problem. These solutions were taken from the existing strategy wall charts, or new solutions were developed which were later added to the charts. When the problem was an unknown word, for instance, Cecilia and the students might have reread the previous paragraph, read the paragraph after the word, or discussed the relative importance of knowing what the word meant. If a student was having difficulty finding the appropriate language for expressing a particular idea, Cecilia and the students brainstormed various ways in which the idea might be expressed and discussed which one was most appropriate. Regardless of what the problem happened to be, Cecilia would "walk the students through" various solutions.

In response conferences, students reacted to a piece of writing using the response strategies illustrated in Table 1. Texts responded to were student drafts as well as published works by students and professional authors. Students discussed what they learned from the text, how the text related to other things they had read, and how the text might be improved if revisions were to be made. In response conferences, Cecilia helped the students learn to "talk" to the author.

As the year progressed and students became comfortable with the problem/solution and response conferences, Cecilia became a less active participant. Students assumed responsibility for leading the conferences and for helping each other work through their problems and respond to what had been read or written.

Evidence of Strategy Internalization

As a participant-observer, I was particularly interested in the effects of the curriculum and the wall charts on students' strategy development. Because I was in the classroom on a regular basis, I had numerous opportunities both to observe and to talk with the children as they engaged in various literacy activities. My observations and field notes focused on the strategies the students used as they interacted with print and the developmental changes that occurred in these interactions throughout the year.

Table 2 presents a summary of the changes in student-text interactions during the year; each column in the table corresponds to one of the four strategy wall charts. Table 3 highlights those instructional events and behaviors that significantly promoted or inhibited strategy internalization. In many respects, the findings in Table 3 challenged my thinking as a researcher throughout the year. I had assumed that the

Table 2. Trends in strategy internalization.

Beginning of the Year

Reading Strategies	Reader Response Strategies	Spelling Strategies	Writing Strategies
Students "sound out" or skip words not recognized; they show little concern for not understanding the ideas in what is being read; when sharing their drafts, many students cannot read what has been written.	There is little or no response to what is read; students refuse to respond voluntarily; they appear puzzled by the open-ended questions; they are reluctant to share their drafts; there are limited responses to student drafts: "I like it"; there are few requests for teacher response to their journals.	Students consistently ask the teacher or other students for spelling assistance; some forget what they want to write when focusing on the spelling of particular words.	Some students use current experiences as writing topics and as sources of information to overcome blocks during free writing; other students retell folktales during free writing so as to avoid blocks.
When sharing their drafts with others, students reread previous portions of their texts when they have difficulty reading what they have written; students begin to engage spontaneously in choral reading.	Responses are general in nature, focus on what is liked about the pictures and what has been learned or what can be recalled; they are unable to discuss what is not liked or how to improve published texts; there are suggestions for revision in student-authored texts: add pictures, write in cursive, write in English; they are unable to see thematic links between texts.	Most students appear not to understand the idea of generating multiple spellings for a word that cannot be spelled conventionally; they stop asking the teacher for spelling assistance; they continue to ask other students for assistance.	Some students use predictable formats such as "The Lost _____" to avoid blocks; there is lack of student involvement during free writing.
In "paired reading" students discuss what strategies to use when they encounter an unknown word; they begin to demonstrate the use of context and rereading when something does not make sense.	Students begin to expand response to books read during teacher reading and filmstrips shown during the themes; suggestions for revisions focus on the pictures, for example, "make them in color."	Some students begin to understand the difference between "drafts" and texts to be published; many students begin to spell "as best they can"; some students continue to believe that each word must be spelled	Some students begin to conference on their own when encountering blocks; they use theme topic or books read during free reading as a source of information to overcome blocks.

continued on next page

Table 2 continued

In "paired reading" students discuss ideas they do not understand.	As student-published texts become available and are read during free reading, students engage in "paired reading" and respond throughout the text; when asked how particular theme books are similar, students focus on physical similarities such as size, shape, and use of pictures; students begin to request teacher response to their journals. Responses become more varied and specific; suggestions for revisions on both student drafts and professionally authored texts focus on the development of ideas, the use of specific pictures to illustrate an idea, and such linguistic changes as using commas instead of a series of "and's," using "my" instead of "a" to indicate ownership, and writing in Spanish; students use both theme and free reading as opportunities to read and respond together. There are numerous volunteers to teacher-asked response questions; students challenge each other's responses; they can discuss thematic links between various books.	conventionally when it is written. A few students begin to generate multiple spellings for words that cannot be spelled conventionally or write the letters they know are in the word and put lines for the other letters; some students use theme books to spell words when engaging in theme-related writing; some students continue to believe that each word must be spelled conventionally when it is written.

End of the Year

strategy wall charts, in conjunction with the problem/solution and response conferences, would serve as the primary agents for strategy internalization. Although this was partially the case, there were also other instructional events, materials, and affective behaviors embedded within the curriculum that either promoted or inhibited strategy internalization.

Reader Response Strategies

As indicated in Table 2, the most significant development in student-text interactions was in the area of reader response. At the beginning of the year, students were unwilling or unable to react to what was read

Table 3. Significant instructional events and behaviors that either promoted or inhibited strategy internalization.

Promoting			
Reading Strategies	*Reader Response Strategies*	*Spelling Strategies*	*Writing Strategies*
Students' oral reading of their drafts to other students	Texts with numerous pictures	Teacher's refusal to provide correct spelling	Theme-related writing
Paired reading	Students responding to student drafts during writing conferences	Understanding the concept of drafts versus publishable texts	Internalization of spelling strategies
	Student response to stories orally read by the teacher		
	Filmstrips		
	Reading student-published texts during free reading		
Inhibiting			
Use of predictable story formats			
Retelling of stories, movies, and personal experiences			
Completion of a text in one class period			
Lack of engagement			

and often appeared puzzled by requests to do so. After a story had been read, either by Cecilia during teacher reading or by the children as part of the theme, few students would verbalize their reactions. In writing conferences, the children were hesitant to share their drafts and would only do so if another child read the draft for them; and responses seldom went beyond, "I like it." Finally, there were few if any requests for Cecilia to respond to the journals that the students kept as part of the school's "homework policy."

Expansion of response strategies tended to develop from the general to the specific and from a concern with the pictures to a concern with the discourse itself. In their responses early in the year, students talked about "liking the pictures" and retold what they could remember from the text. Although unable to suggest "things to improve" in professionally authored texts, reactions to student drafts focused on the addition of pictures and writing in cursive and in English. As the year progressed, the children began to respond more readily to the stories read by Cecilia, to the filmstrips shown as part of a theme, and to student-published texts. The student-published texts, in particular, promoted the most numerous and varied responses and were the most popular texts read and reread during free reading. Students frequently read these texts in pairs, discussed them throughout the entire reading, and shared favorite parts with children who might be sitting nearby.

By the end of the year, students were able to make specific suggestions for change, both in student-authored and professionally authored texts. Suggestions frequently involved further development and elaboration of ideas and modification in language to clarify meanings. Pictures continued powerfully to attract and influence the children; however, their suggestions for the pictures' improvement became more specific and were discussed in terms of what meanings the pictures needed to add to the discourse itself. Although they were part of a transition classroom, the students also valued the ability to write in Spanish and commented that English texts might be improved by translating them into Spanish. Perhaps the most significant overall change was that students were consistently sharing and responding to whatever was being read and written as the school year came to an end.

Reading Strategies

The use of more varied reading strategies was first promoted by the sharing of student drafts and secondly by "paired reading." During writing conferences, each student orally read the draft currently being written for publication. Because many students experienced difficulty reading what they had written, Cecilia encouraged students to read their drafts to themselves before sharing with the group. During both these private and group readings, students could be observed rereading parts of their texts, as well as reading on and then returning to what could not be read. With these texts, students demonstrated the willingness and ability to use contextual clues early in the year, perhaps because they were sharing part of themselves through sharing their drafts.

In the reading of professional authors, the use of various strategies first occurred during paired reading. When a particular book or article was read, Cecilia often paired students. Students in these pairs were given one copy of the text and asked to read it aloud in unison. As blocks were encountered, they were to use the various strategies listed on the reading strategy wall chart. Initial student use of the wall chart focused primarily on the word level. For example, when encountering unknown words, students began to reread portions of the text or continued reading and then returned to the unknown word. Although sounding out continued to be used, it became embedded within the use of contextual clues; that is, the context and letters in the unknown word were used together. Over time, the students came to realize that word identification did not necessarily lead to understanding. In paired reading situations, students began to discuss ideas that they did not understand. Throughout the year, however, there were several students who were unwilling to expand their focus beyond that of sounding out words. In spite of the encouragement to use context as an additional strategy, these students consistently asked other students to identify words they did not recognize. Interestingly, these were the same students who insisted that each word be spelled conventionally when they wrote.

Spelling Strategies

With the few exceptions just mentioned, most children quickly learned at least some of the various spelling strategies presented on the wall chart. One impetus for this was Cecilia's refusal to provide conventional spellings when the children asked for assistance. The initial response of many children to Cecilia's refusal was simply to ask another student for the correct spelling. During this time, Cecilia continued to promote the idea of generating several possible spellings for a word and selecting the one that looked most correct. However, even at the end of the year, most students either appeared not to understand this concept or rejected its utility.

The second impetus that promoted the learning of various spelling strategies was the students' growing understanding of the concept of "draft" versus "publishable" text. Because the students engaged in at least two conferences before a piece of writing was published—the first focusing on meaning, the second on conventions—they came to understand when in the writing process a piece needed to be "polished." This realization resulted in most students simply writing the word "as best they could" and worrying about the spelling immediately before publication.

By the end of the year, different children came to rely on different spelling strategies. A few would generate multiple spellings; some put lines for letters when they were not sure what letters were in a word; and some used theme-related books to locate words when writing theme-related texts. Regardless of the strategy used, spelling was no longer a "block" to the generation of meaning for most of the children. However, as noted, there were several students who resisted the notion of "invented spellings" and who refused to continue writing until they had each word spelled correctly.

Writing Strategies

The extent to which various writing strategies were internalized was largely influenced by the degree of student engagement with the particular piece being written. Contrary to current thinking, when writing theme-related pieces, students tended to be more engaged and experienced fewer blocks than when involved in free writing. This appears to be the case for several reasons. First, in theme-related writing the students had a wealth of knowledge from which to draw. Within the themes, students read numerous and varied texts about the topic, viewed videotapes and filmstrips, and experienced art and music activities. Most students also found the thematic units interesting since they had been consulted as to what topics were to be studied. Finally, many of the themed writing activities tended to be collaborative in nature. Typically, the students and Cecilia would identify a number of theme-related issues to research, and writing teams or expert groups would be formed to investigate each of these issues. These group investigations tended to last several days to several weeks. Most of the written texts that resulted from these investigations were published and shared with the entire class.

In contrast, there was a general lack of student engagement with the texts produced during free writing. This was the case even though these texts received the same status as those texts produced as part of the themes. As with theme writings, students conferenced, published, and shared what they wrote. Perhaps because of this lack of engagement, students experienced writing blocks more frequently, especially in terms of topic selection and elaboration. Although at the beginning of the year many students relied on personal experiences as a source for their writing, these experiences tended to result in little more than written "retellings." Other students retold folktales and movies or used predictable formats, like "The Lost _____," inserting different animals into the blank. As I observed students engaging in this behavior, I was reminded of fill-in-the-blank worksheets. Students circumvented the cognitive demands of meaning elaboration by making free writing into a series of worksheets, each day selecting a different topic to insert into the blank.

Finally, and again in contrast to theme-related writing, most students resisted writing on their topic for more than one day. Each day, students selected new topics and completed the texts by the end of the time allotted for free writing. One group of students even made free writing into a contest, competing to see who could write the most stories a week.

Cecilia's response to these behaviors was to brainstorm with the children possible writing topics, which were written on the inside front cover of the students' writing folders. She also discussed with the class the concept of text ownership and the inappropriateness of putting one's name on a text that was a retelling of a story written by another author. Eventually, some students began to brainstorm topic ideas with one another or used knowledge learned from the themes as information sources. However, many students continued to use predictable formats.

Do Students Want to Be Guided "through" the Literacy Processes?

For all students in the class, the issue of "desire" appeared to be a constant factor in promoting strategy internalization. Cecilia and I began the year exploring the use of instructional techniques that might help students expand their use of various literacy strategies. We believed the wall charts and the problem/solution and response conferences would introduce the students to *what* cognitive strategies were to be learned and *how* the strategies were to be used. We never questioned the students' willingness to learn and use the strategies as long as our demonstrations and mediations were effectively presented.

The students, however, told us in very direct ways that they wanted to know *why* the strategies were to be learned and used. Rather than simply learning the alternate strategies and then applying them when required, the students first had to be convinced that a particular text was worth the effort. When students found the texts interesting, engaging, or felt a degree of ownership, they were more willing to experiment with alternate strategies as they struggled with text meanings. Conferences in which student drafts or student-published texts were the focus typically evoked such engagement, as did texts with numerous pictures and theme-related writing on issues students helped to select.

In contrast, students were reluctant to apply alternate strategies to texts written during free writing, and students used predictable story formats and the retelling of known stories to avoid encountering blocks. Although Cecilia attempted to address the use of predictable formats through brainstorming possible writing topics with the children, the effect was negligible. A more effective response might have involved engaging the children in discussions about where topics of interest might be found. Some children independently discovered theme topics as one possible source for interesting free writing topics.

It would appear that a shift to a process-oriented curriculum and the introduction of various literacy strategies does not guarantee that students will apply what they are being taught. Effective delivery of instruction and student knowledge of the what's and the how's, although necessary, are not sufficient conditions for strategy internalization. Motivation and engagement are also required. As a number of researchers have recently suggested (Krapp, Hidi, & Renninger, 1992; Valsiner, 1992), and Cecilia and I discovered, the well-known construct of interest may provide the critical link between cognition, motivation, and engagement.

Acknowledgments

I would like to thank the Research Foundation of the National Council of Teachers of English (Kucer, 1990) for its financial support of this research, Cecilia Silva for her collaborative spirit, and Laurie Stowell for her helpful critique of my thinking.

REFLECTION: HOW READING AFFECTS WRITING

Editors' Text: How does reading affect writing or writing affect reading? The Goodmans provide some principles for thinking about these relationships.

———————

1. While both oral and written language are transactional processes in which communication between a language producer and a language receiver takes place, the interpersonal aspects of oral language are more pervasively evident than those of written language. Productive and receptive roles are much more interchangeable in a speech act of oral language than in a literacy event of written language. The contribution of listening development to speaking development is easier to identify than the similar contribution of reading to writing. One reason is that oral interaction is more easily observable than written.

2. Both reading and writing develop in relation to their specific functions and use. Again there is greater parity for functions and needs of listening and speaking than for reading and writing.

3. Most people need to read a lot more often in their daily lives than they need to write. Simply, that means they get a lot less practice in writing than reading.

4. Readers certainly must build a sense of the forms, conventions, styles, and cultural constraints of written texts as they become more proficient and flexible readers. But there is no assurance that this will carry over into writing unless they are motivated to produce themselves, as writers, similar types of texts.

5. Readers have some way of judging their effectiveness immediately. They know whether they are making sense of what they are reading. Writers must depend on feedback and response from potential readers which is often quite delayed. They may of course be their own readers, in fact it's impossible to write without reading.

6. Readers need not write during reading. But writers must read and reread during writing, particularly as texts get longer and their purposes get more complex. Furthermore, the process of writing must result in a text which is comprehensible for the intended audience. That requires that it be relatively complete, that ideas be well presented, and that appropriate forms, styles, and conventions be used.

▶

As writing proficiency improves through functional communicative use, there will certainly be a pay-off to reading since all of the schemata for predicting texts in reading are essentially the same as those used in constructing texts during writing.

7. Reading and writing do have an impact on each other, but the relationships are not simple and isomorphic. The impact on development must be seen as involving the function of reading or writing and the specific process in which reading and writing are used to perform those functions. (p. 591)

Source: Goodman, K., & Goodman, Y. (1983). Reading and writing relationships: Pragmatic functions. *Language Arts, 60*(5), 590–599.

REFLECTION: CREATING LITERACY LEARNING ENVIRONMENTS FOR STUDENTS WITH SEVERE LANGUAGE AND LEARNING PROBLEMS

Editors' Note: Principles informing the creation of literacy environments can be applied to a variety of settings and with a variety of students. If such principles are used, collaboration between specialists and classroom teachers can be enhanced.

- Immerse students in a print-filled environment: Print is displayed throughout the rooms through the use of charts, labels, directions, books, signs, and student writing.
- Read to students several times each day. . . .
- Purposely talk about books and information gleaned from books. . . .
- Establish multiple opportunities for students to observe teachers and more proficient peers reading and writing. . . .
- Support students as they construct a personal understanding of print and make connections between themselves and the content of books. . . .

- Support the functions of oral and written language that make the most sense to each child. . . .

- Combine the academic and functional curriculum through the use of theme cycles: Special educators are often interested in how we deal with some of the functional skills that are typically focused upon with students like ours. We have combined an academic curriculum with a functional one. (p. 550)

Source: Cousin, P. T., Weekley, T., & Gerard, J. (1993). The functional uses of language and literacy by students with severe language and learning problems. *Language Arts, 70*(7), 548–556.

REFLECTION: FROM MYTHS TO ASSUMPTIONS—RETHINKING "AT RISK" CHILDREN

Editors' Note: The term "at risk" is often used to label students from nonmainstream backgrounds. Flores and her colleagues, through careful documentation and research, indicate that the concepts contained within the myths can and should be rethought so that each and every learner's learning, language, and culture are valued.

Myths	New Assumptions
Myth 1. "At risk" children have a language problem. Their language and culture is deficient. They lack experiences. These deficits cause them to have learning problems. (p. 370)	Assumption 1: Children are proficient language users and bring many experiences into the classroom. (p. 373)
Myth 2: "At risk" children need to be separated from the regular class and need a structured program based on hierarchical notions of language development. (p. 371)	Assumption 2: Children need opportunities to learn language in rich, integrated settings and can be successful in regular classroom programs. (p. 373)

Myth 3: Standardized tests can accurately identify and categorize students who are at risk for learning/language problems. (p. 372)	Assumption 3: The language development of these students can be effectively monitored by observing their language use in authentic settings across the curriculum. (p. 373)
Myth 4: "At risk" children have problems because parents don't care, can't read, or don't work with them. (p. 372)	Assumption 4: The parents of these children are interested in the achievement and success of their children in the school setting and can be partners in the educational experience of their children. (p. 374)

Source: Flores, B., Cousin, P. T., & Díaz, E. (1991). Transforming deficit myths about learning, language and culture. *Language Arts, 68*(5), 369–379.

25 Testing the Way Children Learn: Principles for Valid Literacy Assessments

Beverly Falk

Editors' text: Many educators would agree that standardized tests provide an impoverished view of literacy learning. To replace them, educators need a principled way to proceed based upon literacy research and theory. Falk offers a set of principles to guide assessment design, along with a description of what should be included in an elementary literacy profile.

Some years ago, when I was the director of a public elementary school, each spring's administration of standardized tests brought anxiety to me and my colleagues. Because important decisions about students' futures are often made on the basis of these tests, and because the educational system and the public rely heavily on test scores as measures of teacher and school accountability, we felt under considerable pressure to make sure that our students were able to perform well.

From our perspective, however, these tests provided only a limited, and sometimes misleading, view of students' proficiencies and their progress. The test questions offered students little opportunity to use higher-order thinking, to problem-solve, or to apply knowledge to real-world problems. The lack of contextualization for the questions often disadvantaged those from culturally and linguistically diverse backgrounds. With "right" or "wrong" answers as the only options, the students' answers gave us little indication of their thinking or the strategies they used in their learning. The response options in the multiple choice format had answers that distracted children and did not take into account their sometimes logical explanations for the choices they made. Overall, information provided by these tests was of little use to our teaching.

This essay appeared in *Language Arts* 76.1 (1998) on pages 57–66.

The shortcomings of standardized tests, documented in numerous studies and analyses (Archbald & Newmann, 1988; Darling-Hammond, 1989, 1991, 1994; Darling-Hammond, Ancess, & Falk, 1995; Edelsky & Harman, 1988; Resnick, 1987a; Sternberg, 1985; Wiggins, 1993), were particularly problematic for students like Akeem, a third grader with whom I worked closely for several years as he struggled to gain literacy skills. When I first knew Akeem, his nationally normed reading scores indicated that he was among the least proficient readers in his grade. Yet, even when he began to improve as a result of the supports he received in our school—when he began to master the range of cueing systems that were needed for making meaning out of print, when he was able to successfully challenge an increasingly wider scope of materials and texts, when he began to persist instead of giving up in the face of difficulty—his test scores essentially remained the same. Because such tests are designed to compare performance with others, rather than demonstrate the degree to which a student has mastered specific criteria, they did not reveal Akeem's actual progress. Although he had improved, so had his peers; so his scores gave the appearance that he was standing still.

This way of evaluating Akeem's literacy learning was particularly frustrating to me and Akeem's teachers because our evaluations of his progress indicated that he was indeed developing as a reader and writer. We noted his changes through a variety of evidence collected in classroom contexts over time: documented observations of his reading, lists of books that he read during the year, and samples of various types of writing. These data showed us what Akeem could do, revealing his strengths as well as his weaknesses. It also offered us information about *how* Akeem was approaching his learning. It helped us to shape our instructional strategies so that we could be responsive to his specific needs (Falk, 1994).

My colleagues and I were troubled by the discrepancies between our school's way of evaluating student learning and the evaluations provided by standardized tests. While we recognized the need of a district and state to have information about students' progress for accountability purposes, we did not understand why the system's methods of evaluation could not utilize some of the assessment strategies that gave us such rich understandings of our students. We wanted tests that would support, not be at odds with, the ways we taught and the ways our students learned.

I got the opportunity to explore these questions several years later when the organization with which I am now affiliated, the National

Center for Restructuring Education, Schools, and Teaching (NCREST), at Teachers College, Columbia University, worked with the New York State Education Department to develop and pilot test assessments for the redesign of the state student assessment system. Our project sought to create assessments that could examine student performance across a large state in a manner that reflected student progress and that provided more useful information to evaluate students like Akeem than the tests currently in use. In the course of this work, we examined assessments from all over the world to find out what possible models existed so that we could utilize the lessons of their experiences. We learned about assessments used in other systems that do not have such great disparities between how children learn and how they are tested (Darling-Hammond, Einbender, Frelow, & Ley-King, 1993; Eckstein & Noah, 1993; Lewy, 1996; Mitchell, 1992; Rothman, 1995; Valencia, Hiebert, & Afflerbach, 1994). In this article, I share some of what we learned from our study. I outline principles for assessments that are supportive of teaching and learning and then discuss qualities that such assessments must have in order to be useful for reporting information to the public. I conclude by introducing a language arts assessment that I have developed with other educators in New York State—The Elementary Literacy Profile. It is designed to embody these principles and qualities so that it will be instructionally supportive as well as useful for accountability.

Validity Principles for Assessments

Assessment should always be in the service of learning. This is the most fundamental principle to guide assessment development and use (Darling-Hammond, 1992; Glaser & Silver, 1994; National Association for the Education of Young Children, 1988; National Forum on Assessment, 1995; Shepard, 1995; Wiggins, 1993). Because assessment results have serious consequences for teachers and students (in many places teachers and schools are subject to sanctions or rewards based on students' test scores; test scores are frequently used to make decisions about students' placements in ability groups, tracks, or grades), they exert a strong influence on instruction and often drive the curriculum (McGill-Franzen & Allington, 1993). Considerable time in many schools is spent on test-taking practice or test-like activities, even when these are recognized as being less useful to learning than other experiences (Darling-Hammond & Wise, 1985). This powerful impact of assessments on curriculum and instruction makes it critically important for assessments to be grounded in good teaching and supportive of meaningful learning.

Guide Assessment Design with Knowledge of Human Development and Learning

If assessments are to genuinely support and reflect learning, they need to incorporate some of the essential understandings about cognition and pedagogy that have evolved from the research of the last several decades. Most important of these understandings is that learning is not transmitted solely through "telling" but rather is constructed through students' interactions with a range of experiences, ideas, and relationships. Connected to this idea is the recognition that learning is not a linear process—with "basic" skills preceding thinking skills—but, rather, proceeds in a cyclical manner, with facts and skills accrued in the course of developing concepts and higher-order thinking. Instruction and assessment that focus on the recall of decontextualized bits of information do not support the way most people learn, nor do they allow students to fully demonstrate what they know and understand. Teaching and assessment are supported best when skills are combined with higher-order thinking, embedded in contexts, and applied to real-world situations (Bruner, 1960; Cohen & Barnes, 1993; Darling-Hammond & Falk, 1997; Falk, 1996; Fosnot, 1989; Piaget, 1970; Resnick, 1987a; Sternberg, 1985; Vygotsky, 1978).

Another understanding about the nature of learning that is important to incorporate into the thinking about and design of assessments is that individual students learn and demonstrate what they know in different ways, at different rates, and from the vantage point of their different experiences (Darling-Hammond, Ancess, & Falk, 1995; Falk, MacMurdy & Darling-Hammond, 1995; Garcia & Pearson, 1994; Gardner, 1983; Kornhaber & Gardner, 1993). Because of this diversity in learners, methods of presenting or assessing knowledge that utilize only one approach to learning, or that call for only one right answer, are not effective for all students. Both teaching and assessment must allow for a variety of forms of learning and expression, not just the linguistic and logico-mathematical emphases that predominate in most schools.

And finally, assessments should utilize understandings about the powerful role of interest and purpose in motivating learning and enabling students to show what they know (Carini, 1986; Eisner, 1991; Perrone, 1991b). This understanding is underscored by a recently released study that followed high school valedictorians for 20 years after graduation—through college, graduate school, and beyond. The long-term achievement of the students in this study, the academic stars of their respective schools, was not anywhere near the professional success of certain peers who were less successful academically in high school but who each nurtured and pursued their own passions as they proceeded through the challenges of their lives (Arnold, 1995).

Taken together, these insights about the nature of the learning process suggest that both teaching and assessment could be more useful were they to support more fully and reveal the complexity and range of students' abilities. Assessments would be greatly enriched if they could:

> measure the use of knowledge and skills in real-world contexts and applications;
>
> require higher-level thinking and complex problem solving;
>
> be embedded in meaningful and purposeful activities;
>
> provide a variety of ways for students to demonstrate what they know, understand, and can do about many dimensions and kinds of learning;
>
> be accessible to students of diverse backgrounds.

Use Multiple Forms of Evidence to Assess Student Progress

Because learning is such a complex and variegated process, especially the process of literacy learning, relying on any one form of evidence to evaluate students' proficiencies and progress offers, at best, a limited view—and sometimes even distorts the picture—of what students actually know and can do. Multiple forms of evidence provide a more accurate picture of students' abilities.

Some interesting insights about the benefits of using multiple forms of evidence to assess student progress are offered in a study that compares teachers' judgments of students' reading abilities derived from a variety of classroom-based assessments with the scores these same students achieved on one standardized reading test (Price, Schwabacher, & Chittenden, 1993). The test that is analyzed in the study utilizes a "cloze" format—it asks students to read a series of passages of increasing difficulty in which words have been omitted throughout. Students are asked to fill in the blanks by selecting the "correct" word from the multiple choice answer form. Students' reading abilities are evaluated by analyzing the number of correct answers in relation to the increasing length and complexity of the text. This evaluation is translated into a Degree of Reading Power (DRP) score. Students who read passages with short words and uncomplicated sentences get lower DRP ratings than those who read passages with lengthier words and more complicated sentences.

Although this formula for measuring reading ability is tidy, it does not adequately reflect the complexities involved in comprehending what is read. Very different kinds of texts can have the exact same DRP rating. For example, the popular young children's book *Blueberries for Sal* (McCloskey, 1948) has the same DRP rating as Hemingway's *Old Man and the Sea* (1952), an adult book that, despite its short length and easy-to-read words, raises pretty hefty questions about the meaning of life. Clearly, the DRP way of measuring reading leaves out important information, especially the degree to which a test taker can analyze, evaluate, or critically respond to a text.

The teachers in the study confirmed this point. They were asked to maintain a list of texts that they could verify their students had read and understood, look up the DRP rating for these texts, and then compare the rating of the texts with the scores the students achieved on the DRP test. Only 50 percent of students had test scores that were similar to the ratings of the books they had read. Of the students whose test scores did not correlate with what they had actually read, correlations were off most for low-scoring students, who were often reading texts that were rated some 20 or more points higher than their test scores indicated. Such a discrepancy raises serious questions about this assessment's validity. It is also troubling because of the consequences associated with low test scores. Because test scores are used to rank schools and to make important decisions about students' lives, relying solely on this one form of evidence for evaluating reading can be misleading and sometimes harmful (Allington & McGill-Franzen, 1992; Darling-Hammond & Falk, 1997; McGill-Franzen & Allington, 1993).

Connect Assessments to the Goals and Purposes of Learning

Valid assessments that are useful to learning provide accurate information about how students are progressing in relation to desired goals. This kind of information is often not evident in the results of large-scale assessments. Most large-scale assessments are norm-referenced, that is, they are designed primarily to rank students in comparison to each other (not to demonstrate how students meet specified criteria). Questions are purposefully placed on such tests to discriminate among students' performance so that results will fall out on a bell curve—only a few students will do really well, only a few will do poorly, the bulk of the students will perform in the mid-range, with "grade level" designated as the average score. To achieve this bell curve, the tests are developed by pretesting questions on a nationally representative sample (i.e., if the test is for third graders it will have been constructed by pretesting items on a sample of third graders who are supposed to represent the diversity of third graders in the nation). If too many students perform well on particular items during the pre-testing phase of test development, these items, even if they are of value, may be discarded by test makers to make sure that the bell curve is maintained.

So, because norm-referenced tests are constructed with items that ensure that performance is distributed along a bell curve, and because average performance is defined as "grade level," it is technically impossible for all students who take a norm-referenced test to achieve "on grade-level," the designated standard of performance in most places. In much the same way that baseball team rankings result in half of the teams being in the bottom of their league (regardless of how well or poorly they perform), norm-referenced tests set the standard as the average, making it inevitable that half of all students will fail (Darling-Hammond, 1994; Darling-Hammond & Falk, 1997; Oakes, 1985).

In contrast, criterion- or standards-referenced tests are designed to assess clear and publicly articulated criteria for what students are expected to know and do in a particular discipline or area (Darling-Hammond, 1991, 1994, 1997; Darling-Hammond & Falk, 1997; Darling-Hammond & Wise, 1985; Falk & Ort, in press; Herman, Aschbacher, & Winters, 1992; New York State Curriculum and Assessment Council, 1994; Resnick, 1995). Items for such tests are constructed and placed on the test on the basis of what students can do in relation to specified criteria, not on the basis of how they perform in relation to others. While items are selected to represent a range of difficulty for existing populations, "grade level" or passing is determined not by the average score, but by the degree to which students meet the criteria. Technically then, on criterion- or standards-referenced tests, if the important information and skills that appear on the test have been taught well by teachers and mastered by students, it would be possible for all students to be "on grade level" and to achieve the desired high standards. And even though comparison is not the force that guides the construction of criterion- or standards-referenced assessments, they can still be used to compare individual students' performance in relation to their peers. Teachers, schools, or districts can aggregate test results to determine what percentage of students achieved the specified criteria at each designated level of performance.

Because criterion- or standards-referenced tests are designed to provide information about how students are progressing toward specific goals, they have the potential to be extremely useful to teaching.

They do this by clearly articulating criteria for the tasks and by describing student work in degrees of proficiency—from beginning to accomplished—in scoring guides that accompany the assessments. In this way, scoring guides provide everyone with a guide to learning. They can be especially helpful to low-performing students who, for a variety of reasons, may have had little exposure to the desired standard of performance and may have previously been pointed to high standards only *after the fact*, through negative responses to their work. Standards-referenced assessments, in contrast, offer everyone a description *in advance* of what constitutes quality work. In this way, they help to "level the playing field" a bit between students who have had vastly unequal opportunities, resources, and supports for their learning (Falk & Ort, in press; Resnick, 1994; Rothman, 1997).

While clear and open expectations contribute to assessments' ability to support teaching and learning, to be most helpful assessments need to articulate and reflect goals in a broad enough way to accommodate diversity in both teachers and students (Darling-Hammond & Falk, 1997). Performance-based assessments do this well by calling on students to apply their knowledge in real-world situations and to demonstrate what they understand. Examples of performance assessments include written essays, projects, experiments, exhibitions, performances, or collections of students' work. These ways of examining what students know and can do enable students with different learning styles and strengths to demonstrate their proficiencies in a variety of ways (Chittenden & Courtney, 1989; Darling-Hammond, Ancess, & Falk, 1995; Falk & Larson, 1995; McDonald, Smith, Turner, Finney, & Barton, 1993; Mitchell, 1992; Perrone, 1991a).

Assessments Should Be a Learning Experience

Assessments need to reveal the process as well as the product of learning in rich and dynamic ways. This kind of information helps teachers shape their instruction in order to respond to students' needs. When assessments demonstrate the process of students' thinking, they encourage teachers to inquire and reflect about their students, about the nature of their discipline, and about the strategies used in teaching. Such assessments guide teachers, students, and their families to a better understanding of progress and growth. Thus, assessment becomes a learning experience for all who are involved (Darling-Hammond, Ancess, & Falk, 1995; Falk & Ort, in press; Shepard, 1995; Wolf, 1989; Wiggins, 1989; Wood & Einbender, 1995).

Assessment Information Should Reveal the Impact of Instruction over Time

Assessments that provide an indication of how students have progressed over time offer a clearer and more valid picture of achievement than those that focus only on outcomes without regard to students' starting points. Because students and groups of students may vary greatly in their levels of performance—due to differences in family backgrounds and/or issues, psychological make-up, and/or language proficiencies—assessment scores, to be most helpful, should indicate who started where and how far each has traveled in the journey toward proficiency. Measuring student progress in this way will furnish a fairer picture of achievement than scores that simply provide information about how students compare to a national norm. Assessments that reveal and recognize the "value-added" from students' educational experiences will more justly credit teachers and schools for the results of their efforts rather than penalize them, as is currently the case, for working with struggling students and communities that have histories of low-performance on tests (Chittenden & Courtney, 1989; Falk & Darling-Hammond, 1993; Falk, MacMurdy & Darling-Hammond, 1995).

Assessments for Accountability Must Also Support Teaching and Learning

The purpose of any assessment or assessment system defines and shapes its structure and format (Herman, Aschbacher, & Winters, 1992). Different types of assessments are designed to fulfill primarily different purposes—some to furnish information that is useful for instruction, some to offer evidence of learning that is the result of a specific instructional experience, some to shed light on individual and group progress in order to address public questions about accountability. These different purposes require assessment forms that possess unique qualities and characteristics.

Assessments that are to be used for reporting (or accountability) have to be standardized enough to mean the same thing in different places—so that what is considered to be "accomplished" work in one locale represents the same level of accomplishment in another. Accountability assessments also need to provide evidence that can translate into manageable and publicly accessible information about the performance of students across locales and groups.

Assessments that are most useful for teaching, however—revealing what students know and can do, the strategies they use, their unique strengths, interests, and needs—are, because of their very nature, difficult to standardize and translate into data that can reveal the performance trends of groups of students. (Student work samples, teacher observations, and/or projects that take place in the classroom are examples of these kinds of assessments.) These kinds of assessments are difficult to standardize and translate into scores because they are highly sensitive to such differences as classroom environments, local resources, and/or teachers' judgments. In addition, such assessments tap into complexities of subject matter and students' thinking that are difficult to measure and compare across groups. Yet it is these very kinds of assessments that reveal the richest picture of student knowledge and learning.

Herein lies a problem that is central to efforts to develop assessments that are useful for reporting and, at the same, are supportive of teaching and learning. Currently, to look reliably at student performance across groups, assessments are standardized in a way that limits their ability to provide information about students that can be beneficial to learning. The push for standardization drives large-scale assessments to focus on what is easiest to measure, rather than what is most important. As a result, these assessments generally measure lower order skills in somewhat artificial formats. To make matters worse, the added pressure to do well on such tests often drives instruction to mimic the tests, thus being at odds with worthy learning goals.

This is the dilemma that needs to be solved: how to develop accountability assessments that can reliably report on student progress while remaining valid and useful to learning. The biggest challenge here is to create assessments that have the uniformity necessary to view progress across groups in trustworthy ways and yet also are sufficiently context-embedded and flexible so as to be responsive to individual differences, represent real-world performance, and capture students' genuine abilities and understandings (Linn, 1987; Linn, Baker, & Dunbar, 1991; Moss, 1994).

Literacy Assessments

A variety of literacy assessments have made significant headway in meeting the challenge of creating measures of individual and group literacy progress that are also useful and supportive to teaching and learning. Notable developments include: *The Primary Language Record* developed in London (Barrs, Ellis, Hester, & Thomas, 1988); the *Learning Record* developed in California (Barr & Cheong, 1993; Barr & Syverson, 1994; Center for Language in Learning, 1995); the Victoria Literacy Profiles (Griffen, Smith, & Burrill, 1995); "First Steps" Developmental Continuums from Western Australia (Education Department of Western Australia, 1994); the Work Sampling System developed at the University of Michigan (Meisels, Liaw, Dorfman, & Fails, 1993); the Reading/Writing Scale of the South Brunswick, New Jersey, Public Schools (1992); the Assessment Framework of the Cambridge Public Schools (1991); and the Elementary Literacy Profile that I have been developing with educators in New York State.

All of these tests represent a shift in thinking about the purposes and uses of assessments. They are designed not only to provide information to support student learning and inform instruction but also to provide the summative evaluation that has heretofore been provided by tests. These assessments differ from tests, however, in that they: (1) look at student learning through multiple forms of evidence, gathered over time, in the natural learning context of the classroom; (2) assess literacy progress in relation to developmental scales that clearly articulate what has been identified as the continuum of literacy development; (3) do not rank and sort students according to their performance in the way that norm-referenced standardized tests do. Rather they provide a variety of audiences with a useful picture of individual students' progress in relation to the individual's own growth as well as in relation to the overall continuum of literacy learning.

These assessments are also grounded in research of the last several decades suggesting that literacy growth is facilitated by:

> focusing on skill development in the context of actual language use rather than in isolated exercises and drills;
>
> providing experiences that are meaningful, purposeful, and engaging to learners;
>
> building on students' prior understandings and strengths in the learning process;
>
> developing students' proficiencies in the use of a variety of strategies and all cueing systems: graphophonic (letter-sound or phonics) cues, semantic (context) cues, syntactic (language structure) cues. All of these are important; none of them alone is sufficient (Bussis, Chittenden, Amarel, & Klausner, 1985; McDonald, et al., 1997; Pearson, 1996; Pressley, Rankin, & Yokoi, 1996; Routman, 1996; Smith, 1988).

The Elementary Literacy Profile

The Elementary Literacy Profile was conceived by educators in 1995 as part of New York State's recent efforts to develop a standards-based performance assessment system. It is an assessment designed to provide information about individual and group progress that is standardized enough to be used for accountability purposes yet flexible enough to be responsive to individual learning differences. The Profile assesses students' progress in reading, writing, speaking, and listening. It is organized around four purposes for language use: (1) information and understanding, (2) literary response and expression, (3) critical analysis and evaluation, and (4) social interaction (New York State Education Department, 1996).

The Elementary Literacy Profile can be used as an ongoing measure of individual progress, as an early identifier of students who need support, as a guide for teachers, students, and their families to the behaviors and skills that comprise literacy learning, and as a way of observing the progress of groups of students in a school or across a district.

In the course of developing the Profile, an effort was made to make it manageable enough so that a broad range of teachers could easily use it, regardless of their past experiences or practices. The Profile is thus comprised of a small set of standardized tasks—a set each for reading, writing, and oral language—that are to be completed by students during the everyday life of their classroom, collected at designated times in the year, and evaluated by examining the collected evidence in relation to scoring guides.

Reading Evidence

Students' reading proficiencies are assessed by examining three pieces of evidence:

> a reading sample—a child reads to the teacher who notes the strategies and behaviors that the child uses, in order to analyze fluency and comprehension;

> a reading list—a list of five books that the child has read to provide evidence about his/her range and experience as a reader;

> a written reading response—the child writes a letter to a friend discussing a book he or she has read to provide additional information about the child's abilities to understand and analyze texts.

This evidence is collected in the fall and the spring and can be evaluated (at these two points in the year) in relation to a Reading Scale that describes eight stages of literacy development, from "emergent" through "advanced experienced" reader. The scale describes what student progress looks like in the following areas: *text difficulty, independence, range of strategies, comprehension*. The stages in the Reading Scale emphasize what students *can* (rather than cannot) do, suggesting that literacy learning is supported most effectively by building on students' strengths rather than by focusing on their deficits.

Writing Evidence

Students' abilities to use written language to express ideas and to communicate effectively are assessed by examining three forms of evidence:

> a story in first draft;
>
> the same story in second draft or another first draft of a different story (for students in early stages of writing development);
>
> reading response—the same one that was completed for the Reading Evidence section.

As with reading, this set of student work is collected and evaluated in the fall and again in the spring in relation to an eight-stage scale that describes a continuum of writing progress from "emergent" to "accomplished" skills. Qualities described in the Writing Scale are *idea development, language use, organization, and conventions.*

Oral Language Evidence

Oral language evidence is assessed through a listening/speaking scale that describes student progress in the following qualities: *responsiveness, participation, clarity,* and *organization.* Four stages of development along a continuum of progress from beginning to accomplished are outlined. Teachers observe students at work in the classroom, once in the fall and again in the spring, to determine the stage each student is at as a listener and a speaker.

Optional Evidence

An optional section of the Profile offers suggestions for other ways of assessing students' literacy growth. Many of these recommendations have been drawn from classroom-based assessment practices that experienced teachers have used as part of their instructional strategies:

> a family conference to find out the family's understandings about the student as a learner as well as to record the goals that the family has for the student's learning during the school year;
>
> a student conference designed to give the student an opportunity to discuss experiences, achievements, and interests with the teacher, to reflect on his or her reading and writing activities, to assess his or her own progress, and to develop a working plan with the teacher for the school year;

additional writing samples and responses to texts;

teachers' recorded classroom observations, miscue analyses, and/or observational checklists;

students' self-assessments;

and/or teachers' narrative summary reports.

Putting Assessment Information to Good Use

The Elementary Literacy Profile can be a useful guide to teachers, students, and their families about the process of learning to read and write and develop oral language. It can also be used for reporting individual and group progress to teachers, administrators, parents, and students. Looking at literacy learning through the Profile can help educators make decisions about how resources should be allocated across a school or district and about what supports may be needed for individual students or groups. Because the Literacy Profile articulates clear standards and includes multiple forms of evidence, it meets the new assessment requirements of Federal Title I Programs. (Grade/stage correlations are suggested in the Profile to indicate when students may need intervention and/or extra support.)

Early Lessons from New York State

Since 1996, draft versions of the Elementary Literacy Profile have been piloted by groups of teachers representing the different regions and populations of New York State. During the 1997–98 school year, hundreds of teachers used the Profile.

Scoring Reliability

Each summer a group of pilot teachers has met to evaluate the Literacy Profile's ability to reflect and support literacy progress and to score the evidence of students' performance provided in the literacy Profiles. Working in groups, the teachers wrestled with how to create assessment formats that use the same criteria to evaluate all students without losing the assessment's capacity to elicit authentic demonstrations of students' abilities. Their discussions have led to refinements of and improvements in the Profile's tasks and scales. The pilot teachers also spent time together scoring student work: They reviewed student work first as a group, talking about it and its relation to the scales, until consensus was reached about a score. Then they scored the work individually through a process designed to determine if two separate raters could reach agreement about a score. The results of these scoring sessions were an 80–90 percent rate of agreement between two different raters. This degree of agreement is well beyond what is considered acceptable for validating the use of a large-scale performance assessment.

Teachers' Responses

In interviews and a survey administered to teachers who have used the Elementary Literacy Profile, responses have been enthusiastic. Nearly every teacher who was surveyed indicated that she or he found the Profile to be a fair and accurate measure of students' abilities *as* language users. In addition, teachers reported that using the Elementary Literacy Profile was a support to their teaching and to their students' learning. The following comment reflects many of the teachers' views:

> This assessment helped my students think about and talk about their learning intelligently. They can now explain what is an example of quality work and why. Their goal setting has become better. They can undertake work with clear expectations. They have become more powerful learners.

Pilot teachers also credited the Literacy Profile with helping them gain insights into their students' learning. Some noted that, as a result of seeing the variety of ways that the Profile demonstrated students' skills and understandings, they developed a better appreciation for students' differences. Other teachers reported that, as a result of using the Literacy Profile, they gained an appreciation for students' strengths that had formerly gone unnoticed. One teacher wrote the following comment: "This assessment is the best way I have to know my students."

Using the Literacy Profile also appeared to be a learning experience for the teachers involved. Many teachers noted that the Profile served as a guide for how to do reading instruction because it describes the literacy behaviors and strategies students need to become proficient readers. One teacher explained it in this way: "This assessment helped me to reflect on what I need to do. It is an enormous stimulus to far better practice."

Next Steps and Challenges in Literacy Assessment

The word *assessment* comes from the Latin *assidere,* which means "to sit by one's side" (Wiggins, 1993). The Elementary Literacy Profile was created in the spirit of this word—to sit by the side of each child in order to support his or her further development.

Much work is still needed to develop assessments that will provide educators with information about student progress that is a genuine and valid representation of reading and writing, means the same thing in very different places, and is supportive to teaching as well as to learning. However, the challenges are not limited just to developing such assessments. The challenges also include making sure that the assessments are put to good use—providing teachers and schools with the resources, professional development, and organizational supports required to use the assessments well. Other challenges include collecting evidence about new assessment efforts to examine assumptions, answer questions, and chart directions for improvements in teaching, and learning practices. A final challenge involves educating the public about assessment issues so that they can be knowledgeable consumers and participants in our nation's educational enterprise.

As I struggle with the challenges involved in this work, the image of Akeem, from the story I related earlier, returns continually to my mind. For the sake of *all* children, but especially those who are negatively affected by the way we evaluate achievement in schools, we need to continue assessment development efforts that measure what is important, not what is easy. We need to create assessments that respect and support how children learn.

REFLECTION: WHAT DO TEST ITEMS TEST?

Editors' Note: Alex Moore found that students' performance on a problem-solving literacy task revealed them to have a much different relationship to literacy than did their performance on standardized tests. He then decided to find out why. The interview reprinted below—one of many that he conducted with students about standardized tests—makes one wonder about the validity of some standardized test items.

AM: Now it said in the test, "It began to 'something' so we put our coats on." The choice was "rain," "bucket," "collar," "dance," and "spare." And you put . . .?

Steven: "Bucket."

AM: "Bucket." . . . Now, why would you think it was "bucket?"

▶

Steven: Because it bucketed, didn't it. Like, it was really heavy.

AM: You wouldn't think it could just be "rain" then?

Steven: No. . . . Well, it could be.

AM: But you don't think so.

Steven: No, 'cause . . . if it was just raining, you probably wouldn't bother to put your coat on. (p. 312)

One of the things the students appear to have been doing was using their own day-to-day language, knowledge, and experience to meet the challenge that had been placed before them. . . . They constructed narratives that would provide more elaborate contexts for them to be able to arrive at what seemed to them quite sensible readings. . . . From the [test] designers' viewpoint, bringing in extra-textual knowledge and understandings to their solutions to the problems was exactly what was not wanted—as is testified to by the very fact that only one correct answer is allowed on the text even though . . . others might have fit just as well. From the designers' viewpoint, it seems clear that it was only the context of the 'immediate sentence' that the children were to make use of. . . . It is partly as a result of this apparent mismatch between the designers' implicit intentions and understandings and those of the children that so many "wrong answers" occurred. (p. 313)

Source: Moore, A. (1996). Assessing young readers: Questions of culture and ability. *Language Arts, 73*(5), 306–316.

REFLECTION: L2 LEARNER WATCHING

Editors' Note: Specialists in the teaching of English as a Second Language children are invaluable resources to classroom teachers in planning for instruction with ESL (or L2) children. Yet, as Genishi reminds us, there is much that can be learned from careful and patient observation.

———— ✧ ————

Observation is . . . the key to discovering *what L2 learners already know about English* and to discovering *what their inclinations and abilities are when they enter our classrooms, or what kind of L2 learners they are.* Thus, the first questions we ask in "L2 learner watching" are, how much

▶

English does she or he already know, and what kind of L2 learner does she or he seem to be?. . .

Listening to interactions and reading written products in a variety of activities gives us evidence about what kind of language users children are becoming. With L2 learners, though, there may at first be little language to hear and see; and an initial assessment about their language use seems impossible. In your class you may have a non-English-speaker who has said nothing, for weeks. . . . Novelist Maxine Hong Kingston (1976), for example, remembers her kindergarten year in a California school:

> During the first silent year I spoke to no one at school, did not ask before going to the lavatory, and flunked kindergarten. My sister also said nothing for three years, silent in the playground and silent at lunch. . . . I enjoyed the silence. At first it did not occur to me I was supposed to talk or to pass kindergarten. . . . It was when I found out I had to talk that school became a misery, that the silence became a misery. . . . (pp. 192–193)

At first there may be nothing to hear; instead there are signs to see, signs that we are barely aware of. We wait for a look in the eyes that indicates interest. To illustrate, a preschool teacher who had six L2 learners in her group watched as they listened to the class's own version of the predictable book *A Dark Dark Tale* (Brown, 1981). . . . The teacher observed that the two silent children in the group of six were enchanted as she read the repetitive story, and, in her words, "their eyes lit up like the sun." (pp. 510–511)

Source: Genishi, C. (1989). Observing the second language learner: An example of teachers' learning. *Language Arts, 66*(5), 509–515.

REFLECTION: THE NATURE OF TEACHER RESEARCH

Editors' Note: Strickland offers her view of the significance of teacher research as well as some idea of how teachers go about teacher research.

Teachers learn in many ways. They learn by reading, by observing in their own classrooms and in the classrooms of others, by reflecting on their observations alone and with others, and by sharing their knowledge and experience. They also learn through the systematic investigation of problems concerning them. Teacher-researchers take advantage of all these ways of learning. Most often their investigations involve a variety of case study methods, including observations, field notes, teacher and pupil diaries, and interviews. Survey studies, using questionnaires as the primary source of data collection, and comparison group studies are also used. The data collection and analysis may be informal or tightly structured. (p. 759)

Source: Strickland, D. S. (1988). The teacher as researcher: Toward the extended professional. *Language Arts, 65*(8), 754–764.

26 Reassessing Portfolio Assessment: Rhetoric and Reality

Mary Louise Gomez, M. Elizabeth Graue, and
Marianne N. Bloch

*Editors' text: Portfolio assessments, which involve the systematic
collection of evidence of literacy from the day-to-day events of classroom
life, are lauded as a sound alternative to standardized tests. Yet portfolio
assessments are not without their own set of difficulties. Gomez and her
colleagues demonstrate the large work commitment that portfolios require
of teachers and the effect that portfolio assessment can have on teachers
and students alike.*

A vase of early daffodils and a photocopy of $12^{1}/_{2}$-year-old Simon's first published book of the year sit atop the stack of audiotapes, interview transcripts, and field notes which surround our desks. Since early autumn, we have studied the struggles of Simon's teacher and 11 other elementary teachers to implement portfolio assessment of their students' learning and achievement in reading and writing. We deliberately choose to say we have observed these teachers' struggles, as their year-long efforts to practice this new form of assessment have been marked by their quest to acquire the requisite resources, knowledge, and skills to do the job. In this article, we lay out the historical and social contexts in which portfolio assessment have developed and examine the encouragements and constraints facing teachers who attempt to use it. To illustrate our arguments, we tell the story of one teacher's efforts. Finally, we provide teachers and administrators with questions to consider when planning for implementation of alternative programs of assessment.

Historical and Social Contexts of Portfolio Assessment

Current widespread enthusiasm for assessment via portfolio is a product of particular historical and social circumstances. Alternative forms

This essay appeared in *Language Arts* 68.8 (1991) on pages 620–628.

of assessment—variously called authentic assessment (Archbald & Newmann, in press; Wiggins, 1989); performance assessment (Stiggins & Bridgeford, 1985); and dynamic assessment (Cioffi & Carney, 1983)— have emerged in the past two decades as a result of parallel movements. On the one hand, there was, during the 1980s, a resurgence of calls for rethinking the general purposes, policies, and procedures of standardized testing; and on the other, a series of conceptual shifts within the field of English language arts.

Recent calls for reform of testing procedures and use grow out of the shift in the rhetoric and uses of test programs. Until the early 1980s, standardized tests were used at a local level for the purposes of pupil tracking, selection for special programs, and for instructional planning. The accountability movement of the Reagan years shifted the purpose of testing to comparisons of students' performance. Testing was seen as a way of helping to increase achievement (see Haney [1984] and Madaus [1985] for a comprehensive review). Unanticipated consequences of this trend toward testing included rising test scores that reflected factors other than increases in achievement (Linn, Graue, & Sanders, 1990) and a narrowing of instruction to match the domain of items on a single achievement test (Shepard, 1990). As a result, critics suggested that assessment should be modified to match more closely the tasks in which students engage in their classroom experience.

In addition, calls for assessment reform have come from those who advocate the empowerment of teachers in decision making. Since the release of the second wave of school reform reports (e.g., Carnegie Task Force on Teaching as a Profession, 1986; The Holmes Group, 1986), teacher empowerment and the restructuring of schools have been a focus of researchers and policymakers. Central to these efforts are the redistribution of power through site-based management of schools and the struggle to give teachers more control of curriculum, instruction, and assessment.

A third faction calling for new assessment practices are groups which have focused on standardized tests as yet another means to maintain the social and economic repression of people of color. For the past two decades, the National Association of Black Psychologists, the National Education Association, the National Association for the Advancement of Colored People, the National Association of Elementary School Principals, and the investigative staff of Ralph Nader have called for varying reforms related to standardized testing that are grounded in standards of the cultural knowledge of one group—white, middle class, native English speakers (see Haney, 1984; Williams, Mosby, & Hinson, 1976).

As these calls for reform of standardized assessments grew, parallel reconceptualizations favoring holism over analysis occurred within the field of English language arts (Sulzby, 1990; Valencia, 1990; White, 1984, 1985). This shift is evident in such developments as process writing theory and practice, calls for assessment of entire student-written products in the evaluation of writing, whole language teaching in reading education, and post-structuralist literary criticism.

These many developments have highlighted problems in assessment procedures that use indirect measures of all students' learning and achievement based on comparisons. Through portfolios, teachers and other school professionals have hoped to locate the means to tie together more closely curriculum, instruction, and assessment for all children. We support these efforts; yet in this article, we argue that the rhetoric of portfolio assessment and the reality of its implementation by elementary classroom teachers may lie far apart.

We caution enthusiasts that little is currently known about the effects and processes of portfolio assessment on teaching and learning, student motivation, or teachers' work. Project Zero at Harvard, the Educational Testing Service, and the Pittsburgh Public Schools were funded by the Rockefeller Foundation in 1985 to investigate the development of portfolio assessment; and a few isolated collections of student work, such as those of the Prospect School and the Craftsbury Academy, now exist. (The state of Vermont portfolio assessment does concern language arts, yet few data are now available concerning that effort's successes and problems.) None of these projects was designed specifically to take a close look at writing and reading portfolios and their effects on students, parents, teachers, principals, superintendents, boards of education, education agency personnel, and state legislators. The issues mentioned above seemed vital to pursue if portfolio assessment were to become part and parcel of the assessment process in education.

The Portfolio Project

So we set out to study portfolio assessment in the context of actual elementary school classrooms. The key questions we addressed were the following:

1. How is teachers' work restructured by adoptions of portfolio assessment procedures? Some argue that demands made upon teachers (most of whom are white, middle-class females in the United States) by school administrators or by national movements toward changed forms of assessment are yet another

means of increasing and controlling teachers' work while appearing to empower teachers' choices (see, for example, Apple, 1988; Casey, 1988; Spencer, 1986; Valli, 1986.)

2. How does the portfolio assessment of writing and reading affect the teaching and learning of those subjects in elementary schools? In recent years, curricula and teaching in the United States have been shaped by the nature of the assessments used to evaluate their worth; "teaching to the test" sums up the outcome of this relationship. Will the products placed in the portfolio to demonstrate student learning become focal in the curriculum? If so, how will this shift in focus affect teachers, students, and parents? And do these outcomes promote or impede the development of writing and reading skills?

3. How are students invited to participate? And further, what is the nature of their participation? On the surface, calls for student participation in constructing portfolios of their work and in using these to enable a clearer understanding of the learning and achievement represented by these products are egalitarian and democratic. Yet, faith in such invitations to students may disregard the variability in their participation at every step of the portfolio process. Not all students have the same opportunities to generate products, and students vary in their ability to choose representations of their own learning. Is the invitation to participate enough?

A local school district developed a project to pilot portfolio assessment of student learnings and achievement in writing and reading in the fall of 1990. Early in the year, teachers in the district's six pilot schools were given notebooks of suggested activities to use for the compilation of student portfolios. They were asked to use activities which appealed to them and to incorporate these into any ongoing compilations of student work already initiated in their classrooms.

In October 1990 we began a study of 12 of these elementary teachers' efforts to use portfolios. We wanted to obtain a picture of how teachers used portfolios and what this process meant for them as well as for their students. We tracked construction of these portfolios in three of the six pilot schools through semi-structured interviews of teachers and administrators, observations twice per month of teachers' writing and reading instruction, observations of the monthly meetings of the district portfolio council (which consisted of teacher representatives of pilot schools and others interested in alternative assessment), and informal conversations with students. It is beyond the scope of this paper to present our findings in full; rather, we tell the story of one teacher's struggle to implement portfolio assessment of her students' writing and reading as an illustration of the challenges that such assessment brings to school.

The portfolios this teacher (and others in the pilot schools) developed contained evidence of students' learning and achievement in reading and writing. The contents of portfolios were negotiated by each teacher rather than mandated by the district and included products, evaluations, and artifacts. Student products were comprised of samples of students' writing, from early drafts to published books. Also included were various types of evaluation such as forms (filled out by the teachers and the children) listing students' reading interests, the books children read and their responses to them, and the skills the students were developing as readers and writers. Finally, the students collected artifacts of their across-the-curriculum project experiences through photographs, journal entries, and other materials individually chosen by the children and their teacher.

The Story of Carolyn Benson

Carolyn Benson is Simon's fifth-grade teacher, one of six teachers (two each at grades 1, 3, and 5) we studied in a large elementary school where poverty encircles the lives of nearly 60 percent of the children. (Ms. Benson is the actual name of the teacher in this report, but the names of the children in her class and the name of the school are pseudonyms). Simon is one of four black children in Ms. Benson's class. Earlier in the year he, his siblings, and his mother were homeless, but now they live in an apartment. Because he was retained in an earlier grade in another city, Simon is a fifth grader and 12 1/2 years old. Like others in Ms. Benson's room, including Pao and Kia, recently arrived Hmong Cambodian refugees, Simon's reading and writing skills are not sufficiently developed to allow him to express his thoughts as eloquently as many other children his age. Nearly 30 percent of the children at Ms. Benson's school are children of color; many are from families who have recently been homeless or highly transient; many more are children of divorced families. In sum, Ms. Benson's students reflect the changing faces and increasing challenges of U.S. schools.

As a teacher, Ms. Benson works hard to meet the needs of all of her students. One of the ways she thinks she most effectively guides their learning is in her daily one-hour writing workshop to which one of us made over 40 visits this year. Drawing on the work of Nancie Atwell, Lucy Calkins, and Donald Graves, she teaches mini-lessons, conferences with individuals and small groups, reads children's work, and helps with spelling and mechanics. These sessions also include organizing a rotating set of peer editors, assisting in the publication of student writing, and monitoring with students their learning and achievement through portfolio assessment. In the following section, we portray how Ms. Benson uses student portfolios to enhance her instruction by tying more closely her teaching to the intricacies of the student learning process.

Super Jack, Jr., 1, 2, 3, 4, 5, and 6

In a midwinter interview, Ms. Benson reflected on the role that students' portfolios had played in her understanding of one child's learning. She explained:

> For weeks now I have been worried about Jack; he writes nothing but stories of the adventures of his alter ego, Super Jack, Jr. There are now six of these in his portfolio, one each for Super Jack, Jr. Goes to World War III; World War IV; World War V; Nuclear War; Alien War; and finally, Monster Mash-Super Jack, Jr. Fights 15,000 Monsters, One Dinosaur, Dragons, and A Robot. While I have been concerned with his engagement in violence all fall, mostly I've worried about whether using the same topic and reiterating the same themes—Super Jack, Jr., is challenged by forces greater than himself and, through personal ingenuity and technological wizardry, he saves himself and the world—will help him develop the skills he needs to master this year. Other than on the topic of Super Jack, Jr., he is not interested in writing.
>
> Well, as soon as I saw what was happening, I began to track, in my spiral notebook, the skills Jack *was* mastering as he wrote these crazy adventures. See, here on October 10, I wrote "Alien Wars, background information"; on October 19, I wrote "Monster Mash, exclamation points." Then I fell behind; I could not focus on Jack so much because then it was clear to me that Simon and Pao were having problems. And tracking down the source of these was going to be tricky! So, I continued to worry but didn't have much time to do anything about it. Then, today, I decided I had to watch—to observe the kids, to step back and not be so involved one-on-one with them. I needed to take time out.
>
> This was very hard on me and the kids because, although they are pretty independent and use each other as sounding boards and as peer editors, it's hard to wean them from me. I'm the favored listener. So, I stand there and kids try to talk to me, think I'm not busy 'cause after all I'm just standing here, and I tell them I can't talk to them. This sounds peculiar! You're the teacher, right, and you're just standing there and you can't talk to me! Well, my last entry on Jack was two months ago. I feel so guilty, but I watched him today, and Donald Graves was right when he said kid watching like this is important. I learned some more. Jack and Bart somehow work together on these stories. Jack talks, draws—he's a good artist—and Bart is the listener, the audience, and his responses seem to give Jack guidance about what to put

in and what to leave out of these stories. Bart is not very engaged in school; he seems too worried about being cool to write or read much. I wonder . . . I have a hunch that Jack and Bart use this as a way to be friends; there's a formula to the story and one to their relationship, too. So, today my notes read "Nuclear War, using story to collaborate, sees value of audience, tests ideas." I still feel guilty. I don't have enough entries for him, and I don't have any for Chuck or Lauren or LaToya. And in just 10 days winter break starts, and I won't have a chance to record anything for another two weeks.

Ms. Benson recognizes that using portfolios has changed her work as a teacher. It has enabled her to change both the ways she thinks about her teaching and the children's learning, and has required that she do so. In the story she tells about her student Jack, she recognizes that keeping the portfolio has allowed her to pursue questions about Jack's skills that would not have been possible if his work were not collected, preserved, and available for her—and him—to revisit. Further, she sees that understanding how and why Jack writes in one genre and on one topic can occur only when she alters her usual practice of constantly interacting with children and makes the conscious effort to observe them interacting with one another. The use of portfolios has afforded Ms. Benson the opportunity to rethink her role as a teacher, to reexamine the activities that drive her daily work and contribute to her thinking about teaching and learning.

Working in these new ways has also made her uncomfortable; she feels that it is difficult for children to understand why a teacher is sitting or standing around, watching, not doing something. She, too, feels strange; quietly watching is not an activity into which teachers are enculturated. She also recognizes that there is little time in the busy school day, as it is currently constructed, to stand back and get the big picture of what is going on in her room, as well as the little pictures about how individual children are working and learning. Once she has enjoyed and benefited from this activity, there seems little opportunity to engage in it.

Finally, although it is not apparent in her story about Jack, Ms. Benson did not choose to use portfolios in her classroom. Her school receives special additional funds from the district for increasing the achievement of minority children, and the implementation of portfolios was a required component of that funding. Although using this new assessment tool has been beneficial, it has also been a struggle. She and her fifth-grade colleagues were funded for one-half day of release time together focusing on portfolios for this entire school year.

Not Equality; Equality Does Not Work

Weeks passed, and Ms. Benson reported one day that all that kid watching she had done in the early winter had begun to pay off. Because her teaching and understanding of Jack's achievement had profited from observation, she recently had made time to do this for Simon and Pao. On this day, her story was about how the observations and subsequent recording of these in her spiral notebook had shown her something about the outcomes of her teaching for different kids. She said:

> I figured my teaching was good for everybody, that the workshop I had put together benefits all the kids. Little did I know! How could I have thought that? I guess before, I thought so much about having high expectations for everybody, about having a sort of democracy, I have always assumed that everybody benefited. But, as I watched Simon and Pao this winter, I began to understand that the teaching that benefited Peter and Jack and Lauren and the others did not equally benefit Simon and Pao.

Ms. Benson began to track how both boys used the freedom of the workshop to avoid writing. She watched as Simon used the option to work in the adjacent library to move in and out of the classroom 3–10 times in any given hour. While he always carried a pencil and paper, Simon rarely landed anywhere long enough to write more than a few words. Rather, he used the workshop time to dance, twirl, leap, and stroll among his classmates, moving restlessly to rhythms often expressed in drumbeats on desktops or recitations of rap music. Through these activities, Simon avoided confronting his inability to write more than simple sentences and very short stories.

Ms. Benson noticed that Pao, too, used the opportunities of the workshop—to talk to peers about writing or to write collaboratively— *only* to tell or talk about stories. She watched as he changed the individuals with whom he worked several times during the winter; moving from collaboration with a group of white boys to partnerships, first with another white boy and then with a black male classmate. By taking advantage of Ms. Benson's invitation to work with peers, Pao orchestrated activities that precluded his composing in the English language, a language that he was still learning to speak as well as write.

As she closely observed Simon's and Pao's behavior, Ms. Benson began to see that what she had purposefully developed as equal opportunities to learn were differently benefiting the children in her class. As one means of providing more equitable instruction, she decided to meet individually with both boys and to set daily goals for class performance. For herself, she set two goals: first, to continue close monitoring (kid watching) of Simon's and Pao's progress, and second, to continue exploring the ways her teaching enhanced or denied the skills and experiences that all children brought to her classroom. "I am convinced," she said, "I had the wrong idea all along. Equality is not the goal; equality does not work."

Although use of standardized test scores has often caused teachers to focus their instruction on the discrete skills measured by the test instruments, we could only speculate about what might occur when teachers used portfolios as a means to examine the consequences of their instruction for students. In this instance, Ms. Benson's teaching changed as a result of her examination of the work in Simon's and Pao's portfolios. First, she determined that they wrote only short pieces and that when Pao did write, he was usually a sort of silent partner for others more skilled in writing than he was. She formed questions: Why was so little writing present in either student's portfolio? What did each child do during the workshop? What were the consequences of those activities? How could she intervene so that each boy could increase his skills in written expression?

Several months have passed since Ms. Benson told this story of her teaching. She continues to monitor closely Simon's and Pao's activities during the workshop. She has tried to limit Simon's unceasing movement and to encourage Pao to take the risk of writing on his own through the use of brief, daily individual conferences in which each sets goals for his writing. While this has worked somewhat, the demands of other students, equally needy of her time and resources, have not permitted Ms. Benson to be as responsive to Simon and Pao as she would have liked. Although teachers can clearly see students' deficits as they are portrayed by test scores and can just as easily devise materials and instruction to remediate these, responding to what is learned from portfolios of student work may be much more complex and challenging.

"I strated wirte story about thing I no."

It is March; insistent wind drives rain against the window panes at Snowcroft School. Rattling old radiators provide a backdrop to children's voices. Ms. Benson sits on the floor at the front of the room, surrounded by three students. She has planned a 30-minute period to work alone with these students. The rest of the class is seated individually or in small groups in various comfortable spots around the room. Peter, Simon, and Pao sit in a semicircle around Ms. Benson, their portfolios before them on the floor. Ms. Benson begins by saying, "I want you to look for changes in your writing that have occurred over time.

Look through all the writing you have done this year and look for changes. For example, when Kia did this, she noticed that when she first started writing this year that she moved quickly from one topic to another. Now she gives more detail and elaborates more about her topics. When Sandy did this, he noticed that his earlier writing did not contain very much conversation, but now there is a lot of talking in his stories."

Ms. Benson turns to Peter: "What have you noticed about your writing, and how has it changed this year? Look through your portfolio and see if you can find changes that have occurred over time."

Peter, Simon, and Pao have all been quietly shuffling through their portfolios as Ms. Benson speaks. Peter responds tentatively, "I think I'm using more descriptive words now than I used to."

"Can you prove it?" she asks. "Look through your stories and try to find places that are different, places where early in the year there was no description and now there is. While you try to find proof, I'll talk to Pao." She turns to Pao who is nervously running his fingers through his hair. "I noticed that in your first story about your fish that you only wrote a few sentences and did not finish it." Pao says he needs more time to look, and Ms. Benson swivels around to where Simon has laid out numerous short stories about his life. "Well," she says, "what do you see?"

Simon beams, "I started making my stories longer and I started getting ideas from other people. I just wrote about things I knew about and things I knew for a long time."

Ms. Benson responds, "Keep on looking, I'll be back to you in a minute; you're doing great!" She turns back to Pao, who has located a story which he believes is longer than others he has written. "Is that what you are looking for?" he asks. "No, not necessarily just longer stories but a place in your writing where you began an idea and completed that, gave the detail, a place where we got to see the whole picture you were painting for our minds." Pao remains puzzled, but Peter insistently picks at Ms. Benson's shirtsleeve.

"I've found one," he yells, and he reads from an early story where he has used little description and follows that with a recent one with great detail.

Ms. Benson asks, "So, what's more descriptive about the second one?"

"You can get a better picture, a better picture in your mind when you read the second one."

"Are there other changes that you can see in your writing? Look for some more." She returns her attention to Simon, who is exploding with excitement. "Yes, Simon, what have you found?"

Simon proudly shows her the written record he has made of the changes he has tracked in his written work this year:

> I strated wirte story about thing I no. I rote 4our book about thing that is ture and fales. I really like wirte book and we got to wirte every day. my classmate say I wirte to many Books so I stop. I cannot thing no more book. I started a new book about Milli Vanilli. I got informant on of a paper.

"That's a neat evaluation of your writing, Simon. You are right, you used to write mostly about your life and what you did in your neighborhood, and last week you wrote your first story about something different. I liked how you used the information in the *Weekly Reader* to help you write about Milli Vanilli."

"Can I read it to you, read it to you and Pao and Peter, read it right now?"

"Yes, Simon," Ms. Benson smiles, "read it to us right now."

Minutes later, the session over, Simon leaps up from the floor and on the way back to his classmates, twirls in a gleeful pirouette. Pao and Peter follow, swaggering a bit; they, too, are pleased with what they have learned. Ms. Benson stretches, glances quickly around the room, and moves briskly to respond to another student's call for help.

What is not apparent in this story is what Ms. Benson did before-hand to enable her to spend this 30-minute period with only three of the children in her class. She explained at lunchtime that day that she had carefully planned the questions she would ask students during these meetings. She had also considered the composition of the small groups that would meet together in this assessment. She noted that all the months of peer collaboration in writing, peer editing, and the freedom to practice making responsible choices for their work time enabled the other students to be somewhat independent on such days. This allowed her to have a quiet and relatively uninterrupted time to work with only a few children. Chuckling, she acknowledged that you also have to be trusting of kids and a little moonstruck to do this sort of thing: "You can't watch all the other kids every minute when you're doing this so intensely with a few. But, it sure feels worth it to me."

What benefits did Simon, Peter, and Pao reap from this activity? That which was clearest was their pleasure in understanding something about their own learning and achievement that they had not recognized before. Peter is one of the most skilled writers in the class, he is very popular with his peers, and his mother supports Ms. Benson's instruction by volunteering in the computer lab so that students can type their final copies on word processors. In a traditionally organized classroom,

Peter would be in the "top group"; he would be more likely to have this opportunity than his lower-skilled peers, both of whom would undoubtedly be placed in the bottom or remedial track. Yet even children like Peter rarely have time in school to make knowledge about themselves as learners, knowledge that informs their understandings and those of their teacher about what they have achieved. Simon and Pao may have gained something additional, as they are children whose academic skills do not afford them many opportunities for positive feedback, for feeling just great about themselves.

Conclusion

We started out this project thinking that we were going to find the answers to our questions about portfolio assessment. Although months of observation in Ms. Benson's classroom have provided us with a rich portrait of the possibilities that portfolios provide language arts teachers, we have generated more questions than answers. We continue to puzzle about the broad areas outlined at the beginning of this paper:

- *How does the use of portfolios affect teachers' work?*

  Ms. Benson's use of portfolios was a very labor-intensive process. It required her to spend untold hours after school and in the evenings planning strategies for integrating their past work into the children's current learning. This effort definitely bore fruit for her students because Ms. Benson was willing and able to use her time in this way. For more common adoption of portfolio use by the majority of teachers, the nature of teacher work must be reconsidered. Schools will need to provide release time during the school day for teachers—alone and in groups—to plan and implement portfolio assessment. In addition, school districts will also need to find ways to support teachers in their use of portfolios through inservice and consultant services from a variety of sources. These include expert teachers and academicians, among others. Portfolio use is such a complex and personal teaching act that the nature of the support we provide teachers must reflect an active construction of the process of assessment that is integral to their conception of learning.

- *What impact does portfolio use have on teachers' curriculum planning and instruction?*

  Ms. Benson's teaching was clearly changed by using portfolios with her students. She learned the value of stepping back to look at the bigger picture of her classroom. She also found that instruction is not a one-size-fits-all proposition. It took careful tracking of student work, both by watching the activity and by analyzing the work in the portfolio, to understand the meaning of each child's learning process. Finally, she found that she must organize her classroom so that she can take time to focus on a few students; this was a zoom lens approach to teaching that allowed her to get deeper into what individuals knew and how they knew it.

- *How do portfolios help students understand themselves as learners?*

    In and of themselves, portfolios will not facilitate learner self-understanding. It is up to individual teachers to pull students into the activity. They must understand both the individual pieces and their place in the composite, to see what each product shows about them and what the group of products says about their trajectory of learning over time. This is a new role for teachers and for students, requiring collaboration in a way that honors learners as makers of knowledge.

The rhetoric of portfolio assessment is unambiguously positive; portfolios are portrayed as solutions to many problems, some related, some not. Our close look at one classroom tells us that there are tensions inherent in portfolio use. As Ms. Benson found, there are few models for the ways that she needed to change her teaching. In addition, the use of portfolios required significant amounts of both in-class and after-school time to reflect on and prepare for her next step in teaching. The promise of portfolio assessment is in its collaborative power for students and teachers, providing a common framework to discuss learning and achievement. It also gives teachers a rich opportunity to reconsider their teaching practice by making a tight connection between instruction and assessment. The reality of portfolio assessment, however, tells us that the responsibility of making this restructured assessment work falls squarely on the shoulders of already burdened teachers.

Acknowledgments

This work was made possible in part by grants from the Robert M. LaFollette Institute for Public Affairs, University of Wisconsin–Madison and the University of Wisconsin System Institute on Race and Ethnicity, University of Wisconsin–Milwaukee.

REFLECTION: "RESISTING (PROFESSIONAL) ARREST"

Editors' Note: Carole Edelsky documents some of the threats to teachers' professional identities.

According to Apple [1983], recent "educational reforms" amount to deprofessionalizing—decreasing teachers' autonomy through deskilling, reskilling, and proletarianization of teaching. *Deskilling* is a process in which occupational skills are redefined so that former skills entailing judgment and intuition and a sense of start-to-finish over large work spheres becomes atomized, then behaviorally described, then appropriated by management. . . . The older more global skills atrophy since they are no longer needed. *Reskilling* refers to the substitution of a required new range of more mechanical, clerical, and management skills for the older, more global skills. Along with reskilling comes intellectual deskilling (e.g., relying on experts to create curricular and teaching goals) and intensification (e.g., increased demand for routine work such as grading more and more pre- and post-tests and worksheets, managing "systems" of objectives and prematched packaged lessons, organizing and reorganizing multiple subgroups of students according to frequent mastery test results, etc.). Intensification frequently leads to "burnout." *Proletarianization* is a process of declining autonomy in an occupation. A key feature of declining autonomy is the separation of conception (e.g., development of instructional goals) from execution (e.g., instruction). What happens, Apple notes, when such a process is underway in education is that teachers' efficiency as managers increases while their control over curriculum decreases. (pp. 397–398)

Source: Edelsky, C. (1988). Research Currents: Resisting (professional) arrest. *Language Arts, 65*(4), 396–402.

REFLECTION: INQUIRY AS ASSESSMENT

Editors' Note: The inquiring stance of a teacher researcher is key to effective assessment of individual learners. Stephens and her colleagues offer a brief

▶

glimpse of one teacher's approach to learning more about a student in her classroom.

———————— ✺ ————————

Curricular decisions are plans we make that will enable us to test out our hypotheses. The goal is to understand better the child as learner. Very often these plans include observing more, listening more, and spending more time with the child and texts. Stephanie, for example, decided to talk to Virgie and her mother about Virgie's hearing and about Virgie's experiences with English and possibly with other languages. She talked to Virgie, her mother, and her teacher about Virgie as a reader. She tried to understand how much reading Virgie did and of what kinds of texts. She recorded and analyzed miscues. She observed Virgie in a variety of reading situations to try to understand her confidence and her willingness to take risks. She talked to Virgie about what she was reading so she could better understand Virgie's meaning-making process. (p. 109)

Source: Stephens, D., et al. (1996). When assessment is inquiry. *Language Arts*, 73(2), 105–112.

REFLECTION: THE UNDERSIDE OF PARENT INVOLVEMENT

Editors' Note: One of the concerns about the family literacy "movement" is the degree to which some of these programs threaten to transform parents' role from mother or father to "teacher" and transform homes in the image of schooling. Former Language Arts *editor David Dillon expressed these concerns in this excerpt from one of his editorials.*

———————— ✺ ————————

Instead of educators collaborating with parents as equal partners, I see educators trying to *educate*—or sometimes just *train*—parents, trying to enlist them in educators' enterprises. The thrust seems to be to get parents to help us educators with our jobs, not just by helping in the classroom but also by extending the classroom into the home through the parents' efforts—and the educators' guidance. Funny that for "collaboration," the rhetoric seems so one-way. Edu-

▶

cators writing articles for parents, educators giving presentations to parents, educators organizing parents—to inform them of what we educators are doing with their children, *and* what they can do with their children to help us. As I look and listen carefully, I don't hear the voices of parents in this "dialogue." I don't see any parents writing articles for educators, or parents giving presentations to educators, or parents organizing educators—to inform educators of what they are doing with their own children, *and* what the educators can do to help them. . . . If it doesn't look like collaboration or act like collaboration or sound like collaboration, chances are . . . (p. 7)

Things started off innocently—if problematically—enough when we suggested to parents that they have lots of print in the home, that they read to and with their children, that they read and write themselves, that they answer their kids' questions about print, and so on. However, more and more I'm seeing educators suggest to parents what I can only call "instructional activities"—dialogue journals, writing conferences, the use of not just any print, but of literature, and not just any literature, but "good quality" literature (i.e., the kind we use in school). The not-so-hidden message about how to help your child succeed in school is to turn the home into an extension of the classroom. Is this "collaboration" or "partnership"? Sounds more like "co-opting" at best, and "exploiting" at worst. (p. 9)

Source: Dillon, D. (1989). Dear Readers. *Language Arts, 66*(1), 7–9.

STRATEGIES: KEYS TO COLLABORATING WITH PARENTS

Editors' Note: Carolyn Burke offers three keys to establishing collaborative relationships with parents.

———— ✍ ————

1. Within a collaborative relationship each participant is accepted as an equal among equals. (p. 840)
2. Within a collaborative relationship consensus becomes the preferred form of problem solving. (p. 841)

▶

3. Within a collaborative relationship all responsibilities are shared. (p. 841)

Source: Burke, C. (1985). Parenting, teaching, and learning as a collaborative venture. *Language Arts, 62*(8), 836–843.

References

Editors' Note: Entries listed as "in press" in the Language Arts *articles reprinted in this book have been updated here to indicate their publication dates. (The "in press" citation has been retained in the text of the book's chapters and is also included here alongside the date in order to help readers match entries to citations in the text.)*

Adams, M. J. (1990). *Beginning to read: Thinking and learning about print.* Cambridge, MA: MIT Press.

Agar, M. (1994). *Language shock: Understanding the culture of conversation.* New York: Morrow.

Aliki. (1989). *The king's day: Louis XIV of France.* New York: Crowell.

Allen, R., & Allen, C. (1976). *Language experience activities.* Boston: Houghton Mifflin.

Allen, J., Cary, M., & Delgado, L. (1995). *Exploring blue highways: Literacy reform, school change and the creation of learning communities.* New York: Teachers College Press.

Allen, J. B., & Mason, J. M. (Eds.). (1989). *Risk makers, risk takers, risk breakers: Reducing the risks for young literacy learners.* Portsmouth, NH: Heinemann.

Allen, R. V. (1976). *Language experiences in communication.* Boston: Houghton Mifflin.

Allington, R. L., & McGill-Franzen, A. (1992). Unintended effects of educational reform in New York. *Educational Policy, 6,* 397–414.

Altwerger, B., Edelsky, C., & Flores, B. (1987). Whole language: What's new? *The Reading Teacher, 41,* 144–154.

Altwerger, B., & Ivener, B. L. (1994). Self-esteem: Access to literacy in multicultural and multilingual classrooms. In K. Spangenberg-Urbschat & R. Pritchard (Eds.), *Kids come in all languages: Reading instruction for ESL students* (pp. 65–81). Newark, DE: International Reading Association.

Ammon, R. (1989). *Growing up Amish.* New York: Atheneum.

Ancona, G., & Anderson, J. (1989). *The American family farm.* New York: Harcourt Brace Jovanovich.

Ancona, G., & Beth, M. (1989). *Handtalk zoo.* New York: Four Winds Press.

Anderson, J., & Gunderson, L. (1997). Literacy learning from a multicultural perspective. *The Reading Teacher, 50,* 514–516.

Anyon, J. (1984). Intersection of gender and class: Accommodation and resistance by working-class and affluent females to contradictory sex-role ideologies. *Journal of Education, 166,* 25–48.

Apple, M. W. (1988). *Teachers and texts: A political economy of class and gender relations in education.* London: Routledge and Kegan Paul.

Applebee, A. (1993). *Beyond the lesson: Reconstruing curriculum as a domain for culturally significant conversations. Report Series 1.7.* Albany: National Research Center on Literature Teaching & Learning.

Applebee, A. N., & Langer, J. A. (1983). Instructional scaffolding: Reading and writing as natural language activities. *Language Arts, 60,* 176–183.

Archbald, D. A., & Newmann, F. M. (in press/1988). *Beyond standardized testing: Assessing authentic academic achievement in the secondary school.* Reston, VA: National Association of Secondary School Principals.

Archbald, D. A., & Newmann, F. M. (in press/1992). Approaches to assessing authentic academic achievement. In H. Berlak (Ed.), *Assessing achievement: Toward the development of a new science of educational testing.* Albany: State University of New York Press.

Aristotle. (1952). *The works of Aristotle: Vol. 11. Rhetorica, De rhetorica ad Alexandrum, Poetica* (W. D. Ross, Ed.; I. Bywater, Trans.). Oxford: Clarendon Press.

Arnold, K. (1995). *Lives of promise: What becomes of high school valedictorians.* San Francisco: Jossey-Bass.

Atwell, N. (1987). *In the middle: Writing, reading, and learning with adolescents.* Portsmouth, NH: Heinemann.

Atwell, N. (Ed.). (1990). *Coming to know: Writing to learn in the intermediate grades.* Portsmouth, NH: Heinemann.

Atwell, N. (1991). *Side by side: Essays on teaching to learn.* Portsmouth, NH: Heinemann.

Au, K. (1993). *Literacy instruction in multicultural settings.* Orlando: Harcourt Brace.

Babcock, B. (1993). "At home, no womens are storytellers": Ceramic creativity and the politics of discourse in Cochiti Pueblo. In S. Lavie, K. Narayan, & R. Rosaldo (Eds.), *Creativity/anthropology* (pp. 70–99). Ithaca: Cornell University Press.

Bakhtin, M. (1981). *The dialogic imagination.* Austin, TX: The University of Texas Press.

Barnes, D. (1973). *Language in the classroom.* Milton Keynes: Open University.

Barnes, D. (1976). *From communication to curriculum.* Toronto: Penguin Education.

Barnes, D. (1992). *From communication to curriculum* (2nd ed.). Portsmouth, NH: Heinemann.

Barnes, D., et al. (1969). *Language, the learner and the school.* Harmondsworth: Penguin.

Barnes, D., & Todd, F. (1977). *Communication and learning in small groups.* London: Routledge and Kegan Paul Ltd.

Barr, M., & Cheong, J. (1993, March). Achieving equity: Counting on the classroom. Paper presented at the *Equity and Educational Testing and Assessment* symposium, Washington, DC.

Barr, M., & Syverson, M. (1994). *Overview of the California learning record: Report on regional moderation readings.* La Jolla, CA: The Center for Language in Learning.

Barrs, M., Ellis, S., Hester, H., & Thomas, A. (1988). *The primary language record.* London: ILEA/Centre for Language in Primary Education.

Bartel, R. (1983). *Metaphor and symbols: Forays into language.* Urbana, IL: National Council of Teachers of English.

Barthes, R. (1975). *The pleasure of the text* (R. Miller, Trans.). New York: Hill and Wang.

Bartlett, E. J., & Scribner, S. (1981). Text and content: An investigation of referential organization in children's written narratives. In E. J. Bartlett & S. Scribner (Eds.), *Writing: The nature, development, and teaching of written communication* (Vol. 2). Hillsdale, NJ: Erlbaum.

Bartolomé, L. I. (1994). Beyond the methods fetish: Toward a humanizing pedagogy. *Harvard Educational Review, 64,* 173–194.

Barton, D., & Hamilton, M. (1998). *Local literacies: Reading and writing in one community.* New York: Routledge.

Bates, E. (1979). *The emergence of symbols.* New York: Academic Press.

Bean, W., & Bouffler, C. (1987). *Spell by writing.* Sydney, Australia: Primary English Teaching Association.

Bean, W., & Bouffler, C. (1997). *Spelling: An integrated approach.* Armadale, Victoria, Australia: Eleanor Curtain Publishing.

Bear, D. R. (1989). Why beginning reading must be word-by-word: Disfluent oral reading and orthographic development. *Visible Language, 23,* 353–367.

Bear, D. R. (1991). "Learning to fasten the seat of my union suit without looking around": The synchrony of literacy development. *Theory into Practice, 30*(3), 149–157.

Bear, D., Templeton, S., Invernizzi, M., & Johnston, F. (1996). *Words their way: Word study for phonics, vocabulary, and spelling instruction.* Upper Saddle River, NJ: Merrill.

Beers, J. (1980). Developmental strategies of spelling competence in primary children. In E. H. Henderson & J. Beers (Eds.), *Developmental and cognitive aspects of learning to spell: A reflection of word knowledge* (pp. 36–45). Newark, DE: International Reading Association.

Beers, J., Beers, C., & Grant, K. (1977). The logic behind children's spelling. *The Elementary School Journal, 77,* 238–242.

Bernstein, B. (1972). A critique of the concept "compensatory education." In C. B. Cazden, D. Hymes, & V. John. (Eds.), *Functions of language in the classroom.* New York: Teachers College Press.

Bloome, D. (1987). Reading as a social process in a middle school classroom. In D. Bloome (Ed.), *Literacy and schooling* (pp. 123–149). Norwood, NJ: Ablex.

Bloome, D., & Green, J. (1982). *Capturing social contexts of reading for urban junior high school students in home, school, and community settings.* (Final Report of Grant No. 34-21-2915-02). Washington, DC: National Institute of Education.

Bloome, D., & Green, J. (1984). Directions in the sociolinguistic study of reading. In P. D. Pearson, R. Barr, M. Kamil, & P. Mosenthal (Eds.), *Handbook of reading research* (pp. 395–421). New York: Longman.

Blumberg, R. (1989). *The great American gold rush.* New York: Bradbury Press.

Boyle, O. F., & Peregoy, S. F. (1990). Literacy scaffolds: Strategies for first- and second-language readers and writers. *The Reading Teacher, 44,* 144–200.

Britton, J., Burgess, T., Martin, N., McLeod, A., & Rosen, H. (1975). *The development of writing abilities (11–18).* London: Macmillan.

Brown, J., Goodman, K., & Marek, A. (1996). *Studies in miscue analysis: An annotated bibliography.* Newark, DE: International Reading Association.

Brown, R. (1981). *A dark, dark tale.* New York: Dial Books.

Bruner, J. (1960). *The process of education.* Cambridge, MA: Harvard University Press.

Bruner, J. (1975). The ontogenesis of speech acts. *Journal of Child Language, 2,* 1–19.

Bruner, J. (1983). *Child's talk.* London: Oxford University Press.

Bruner, J. (1986). *Actual minds, possible worlds.* Cambridge, MA: Harvard University Press.

Bruner, J., & Ratner, N. (1978). Games, social exchange and the acquisition of language. *Journal of Child Language, 5,* 391–401.

Bussis, A., Chittenden, E., Amarel, M., & Klausner, E. (1985). *Inquiry into meaning: An investigation of learning to read.* Hillsdale, NJ: Lawrence Erlbaum.

Butler, A., & Turbill, J. (1984). *Towards a reading-writing classroom.* Sydney: Primary English Teaching Association.

Calabro, M. (1989). *Operation grizzly bear.* New York: Four Winds Press.

Calkins, L. (1986). *The art of teaching writing.* Portsmouth, NH: Heinemann.

Calkins, L. M. (1994). *The art of teaching writing* (2nd ed.). Portsmouth, NH: Heinemann.

Cambourne, B. (1988). *The whole story.* New York: Scholastic.

Cambourne, B., & Turbill, J. (1987). *Coping with chaos.* Sydney: Primary English Teaching Association.

Cambourne, B., & Turbill, J. (1991). Teacher-as-co-researcher. How an approach to research became the methodology for staff development. In

J. Turbill, A. Butler, & B. Cambourne (Eds.), *Frameworks: Theory of others* (4th ed.) (pp. 1–10). Stanley, NY: Wayne Finger Lakes Board of Cooperative Educational Services.

Cambridge Public Schools. (1991). *Documentation and assessment of student progress.* Unpublished report. Cambridge, MA: Author

Carey, S. (1978). The child as word learner. In M. Halle, J. Bresnan, and G. A. Miller (Eds.), *Linguistic theory and psychological reality.* Cambridge, MA: MIT Press.

Carini, P. (1986). Building from children's strengths. *Journal of Education, 168,* 13–24.

Carnegie Task Force on Teaching as a Profession. (1986). *A nation prepared: Teachers for the 21st century.* New York: Carnegie Forum on Education and the Economy.

Casey, K. (1988). *Teacher as author: Life history narratives of contemporary women teachers working for social change.* Unpublished doctoral dissertation, University of Wisconsin–Madison.

Cazden, C. (1979). Peekaboo as an instructional model: Discourse development at home and at school. *Papers and Reports on Child Language Development, 17,* 1–19.

Cazden, C. (1981). Keynote address to Canadian Council of Teachers of English, Vancouver, B.C.

Cazden, C. B. (1982). Contexts for literacy: In the mind and in the classroom. *Journal of Reading Behavior, 14,* 413–427.

Cazden, C. (1992a). Play with language and metalinguistic awareness. *Whole language plus: Essays on literacy in the United States and New Zealand* (pp. 59–74). New York: Teachers College Press.

Cazden, C. (1992b). *Whole language plus.* New York: Teachers College Press.

Cazden, C. B., Michaels, S., & Tabors, P. (in press/1985). Self-repair in sharing time narratives: The intersection of metalinguistic awareness, speech event and narrative style. In S. W. Freedman (Ed.), *The acquisition of writing: Response and revision.* Norwood, NJ: Ablex.

Center for Language in Learning. (1995). *Connecting classroom and large scale assessment: The CLR moderation process.* El Cajon, CA: Author.

Chall, J. (1967). *Learning to read: The great debate.* New York: McGraw Hill.

Chall, J. (1991, May 13). As quoted in "Armed with pen and lots to say." *Washington Post,* p. A 16.

Chew, C. R. (Ed.). (1991). *Whole language in urban classrooms.* Roslyn, NY: Berrent Publications.

Chittenden, E., & Courtney, R. (1989). Assessment of young children's reading: Documentation as an alternative to testing. In D. S. Strickland & L. M. Morrow (Eds.), *Emerging literacy: Young children learn to read and write* (pp. 107–120). Newark, DE: International Reading Association.

Chomsky, C. (1980). Developing facility with language structure. In G. S. Pinnel (Ed.), *Discovering language with children* (pp. 56–59). Urbana, IL: National Council of Teachers of English.

Christenbury, L., & Kelly, P. (1983). *Questioning: A path to critical thinking*. Urbana, IL: National Council of Teachers of English.

Cioffi, G., & Carney, J. J. (1983). Dynamic assessment of reading disabilities. *The Reading Teacher, 36*, 764–768.

Clark, M. (1989). *The great divide: The construction of gender in the primary school*. Canberra, ACT, Australia: Curriculum Development Centre.

Cleary, B. (1952). *Henry and Beezus*. New York: Dell.

Cochran-Smith, M. (1984). *The making of a reader*. Norwood, NJ: Ablex.

Cohen, D. K., & Barnes, C. A. (1993). Conclusion: A new pedagogy for policy? In D. K. Cohen, M. W. McLaughlin, & J. E. Talbert (Eds.), *Teaching for understanding: Challenges for policy and practice* (pp. 240–275). San Francisco: Jossey-Bass.

Collins, J. (1989). Hegemonic practice: Literacy and standard language in public education. *Journal of Education, 171*, 9–34.

Connell, R., Ashenden, D. J., Kessler, S., & Dowsett, G. W. (1982). *Making the difference: Schools, families, and social division*. Sydney, Australia: Allen & Unwin.

Connor, S. (1992). Aesthetics, pleasure and value. In S. Regan (Ed.), *The politics of pleasure: Aesthetics and cultural theory* (pp. 203–220). Philadelphia: Open University Press.

Cook-Gumperz, J. (Ed.). (1986). *The social construction of literacy*. Cambridge: Cambridge University Press.

Creech, S. (1994). *Walk two moons*. New York: HarperCollins.

Cullinan, B. (Ed.). (1992). *Invitation to read. More children's literature in the reading program*. Newark, DE: International Reading Association.

Cullinan, B., Scala, M., & Schroder, V. (1995). *Three voices: An invitation to poetry across the curriculum*. York, ME: Stenhouse.

Cummins, J. (1994). The acquisition of English as a second language. In K. Spangenberg-Urbschat & R. Pritchard (Eds.), *Kids Come in All Languages: Reading Instruction for ESL Students* (pp. 36–62). Newark, DE: International Reading Association.

Cushman, K. (1994). *Catherine, called Birdy*. New York: Clarion.

Dahl, K., Purcell-Gates, V., & McIntyre, E. (1989). *An investigation of the ways low-SES learners make sense of instruction in reading and writing in the early grades*. Final Report to the U.S. Department of Education, Office of Educational Research and Information (Grant No. G008720229). Cincinnati: University of Cincinnati.

Darling-Hammond, L. (1989). Curiouser and curiouser: Alice in testingland. *Rethinking Schools, 3*(1), 17.

Darling-Hammond, L. (1991). The implications of testing policy for quality and equality. *Phi Delta Kappan, 73,* 220–225.

Darling-Hammond, L. (1992). *Standards of practice for learner-centered schools.* New York: National Center for Restructuring Education, Schools, and Teaching (NCREST).

Darling-Hammond, L. (1993a). *Federal policy options for Chapter 1: An equity agenda for school restructuring.* New York: National Center for Restructuring Education.

Darling-Hammond, L. (1993b). Reframing the school reform agenda. *Phi Delta Kappan, 74,* 753–761.

Darling-Hammond, L. (1994). Performance-based assessment and educational equity. *Harvard Educational Review, 64,* 5–30.

Darling-Hammond, L. (1997). *The right to learn: A blueprint for creating schools that work.* San Francisco: Jossey-Bass.

Darling-Hammond, L., Ancess, J., & Falk, B. (1995). *Authentic assessment in action.* New York: Teachers College Press.

Darling-Hammond, L., Einbender, L., Frelow, F., & Ley-King, J. (1993). *Authentic assessment in practice: A collection of portfolios, performance tasks, exhibitions, and documentation.* New York: National Center for Restructuring Education, Schools, and Teaching (NCREST).

Darling-Hammond, L., & Falk, B. (1997). Policy for authentic assessment. In A. Lin Goodwin (Ed.), *Assessment for equity and inclusion* (pp. 51–75). London: Routledge.

Darling-Hammond, L., & Falk, B. (1997). Using standards and assessments to support student learning. *Phi Delta Kappan, 79,* 190–199.

Darling-Hammond, L., & Wise, A. E. (1985). Beyond standardization: State standards and school improvement. *The Elementary School Journal, 85,* 315–336.

Delacre L. (1993). *Vejigante masquerader.* New York: Scholastic.

Delpit, L. (1988). The silenced dialogue: Power and pedagogy in educating other people's children. *Harvard Educational Review, 58,* 280–298.

Delpit, L. (1995). *Other people's children.* New York: The New Press.

Denman, G. (1988). *When you've made it your own . . . : Teaching poetry to young people.* Portsmouth, NH: Heinemann.

Derrida, J. (1978). *Writing and difference.* London: Routledge and Kegan Paul.

Dethier, B. (1994). Eddie's full service rewrite. *English in Texas, 25,* 43.

Diamond, B. J., & Moore, M. A. (1995). *Multicultural literacy: Mirroring the reality of the classroom.* White Plains, NY: Longman.

Dickinson, J. (1993). Children's perspectives on talk: Building a learning community. In K. M. Pierce & C. J. Gilles (Eds.), *Cycles of meaning: Exploring the potential of talk in learning communities* (pp. 99–118). Portsmouth, NH: Heinemann.

Dickson, R. (1998). Horror: To gratify, not edify. *Language Arts, 76*(2), 115–122.

Dix, T. (1993). Cycles of professional growth: Evaluating literature discussion groups. In K. M. Pierce & C. J. Gilles (Eds.), *Cycles of meaning: Exploring the potential of talk in learning communities* (pp. 315–329). Portsmouth, NH: Heinemann.

Donaldson, M. (1978). *Children's minds.* Glasgow: William Collins Sons.

Dorr-Bremme, D. W. (1982). *Behaving and making sense: Creating social organization in the classroom.* Doctoral dissertation, Harvard University. (UMI #82-23,203)

Dove, R. (1994). Rita Dove. In R. Carroll (Ed.), *I know what the red clay looks like: The voice and vision of Black women writers* (pp. 83–90). New York: Crown Trade Paperbacks.

Dowhower, S. (1987). Effects of repeated reading on second-grade transitional readers' fluency and comprehension. *Reading Research Quarterly, 22,* 389–406.

Dowhower, S. (1994). Repeated reading revisited: Research into practice. *Reading and Writing Quarterly: Overcoming Learning Difficulties, 10,* 343–358.

Downs, J., & Morin, S. (1990). Improving reading fluency. *Teaching Exceptional Children, 22*(3), 38–40.

Duckworth, E. (1982). Understanding children's understanding. In V. Windley, M. Dorn, & L. Weber (Eds.), *Building on the strengths of children.* New York: City College.

Duffy, G. G., Roehler, L., & Rackliffe, G. (1986). How teachers' instructional talk influences students' understanding of lesson content. *The Elementary School Journal, 87,* 3–16.

Dyson, A. H. (1982). Reading, writing, and language: Young children solving the written language puzzle. *Language Arts, 59,* 829–839.

Dyson, A. H. (1984). Learning to write/Learning to do school. *Research in the Teaching of English, 18,* 233–266.

Dyson, A. H. (1986). Transitions and tensions: Interrelationship between the drawing, talking, and dictating of young children. *Research in the Teaching of English, 20,* 379–409.

Dyson, A. H. (1989). *Multiple worlds of child writers: Friends learning to write.* New York: Teachers College Press.

Dyson, A. H. (1993). *Social worlds of children learning to write in an urban primary school.* New York: Teachers College Press.

Dyson, A. H. (1994). The ninjas, the X-Men, and the ladies: Playing with power and identity in an urban primary school. *Teachers College Record, 96,* 219–239.

Dyson, A. H. (1995). Writing children: Reinventing the development of childhood literacy. *Written Communication, 12,* 4–46.

Eckstein, M., & Noah, H. (1993). Secondary school examinations. New Haven: Yale University Press.

Edelsky, C. (1989). Putting language variation to work for you. In P. Rigg & V. G. Allen (Eds.), *When they don't all speak English: Integrating the ESL student into the regular classroom* (pp. 96–107). Urbana, IL: National Council of Teachers of English.

Edelsky, C. (1991). *With literacy and justice for all: Rethinking the social in language and education.* London: Falmer Press.

Edelsky, C., Altwerger, B., & Flores, B. (1991). *Whole language: What's the difference?* Portsmouth, NH: Heinemann.

Edelsky, C., & Harman, S. (1988). One more critique of reading tests—With two differences. *English Education, 20,* 157–171.

Education Department of Western Australia. (1994). *First Steps.* Melbourne, Australia: Longman.

Edwards, A. D., & Furlong, V. J. (1978). *The language of teaching: Meaning in classroom interaction.* London: Heinemann Educational Books.

Edwards, D., & Mercer, N. (1987). *Common knowledge.* New York: Routledge.

Ehlert, L. (1992). *Moon rope: A Peruvian folktale* (A. Prince, Trans.). New York: Scholastic.

Eisner, E. W. (1991). What really counts in schools. *Educational Leadership, 48,* 10–17.

Emig, J. (1971). *The composing processes of twelfth graders.* Urbana, IL: National Council of Teachers of English.

Epstein, J. L. (1985). After the bus arrives: Resegregation in desegregated schools. *Journal of Social Issues, 41,* 23–43.

Ernst, G., & Richard, K. J. (1994/95). Reading and writing pathways to conversation in the ESL classroom. *The Reading Teacher, 48,* 320–326.

Falk, B. (1994). *The Bronx New School: Weaving assessment into the fabric of teaching and learning.* New York: National Center for Restructuring Education, Schools, and Teaching (NCREST).

Falk, B. (1996). Teaching the way children learn. In M. McLaughlin & I. Oberman (Eds.), *Teacher learning* (pp. 22–29). New York: Teachers College Press.

Falk, B., & Darling-Hammond, L. (1993). *The Primary Language Record at P.S. 261: How assessment transforms teaching and learning.* New York: National Center for Restructuring Education, Schools, and Teaching (NCREST).

Falk, B., & Larson, J. (1995, April). *An invitation to invention: Top-down support for bottom-up reform of assessment in New York State.* Paper presented at the Annual Meeting of the American Educational Research Association, San Francisco, CA.

Falk, B., MacMurdy, S., & Darling-Hammond, L. (1995). *Taking a different look: How the Primary Language Record supports teaching for diverse learners.* New York: National Center for Restructuring Education, Schools, and Teaching (NCREST).

Falk, B., & Ort, S. (in press/1998). Sitting down to score: Teacher learning through assessment. *Phi Delta Kappan, 80,* 59–64.

Farr, J. (1996). *I never came to you in white: A novel.* Boston: Houghton Mifflin.

Fasick, A. M., Johnston, M., & Osler, R. (Eds.). (1990). *Lands of pleasure: Essays on Lillian H. Smith and the development of children's libraries.* Metuchen, NJ: Scarecrow Press.

Feeley, J., Strickland, D. S., & Wepner, S. (Eds.). (1991). *Process reading and writing: A literature-based approach.* New York: Teachers College Press.

Feitelson, D. (1988). *Facts and fads in beginning reading: A cross-language perspective.* Norwood, NJ: Ablex.

Ferdman, B. M. (1990). Literacy and cultural identity. *Harvard Educational Review, 60,* 181–204.

Fisher, C. J. (1994). Sharing poetry in the classroom: Building a concept of poem. In J. Hickman, S. Hepler, & B. E. Cullinan (Eds.), *Children's literature in the classroom: Extending Charlotte's web* (pp. 53–65). Norwood, MA: Christopher-Gordon.

Fleischer, C., & Schaafsma, D. (1998). Introduction: Further conversations: Jay Robinson, his students, and the study of literacy. In C. Fleischer & D. Schaafsma (Eds.), *Literacy and democracy: Teacher research and composition studies in pursuit of habitable spaces* (pp. xiii–xxxii). Urbana, IL: National Council of Teachers of English.

Fleischman, P. (1988). *Joyful noise: Poems for two voices.* New York: Harper & Row.

Flores, B., Cousin, P., & Díaz, E. (1991). Transforming deficit myths about learning, language, and culture. *Language Arts, 68,* 369–379.

Flower, L., & Hayes, J. (1981). A cognitive process theory of writing. *College Composition and Communication, 32,* 365–387.

Fordham, S. (1994). "Those loud black girls": (Black) women, silence, and gender "passing" in the academy. *Anthropology & Education Quarterly, 24,* 3–32.

Forman, E. A., & Cazden, C. B. (1994). Exploring Vygotskian perspectives in education: The cognitive value of peer interaction. In R. B. Ruddell, M. R. Ruddell, & H. Singer (Eds.), *Theoretical models and processes of reading* (4th ed.) (pp. 155–178). Newark, DE: International Reading Association.

Farnan, N., Lapp, D., & Flood J. (1992). Changing perspectives in writing instruction. *Journal of Reading, 35,* 550–556.

Fosnot, C. T. (1989). *Enquiring teachers, enquiring learners.* New York: Teachers College Press.

Fox, C. (1983). Talking like a book: Young children's oral monologues. In M. Meek et al. (Eds.), *Opening Moves*. Bedford Way Papers 17. London: Institute of Education, University of London.

Frank, A. (1958). *Anne Frank: The diary of a young girl*. New York: Simon & Schuster.

Freedman, L. (1993). Teacher talk: The role of the teacher in literature discussion groups. In K. M. Pierce & C. J. Gilles (Eds.), *Cycles of meaning: Exploring the talk in learning communities* (pp. 219–235). Portsmouth, NH: Heinemann.

Freedman, R. (1980). *Immigrant kids*. New York: Dutton.

Freeman, D. E., & Freeman, Y. S. (1993). Strategies for promoting the primary languages of all students. *The Reading Teacher, 46*, 552–558.

Freire, P. (1970). *Pedagogy of the oppressed*. New York: Continuum.

Fresch, M. J., & Wheaton, A. (1997). Sort, search, and discover: Spelling in the child-centered classroom. *The Reading Teacher, 51*, 20–31.

Frost, R. (1968). The constant symbol. In H. Cox & E. C. Lathem (Eds.), *Selected prose of Robert Frost* (pp. 23–29). New York: Collier Books.

Galda, L., Cullinan, B., & Strickland, D. (1993). *Language, literacy, and the child*. Orlando, FL: Harcourt Brace.

Gallas, K. (1992). When the children take the chair: A study of sharing time in a primary classroom. *Language Arts, 69*(3), 172–182.

Gallas, K. (1997). Story time as a magical act open only to the initiated: What some children don't know about power and may not find out. *Language Arts, 74*(4), 248–254.

Gallas, K. (1998). *Sometimes I can be anything: Power, gender, and identity in a primary classroom*. New York: Teachers College Press.

Gamberg, R., Kwak, W., Hutchings, M., & Altheim, J. (1988). *Learning and loving it: Theme studies in the classroom*. Portsmouth, NH: Heinemann.

Gannet, R. (1948). *My father's dragon*. New York: Random House.

Garcia, G. E., & Pearson, P. D. (1994). Assessment and diversity. In L. Darling-Hammond (Ed.), *Review of Research in Education 20* (pp. 337–391). Washington, DC: American Educational Research Association.

Gardner, H. (1983). *Frames of mind: The theory of multiple intelligences*. New York: Basic Books.

Gentry J. (1978). Early spelling strategies. *The Elementary School Journal, 79*, 88–92.

Gentry, J. R. (1981). Learning to spell developmentally. *The Reading Teacher, 34*, 378–381.

Gentry J. (1997). *My kid can't spell*. Portsmouth, NH: Heinemann.

Gentry, J., & Gillet, J. (1993). *Teaching kids to spell*. Portsmouth, NH: Heinemann.

Gibbons, G. (1984). *Tunnels.* New York: Holiday House.

Gibbons, G. (1989). *Whales.* New York: Holiday House.

Giblin, J. C. (1982). *Chimney sweeps: Yesterday and today.* Illustrations by M. Tomes. New York: Harper & Row.

Giblin, J. C. (1990). *The riddle of the Rosetta Stone.* New York: Harper & Row.

Gilbert, P. (1994). "And they lived happily ever after": Cultural storylines and the construction of gender. In A. H. Dyson & C. Genishi (Eds.), *The need for story: Cultural diversity in classroom and community* (pp. 124–144). Urbana, IL: National Council of Teachers of English.

Gilles, C. (1991). *Negotiating the meanings: The uses of talk in literature study groups by adolescents labeled learning disabled.* Unpublished doctoral dissertation, University of Missouri, Columbia.

Gillet, J. W., & Kita, M. J. (1980). Words, kids, and categories. In E. Henderson & J. Beers (Eds.), *Developmental and cognitive aspects of learning to spell* (pp. 120–126). Newark, DE: International Reading Association.

Giroux, H. (1992). Educational leadership and the crisis of democratic government. *Educational Researcher, 21*(4), 4–11.

Glaser, R., & Silver, E. (1994). Assessment, testing and instruction: Retrospect and prospect. In L Darling-Hammond (Ed.), *Review of Research in Education 20* (pp. 393–419). Washington, DC: American Educational Research Association.

Goodman, K. S. (1967). Reading: A psycholinguistic guessing game. *Journal of the Reading Specialist, 6,* 126–135.

Goodman, K. S. (1970). Behind the eye. In K. S. Goodman & O. Niles, *Reading process and program.* Urbana, IL: National Council of Teachers of English.

Goodman, K. (1985). Unity in reading. In H. Singer & R. Ruddell (Eds.), *Theoretical models and processes of reading* (pp. 813–840). Newark, DE: International Reading Association.

Goodman, K. S. (1986). *What's whole in whole language?* Portsmouth, NH: Heinemann

Goodman, K. (1991, August). *Helping learners become whole.* Speech given at the Second Whole Language Umbrella Conference, Phoenix, Arizona.

Goodman, K. (1994). Reading, writing, and written texts: A transactional sociopsycholinguistic view. In R. Ruddell, M. Ruddell, & H. Singer (Eds.), *Theoretical models and processes of reading* (pp. 1093–1130). Newark, DE: International Reading Association.

Goodman, K. (1996a). *On reading.* Portsmouth, NH: Heinemann.

Goodman, K. (1996b). Principles of revaluing. In Y. Goodman & A. Marek (Eds.), *Retrospective miscue analysis: Revaluing readers and reading* (pp. 13–20). Katonah, NY: Richard C. Owen.

Goodman, K., & Gollasch, F. (1981). *Word level omissions in reading: Deliberate and non-deliberate implications and applications* (Occasional Paper No. 2). Tucson: University of Arizona, College of Education.

Goodman, K. S., & Goodman, Y. (1976). *Learning to read is natural.* Paper presented at Conference on Theory and Practice of Beginning Reading, University of Pittsburgh.

Goodman, K. S., & Goodman, Y.M. (1979). Learning to read is natural. In L. B. Resnick & P. A. Weaver (Eds.), *Theory and practice of early reading*, Vol. 1 (pp. 137–154). Hillsdale, NJ: Erlbaum.

Goodman, K. S., Shannon, P., Freeman, Y., & Murphy, S. (1988). *Report card on basal readers.* New York: Richard C. Owen Publishers.

Goodman, Y. (1978). Kid watching: An alternative to testing. *National Elementary Principal, 57*(4), 41–45.

Goodman, Y. M., & Burke, C. L. (1972). *Reading miscue inventory: Procedure for diagnosis and evaluation.* New York: Macmillan Company.

Goodman, Y., Watson, D., & Burke, C. (1987). *Reading miscue inventory: Alternative procedures.* New York: Richard C. Owen.

Goodrich, F., & Hackett, A. (1989). The diary of Anne Frank. In R. D. Pearson, D. Johnson, I. Clymen, R. Indrisano, R. Venezky, J. Bauman, E. Hiebert, & M. Toth (Series Eds.), *World of reading* series: *Level 13—Star walk* (pp. 74–98). Morristown, NJ: Silver, Burdett & Ginn.

Gosling, J. C. B., & Taylor, C. C. W. (1982). *The Greeks on pleasure.* Oxford: Clarendon Press.

Grace, D. J., & Tobin, J. (1997). Carnival in the classroom: Elementary students making videos. In J. Tobin (Ed.), *Making a place for pleasure in early childhood education* (pp. 159–187). New Haven: Yale University Press.

Graves, D. H. (1981). Patterns of child control of the writing process. In R. D. Walshe (Ed.), *Donald Graves in Australia: "Children want to write"* (pp. 17–28). Rozelle, NSW, Australia: Primary English Teaching Association.

Graves, D. (1983). *Writing: Teachers and children at work.* Portsmouth, NH: Heinemann.

Graves, D. H. (1989). *Investigate nonfiction.* Portsmouth, NH: Heinemann.

Graves, D. H. (1994). *A fresh look at writing.* Portsmouth, NH: Heinemann.

Graves, D., & Hansen, J. (1983). The author's chair. *Language Arts, 60,* 176–183.

Greene, M. (1988). *The dialectic of freedom.* New York: Teachers College Press.

Griffen, P., Smith, P., & Burrill, L. (1995). *The American literacy profile scale: A framework for authentic assessment.* Portsmouth, NH: Heinemann.

Gundlach, R. (1982). Children as writers: The beginnings of learning to write. In M. Nystrand (Ed.), *What writers know: The language, process, and structure of written discourse* (pp. 129–148). New York: Academic Press.

Gutierrez, K. (1993). Biliteracy and the language-minority child. In O. Saracho & B. Spodek (Eds.), *Language and literacy in early childhood education* (pp. 82–101). New York: Teachers College Press.

Hall, D. (1982). Goatfoot, milktongue, and twinbird: The psychic origins of poetic form. In D. Hall (Ed.), *Claims for poetry* (pp. 141–150). Ann Arbor, MI: University of Michigan Press.

Hall, S. (1981). Notes on deconstructing "the popular." In R. Samuel (Ed.), *People's history and socialist theory* (pp. 227–239). London: Routledge & Kegan Paul.

Halliday, M. A. K. (1973). *Explorations in the functions of language.* London: Edward Arnold.

Haney, W. (1984). Testing reasoning and reasoning about testing. *Review of Educational Research, 54,* 597–654.

Harris, I. B. (1993, Spring). Education—Does it make a difference when you start? *Aspen Institute Quarterly, 5,* 30–52.

Harste, J., Burke, C., and Woodward, V. (1982). Children's language and world: Initial encounters with print. In J. A. Langer & M. T. Smith-Burke (Eds.), *Reader meets author / Bridging the gap: A psycholinguistic and sociolinguistic perspective.* Newark, DE: International Reading Association.

Harste, J., Burke, C., & Woodward, V. (1983). *The young child as writer-reader and informant.* (Final Report of NIE-G-80-0121). Bloomington, IN: Language Education Department.

Harste J., Short, K., & Burke, C. (1988). *Creating classrooms for authors.* Portsmouth, NH: Heinemann.

Harste, J., Woodward, V. A., & Burke, C. L. (1984). *Language stories & literacy lessons.* Portsmouth, NH: Heinemann.

Hartford, J. (1986). *Steamboat in a cornfield.* New York: Crown.

Hasan, R. (1986). The ontogenesis of ideology: An interpretation of mother-child talk. In T. Threadgold, E. A. Grosz, G. Kress, & M. A. K. Halliday (Eds.), *Semiotics, ideology and language* (pp. 125–146). Sydney, NSW, Australia: Sydney Association for Studies in Society and Culture.

Hazen, B. S. (1979). *Tight times.* New York: Viking.

Heard, G. (1993). Living like a poet. *The New Advocate, 6*(2), 115–122.

Heath, S. B. (1983). *Ways with words: Language, life, and work in communities and classrooms.* Cambridge: Cambridge University Press.

Hemingway, E. (1952). *Old man and the sea.* New York: Scribner.

Henderson, E. (1990). *Teaching spelling* (2nd ed.). Boston: Houghton Mifflin.

Henderson, E. H., & Templeton, S. (1986). A developmental perspective of formal spelling instruction through alphabet, pattern, and meaning. *Elementary School Journal, 86,* 305–316.

Herman, J., Aschbacher, P. R., & Winters, L. (1992). *A practical guide to alternative assessment.* Alexandria, VA: Association for Supervision and Curriculum Development.

Hickman, J. (1981). A new perspective on response to literature: Research in an elementary school setting. *Research in the Teaching of English, 15,* 343–354.

Hiebert, E. H. (Ed.). (1991). *Literacy for a diverse society.* New York: Teachers College Press.

Ho, C. S. H., & Bryant, P. (1997). Learning to read Chinese beyond the logographic phase. *Reading Research Quarterly, 32,* 276–289.

Hodgkinson, H. (1991). Reform versus reality. *Phi Delta Kappan, 73,* 8–16.

Hoffman, J., & Isaacs, M. E. (1991). Developing fluency through restructuring the task of guided oral reading. *Theory into Practice, 30*(3), 185–194.

Hollingsworth, S. (1994). *Teacher research and urban literacy education: Lessons and conversations in a feminist key.* New York: Teachers College Press.

The Holmes Group. (1986). *Tomorrow's teachers: A report from the Holmes Group.* East Lansing, MI: The Holmes Group.

Homan, S., Klesius, J., & Hite, C. (1993). Effects of repeated readings and nonrepetitive strategies on students' fluency and comprehension. *Journal of Educational Research, 87*(2), 94–99.

hooks, b. (1990). Talking back. In R. Ferguson, M. Gever, T. Minh-ha, & C. West (Eds.), *Out there: Marginalization and contemporary cultures* (pp. 337–340). New York: The New Museum of Contemporary Art, & Cambridge, MA: MIT Press.

Hopkins, L. B. (1987). *Pass the poetry, please!* (Rev. ed.). New York: HarperCollins.

Hoskisson, K. (1975). Many facets of assisted reading. *Elementary English, 52,* 312–315.

Howell, K., & Lorson-Howell, K. (1990). Fluency in the classroom. *Teaching Exceptional Children, 22*(3), 20–23.

Hoyt-Goldsmith, D. (1990). *Totem pole.* Photographs by L. Migdale. New York: Holiday House.

Huck, C. (1992). Literature and literacy. *Language Arts, 69,* 520–526.

Hudelson, S. (1990). Bilingual/ESL learners talking in the English classroom. In S. Hynds & D. L. Rubin (Eds.), *Perspectives on talk and learning* (pp. 267–283). Urbana, IL: National Council of Teachers of English.

Hudelson, S. (1994). Literacy development of second language children. In F. Genesse, (Ed.), *Educating second language children* (pp. 129–158). New York: Cambridge University Press.

Hughes, M., & Searle, D. (1997). *The violent E and other tricky sounds: Learning to spell from kindergarten through grade 6.* York, ME: Stenhouse.

Hunt, J. (1989). *Illuminations.* New York: Bradbury.

Hurst, K. (1988). Group discussion of poetry. In M. Benton, J. Teasy, R. Bell, & K. Hurst (Eds.), *Young readers responding to poems* (pp. 175–189). New York: Routledge.

Hutchins, P. (1968). *Rosie's walk*. New York: Macmillan.

Innocenti, R. (1985). *Rose Blanche*. Mankato, MN: Creative Education.

Invernizzi, M., Abouzeid, M., & Gill, J. T. (1994). Using students' invented spellings as a guide for spelling instruction that emphasizes word study. *The Elementary School Journal, 95*, 155–167.

Ishiguro, K. (1989). *The remains of the day*. New York: Knopf.

Jameson, F. (1983). Pleasure: A political issue. In Formations Editorial Collective (Eds.), *Formations of pleasure* (pp. 1–4). London: Routledge & Kegan Paul.

Jensen, J. (1993). What we know about the writing of elementary school children. *Language Arts, 70*, 290–294.

Jiannan, F. (Ad. and Ill.). (1991). *Jingwei filling the sea*. Beijing: Dolphin Books.

Juel, C. (1995). The messenger may be wrong, but the message may be right. *Journal of Research in Reading, 18*(2), 146–153.

Keats, E. J. (1962). *The snowy day*. New York: Viking.

Kelly, P. R., & Farnan, N. (1991). Promoting critical thinking through response logs: A reader-response approach with fourth graders. In J. Zutell & S. McCormick (Eds.), *Learner factors/teacher factors: Issues in literacy research and instruction* (pp. 297–303). Chicago, IL: The National Reading Conference.

Kerr, W. (1962). *The decline of pleasure*. New York: Simon and Schuster.

Kiefer, B. Z., & DeStefano, J. S. (1985). Cultures together in the classroom: "What You Saying?" In A. Jagger & T. Smith-Burke (Eds.), *Observing the language learner* (pp. 159–171). Newark, DE: International Reading Association.

Kimmel, E. A. (1977). Confronting the ovens: The Holocaust and juvenile fiction. The *Horn Book Magazine, 53*, 84–91.

Kingston, Maxine Hong. (1977). *The woman warrior: Memoirs of a girlhood among ghosts*. New York: Vintage Books.

Kline, S. (1993). *Out of the garden: Toys, TV, and children's culture in the age of marketing*. London: Verso.

Knapp, M. S., & Turnbull, B. J. (1990). *Better schooling for the children of poverty: Alternatives to conventional wisdom*. Washington, DC: U.S. Department of Education.

Koch, K. (1970). *Wishes, lies, and dreams: Teaching children to write poetry*. New York: Harper & Row.

Kornhaber, M., & Gardner, H. (1993). *Varieties of excellence: Identifying and assessing children's talents*. New York: National Center for Restructuring Education, Schools, and Teaching (NCREST).

Krapp, A., Hidi, S., & Renninger, K. A. (1992). Interest, learning, and development. In K. A. Renninger, S. Hidi, & A. Krapp (Eds.), *The role of interest in learning and development* (pp. 3–25). Hillsdale, NJ: Lawrence Erlbaum.

Kreeft, J. (1984). Dialogue writing—Bridge from talk to essay writing. *Language Arts, 61*, 141–150.

Kucer, S. B. (1990). *Investigating the development, implementation, and effects of an integrated literacy curriculum within a third-grade bilingual classroom.* (Final Report to the National Council of Teachers of English Research Foundation). Los Angeles: University of Southern California, School of Education.

Kucer, S. B. (1993). Helping students become independent readers, writers, and thinkers. In M. Lewison (Ed.), *Language arts teacher resource materials grade 3–5* (pp. 17–19). Los Angeles: Galaxy Institute for Education.

Kucer, S. B. (1998). Engagement, conflict, and avoidance in a whole language classroom. *Language Arts, 75*(2), 90–96.

Labbo, L., Hoffman, J., & Roser, N. (1995). Ways to unintentionally make writing difficult. *Language Arts, 72*, 164–170.

Lane, B. (1993). *After the end: Teaching and learning creative revision.* Portsmouth, NH: Heinemann.

Lane, M. (1981). *The squirrel.* New York: Dial Press.

Langer, J. (1992). *Literature instruction: A focus on student response.* Urbana, IL: National Council of Teachers of English.

Lasky, K. (1983). *Sugaring time.* Photographs by C. Knight. New York: Macmillan.

Lauber, P. (1986). *Volcano: The eruption and healing of Mount St. Helens.* New York: Bradbury Press.

Lee, H. V. (1994a). *At the beach.* New York: Henry Holt & Co.

Lee, H. V. (1994b). *Snow.* New York: Henry Holt & Co.

Lee, S. (Author & Ill.). (1963). *The X-Men.* New York: Marvel Entertainment Group.

Lensmire, T. (1994). *When children write.* New York: Teachers College Press.

Lewy, A. (1996). Postmodernism in the field of achievement testing. *Studies in Educational Evaluation, 22*, 223–244.

Lim, H. L., & Watson, D. J. (1993). Whole language content classes for second-language learners. *The Reading Teacher, 46*, 384–393.

Lindfors, J. (1987). *Children's language and learning* (2nd ed.). Englewood Cliffs, NJ: Prentice-Hall.

Lindwer, W. (1992). The last days of Anne Frank. *READ Magazine, 41*(15), 4–13.

Linn, R. L. (1987). Accountability: The comparison of educational systems and the quality of test results. *Educational Policy, 1*, 181–198.

Linn, R. L., Baker, E. L., & Dunbar, S. B. (1991). Complex, performance-based assessments: Expectations and validation criteria. *Educational Researcher, 20*, 15–21.

Linn, R. L., Graue, M. E., & Sanders, N. M. (1990). Comparing state and district test results to national norms: The validity of the claims that "everyone is above average." *Educational Measurement: Issues and Practice, 9*, 5–14.

Lipson, M., & Lang, L. B. (1991). Not as easy as it seems: Some unresolved questions about fluency. *Theory into Practice, 30*(3), 218–227.

Lipson, M. Y., Valencia, S. W., Wixson, K. K., & Peters, C. W. (1993). Integration and thematic teaching: Integration to improve teaching and learning. *Language Arts, 70*, 252–263.

Livingston, M. C. (1990). The poem on page 81. In M. C. Livingston (Ed.), *Climb into the bell tower* (pp. 3–24). New York: Harper & Row.

Lucas, C. K. (1988a). Toward ecological evaluation. *The Quarterly Newsletter of the National Writing Project and the Center for the Study of Writing, 10*(1), 1–17.

Lucas, C. K. (1988b). Toward ecological evaluation, part 2. *The Quarterly Newsletter of the National Writing Project and the Center for the Study of Writing, 10*(2), 4–20.

MacGinitie, W. H. (1991). Reading instruction: Plus ca change. . . . *Educational Leadership, 48*, 55–58.

MacGinitie, W. H., & MacGinitie, R. K. (1989). *Gates-MacGinitie Reading Tests* (3rd ed.). Chicago: Riverside.

Madaus, G. F. (1985). Test scores as administrative mechanisms in educational policy. *Phi Delta Kappan, 66*, 611–617.

Madraso, J. (1993). Proofreading: The skill we've neglected to teach. *English Journal, 82*, 32–41.

Marland, M. (1983). School as a sexist amplifier. In M. Marland (Ed.), *Sex differentiation and schooling* (pp. 1–7). London: Heinemann.

Matthews, D. (1989). *Polar bear cubs*. Photographs by D. Guravich. New York: Simon and Schuster.

Matthewson, G. C. (1976). The function of attitude in the reading process. In H. Singer & R. B. Ruddell (Eds.), *Theoretical models and processes of reading* (2nd ed.) (pp. 841–856). Newark, DE: International Reading Association.

Mazer, H. (1973). *Snowbound*. New York: Dell.

McBride, R. L. (1996). The bliss point and pleasure. In D. M. Warburton & N. Sherwood (Eds.), *Pleasure and quality of life* (pp. 147–154). New York: John Wiley.

McCloskey, R. (1948). *Blueberries for Sal*. New York: Viking.

McClure, A., Harrison, P., & Reed, S. (1990). *Sunrises and songs: Reading and writing poetry in an elementary classroom*. Portsmouth, NH: Heinemann.

McDonald, R., Pressley, M., Rankin, J., Mistretta, J., Yokoi, L., & Ettenberger, S. (1997). Effective primary-grades literacy instruction = Balanced literacy instruction. *The Reading Teacher, 50,* 1–14.

McDonald, J., Smith, S., Turner, D., Finney M., & Barton, E. (1993). *Graduation by exhibition.* Alexandria, VA: Association for Supervision and Curriculum Development.

McGill-Franzen, A., & Allington, R. L. (1993). Flunk 'em or get them classified: The contamination of primary grade accountability data. *Educational Researcher, 22,* 19–22.

McIntyre, E. (1990, April). *Young children's reading behaviors in various classroom contexts: Their relationship to instruction.* Paper presented to the American Educational Research Association, Boston, MA.

McIntyre, E. (1995a). The struggle for developmentally appropriate literacy instruction. *Journal of Research in Childhood Education, 9*(2), 145–156.

McIntyre, E. (1995b). Teaching and learning writing skills in a low-SES, urban primary classroom. *Journal of Reading Behavior, 27*(2), 213–242.

McKissack, P., & McKissack, F. (1989). *A long hard journey: The story of the pullman porter.* New York: Walker.

McLerran, A. (1990). *Roxaboxen.* New York: Lothrop, Lee, & Shepard.

Mehan, H. (1979). *Learning lessons.* Cambridge, MA: Harvard University Press.

Meisels, S., Liaw, F., Dorfman, A., & Fails, R. (1993, April). *The work sampling system: Reliability and validity of a performance assessment for young children.* Paper presented at the Annual Meeting of the American Educational Research Association, Atlanta, GA.

Mendoca, C. O., & Johnson, K. E. (1994). Peer review negotiations: Revision activities in ESL writing instruction. *TESOL Quarterly, 28,* 745–769.

Menosky, D. M. (1971). *A psycholinguistic analysis of oral reading miscues generated during the reading of varying positions of text by selected readers from grades two, four, six, and eight.* Unpublished doctoral dissertation, Wayne State University, Detroit, MI.

Mercer, C. (1983). A poverty of desire: Pleasure and popular politics. In Formations Editorial Collective (Eds.), *Formations of pleasure* (pp. 84–100). London: Routledge & Kegan Paul.

Michaels, S. (1981). "Sharing time": Children's narrative styles and differential access to literacy. *Language in Society, 10,* 423–442.

Michaels, S., & Cazden, C. B. (in press/1986). Teacher/child collaboration as oral preparation for literacy. In B. B. Schieffelin and P. Gilmore (Eds.), *The acquisition of literacy: Ethnographic perspectives.* Norwood, NJ: Ablex.

Michell, L., & Peel, E. (1977). A cognitive dimension in the analysis of classroom discourse. *Educational Review, 29,* 255–266.

Miller, P. (1982). *Amy, Wendy, and Beth: Learning language in South Baltimore.* Austin, TX: University of Texas Press.

Mitchell, R. (1992). *Testing for learning: How new approaches to evaluation can improve American schools.* New York: The Free Press.

Moffett, J., & Wagner, B. J. (1976). *Student-centered language arts and reading. A handbook for teachers* (2nd ed.). Boston: Houghton Mifflin.

Moll, L. C. (1988). Some key issues in teaching Latino students. *Language Arts, 65,* 465–472.

Moll, L. (Ed.). (1990). *Vygotsky and education.* New York: Cambridge University Press.

Moll, L. C., & González, N. (1994). Lessons from research with language minority children. *Journal of Reading Behavior, 26,* 439–456.

Moll, L. C., & Greenberg, J. B. (1990). Creating zones of possibilities: Combining social contexts for instruction. In L. C. Moll (Ed.), *Vygotsky and education* (pp. 319–348). New York: Cambridge University Press.

Moll, L., & Whitmore, K. (1993). Vygotsky in classroom practice: Moving from individual transmission to social transaction. In E. A. Forman, N. Minick, & C. A. Stone (Eds.), *Contexts for learning: Sociocultural dynamics in children's development* (pp. 19–42). New York: Oxford University Press.

Morgan, N., & Saxton, J. (1991). *Teaching, questioning, and learning.* New York: Routledge.

Moss, P. A. (1994). Can there be validity without reliability? *Educational Researcher 23,* 5–12.

Murphy, S., & Dudley-Marling, C. (1997). Whole language: Is there anybody out there? *Talking Points, 9*(1), 21–26.

Murphy S., & Dudley-Marling, C. (Eds.) (1999). Doing teacher research (themed issue of journal). *Language Arts, 77*(1).

Murray, D. M. (1978). Internal revision: A process of discovery. In C. R. Cooper & L. Odell (Eds.), *Research on composing: Points of departure* (pp. 85–103). Urbana, IL: National Council of Teachers of English.

Musgrove, M. (1976). *Ashanti to Zulu.* Illustrated by L. Dillon & D. Dillon. New York: Dial.

Musker, J., & Clements, R. (Producers & Directors). (1992). *Aladdin.* Burbank, CA: Walt Disney Pictures.

Myers, W. D. (1988). *Fallen angels.* New York: Scholastic.

Natarella, M. (1980). Sharing literature with the young child. In G. S. Pinnell (Ed.), *Discovering language with children* (pp. 48–51). Urbana, IL: National Council of Teachers of English.

National Association for the Education of Young Children. (1988). NAEYC position statement on developmentally appropriate practice in the primary grades, serving 5 through 8 year olds. *Young Children, 43*(2), 64–84.

National Council of Teachers of English and International Reading Association. (1996). *Standards for the English language arts*. Urbana, IL: National Council of Teachers of English, and Newark, DE: International Reading Association.

National Forum on Assessment. (1995). *Principles and indicators for student assessment systems*. Cambridge, MA: FairTest.

Nelms, B. (1988). *Literature in the classroom: Readers, texts and contexts*. Urbana, IL: National Council of Teachers of English.

Newkirk, T. (1989). *More than stories*. Portsmouth, NH: Heinemann.

New York State Curriculum and Assessment Council. (1994). *Learning-centered curriculum and assessment for New York State*. Albany: New York State Education Department.

New York State Education Department. (1996). *Learning standards for the English Language Arts*. Albany: Author.

Nicolopoulou, A., Scales, B., & Weintraub, J. (1994). Gender differences and symbolic imagination in the stories of four-year-olds. In A. H. Dyson & C. Genishi (Eds.), *The need for story: Cultural diversity in classroom and community* (pp. 102–123). Urbana, IL: National Council of Teachers of English.

Nieto, S. (1996). *Affirming diversity*. White Plains, NY: Longman Publishers.

Norman, K. (1992). *Thinking voices: The work of the National Oracy Project*. London: Hodder & Stoughton.

Norton, D. E. (1992). *The impact of literature-based reading*. New York: Macmillan.

NSW Department of Education and Training (1998). *Teaching Spelling K–6*. Sydney, Australia: Author.

Nurss, J. R., & Hough, R. A. (1992). Reading and the ESL student. In S. J. Samuels & A. E. Farstrup (Eds.), *What research has to say about reading instruction* (pp. 277–313). Newark, DE: International Reading Association.

Nye, N. S. (1994). *Red suitcase*. Brockport, NY: BOA Editions, Ltd.

Nye, N. S. (1997). Dia de dulce/Sweet day: Using Paz, Pacheco, Gutierrez, Deltoro, and Blanco. In J. Marzan (Ed.), *Luna, luna: Creative writing ideas from Spanish, Latin American, and Latino literature* (pp. 183–192). New York: Teachers & Writers Collaborative.

Oakes, J. (1985). *Keeping track: How schools structure inequality*. New Haven, CT: Yale University Press.

O'Keefe, S. (1989). *One hungry monster: A counting book in rhyme*. Boston: Joy Street Books.

Ortony, A. (1975). Why metaphors are necessary and not just nice. *Educational Theory, 25*, 45–53.

O'Shea, L., Sindelar, P., & O'Shea, D. (1985). The effects of repeated readings and attentional cues on reading fluency and comprehension. *Journal of Reading Behavior, 17*(2), 129–142.

Pappas, C. C. (1993). Is narrative primary? Some insights from kindergart-ners' pretend readings of stories and information books. *Journal of Reading Behavior, 25,* 97–129.

Pappas, C. C. (1997). Making "collaboration" problematic in collaborative school-university research: Studying with urban teacher researchers to transform literacy curriculum genres. In J. Flood, S. B. Heath, & D. Lapp (Eds.), *Handbook of research on teaching literacy through communicative and visual arts* (pp. 215–231). New York: Macmillan.

Pappas, C. C., Kiefer, B. Z., & Levstick, L. S. (1994). *An integrated language perspective in the elementary school.* White Plains, NY: Longman.

Pappas, C., Ouler, C., Barry, A., & Rassel, M. (1993). Focus on research: Collaborating with teachers developing integrated language arts programs in urban schools. *Language Arts, 70,* 297–303.

Pappas, C. C., & Pettegrew, B. S. (1998). The role of genre in the psycholinguistic guessing game of reading. *Language Arts, 75*(1), 36–44.

Pappas, C. C., & Zecker, L. B. (in press/2001a). *Teacher inquiries in literacy teaching-learning.* Mahwah, NJ: Erlbaum.

Pappas, C. C., & Zecker, L. B. (in press/2001b). *Working with teacher-researchers in urban classrooms.* Mahwah, NJ: Erlbaum.

Patterson, L., Santa, C. M., Short, K. G., & Smith, K. (Eds.). (1993). *Teachers are researchers: Reflection and action.* Newark, DE: International Reading Association.

Pearson, P. D. (1996). Six ideas in search of a champion: What policymakers should know about the teaching and learning of literacy in our schools. *Journal of Literacy Research, 28,* 302–309.

Peetom, A. (1993, August). *Whole language teachers: Amateurs rather than professionals.* Address at the Whole Language Umbrella Conference, Winnipeg, Canada.

Peregoy, S. F., & Boyle, O. (1993). *Reading, writing and learning in ESL.* New York: Longman.

Perl, L. (1989). *The great ancestor hunt: The fun of finding out who you are.* New York: Clarion.

Perrone, V. (Ed.). (1991a). *Expanding student assessment.* Alexandria, VA: Association for Supervision and Curriculum Development.

Perrone, V. (1991b). *A letter to teachers: Reflections on schooling and the art of teaching.* San Francisco: Jossey-Bass.

Perry, D. L. (1967). *The concept of pleasure.* The Hague: Mouton and Company.

Peterson, R. (1992). *Life in a crowded place.* Portsmouth, NH: Heinemann.

Peterson, R., & Eeds, M. (1990). *Grand conversations: Literature groups in action.* New York: Scholastic.

Phillips, A. (1990). Thinking on the inside: Children's poetry and inner speech. Unpublished manuscript, Harvard Graduate School of Education, Cambridge.

Piaget, J. (1970). *The science of education and the psychology of the child.* New York: Penguin.

Pierce, K., & Gilles, C. (1993). *Cycles of meaning: Exploring the potential of talk in learning communities.* Portsmouth, NH: Heinemann.

Pinnell, G., Fountas, I., & Giacobbe, M. (1998). *Word matters: Teaching phonics and spelling in the reading/writing classroom.* Portsmouth, NH: Heinemann

Pontecorvo, C., Orsolini, M., Burge, B., & Resnick, L. (1996). *Children's early text construction.* Mahwah, NJ: Lawrence Erlbaum.

Potok, C. (1967). *The chosen.* New York: Simon and Schuster.

Prelutsky, J., & Brown, M. (Eds.). (1986). *Read-aloud rhymes.* New York: Alfred A. Knopf.

Pressley, M., Rankin, J., & Yokoi, L. (1996). A survey of instructional practices of primary teachers nominated as effective in promoting literacy. *The Elementary School Journal, 96,* 363–384.

Price, J., Schwabacher, S., & Chittenden, E. (1993). *The multiple forms of evidence study.* New York: The National Center for Restructuring Education, Schools, and Teaching (NCREST).

Provensen, A., & Provensen, M. (1984). *Leonardo da Vinci.* New York: Viking.

Purcell-Gates, V., & Dahl, K. (in press/1991). Low-SES children's success and failure at early literacy learning in skills-based classrooms. *Journal of Reading Behavior, 23*(1), 1–34.

Quintero, E., & Huerta-Macias, A. (1990) All in the family: Bilingualism and biliteracy. *The Reading Teacher, 44,* 306–312.

Rasinski, T. (1990a). Effects of repeated reading and listening-while-reading on reading fluency. *Journal of Educational Research, 83*(3), 147–150.

Rasinski, T. (1990b). Investigating measures of reading fluency. *Educational Research Quarterly, 14*(3), 37–44.

Rasinski, T., & Zutell, J. (1990). Making a place for fluency instruction in the regular reading curriculum. *Reading Research and Instruction, 29*(2), 85–91.

Rawls, W. (1961). *Where the red fern grows.* New York: Bantam.

Read, C. (1971). Pre-school children's knowledge of English phonology. *Harvard Educational Review, 41,* 1–34.

Reiser, L. (1993). *Margaret and Margarita, Margarita y Margaret.* New York: Scholastic.

Resnick, L. B. (1987a). *Education and learning to think.* Washington, DC: National Academy Press.

Resnick, L. (1987b). Learning in school and out. *Educational Researcher, 16,* 13–20.

Resnick, L. B. (1994, August). Performance puzzles. *American Journal of Education, 102,* 511–526.

Resnick, L., & Nolan, K. (1995). Standards for education. In D. Ravitch (Ed.), *Debating the future of American education* (pp. 94–119). Washington, DC: The Brookings Institution.

Reutzel, D. R., & Hollingsworth, P. M. (1993). Effects of fluency training on second graders' reading comprehension. *Journal of Educational Research, 86*(6), 325–331.

Reyes, M. de la Luz. (1991). A process approach to literacy instruction for Spanish-speaking students: In search of a best fit. In E. H. Hiebert (Ed.), *Literacy for a diverse society* (pp. 157–171). New York: Teachers College Press.

Rhodes, L. K., & Shanklin, N. L. (1993). *Windows into literacy: Assessing learners, K–8.* Portsmouth, NH: Heinemann.

Rief, L. (1992). *Seeking diversity.* Portsmouth, NH: Heinemann.

Rigg, P., & Allen, V. G. (1989). *When they don't all speak English: Integrating the ESL student into the regular classroom.* Urbana, IL: National Council of Teachers of English.

Robertson, H. (1998). *No more teachers, no more books: The commercialization of Canada's schools.* Toronto: McClelland and Stewart.

Roop, P., & Roop, C. (1990). *I, Columbus: My journal.* Illustrated by P. E. Hanson. New York: Walker.

Rosaldo, R. (1989). *Culture and truth: The remaking of social analysis.* Boston: Beacon Press.

Rosaldo, R., Lavie, S., & Narayan, K. (1993). Introduction: Creativity in anthropology. In S. Lavie, K. Narayan, & R. Rosaldo (Eds.), *Creativity/anthropology* (pp. 1–10). Ithaca, NY: Cornell University Press.

Rosen, H. (1982). *The nurture of narrative.* Paper presented to the annual meeting of the International Reading Association, Chicago.

Rosenblatt, L. M. (1976). *Literature as exploration.* New York: Noble and Noble.

Rosenblatt, L. M. (1978). *The reader, the text, the poem: The transactional theory of the literary work.* Carbondale, IL: Southern Illinois University Press.

Rosenblatt, L. (1980). "What facts does this poem teach you?" *Language Arts, 57,* 386–394.

Rosenblatt, L. M. (1983). *Literature as exploration.* (4th ed.). New York: Modern Language Association.

Rosenblatt, L. M. (1989). Writing and reading: The transactional theory. In J. M. Mason (Ed.), *Reading and writing connections* (pp. 153–176). Boston: Allyn and Bacon.

Rothman, R. (1995). *Measuring up: Standards, assessment, and school reform.* San Francisco, CA: Jossey-Bass.

Rothman, R. (1997). *Organizing schools so that all children can learn.* New York: National Center on Education and the Economy.

Routman, R. (1991). Transitions. Portsmouth, NH: Heinemann.

Routman, R. (1996). *Literacy at the Crossroads.* Portsmouth, NH: Heinemann Press.

Rummelhart, D. (1985). Toward an interactive model of reading. In H. Singer & R. Ruddell (Eds.), *Theoretical models and processes of reading* (pp. 722–750). Newark, DE: International Reading Association.

Sabin, R. (1985). *Jackie Robinson.* New York: Troll.

Samuels, S. J. (1979). The method of repeated readings. *The Reading Teacher, 32,* 403–408.

Sattler, H. R. (1989). *The book of eagles.* Illustrated by J. D. Zallinger. New York: Lothrop, Lee and Shepard.

Schlagal, R. C., & Schlagal, J. H. (1992). The integral character of spelling: Teaching strategies for multiple purpose. *Language Arts, 69,* 418–424.

Schreiber, P. (1980). On the acquisition of reading fluency. *Journal of Reading Behavior, 12*(3), 177–186.

Schwartz, D. M. (1989). *If you made a million.* Illustrated by Steven Kellogg. New York: Lothrop, Lee and Shepard.

Scieszka, J. (1991). *The frog prince continued.* New York: Penguin.

Scollon, R. (1976). *Conversations with a one-year-old. A case study of the developmental foundations of syntax.* Honolulu: University Press of Hawaii.

Scribner, S., & Cole, M. (1981). *The psychology of literacy.* Cambridge, MA: Harvard University Press.

Searle, D. (1981). *Two contexts for adolescent language, classroom learning and the discussion of extra-school experience.* Unpublished Ph.D. dissertation, University of London.

Searle, D., & Dillon, D. (1981). *The role of language in the classroom.* Paper presented at the annual meeting of the American Educational Research Association, Los Angeles.

Shanahan, T. (Ed.). (1990). *Reading and writing together: New perspectives for the classroom.* Norwood, MA: Christopher-Gordon.

Shannon, P. (1990). *The struggle to continue: Progressive reading instruction in the United States.* Portsmouth, NH: Heinemann.

Shepard, L. A. (1990). Inflated test score gains: Is the problem old norms or teaching the test? *Educational Measurement: Issues and Practice, 9,* 15–22.

Shepard, L. (1991). Negative policies for dealing with diversity: When does assessment and diagnosis turn into sorting and segregation? In E. H. Hiebert (Ed.), *Literacy for a diverse society* (pp. 279–298). New York: Teachers College Press.

Shepard, L. (1995). Using assessment to improve learning. *Educational Leadership, 52*, 38–43.

Short, K., & Burke, C. (1991). *Creating curriculum: Teachers and students as a community of learners.* Portsmouth, NH: Heinemann.

Short, K., & Pierce, K. (1990). *Talking about books: Creating literate communities.* Portsmouth, NH: Heinemann.

Shuy, R. (1981). What the teacher knows is more important than text or test. *Language Arts, 58*, 919–929.

Silver, M. (1995). "Horrors! It's R. L. Stine." *U.S. News & World Report, 119*(16), 95–96.

Slesinger, B., & Busching, B. (1995). Practicing democracy through student-centered inquiry. *Middle School Journal, 26*(5), 50–56.

Smith, E. B., Goodman, K. S., & Meredith, R. (1970). *Language and thinking in school.* New York: Holt, Rinehart and Winston.

Smith, F. (1973).Twelve easy ways to make learning to read difficult. In F. Smith, *Psycholinguistics and reading.* New York: Holt, Rinehart and Winston.

Smith, F. (1975). *Comprehension and learning: A conceptual framework for teachers.* New York: Holt, Rinehart and Winston.

Smith, F. (1981a). Demonstrations, engagement and sensitivity: A revised approach to language learning. *Language Arts, 58*, 103–112.

Smith, F. (1981b). *Writing and the writer.* New York: Holt, Rinehart and Winston.

Smith, F. (1982). *Understanding reading* (3rd ed.). New York: Holt, Rinehart and Winston.

Smith, F. (1985). *Reading* (2nd ed.). Cambridge: Cambridge University Press.

Smith, F. (1998). *Understanding reading.* Hillsdale, NJ: Lawrence Erlbaum.

Smith, J., & Parkes, B. (1987). *Jack and the beanstalk.* Crystal Lake, IL: Rigby.

Smith, K. (1993). *A descriptive analysis of the responses of six students and their teacher in literature study sessions.* Unpublished doctoral dissertation, Arizona State University, Tempe.

Snowball, D., & Bolton, F. (1999). *Spelling K–8: Planning and teaching.* York, ME: Stenhouse Publishers.

Sobol, D. (1986). *Encyclopedia Brown and the case of the mysterious handprints.* New York: Bantam Skylark.

Sommers, N. (1980). Revision strategies of student writers and experienced adult writers. *College Composition and Communication, 31*, 378–388.

South Brunswick, New Jersey, Public Schools. (1992). *The K–2 reading/writing scale.* South Brunswick, NJ: Author.

Spencer, D. A. (1986). *Contemporary women teachers: Balancing school and home.* New York: Longman.

Spencer, M. M. (1982). *Learning to read*. London: Bodley Head.

Spiegel, D. L. (1981). *Reading for pleasure: Guidelines*. Newark, DE: International Reading Association, and Urbana, IL: ERIC Clearinghouse on Reading and Communication Skills.

Spier, P. (1980). *People*. New York: Doubleday.

Squire, J. R. (1991). The history of the profession. In J. Flood, J. M. Jensen, D. Lapp, & J. R. Squire (Eds.), *Handbook of research on teaching the English language arts* (pp. 3–17). New York: Macmillan Publishing Company.

St. George, J. (1989). *Panama Canal: Gateway to the world*. New York: Putnam.

Stafford, W. (1978). Dreams to have: An interview with Cynthia Lofsness. In W. Stafford, *Writing the Australian crawl* (pp. 85–113). Ann Arbor, MI: University of Michigan Press.

Stanovich, K. (1991). The psychology of reading: Evolutionary and revolutionary developments. *Annual Review of Applied Linguistics, 12*, 3–30.

Stanovich, K., & Stanovich, P. (1995). How research might inform the debate about early reading acquisition. *Journal of Research in Reading, 18*(2), 87–105.

Stauffer, R., & Harrell, M. (1975). Individualizing reading-thinking activities. *Reading Teacher, 28*, 765–769.

Steig, W. (1971). *Amos and Boris*. New York: Farrar, Straus and Giroux.

Steiner, W. (1995). *The scandal of pleasure: Art in an age of fundamentalism*. Chicago: University of Chicago Press.

Sternberg, R. J. (1985). *Beyond IQ*. New York: Cambridge University Press.

Stevens, R. (1912). *The question as a measure of efficiency in instruction: A critical study of classroom practice*. New York: Teachers College Press.

Stiggins, R. J., & Bridgeford, N. J. (1985): The ecology of classroom assessment. *Journal of Educational Measurement, 22*, 271–286.

Stoddard, K., Valcante, G., Sindelar, P., O'Shea, L., & Algozzine, B. (1993). Increasing reading rate and comprehension: The effects of repeated readings, sentence segmentation, and intonation training. *Reading Research and Instruction, 32*(4), 53–65.

Storey, J. (1993). *An introductory guide to cultural theory and popular culture*. Athens, GA: University of Georgia Press.

Strickland, D. S., & Ascher, C. (1992). Low income African-American children and public schooling. In P.W. Jackson (Ed.), *Handbook of research on curriculum* (pp. 609–625). New York: Macmillan.

Strickland, D. S., & Strickland, M. R. (1997). Language and literacy: The poetry connection. *Language Arts, 74*, 201–205.

Strom, Y. (1990). A tree still stands: Jewish youth in Eastern Europe today. New York: Philomel Books.

Sudol, D., & Sudol, P. (1991). Another story: Putting Graves, Calkins, and Atwell into practice and perspective. *Language Arts, 68*, 292–300.

Sudol, D., & Sudol, P. (1995). Yet another story: Writers workshop revisited. *Language Arts, 72,* 171–178.

Sulzby, E. (1980). Word concept development activities. In E. Henderson & J. Beers (Eds.), *Developmental and cognitive aspects of learning to spell* (pp. 127–137). Newark, DE: International Reading Association.

Sulzby, E. (1985). Kindergartners as writers and readers. In M. Farr (Ed.), *Advances in writing research, vol. 1: Children's writing development* (pp. 127–199). Norwood, NJ: Ablex Publishing Corporation.

Sulzby, E. (1990). Assessment of emergent writing and children's language while writing. In L. Morrow & J. Smith (Eds.), *The role of assessment in early literacy instruction* (pp. 83–109). Englewood Cliffs, NJ: Prentice-Hall.

Sulzby, E., Barnhart, J., & Hieshima, J. A. (1989). Forms of writing and rereading from writing: A preliminary report. In J. Mason (Ed.), *Reading and writing connections* (pp. 31–63). Boston: Allyn and Bacon.

Sutton, C. (1989). Helping the nonnative English speaker with reading. *The Reading Teacher, 42*(9), 684–688.

Talk: A Journal of the National Oracy Project. (Available from National Curriculum Council, Albion Sharf, 25 Skeldergate, York, England, Y01 2XL.)

Taylor, D., & Dorsey-Gaines, C. (1988). *Growing up literate: Learning from inner-city families.* Portsmouth, NH: Heinemann.

Tchudi, S. (1987). *The young writer's handbook.* New York: Macmillan.

Teale, W. H. (1991). A conversation with Lisa Delpit. *Language Arts, 68,* 541–547.

Teale, W. H., & Sulzby, E. (1986). *Emergent literacy: Writing and reading.* Norwood, NJ: Ablex.

Temple, C. A., Nathan, R., & Burris, N. (1982). *The beginnings of writing.* Boston: Allyn and Bacon.

Templeton, S., Ganske, K., Invernizzi, M., Bear, D., Abouzeid, M., & Zutell, J. (1994). *Word sort: An alternative to phonics, spelling and vocabulary.* Symposium presented at National Reading Conference, San Diego, CA.

Thwaite, M. F. (1963). *From primer to pleasure.* London: The Library Association.

Trevarthen, C. (1980). The foundation of intersubjectivity. In D. Olson (Ed.), *The social foundations of language and thought.* New York: W. W. Norton.

Turbill, J. (1983). *Now, we want to write!* Sydney, Australia: Primary English Teaching Association.

Turbill, J., Butler, A., & Cambourne, B. (1999). Peer proofreading. In J. Turbill, A. Butler, & B. Cambourne (Eds.), *Frameworks language and literacy course: Professional readings* (4th ed.) (pp. 156–160), Newark, New York: Wayne-Finger Lakes Board of Cooperative Educational Services (BOCES).

Urzúa, C. (1980). Doing what comes naturally: Recent research in second language acquisition. In G. S. Pinnell (Ed.), *Discovering language with children* (pp. 33–38). Urbana, IL: National Council of Teachers of English.

Urzúa, C. (1989). I grow for a living. In P. Rigg & V. Allen (Eds.), *When they don't all speak English: Integrating the ESL student into the regular classroom* (pp. 15–38). Urbana, IL: National Council of Teachers of English.

Urzúa, C. (1992). Faith in learners through literature studies. *Language Arts, 69*, 492–501.

Valencia, S. (1990). A portfolio approach to classroom reading assessment: The whys, whats, and hows. *The Reading Teacher, 43*, 338–340.

Valencia, S., Hiebert, E., & Afflerbach, P. (1994). *Authentic reading assessment: Practices and possibilities.* Newark, DE: International Reading Association.

Valencia, S., McGinley, W., & Pearson, P. D. (1988). Assessing reading and writing. In G. Duffy (Ed.), *Reading in the middle school* (2nd ed.) (pp. 124–153). Newark, DE: International Reading Association.

Valli, L. (1986). *Becoming clerical workers.* Boston: Routledge and Kegan Paul.

Valsiner, J. (1992). Interest: A metatheoretical perspective. In K. A. Renninger, S. Hidi, & A. Krapp (Eds.), *The role of interest in learning and development* (pp. 27–41). Hillsdale, NJ: Lawrence Erlbaum.

Veatch, J. (1978). *Reading in the elementary school* (2nd ed.). Katonah, NY: Richard C. Owen.

Vygotsky, L. (1978). *Mind in society: The development of higher psychological processes.* Cambridge, MA: Harvard University Press.

Waber, B. (1987). *Funny, funny Lyle.* Boston: Houghton Mifflin.

Walker, A. (1983). "Reassurance." In *In search of our mother's gardens* (p. 40). San Diego: Harcourt Brace Jovanovich.

Wallace, L. (1984). *Pleasure and frustration: A resynthesis of clinical and theoretical psychoanalysis.* New York: International Universities Press.

Waters, K., & Slovenz-Low, M. (1990). *Lion dancer. Ernie Wan's Chinese New Year.* New York: Scholastic.

Watson, D., Burke, C., & Harste, J. (1989). *Whole language: Inquiring voices.* Richmond Hill, Ont.: Scholastic-TAB.

Watson, K. (1980). A close look at whole-class discussion. *English in Education, 14*, 39–46.

Watson, K., & Young, B. (1980). Teacher reformulations of pupil discourse. *Australian Review of Applied Linguistics, 3*, 37–47.

Weinstein, G., & Cooke, N. L. (1992). The effects of two repeated reading interventions on generalization of fluency. *Learning Disability Quarterly, 15*, 21–28.

Wells, G. (Ed.).(1981). *Learning through interaction: The study of language development.* Cambridge: Cambridge University Press.

Wells, G. (1986). *The meaning makers: Children learning language and using language to learn.* Portsmouth, NH: Heinemann.

Wells, G. (1990). Talk about text: Where literacy is learned and talked. *Curriculum Inquiry, 20,* 369–405.

Wells, G., & Chang-Wells, G. L. (1992). *Constructing knowledge together: Classrooms as centers of inquiry and literacy.* Portsmouth, NH: Heinemann.

Welty, E. (1984). *One writer's beginnings.* Cambridge: Harvard University Press.

Westwood, P. (1994). Issues in spelling instruction. *Special Education Perspectives, 3,* 31–44.

White, E. B. (1952). *Charlotte's web.* New York: Harper & Row.

White, E. M. (1984). Holisticism. *College Composition and Communication, 35,* 400–409.

White, E. M. (1985). *Teaching and assessing writing.* San Francisco: Jossey-Bass.

Wigfield, A., & Asher, S. R. (1984). Social and motivational influences on reading. In P. D. Pearson, R. Barr, M. Kamil, & P. Mosenthal (Eds.), *Handbook of reading research* (pp. 423–452). New York: Longman.

Wiggins, G. (1989). Teaching to the (authentic) test. *Educational Leadership, 46,* (7), 41–47.

Wiggins, G. (1989). A true test: Toward more authentic and equitable assessment. *Phi Delta Kappan, 70,* 703–713.

Wiggins, G. (1993). *Assessing student performance: Exploring the purpose and limits of testing.* San Francisco: Jossey-Bass.

Wilder, L. I. (1989). *Little house in the big woods.* Santa Barbara, CA: Cornerstone Books.

Wilde, S. (1990). A proposal for a new spelling curriculum. *The Elementary School Journal, 90,* 275–289.

Wilde, S. (1992). *You kan red this!: Spelling and punctuation for whole language classrooms K–6.* Portsmouth, NH: Heinemann.

Wildsmith, B. (1971). *The owl and the woodpecker.* London: Oxford University Press.

Wildsmith, B. (1974). *Squirrels.* London: Oxford University Press.

Wilen, W. W. (1987). *Questions, questioning techniques, and effective teaching.* Washington, DC: National Education Association.

Williams, R. L., Mosby, D., & Hinson, V. (1976). *Critical issues in achievement testing of children from diverse educational backgrounds.* Paper presented at the Invitational Conference on Achievement Testing of Disadvantaged and Minority Students for Educational Program Evaluation. Washington, DC: U.S. Office of Education.

Williamson, J. (1981/82). How does girl number twenty understand ideology? *Screen Education, 40,* 80–87.

Willinsky, J. (1990). *The new literacy: Redefining reading and writing in the schools.* New York: Routledge.

Willis, P. (1990). Common culture. Boulder, CO: Westview Press.

Willis, S. (1993, November). Whole language in the '90s. *ASCD Update, 35*(9), pp. 1, 5, 6, 8. Alexandria, VA: Association for Supervision and Curriculum Development.

Winterson, J. (1995). *Art objects: Essays on ecstasy and effrontery.* Toronto: Alfred A. Knopf.

Wolf, D. P. (1989). Portfolio assessment: Sampling student work. *Educational Leadership, 46,* 35–39.

Wood, D., & Einbender, L. (1995). *An authentic journey: Teachers' emergent understandings about authentic assessment and practice.* New York: National Center for Restructuring Education, Schools, and Teaching (NCREST).

Yolen, J. (1988). *The devil's arithmetic.* New York: Puffin Books.

Zapater, B. M. (1992). *Three kings' day.* Cleveland, OH: Modern Curriculum Press.

Zhang, S. (1995). Reexamining the affective advantage of peer feedback in the ESL writing class. *Journal of Second Language Writing, 4,* 209–222.

Zutell, J. (1975). *Spelling strategies of primary school children and their relationships to the Piagetian concept of decentration.* Doctoral dissertation, University of Virginia, Charlottesville.

Zutell, J. (1990). Reading-spelling links. *The Reading Teacher, 43,* 608–609.

Zutell, J. (1996). The directed spelling thinking activity (DSTA): Providing an effective balance in word study instruction. *The Reading Teacher, 50,* 98–108.

Zutell, J., & Rasinski, T. (1991). Training teachers to attend to their students' oral reading fluency. *Theory into Practice, 30*(3), 211–217.

Index

Editors

Sharon Murphy is professor of education and associate dean of the faculty of graduate studies at York University in Toronto, Canada. A past coeditor of *Language Arts,* she has written on assessment, reading materials, and classroom discourse. Among her recent publications are the books *Telling Pieces: Art as Literacy in Middle Grade Classes,* co-authored with Peggy Albers, and *Fragile Evidence: A Critique of Reading Assessment,* written with Patrick Shannon, Peter Johnston, and Jane Hansen. Murphy has served as a member of the Reading Commission of the National Council of Teachers of English and as president of the Whole Language Umbrella. Her current research interests are focused on values and assessment.

Curt Dudley-Marling is a former elementary and special education teacher who now teaches in the Lynch School of Education at Boston College in Chestnut Hill, Massachusetts. Dudley-Marling is a former coeditor of *Language Arts* and is currently a member of NCTE's Elementary Section Steering Committee. He is also on the Board of Directors of the Massachusetts Reading Association (MRA) and is chair of MRA's Parents and Reading Committee. Dudley-Marling's research focuses on students for whom learning to read and write has been a struggle, as well as their parents. His book *Living with Uncertainty: The Messy Reality of Classroom Practice* was the winner of the 1999 James N. Britton Award for Inquiry in the English Language Arts.

Contributors

Editors' Note: The biographical entries below are based on information that was current when each author's essay was published in Language *Arts.*

In 1998, **Suzette Abbott** was teaching first grade at the Agassiz School in Cambridge, Massachusetts, and had been an early childhood resource consultant for the Cambridge School Department.

In 1999, **Laura Apol** was assistant professor at Michigan State University, where she taught courses and conducted research on children's literature, literary theory, and creating writing. She is also a poet whose work has appeared in a number of literary journals and poetry anthologies.

In 1991, **Marianne N. Bloch** was professor in the Department of Curriculum and Instruction at the University of Wisconsin–Madison. Her teaching and research interests at that time focused on cultural differences and learning in the elementary school.

In 1995, **Beverly A. Busching** was a language arts specialist in the Department of Instruction and Teacher Education at the University of South Carolina and was director of the Midlands Writing Project.

In 1985, **Courtney B. Cazden** was professor of education and chairperson of the Department of Teaching, Curriculum, and Learning Environments at the Harvard Graduate School of Education.

In 1998, **Sarah Cohen** taught second grade at Inter-American Magnet School in Chicago. At that time she indicated that she would continue to document and reflect on possible ways to collaborate with her students in the construction of their literacy curriculum.

In 1995, **Karin L. Dahl** was associate professor in the literacy program at the University of Cincinnati, where she taught courses in reading research and writing instruction in the elementary grades.

In 1994, **Jean Dickinson** taught grade 5/6 at Cherokee Trail School in Parker, Colorado.

In 1995, **Anne Haas Dyson** was professor of education at the University of California, Berkeley, and described herself as a student of the social lives and literacy learning of school children.

In 1998, **Beverly Falk** was the associate director of the National Center for Restructuring Education, Schools, and Teaching (NCREST) at Teachers College, Columbia University. She is coauthor of *Authentic Assessment* *in Action* and *A Teacher's Guide to Standardized Reading Tests: Knowledge Is Power.*

In 1991, **Evelyn B. Freeman** was associate professor of education at Ohio State University Newark.

In 1995, **Penny A. Freppon** was assistant professor in the literacy program at the University of Cincinnati, where she taught courses in language arts and children's literature.

In 2000, **Mary Jo Fresch** was assistant professor in the School of Teaching and Learning at Ohio State University at Marion.

In 1994, **Carol Gilles** worked with teachers as a member of the Departments of Curriculum and Instruction and Continuing Professional Education at the University of Missouri–Columbia.

In 1991, **Mary Louise Gomez** was assistant professor in the Department of Curriculum and Instruction at the University of Wisconsin–Madison, where she co-directed an experimental program that prepared prospective elementary teachers to teach diverse student populations and conducted research on teacher education, with particular emphasis on multicultural education and literacy.

In 1977, **Yetta Goodman** taught at the University of Arizona in Tucson.

In 1991, **M. Elizabeth Graue** was assistant professor in the Department of Curriculum and Instruction at the University of Wisconsin–Madison, where she studied early childhood and assessment policy and taught courses in early childhood education and research methodology.

In 1998, **Claudia Grose** was a member of the graduate faculty of Bank Street College of Education in New York and a reading and literacy consultant based in Cambridge, Massachusetts, where she had recently directed the Intergenerational Literacy Program for the Cambridge School Volunteers.

In 1997, **Laura Harper** taught seventh-grade English, reading, and social studies at Toppenish Middle School in Toppenish, Washington.

In 1999, **Jodi Harris** was a fifth-grade teacher at Grosse Pointe Park Elementary School. During the 1998–1999 school year, she was on sabbatical to continue her doctoral studies in the teacher education program at Michigan State University.

In 1995, **Stephen B. Kucer** was professor of language and literacy education at California State University, San Marcos.

In 1984, **Judith Wells Lindfors** was associate professor of curriculum and instruction at the University of Texas at Austin.

In 1997, **Prisca Martens** was assistant professor in language education at Indiana University, Indianapolis. At that time she described herself as researching, writing, and speaking in the areas of early literacy, miscue analysis, and retrospective miscue analysis.

In 1994, **Cheryl McBride** had been teaching first grade for fifteen years in Sedalia, Missouri.

In 1998, **Christine C. Pappas** was professor in the College of Education at the University of Illinois at Chicago, where she taught language and literacy courses. Her interests involve the research and teaching-learning of genre and teacher inquiry.

In 1991, **Louise M. Rosenblatt** was professor emerita of English education at New York University.

In 1984, **Dennis Searle** was associate professor of language education at York University in Toronto, Canada.

In 1995, **Betty Ann Slesinger** was teaching seventh-grade language arts classes at Irmo Middle School Campus R and was active in the rural teachers' network of the Breadloaf School of English.

In 1981, **Frank Smith** was Lansdowne Professor of Language in Education at the University of Victoria, British Columbia, Canada.

In 1994, **Dorothy S. Strickland** was the State of New Jersey Professor of Reading at Rutgers University, New Brunswick, New Jersey.

In 1991, **David Sudol** was completing a Ph.D. in English education at the University of Arizona. His dissertation was an ethnographic study of the teaching of elementary school writing.

In 1991, **Peg Sudol** was teaching fifth grade at Ironwood Elementary School in the Marana Unified School District, Tucson, Arizona.

In 2000, **Jan Turbill** was a senior lecturer in language and literacy education at the University of Wollongong, NSW, Australia.

In 1994, **Marc VanDover** was teaching seventh, eighth, and ninth graders labeled "learning disabled" at Jefferson Junior High in Columbia, Missouri.

In 1977, **Dorothy J. Watson** was teaching at the University of Missouri–Columbia.

In 1986, **Ken Watson** was teaching in the department of education at the University of Sydney in Australia.

In 1986, **Bob Young** was teaching in the department of education at the University of Sydney in Australia.

In 1998, **Liliana Barro Zecker** was assistant professor in the School of Education at DePaul University, where she taught courses on literacy and language development. She worked with pre- and inservice teachers, documenting the articulation between the theory and practice of literacy learning and instruction as it is realized in classrooms.

This book was typeset in Palatino and Helvetica by Electronic Imaging.
The typefaces used on the cover were Agenda Light Ultra Condensed,
Myriad Condensed, and Tempus Sans ITC.
The book was printed on 50-lb. Williamsburg Offset by Victor Graphics, Inc.